Anonymous

Anecdota Oxoniensia

The English Manuscripts of The Nicomachean Ethics

Anonymous

Anecdota Oxoniensia
The English Manuscripts of The Nicomachean Ethics

ISBN/EAN: 9783743417250

Manufactured in Europe, USA, Canada, Australia, Japa

Cover: Foto ©Lupo / pixelio.de

Manufactured and distributed by brebook publishing software (www.brebook.com)

Anonymous

Anecdota Oxoniensia

Anecdota Oxoniensia

TEXTS, DOCUMENTS, AND EXTRACTS

CHIEFLY FROM

MANUSCRIPTS IN THE BODLEIAN

AND OTHER

OXFORD LIBRARIES

CLASSICAL SERIES. VOL. I—PART I

*THE ENGLISH MANUSCRIPTS OF THE
NICOMACHEAN ETHICS*

DESCRIBED BY

J. A. STEWART, M.A.

Oxford
AT THE CLARENDON PRESS
1882

PREFACE.

IN the following pages I have embodied my collations of six English MSS. of the Ethics. Of three of these MSS. collations have not, so far as I am aware, been hitherto published; while the only independent account published of the other three—by Wilkinson in 1715—is a meagre list of readings selected almost at random, and often inaccurately recorded, not a collation in the modern acceptation of the term.

The form in which my collations are presented I adopted with the object of assigning, if possible, each MS. to its genealogical place. If I succeed in thus throwing, by means of a natural classification of the English MSS, some light upon the general problem of the genealogy of the MSS. of the Ethics, I shall repay but a small part of the debt which I owe to Professor Rassow; for without the leading idea contained in the first section of his 'Forschungen über die Nicomachische Ethik,' I should hardly have attempted this work at all.

To the labours of Professor Susemihl I also owe much. His extensive notices of later corrections in Bekker's MSS, especially in K^b, have been of invaluable service to me. My citations from the Aldine Edition are chiefly borrowed from him,—either as its readings are actually given by him, or as I inferred them from his silence; although in a good many cases I examined the Edition for myself.

In the Fifth Book I found Mr. H. Jackson's collations useful.

In all cases, taking Bekker's collation (Berlin, 1831) as basis, I have accepted subsequent corrections of that collation by Professor Schöll, Professor Susemihl, or Mr. Jackson.

The text with which I collated all my MSS. was Bekker's (Berlin, 1845) as reprinted by Parker (Oxford, 1871).

It only remains that I should thank all who have assisted me in this work—the authorities of the University of Cambridge, of Corpus

PREFACE.

Christi College, Oxford, and of New College, Oxford, for their liberality in lending me their respective MSS; the authorities of the British Museum, and of the Bibliothèque nationale at Paris for kindly permitting me to examine theirs; Professor Vitelli and Dr. Meyncke for consulting, at my request, MSS. in Florence and Rome; and lastly, the two friends who have done me the important service of revising the proofs—Mr. John Rankine, Advocate, Edinburgh, and my colleague Mr. J. H. Onions of Christ Church.

J. A. S.

JAN. 12, 1882.

THE
ENGLISH MANUSCRIPTS
OF
THE NICOMACHEAN ETHICS.

ENGLISH MSS.

A = Manuscript in the Cambridge University Library (No. 1879, I i. v. 44), sec. xiii; the Eliensis of Wilkinson, Zell, and Michelet, O² of Susemihl.
B¹= Brit. Mus. Add. MS. 14080, sec. xv; not before collated.
B²= Brit. Mus. Add. MS. 6790, sec. xv; not before collated.
B³= Brit. Mus. Royal MS. 16 C. xxi, sec. xvi; not before collated (see Appendix).
C = Manuscript in the Library of Corpus Christi College, Oxford (112), sec. xv; the CCC of Wilkinson, Zell, and Michelet, O¹ of Susemihl.
D = Manuscript in the Library of New College, Oxford (227), sec. xv; the NC of Wilkinson, Zell, and Michelet, O³ of Susemihl.

BEKKER'S MSS.

(See F. Susemihl, Die Bekkerschen Hss. der Nicom. Ethik [Neue Jahrbücher für Philologie und Pädagogik, 1878, pp. 625 ff.]).

K^b = Laurent. 81. 11, sec. x.
L^b = Par. 1854, sec. xii.
M^b = Marc. 213, sec. xv ineunte.
O^b = Riccard. 46, sec. xiv.
N^b = Marc. append. 4. 53, sec xiv.
H^a = Marc. 214, sec. xiv.
P^b = Vatic. 1342, sec. xiv (xiii?).

ENGLISH MANUSCRIPTS

OF

THE NICOMACHEAN ETHICS.

THERE are two varieties of the Text of the Nicomachean Ethics represented by the two oldest MSS., K^b (Laurent. 81. 11) and L^b (Paris. 1854) respectively. The term *varieties* is better fitted than the term *recensions* to indicate the nature of the process by which K^b and L^b seem to have been differentiated, not by the conscious agency of critical editors, but by the gradual accumulation of accidental departures from a common archetype.

The points in which K^b and L^b differ, exclusive of obvious blunders, are very numerous, but are seldom, if ever, of material importance, being substitutions, omissions, and insertions of a purely verbal character.

In each of the two later MSS. fully collated by Bekker,—M^b (Marc. Ven. 213) and O^b (Riccard. 46),—although the text is considerably mixed, parts can be distinguished as belonging on the whole either to the K^b variety or to the L^b variety; O^b generally following L^b in those parts in which M^b follows K^b, and M^b following L^b where O^b follows K^b.

That K^b and L^b represent two varieties or families, and that M^b and O^b are related in the manner described to K^b and L^b, was pointed out by Rassow in his Forschungen über die Nic. Eth., 1874, the law being formulated by him for five books, as follows (p. 7):—

B. iii and iv K^bO^b—L^bM^b,
B. vi, vii, ix K^bM^b—L^bO^b.

The other five books he does not venture to include in a similar formula. 'In den übrigen fünf Büchern dagegen hat, ungeachtet auch hier zwischen einigen Handschriften eine grössere Verwandtschaft hervortritt, dennoch schon eine so grosse Vermischung Statt gefunden, dass es nicht mehr möglich ist, den Typus der beiden Familien genau zu unterscheiden.'—p. 7.

Susemihl in his Dissertationes II de recognoscendis Ethicis Nicomacheis, 1878–9, and in his critical edition of the Eth. Nic., Teubner, 1880, accepting Rassow's conclusions regarding Books iii, iv, vi, vii, and ix, endeavours, partly by means of the Vetusta Translatio (Γ) and the Aldine Edition, to distinguish Families in the remaining five Books also. 'Constat,' he says (Eth. Nic., pref. p. viii), 'altera familia (Π^1) per libros i, ii, vi, vii, ix, x, ex K^b et M^b, per libros iii, iv, viii ex K^b et O^b, altera (Π^2), per i, ii, vi, vii, ix ex L^b et O^b, per iii, iv ex L^b et M^b, per viii ex ΓM^{b}Ald., per x ex ΓL^{b}Ald., in libro autem v modo ab altera parte K^bL^b (Π^1) et ab altera M^bO^b (Π^2) modo ab altera K^bO^b (Π^a) et ab altera L^bM^b (Π^b) stare videntur.'

In the following pages I have embodied the results of my collations, complete and partial, of five English MSS., in the hope that, like Susemihl's collations of Γ and Ald., they may throw some light on Rassow's general problem. I have thought it advisable to classify the readings of my MSS. as they agree, in the several Books, with K^bO^b or L^bM^b, and K^bM^b or L^bO^b. Accordingly, I have given complete lists of the K^bO^b— L^bM^b, and K^bM^b—L^bO^b readings in the Ethics, appending the symbols of my own MSS. where they agree, as well as those of the Vetusta Translatio and the Aldine Edition. These lists, apart from the information which they give concerning my MSS., may, I hope, be useful, as enabling the eye easily to take in the quality of the various resemblances and differences on which Rassow and Susemihl found their conclusions. In the meantime the quantitative aspect of these resemblances and differences may be seen from the following table, in which the figures denote the number of cases in each Book of the agreement of two of Bekker's four MSS. against the other two [1]:—

	Book I	II	III	IV	V	VI	VII	VIII	IX	X
K^bM^b—L^bO^b	38	29	12	5	8	58	80	29	67	43
K^bO^b—L^bM^b	7	6	71	78	18	10	17	25	8	17
K^bL^b—M^bO^b	14	5	5	5	31	7	3	9	5	12

[1] I had compiled this table for my own use, to supply the numerical data absent from Rassow's Forschungen, before I studied the statistics given in Susemihl's Dissertationes. It will be found on the whole to be in substantial agreement with them.

Thus in Book i there are thirty-eight cases of variation between K^b and L^b in which M^b follows K^b, and O^b follows L^b; and only seven in which O^b follows K^b and M^b follows L^b. Going through the other columns of the table, we find that in all the Books, except viii, and perhaps also v, M^b and O^b show a decided preference for either K^b or L^b, where M^b prefers the one, O^b preferring the other.

The conclusions fairly suggested by the foregoing figures are that in Books i, ii, vi, vii, ix, and x, O^b is descended from a MS. of the L^b variety, and M^b from one of the K^b variety; and that in Books iii and iv, O^b is descended from a MS. of the K^b variety, and M^b from one of the L^b variety.

With respect to the cause which produced this curiously alternating relationship of M^b and O^b to K^b and L^b I have no definite theory to offer; but the following pages show that a similar effect, presumably due to a similar cause, is noticeable in the English MSS. One remark, however, I will allow myself to make here; that, although *correction* has evidently played an important part in producing similarity between MSS., it cannot by itself explain that similarity in all cases. For example, O^b resembles L^b largely in Books i, ii, vi, vii, ix, x, while in Books iii, iv, v it resembles K^b largely. Its resemblance to K^b, it seems to me, cannot be explained as the result of the mere *correction*, in these three particular Books, of a MS. of the L^b family by means of a MS. of the K^b family. Its K^b readings, consisting of blunders, many of them of omission, too numerous to be coincidences, cannot possibly have come in as corrections. They are rather 'rudimentary organs or characters,' with a genealogical significance. One of the English MSS. to be described in the following pages, C, a MS. elsewhere related to L^b or only distantly to K^b, has a well defined mass of text beginning in the middle of one Book and ending in the middle of the next but one, which reproduces the minutest blunders of K^b—a fact which cannot be explained by correction. Again, another English MS., A, which belongs uniformly to the K^b variety, has four leaves with a text of the L^b variety inserted later to supply a lacuna in the original volume. It seems to me, in the light of these two cases, that the curiously alternating relationship of M^b and O^b to K^b and L^b may be due to some such cause as the possession by one copyist of stray leaves the absence of which obliged another copyist to leave a lacuna to be afterwards supplied from a MS. of a different family. It is certainly a curious coincidence that the K^bO^b—L^bM^b part of the Ethics practically coincides with the part in which C agrees so minutely with K^b. In conclusion, it may be pointed out that, even if we grant that the correction-hypothesis explains the K^b-character of O^b in Books iii, iv, and v, it cannot at the same time explain the L^b-character of M^b in these Books. Why should an ascendant of M^b have been corrected from a MS. of the L^b-variety exactly and only where an ascendant of O^b was corrected from a MS. of the K^b-variety? The alternation of O^b and M^b in relation to K^b and L^b (O^b following L^b only where M^b follows K^b, and *vice versa*) carries us necessarily back, it seems to me, to the defective condition of a single MS.

The MSS. which I have to report upon are (1) one in the Cambridge University Library, which I call A; (2) one in the Library of Corpus Christi College, Oxford, C; (3) one in the Library of New College, Oxford, D; and two in the Library of the British Museum, viz. (4) Addit. MSS. 14080, which I call B^1, and (5) Addit. MSS. 6790, which I call B^2.

A I have collated word for word with Bekker's text (Parker's reprint, Oxford, 1871) in Book x, and in the other Books have examined very fully, i.e. in nearly all places where the other MSS.—Bekker's and the English MSS.—give variants, as well as in many other places, as will be seen from the following pages. I have had unusual means of making a careful study of this MS., as the University of Cambridge lent it to me in Oxford, for which act of liberality I take this opportunity of recording my grateful thanks.

C I have collated word for word throughout the Ethics with Bekker's text (Parker's reprint, Oxford, 1871).

D I have collated word for word with the same text in Books v and x; and in the other Books have examined very fully, i.e. in nearly all places where the other MSS.—Bekker's and the English MSS.—give variants, as well as in many other places. My examination of D was as continuous as my examination of C, but, in all except Books v and x, not quite so minute. I must not omit to mention here that while I was examining D I had the advantage of the use of an excellent collation of that MS. made by the late Rev. W. M. Hatch, and kindly placed at my disposal by his brother the Rev. Edwin Hatch. I take this opportunity of gratefully acknowledging that I derived much benefit from its guidance. All the D readings, however, which I have recorded I have seen for myself in the MS.

B¹ and B² I have examined, with about the same minuteness in each case, throughout the Ethics—i.e. in all the places which bear upon the family to which a MS. is to be assigned, as well as in many other places—in all in about 800 places in each MS.

A (quoted by Wilkinson, Zell, and Michelet as El., it having formerly belonged to the Library of More, Bishop of Ely) is described in the Catalogue of MSS. belonging to the University Library of Cambridge as 'a moderate-sized quarto on vellum of one hundred and forty-seven leaves, each page containing about twenty-six lines written in a cursive hand of the latter part of the thirteenth century, abounding with contractions. ... From fol. 81-90 the MS. is written in a different hand, which appears to belong to the fifteenth century.' Cat. vol. iii. p. 495. In the subscription at the end of the volume (which contains the Mor. Magna, the Eth. Nic., Eth. Eud., and Œconom.), we are told that it was written διὰ χειρὸς Νικολάου εὐτελοῦς ἀναγνώστου τῶν ὡρῶν, αἰτήσει τοῦ θεοτιμήτου μοναχοῦ κυρίου Ἰακὼβ σκευοφύλακτος μάνδρας ἀκρωτηρίου μηνὶ Ἰουνίου ις, ἰνδ. β, ἔτει ϛψπζ, i.e. A.D. 1279.

C (quoted by Wilkinson, Zell, and Michelet as CCC) is thus described in Coxe's Catalogue of the MSS. in the Oxford College Libraries, under the head of Corpus Christi College, 'cxii. Codex chartaceus in folio, ff. 174, sec. xv.:—

1. Aristotelis Ethicorum Nicomacheorum libri decem, fol. 1.
2. Ejusdem Aristotelis Magnorum Moralium libri duo, fol. 48.
3. Moralium ad Eudemum libri i, ii, iii, vii, fol. 65ᵇ.
4. De Virtutibus libellus, fol. 86ᵇ.
5. Œconomicorum libri duo, fol. 88.
6. Politicorum libri octo, fol. 94ᵇ.
7. Ad Alexandrum Rhetorica, fol. 156ᵇ.
8. Alexandri Regis ad Aristotelem Epistola cum responsione, foL 174.
9. Aristotelis ad Olympiadem Epistola, fol. 174.
10. Platonis ad Archytam Tarentinum Epistola, fol. 174ᵇ.

In fronte codicis, "Orate pro anima Joannis Claimondi, coll. corporis Christi primi praesidis, qui hunc librum eidem condonavit."[1] [Claimond was President of Corpus from 1517 to 1537.]

C has uniformly thirty-eight lines to the page, and about seventy-five letters to the line.

D (quoted by Wilkinson, Zell, and Michelet as NC) is described by Coxe as follows, under the head of New College :—'227. Chartaceus in folio, ff. 141, sec. xv; olim Gulielmi Man. Aristotelis Ethicorum, sive de moribus, ad Nicomachum, libri decem. Praemittitur notitia, "Liber Collegii Sanctae Mariae Wynton. in Oxon. ex dono Gulielmi Man, anno Domini 1589, Septembris 31."[1]

D has twenty-four lines to the page, and about thirty-five letters to the line.

It has a long lacuna (not due to the loss of leaves), and exhibits considerable confusion, due apparently to the binder. The following are the details of the order in which the books stand:—Books i, ii, iii, iv to ch. 9. § 2. 1128 b 14 ὠχριῶσιν, vi from ch. 2. § 5. 1139 b 2 καὶ οὐ τέλος, vii, viii to ch. 11. § 7. 1161 b 8 ἄνθρωπος, ix from ch. 12. § 1. 1171 b 35 τῷ συζῆν, x to ch. 5. § 6. 1175 b 31 τοῖς, iv from ch. 9. § 2. 1128 b 14 σωματικά, v, vi to ch. 2. § 5. 1139 b 2 ποιῶν, x from ch. 5. § 6. 1175 b 31 χρόνοις.

D thus proceeds correctly up to 1128 b 14 ὠχριῶσιν inclusive, this being the last word of fol. 60ᵛ. Fol. 61ʳ begins with 1139 b 2 καὶ οὐ τέλος. The mass of text thus omitted is inserted in Book x after 1175 b 31, τοῖς, which is the last word of fol. 110ᵛ. Σωματικά 1128 b 14 is the first word of fol. 111ʳ. Χρόνοις 1175 b 31 is the first word of fol. 130ʳ. Thus nineteen leaves have been misplaced.

The lacuna in D extends from viii. 11. 7 to ix. 12. 1. Ἄνθρωπος 1161 b 8 ends the fifth line from the bottom of a page; and τῷ 1171 b 35 begins the fourth line, there being no difference in hand or ink, and the scribe showing no consciousness of the omission. Mr. H. Jackson (Fifth Book, introduction, p. xii) supposes D to be a copy of Par. 1853, which has a lacuna of the same extent here.

But a special examination of Parisiensis 1853, in relation to the peculiarities of D, has satisfied me that Mr. Jackson's supposition is untenable, being precluded by an important difference (presented in the

NICOMACHEAN ETHICS. 7

following parallel columns) between the two MSS. in respect of the lacuna 1161 b 7—1171 b 34, i.e. viii. 11. 7—ix. 12. 1.

Par. 1853.	New Coll.
1161 b 6 δοκεῖ γὰρ εἶναί τι δίκαιον παντὶ ἀνθρώπῳ πρὸς πάντα τὸν	1161 b 6 δοκεῖ γὰρ εἶναί τι δίκαιον παντὶ ἀνθρώπῳ πρὸς πάντα τὸν
1171 b 34 δυνάμενον ‖ ὅτι ἐστὶν αἱρετὴ καὶ περὶ τὸν φίλον δὴ ἡ δ' ἐνέργεια γίνεται αὐτῆς ἐν τῷ συζῆν ὥστε εἰκότως τούτου ἐφίενται καὶ ὅσοτε ἐστὶν ἑκάστοις τὸ εἶναι ἢ οὗ χάριν...	1171 b 34 δυνάμενον ‖ ὅτι ἐστὶν αἱρετὴ καὶ περὶ τὸν φίλον δὴ ἡ δ' ἐνέργεια γίνεται αὐτῆς ἐν [κοινωνῆσαι νόμου καὶ συνθήκης (sic) καὶ φιλίας δὴ καθ' ὅσον ἄνθρωπος 1161 b 7, 8] τῷ συζῆν ὥστε εἰκότως τούτου ἐφίενται καὶ ὅποτε ἐστὶν ἑκάστοις τὸ εἶναι ἢ οὗ χάριν...

[Neither scribe displays any consciousness (in text, by leaving a blank, or on margin) of the lacuna at ‖, which occurs in each MS. in the middle of a page.]

Par. 1853, it will be observed, entirely omits the words κοινωνῆσαι νόμου καὶ συνθήκης καὶ φιλίας δὴ καθ' ὅσον ἄνθρωπος: nor does it supply them on the margin. The New College MS., on the other hand, while it omits them in their proper place in Book viii, incorporates them in the text of the first sentence of Book ix, which it preserves. I infer accordingly that the New Coll. MS. was not copied from Par. 1853, but from a MS. which had, in some form or other, the words κοινωνῆσαι νόμου καὶ συνθήκης καὶ φιλίας δὴ καθ' ὅσον ἄνθρωπος non-existent in Par. 1853. The agreement, however, between Par. 1853 and the New Coll. MS. is so close throughout all the books of the Ethics that we must suppose either that Par. 1853 is a copy of the New Coll. MS., or that both are descended from a common defective (1161 b 7—1171 b 34) archetype. The latter supposition seems to me to be favoured by the evidence which my examination of Par. 1853 in relation to the New Coll. MS. has brought to light. Par. 1853 probably omitted the words κοινωνῆσαι νόμου καὶ συνθήκης καὶ φιλίας δὴ καθ' ὅσον ἄνθρωπος in the common archetype on account of the peculiarity, whatever it was, which induced the New College scribe to incorporate them in his text out of their proper place. Par. 1853 is the E of Bekker. It is written in a hand or hands of the tenth century from fol. 1 to the bottom of fol. 344ᵛ, where Bekker's collation ends (De Part. Animal. 680 b 36). From the top of fol. 345ʳ to the end of the volume, viz. fol. 453ʳ, it is written in a fifteenth century hand, and contains the latter part of the treatise de Part. Animal., de Gener. Animal., Eth. Nic., and Mor. Mag.

From the following list of their readings, extending throughout all the books of the Ethics, it will be seen, I think, that both Par. 1853 and the New Coll. MS. are descended from a common archetype.

[Par. 1853 = P, New Coll. MS. = D. Readings peculiar to P and D (so far as I know) are marked †].

1095 b 10   νοήσῃ ἐσθλός PD. Post νοήσῃ add. P marg. rec. φρασσάμενος τά κ' ἔπειτα καὶ εἰς τέλος ᾖσιν ἀμείνω.
1096 a 23   τἀγαθόν] τὰ ἀγαθά PD†.
        24   λέγεται] λέγονται PD†.
1098 a 21   περιγεγράφθω μὲν οὖν] περιγράφομεν οὖν D, περιγράφθω μὲν οὖν P, sed γε inter γ et ρ suppl. man. rec.
1099 b 5   ἢ φίλοι om. PD.
1100 a 12   ἐστιν om. pr. D, habet P.
1103 b 14   τά om. P, habet D.
1105 b 10   γίνεται] λέγεται PD†.
1106 a 8   πάσχειν ἁπλῶς] πάσχειν PD† [πάσχειν, non, ut dicit Susem., πράττειν habet D].
     b 12   τῆς δὲ μεσότητος σωζούσης] τῆς μεσότητος δὲ φυλαττούσης D, τῆς μεσότητος δὲ φθειρούσης pr. P, οὐ ante φ.θειρούσης suppl. man. rec.
        13   ὡς] ὡς δή PD†.
1107 a 28   τοῦτο μή] μὴ τοῦτο P, om. μή D.
     b 7, 8   διώπερ οὐδ' ὀνόματος τετύχηκεν οὐδ' ὁ τοιοῦτος ἔστω δὲ ἀναίσθητος PD†.
1108 a 11   μέν om. PD†.
1109 a 29   ὅπερ ἐστὶ τὸ εὖ καὶ σπάνιον ὁ καὶ ἐπαινετὸν καὶ καλόν PD†.
        32   τούτου μέν] τὸ μὲν τοῦ D, τὸ τοῦ μέν P.
1112 b 21   διάγραμμα] διαγραμματου (sic) pr. P, διὰ γραμμάτων D.
1113 a 1   ἢ πέπτηται ὡς δεῖ] ἢ πέπτηται ὡς δεῖ ἢ πεπυίωται P, ἢ πέπτεται ἢ πεποίωται ὡς δεῖ D.

1113 b 24   ὅσοι μὴ βίᾳ] ὅσοι μὴ βίαν PD†; suppl. διά ante βίαν man. rec. D.
1116 b 19   Ἑρμαίῳ συνέβη] Ἑρμαίῳ τῷ ἐν Κορώνῃ τῆς Βοιωτίας συνέβη D.   Verba τῷ
            .... Βοιωτίας suppl. manus prima ad oram P.
         26 ἰητικώτατον P, τὸ ὁρμητικώτατον ἰητικώτατον D, ἰητικώτατον τὸ ὁρμητικώτα-
            τον manus prima ad oram P.
1117 b 6, 7 μικρὸν ὂν τὸ οὗ ἕνεκα οὐδὲν ἡδὺ φαίνεται ἔχειν om. D, habet P.
1118 b 17   ὑπερπλησθῇ] ὑπερπλησθείς D, ὑπερπλησθῇ P, sed -ησθῇ, excepto accentu,
            in ras.
1119 b 19   λέγωμεν P, λέγομεν D.
         34 ἕν τι] sic PD.
1120 a   4 τις post χρεία PD.
         6 τοῦτο] ἕκαστον PD.
       b 4 καὶ ὅτε καὶ οὗ καλόν] sic PD.
         9 δή] δέ PD.
         22 ταῦτα] αὐτά PD.
1121 a   4 καί] sic PD.
        16 συνδυάζεται] συναύξεται PD.
        18 διδόντας ἰδιώτας PD.
        24, 25 δώσει γὰρ οἷς δεῖ καὶ οὐ λήψεται ὅθεν οὐ δεῖ PD.
        33 τοῦτο ποιεῖν μὴ δύνασθαι PD.
       b 4 αὐτοῦ post τούτου habent PD.
        33 καί post ἐργαζόμενοι add. PD.
1122 a 14 ἐστι κακόν PD.
        34 περί PD.
       b 15, 16 κτῆμα μὲν γὰρ τὸ πλεῖστον ἄξιον καὶ τιμιώτατον PD.
        20 τοὺς θεούς PD.
        21 ὅσα habent PD.
        30 τὰ τοιαῦτα] ταῦτα PD.
        30 διά post ἤ habent PD.
        34 δαπανήμασιν] δαπανήσει PD†.
1123 a   2 πᾶσα ἡ PD.
        15 ἔχει μεγαλοπρέπειαν PD.
1124 b   8 ἀφειδής] ἀφειδεῖ PD. [Hanc lectionem exhibent Coraes p. 249, manus
            recentior apud cod. C, Aspasius.]
        21 ἐν PD.
        29, 30 φανερῶς· παρρησιαστὴς (παρησιαστὴς P) γὰρ διὰ τὸ καταφρονητικὸς εἶναι
            καταφρονητικὸς δὲ διὰ παρρησιαστικὸς καὶ ἀληθευτικὸς πλὴν ὅσα μὴ δι᾽
            εἰρωνείαν PD.

c   [I. 1.]

1125 a 1 πρὸς post ἢ habent PD.
     34 χείρων PD.
   b 7 ἐν τιμῆς ὀρέξει PD.
     9 καί ante μᾶλλον habent PD.
     15 δεῖ φέρομεν PD.
     19 δὲ τιμῆς PD.
     32 καί ante ὡς habent PD.
1126 a 17 ἀνταποδιδόασιν PD.
     20 ὀργίζονται PD.
1127 a 8 διά τι ἄλλο PD.
   b 3, 4, 5 ὁ γὰρ φιλαλήθης καὶ ἐν οἷς διαφέρει ἀληθεύων ἀληθεύσει (ἀληθήσι D) καὶ ἐν οἷς μὴ διαφέρει ἔτι μᾶλλον PD†.
     31 καί ante ἀντικεῖσθαι non habent PD.
1128 b 11 γοῦν PD.
     18 δὲ κωλύεσθαι] γὰρ κεκωλύσθαι PD soli excepta man. rec. apud cod. C.
     28 ἑκουσίοις] ἀκουσίοις PD.
1129 a 33 ὁ ante ἄνισος om. PD.
1129 b 1 καί ante πλεονέκτης om. PD.
     17 τοιοῦτον] om. D. Post τοιοῦτον add. P ὥστε ἵνα μὲν τρόπον τινὰ τοιοῦτον, sed, linea ducta, correx.; mox ὥστε κ.τ.λ.
     20 μηδὲ φεύγειν om. PD†.
1130 a 13 τοιάδε] τοιαύτη PD†.
   b 10—13 ἐπεὶ δὲ τὸ ἄνισον καὶ τὸ παράνομον οὐ ταὐτὸν ἀλλ' ἕτερον ὡς μέρος πρὸς ὅλον τὸ μὲν γὰρ ἄνισον ἅπαν παράνομον τὸ δὲ παράνομον οὐχ ἅπαν ἄνισον τὸ μὲν γὰρ πλέον ἅπαν ἄνισον τὸ δὲ ἄνισον οὐ πᾶν πλέον PD.
1135 b 18 ὅταν ἐν ἑαυτῷ ἡ ἀρχὴ ᾖ τῆς αἰτίας PD.
     25 μοχθηρός P, μοχθηρά D.
1136 a 8—10 δὲ μήτε—περί om. D, habet P.
1137 a 3 πλέον ἔχει P, πλεονάζει D.
   b 29 ψηφίσματος] ψηλαφίσματος PD.
1138 b 2 πλευρίτιν ἔχει μείζω νόσον P, πλευρήτην ἔχει μείζων νόσον D.
     10 δή P, δεῖ D.
1141 a 21 γὰρ εἴ] γὰρ εἰδέναι εἰ PD†.
1142 a 25 ἀντίκεισται] ἀπτικοί PD.
   b 19 ἰδεῖν] καὶ σκέψασθαι δεῖν PD†.
1143 b 36—1144 a 1 νῦν μὲν γὰρ ἠπόρηται περὶ αὐτῶν μόνον. πρῶτον μὲν οὖν λέγομεν ὅτι καθ' αὑτάς om. PD†.
1144 a 1 αἱρετάς] ἀρετάς PD†.

NICOMACHEAN ETHICS. 11

1146 a 34 ή] ᾧ PD†.
35 ὅταν τὸ ὕδωρ πνίγῃ τί δεῖ ἐπιπίνειν P, ὅταν τὸ ὕδωρ τὸν φάρυγγα πνίγῃ τί δεῖ ἔτι πίνειν D.
1147 a 19 post σημεῖον add. τοῦ ἐνεργεῖν κατὰ τὴν ἐπιστήμην PD.
34 ἐνοῦσα P, ἐροῦσα D.
1148 b 28 τρώξεις] ἐκτρώξεις P, ἐκτρώσεις D.
1155 b 17 φανερὸν περὶ αὐτῶν PD.
17 γνωρισθέντος P, γνωσθέντος D.
1158 a 2 γίνεται] τοσούτῳ PD†.
b 13 παντὸς ἄρχοντος PD†.
1160 a 36 δ' ἡ τιμοκρατία] δ' ἡμοκρατία (sic) D, δ' ἡ "μοκρατία P, sed eadem, ut videtur, manus vι suppl.
1161 a 1 ἐπίκληροι] ἐπίσκληροι PD†.
13 εὖ πράττωσιν] εὖ πραγῶσιν P, εὐπραγῶσιν D.
26 ὁμοπαθεῖς] οἱ μονωθεῖς PD†.
1172 a 5 τούτῳ] τούτοις PD†.
5 δ τί περ] ὅπερ PD†.
8 συζῆν] ζῆν PD†.
12 ὑπομάττονται PD†.
14 ἄρ' om. PD†.
28, 29 λέγουσιν—πεπεισμένοι om. D, habet P.
30 πρὸς τὸν βίον εἶναι PD†.
b 2 ὡς οὐ τοιαύτην PD.
12 φέρεσθαι μηνεύειν ὡς πᾶσι τοῦτα ἄριστον] φέρεσθαι ὡς πᾶσιν ἄριστον μηνεύει PD.
25 αὐτό om. PD.
27 ἑτέρου om. P spatio relicto, habet D.
28 Πλάτων om. D, et P spatio relicto.
30 μετὰ φρονήσεως τὸν ἡδὺν βίον PD.
30 ἢ χωρίς habet D, om. P spatio relicto.
32 αὐτό] αὐτῷ PD.
1173 a 2 πιστοτέραν PD†.
2 ὠρέγετο PD.
33 τῇ τοῦ] τὸ τοῦ PD.
b 6 εἰς τοῦτο διαλύεσθαι καί] εἰς τοῦτο διαλύεσθαι εἰς τοῦτο καί PD†.
33 ἡ διαφόρους εἴδει om. PD†.
1174 a 15 οὐδενός] τινός PD†.
24 καὶ αὗται τῆς τοῦ ναοῦ ποιήσεως om. PD†.
b 3 οὐκ ἐν] οὐδ' ἐν P, οὐδέν D†.

C 2

1174 b 21   ἡ τελειοτάτη] ἡ τελειότης PD†.
1175 a 4   ἀδυνατεῖ] καὶ ἀδυνατεῖ P, καὶ οὐ δυνατεῖ D.
        7   διά om. PD†.
      b 15,16 αἱ δ' ἀλλότριαι λυμαίνονται δῆλον ὡς πολὺ διιστᾶσιν σχεδὸν γάρ om. D, habet P.
       17   φθείρουσι γὰρ τὰς ἐνεργείας αἱ οἰκεῖαι λῦπαι om. PD.
1176 a 30   εἰρημένων. Here D leaves space for two lines blank, and then begins a new section headed περὶ εὐδαιμονίας in red ink. P goes on without a break.
      b 32 δέ P] γάρ D in textu ; δέ superscr. manus haud scio an prima.
1177 a 20   ὁ νοῦς τῶν ἐν ἡμῖν om. P spatio ix litt. relicto, habet D.
       22   ἡ πράττειν om. P spatio relicto, habet D.
      b 13 περιποιουμένη] περιποιουμένου P, syll. ult. in ras. Περιποιουμέναις D.
       23   τῷ μακαρίῳ P, τῶν μακαρίων D.
1178 a 24   χορηγίας P, om. D.
      b 20 ἀφῃρημένῳ PD.
1179 a 11   τά ante κάλλιστα om. PD.
       12   ὡς ᾤετο om. PD†.
       18   τὸ δ' ἀληθὲς ἐν] τἀληθὲς δ' ἐν P, τὰ δ' ἀληθὲς δ' ἐν D.
1180 a 11   ὀρεγόμενον] παρεχόμενον PD†.
      b 23 αἱ ἐπιστῆμαι] αἰπιστῆμαι PD†.
1181 a 10   ἄν P] ἀλλά D.

While the hypothesis that D is a copy of P seems to me to be discountenanced by much in the foregoing list, and to be absolutely excluded by the occurrence in D of the words κοινωνῆσαι νόμου κ.τ.λ., 1161 b 7, 8; the counter hypothesis, that P is a copy of D, is inadmissible in view of such differences between the two MSS. as those which meet us at 1100 a 12; 1117 b 6, 7; 1136 a 8–10; 1172 a 28, 29; 1172 b 27; 1172 b 30; 1175 b 15, 16; 1177 a 20. The great similarity however (in omissions and other blunders) between the two MSS. warrants us in supposing that they are both copies of one original. P was probably copied directly from it; D, through an intermediate MS. altered in such places as 1098 a 21; 1112 b 21; 1137 a 3; 1146 a 35; 1172 b 27; 1172 b 30; 1175 a 4; 1177 a 20; 1177 a 22.

Brit. Mus. addit. 14080 (B¹) is a codex with twenty-seven lines to the page and about thirty letters to the line. It is described in the

Catalogue as follows—'Aristotelis Ethicorum ad Nicomachum libri decem; ejusdem Moralium Magnorum libri duo, *Graece*. On vellum, xvth cent. octavo. From the Monastery of S. Leonard, near Verona [14080].'

Addit. 6790 (B⁴) is a cod. membr. quarto, containing the Nic. Ethics only, sec. xv. It has twenty-six lines to the page and about thirty-six letters to the line.

A and C in the Eth. Nic. and D were collated by Wilkinson in 1715 in an extremely inaccurate and meagre fashion. Zell, Michelet, and lastly Susemihl, derive their information regarding the MSS., which they quote frequently, from Wilkinson[1]. Wilkinson never, I may say, notices omissions, long or short, which are evidently blunders—the long lacuna in D from 1161 b 8 to 1172 a 1 he actually passes over in silence, betraying Michelet, and after him Susemihl, into an inferential quotation, 1166 b 12, from that MS. in a part which does not exist;—nor does he notice the fact that in A there are four leaves of inferior vellum in an obviously later hand; he more often than not gives a later correction as the original reading; he never notes erasures: his constant habit is to quote two of his three MSS. (CCC=C, NC=D, El.=A) for a various reading, and leave it to be inferred that the reading of his text is that of the third, which is by no means always, or even often, the case; and finally, while it is always dangerous to draw inferences from his silence, as Michelet too often does, his distinct references to his MSS., even if they were accurate, are too few to be of much use. But the following notes made at random will show the character of a collation in which subsequent editors have placed too much confidence.

In the First Book I have counted only twenty-eight places in which Wilkinson gives distinctly and correctly the readings of C (CCC); whereas I have noted 150 places in this Book remarkable for readings peculiar to the MS. or common to it with one or two others. In some of the other Books his references to C (CCC) and D (NC) are even less numerous.

---

[1] Bekker quotes C four times—p. 1099 correctly; 1118 correctly; 1125, where his quotation is not distinct. C has—παρρησιαστὴς γὰρ διὰ τὸ καταφρονητικὸς εἶναι καταφρονητικὸς δὲ διὸ παρρησιαστικὸς καὶ ἀληθευτικὸς πλὴν ὅσα μὴ δι' εἰρωνείαν κ.τ.λ.; 1170 incorrectly. C has in marg. ἐσθλῶν μὲν ἀπ' ἐσθλά, not ἐσθλὰ μὲν ἀπ' ἐσθλῶν.

In 1096 a 20 Wilkinson's text has ἐν τῷ τί ἐστιν, and his note is
'ἐστι deest NC, El. et Ven. 2.' From this one might suppose that
CCC reads ἐστιν, but it omits it.

In 1113 a 1 Wilkinson's text has ἢ πέπεπται ἢ πεποίωται ὡς δεῖ.
His notes are 'ἢ πέπεπται El. non habet (it has);' and 'πεποίηται
Andron. et Bas. ἢ πεποίωται Camerarius omittit.' Michelet's inference
from this is 'Sic vulgatam tueri videntur soli NC et CCC.' NC
indeed has ἢ πέπτεται (sic) ἢ πεποίωται ὡς δεῖ, but CCC omits ἢ πεποίωται
altogether, and for πέπεπται has πεπαισθαι, corrected by a later hand to
πεπαιοται.

In 1102 b 8 CCC has ἢ οὐ λέγεται—the accent and breathing
above the η being on an erasure, and the οὐ having been crossed out.
Wilkinson, who reads ἢ λέγεται, says in his note 'ἢ λέγεται CCC, ἢ οὐ
λέγεται NC,' which Michelet reproduces. The NC reading is correctly
given.

In 1110 a 6, 7 Wilkinson says 'πράξαντες μὲν σώζοιντο, μὴ πράξαντες
δὲ ἀποθνήσκοιεν nostri MSS.'—a statement quoted by Michelet. CCC
reads πράξαντος in both places, and πράξαντες is a later correction. NC,
however, has πράξαντες.

In 1116 b 24 Wilkinson reads ἐπιφέρουσιν and says in a note that
El. and CCC marg. have ἀναφέρουσι. This is repeated by Michelet.
The truth, however, is that CCC has in the text φέρουσιν with K^b alone;
ἐπι stands above the line in a later hand; and ἀναφέρουσι on the margin.
NC has ἀναφέρουσιν, and El. has φέρουσιν by prima man., and ἀναφέρουσι
by later correction.

In 1131 b 31 Wilkinson reads τὰ εἰσενεχθέντα, and says in his note
(correctly) 'προσενεχθέντα El.,' leaving it to be supposed that CCC has
εἰσενεχθέντα, but it has προσενεχθέντα with K^b and P^b, which has been
changed by a later hand into εἰσενεχθέντα. NC, however, has εἰσενεχθέντα.

Of the numerous omissions and other blunders in Books iii, iv,
and v of CCC, which, as we shall see afterwards, establish such a close
connection between that MS. and K^b, Wilkinson scarcely records three
or four.

The following mistakes with regard to the readings of C (O^1) and
D (O^2) require correction in Susemihl's edition of the Eth. Nic. :—

NICOMACHEAN ETHICS. 15

'1106 a 8   πάσχειν] πράττειν O² (=D).' D reads πάσχειν. C has πράττειν.
'1107 a 30 κενώτεροι pr O¹ (=C), κοινότεροι O².' C has κενότεροι p. m., and corr.
             later κενώτεροι; and above the line γρ. κοινότεροι. D has καινότεροι.
'1107 b 11 δι' αὐτάς O².' D has δ' ἑαυτάς.
'1109 a 31 ἡ Καλυψώ] ἡ κίρκη O¹.' C has in the text ἡ κίρκη καλυψώ. A line has
             been drawn through καλυψώ, which, however, a later hand has again
             supplied on the margin.
'1111 b 2   ἔτι καὶ οἱ mg. O¹.' C reads οἱ δέ, and on the margin in a later hand
             has γρ. ὥστε καὶ οἱ.
'1121 a 33 τοῦτο ποιεῖν O¹.' C has μὴ τοῦτο ποιεῖν with K^b alone.
'1125 a 24 νωθροί O¹.' C has ὀκνηροί with γρ. νωθροί on the margin.
1129 b 10   The clause καὶ παράνομος after κοινόν is on the margin of C, but not
             obviously later.
'1145 b 15 πάντας O¹.' C has πάντως.
'1147 a 19 post σημεῖον add. τοῦ εἰδέναι O².' D adds τοῦ ἐνεργεῖν κατὰ τὴν ἐπιστήμην.
'1151 b 21 ἐστὶν ἀκόλαστος οὔτε φαῦλος οὔτε mg. O¹, ἐστὶν ἀκόλαστος εἴτε φαῦλος εἴτε
             pr. O¹.' C has in the text ἢ ἀκόλαστος εἴτε φαῦλος εἴτ', corrected by
             a later hand to οὔτε ἀκόλαστος οὔτε φαῦλος οὔτ'.
'1155 a 17 πρὸς—γεννηθέντι add. O¹.' C omits in the text καὶ πρὸς—γεννηθέντι, but
             adds these words on the margin in a hand not obviously different.
'1157 a 24 ἄλλαις ἑταιρίαις O².' D has ἄλλαις ἑτερίαις.
'1166 b 12 μισοῦσί τε καί O².' I have already pointed out that this is an inference
             from Wilkinson's silence. D is non-existent here. See p. 13.

I now proceed to present the results of my collations of A, B¹, B², C,
and D, arranging the readings of these MSS. as they agree with K^bM^b
or L^bO^b and K^bO^b or L^bM^b, in the various Books of the Ethics. Where
it seems necessary for the determination of the problem of relationship,
I shall also give their readings as they agree with, or differ from, those
of other groups and of single MSS. The readings quoted from Ald.
in the following lists are given mainly on the authority of Susemihl's
actual citations from that edition, and on the strength of my own
inferences from his silence, it being assumed that his collation was a
verbatim one. I had a copy of the Ald. edition beside me, however,
when I made these lists, and was able to verify and, in some cases,
correct my inferences. But as I did not do so quite systematically,
some errors—I hope not many—may have crept into my lists.

BOOK I.

K^bM^b.   L^bO^b.

1094 a 8 om. AD.   καί CAld.B¹B².
   13 κατὰ τόν A.   τόν CDAld.B¹B².
  b 8 τε AC.   γε Ald.B¹B²D.
   23 ἕκαστα A   ἕκαστον B¹B²CDAld.
1095 a 27 τούτοις πᾶσι τοῦ εἶναι ἀγαθὰ   τοῖσδε πᾶσιν αἴτιόν ἐστιν τοῦ εἶναι ἀγαθά
     αἴτιόν ἐστιν A.   CB¹B¹DAld.
   32 ὁ πλάτων A.   πλάτων CDB¹B²Ald.
  b 23 τοῦτο CD.   τοῦτο τό Ald.AB¹B².
   27 εἶναι ἀγαθούς A.   ἀγαθοὺς εἶναι CDAld.B¹B².
1096 a 9 καί.   καίτοι B¹B²CAAld.D.
   23 τούτοις.   τούτων B¹B²CAAld.D.
  b 1 ἐν ἀνθρώπῳ A.   ἀνθρώπῳ CB¹B²Ald.D.
   8 ἔσται AB¹B².   ἔστω CDAld.
   10 ποιεῖσθαι A.   εἰρῆσθαι CB¹B²DAld.
   26 om. A.   γε B¹B²CDAld.
   32 om. AAld.   καί CB¹B²D.
   32 καί A.   τό CDAld.B¹B².
   33 αὐτό τι A.   τι αὐτό CDAld.B¹B².
1097 a 4 τινὰ ἔχει A.   ἔχει τινά CDAld.B¹B².
   7 τοὺς τεχνίτας ἅπαντας A.   ἅπαντας τοὺς τεχνίτας B¹B²DCAld.
   26 ἕτερον A.   ἕτερα B¹B²CDAld.
  b 10 γυναικί.   γυναικί ACB¹B²Ald.D.
1098 a 3 δέ.   δή ACAld.
1099 a 10 φιλοθεώρῳ ACDAld.B¹B².   φιλοθεάμονι.
   14 δ' ἀεὶ αἱ A.   δ' αἱ CB¹B²DAld.
   30 τὴν ἀρίστην AAld.B¹B².   ἀρίστην D.
     τὴν ἀρετήν C.
  b 9 ἢ καὶ ἄλλως.   ἢ ἄλλως AB¹B²DAld.C in ras.
   20 ἢ τὸ διά.   ἢ διά ACB¹B²DAld.
1100 a 8 ἡρωικοῖς   ἡρωικοῖς ACB¹B²Ald.D.
   17 τῶν post καί A.   om. CDAld.B¹B².
  b 35 καὶ τὰ φαῦλα A.   καὶ φαῦλα CDAld.B¹B².
1101 a 21 μέν ACDB¹B².   om.
  b 12 δή ACAld.B¹B²D.   δέ.
   29 κρείττων D.   κρεῖττον ACB¹B²Ald.
1102 a 5 ἐπεί ACDAld.B¹B².   εἰ.

1102 a 12	ἡ σκέψις αὕτη CAld.B¹B².		αὕτη ἡ σκέψις.
	[ἡ ἐπίσκεψις αὕτη A.]		
b 13	τῆς ACDAld.B¹B².		om.
14	ἀκρατοῦς καὶ ἐγκρατοῦς A.		ἐγκ. καὶ ἀκρ. B¹B²CAld.
17	τε.		om. ACB¹B²D.
	K^bO^b.		L^bM^b.
1095 a 3	πράξεων ACB¹B²DAld.		πραγμάτων.
b 4	ἔθεσιν AD.		ἤθεσιν CAld.
7	ἔχει C [ὁ δὲ τοιοῦτος ἔχων λάβοι ἂν A].		ἔχοι.
13	βάλληται AD.		βάληται CAld.
1100 a 28	συμμεταβάλοι Ald.K^bO^b.		συμμεταβάλλοι L^bM^b.
	συμμεταβάλλει C.		συμμεταβάλλει AD.
1101 a 26	καθ' ἕκαστον AAld.		καθ' ἕκαστα CD.
1102 a 19	ψυχῆς.		ψυχήν ACDAld.

The following list contains the C readings in Book i. which I have noted as agreeing with Ald. in other connexions than those recognised in the lists just given. Where D is not cited either as agreeing with C Ald. or differing from them, I have not ascertained its reading.

CAld.

1094 a 10   ἀρετήν B¹B² [δύναμιν AD].
      27   δὴ καὶ ἡ N^bΓ [δ' ἡ D].
    b 22   δί O^b [δὴ D].
1095 b 10   post νοήσῃ add. φρασσάμενος τά κ' ἔπειτα καὶ ἐς τέλος ᾖσιν ἀμείνω B¹B²M^b [om. AD].
1096 a 18   τό post καί add. M^bO^bD.
1097 a 18   ἑκάστῃ O^bΓD.
      24   τὸ αὐτό.
1098 a 22   ἀναγράφειν M^bO^bB¹B² [ἀπογράψαι AD].
    b 26   συμπεριλαμβάνουσι M^bO^bD.
      29   ἀλλ' ἐπί τι καὶ τὰ πλεῖστα M^bO^b [ἀλλ' ἔν γε τι ἤ καὶ τὰ πλεῖστα D, ἀλλ' ἔν γέ τι ἤ πλεῖστα A].
1099 a 30   εἰναί φαμεν H^aM^bP²DB¹B².
    b 11   θεῶν ἐστί H^aM^bO^bP²D.
1101 a 8   γε M^bP²D.
      10   οὐθ' H^aL^bO^b [οὐδ' M^bP²D].

11 ἐκ τῶν τοιούτων δ' οὐκ L^{b}D.
19 καί post πάντῃ add. O^b [om. D].
1102 a 2 ἀρχήν M^{b}O^b [ἀρχή D].
3 πάντα post πάντες H^{a}O^{b}P^a.

The following list contains the C readings which I have noted as differing from Ald. in other connexions than those recognised in the K^{b}M^b—L^{b}O^b and K^{b}O^b—L^{b}M^b lists:—

C.	Ald.
1097 b 21 τῶν.	πάντων τῶν M^b pr. P^a.
1098 b 7 δοκεῖ οὖν γάρ.	δοκεῖ οὖν [δοκεῖ γάρ D].
7 ἤ D.	ἤ τό H^{a}P^a.
7 συμφανῆ.	ἐμφανῆ M^b.
1099 a 22 ἀλλὰ μὴν γε ἀγαθαί καὶ καλαί M^b.	ἀλλὰ μὴν καὶ ἀγαθαί γε καὶ καλαί O^{b}P^{a}C m. rec. [AD=Bekker].
28 οὔ τις ἐρᾶται τυχεῖν H^{a}M^{b}N^b P^{a}A [οὔ τις ἐρᾷ τυχεῖν D].	δὲ τυχεῖν οὔ τις ἕκαστος ἐρᾷ.
1099 b 1 διά.	ἡ διά.
6 ἡ L^{b}M^{b}O^b.	om. K^b.
33 ἄλλο τι τῶν H^{a}M^{b}O^{b}P^a.	ἄλλο τῶν D.
1101 b 15 τὰ ἔργα καὶ τὰς πράξεις H^{a}L^b M^{b}O^{b}D.	τὰς πράξεις καὶ τὰ ἔργα K^b.
1102 a 25 πλεῖον.	πλεῖστον L^{b}D.
33 τοῦ αὔξεσθαι D.	τοῦ αὐξάνεσθαι.
b 5 διάδηλοι.	διάδηλος P^a.
13 δὴ K^{b}L^b.	δή H^{a}M^{b}O^{b}P^{a}Γ.

I have noted only two readings in which C agrees with K^b where the latter seems to be unique among Bekker's MSS. and Susemihl's other authorities, viz. 1098 a 11, τό ante κιθαρίζειν om. K^b C (habent B^1 B^2); and 1100 b 33, αἱ om. K^b C D. In 1101 b 2, C reads ἀφαυρόν, with one letter, however, erased after φ. On the margin a later hand has placed γρ. φλαῦρον, which is the reading of K^b A and B^1. Coraes, to whom K^b does not seem to have been known, gives φλαῦρον as a various reading (ἠθ. νικ. p. 222). B^2 has ἀφαυρόν. I have noted only two cases of the agreement of C with L^b where the latter seems to stand quite alone, viz. 1094 b 6, τά] τό L^{b}C, and 1096 a 13, τοιαύτης] om. L^{b}CB^{1}B^2. In 1101 a 20, C reads (as Michelet correctly states) μακαρίους δ' ὡς ἀνθρώπους, with Par. 2023 (Susemihl's P^1), the Paraphrast, Eustratius, and Γ. All other authorities (including A B^1 B^2 D) omit ὡς. The word is described by Michelet as prima manu superscriptum in Par. 2023; but Susem. simply says corr. P^1. In C a dot has been placed below ὡς. Coraes reads ὡς without note.

The following list contains a large selection of the cases in which K^b is unique among Bekker's MSS. in Book i, and is given in order to show the extent of the agreement of A with these unique readings:—

1094 b 9 γάρ A, om. K^b.
1095 a 5 ἀκούσεται A, ἀκούεται pr. K^b.
       13 προοιμιάσθω K^b, πεπροοιμιάσθω A [B^{1}B^2=Bek.].
     b 32 καί om. K^{b}A.
1096 a 5 ἐχομένοις K^{b}A [B^{1}B^2=Bek].
       31 ἦν A, εἴη K^{b}D.
     b 20 πλεῖον K^b, πλήν A (but ἦν in ras.) B^{1}B^2.
1098 a 11 κιθαρίζειν K^b, τὸ κιθαρίζειν AB^{1}B^2.
     b 8 δί K^b, δή A.
        9 ἐκ τοῦ A, ἑκάστου K^b.
       11 συνήδει A, συνδεῖ K^b.
       17 ὑπὸ τῶν φιλοσοφούντων ὀρθῶς δὴ καί om. K^{b}A.
       30 συνοδός AD, σύνορός K^b.
1099 a 6 ἐπίβολοι K^{b}AB^2.
    10, 11 τὸν αὐτὸν δὲ τρόπον καὶ τὰ δίκαια τῷ φιλοδικαίῳ om. K^b, habet A.
       13 τοιαῦται K^{b}B^{1}B^{2}D, τοιαῦτα A.
       22 ἀλλὰ μὴν καὶ ἀγαθαί γε καὶ καλαί A.
           ἀλλὰ μὴν καὶ ἀγαθαί τε καὶ καλαί K^b.
1100 a 32 τό post δή add. K^b, om. AB^{1}B^{2}CD.
1101 a 13 τελείῳ AB^{1}B^2, ὀλίγῳ K^b.
1102 a 6 post ἐπισκεπτέον add. ἂν εἴη K^{b}A [om. B^{1}B^{2}CD].
       12 ἀλλότριον K^b, ἄμοιρον A.
     b 34 πᾶσα ἡ K^b, πᾶσα A.
1103 a 7 ἤ A, καί K^b.

The results for Book i. may be summed up as follow—K^b and M^b agreeing in thirty-eight places against L^b and O^b, C agrees with L^b and O^b in twenty-nine of them, and with K^b and M^b in nine. Ald. agrees with L^b

and O[b] also in twenty-nine of these thirty-eight places—twenty-seven times in company with C—and with K[b] and M[b] in six—five times in company with C. Under the K[b]O[b]—L[b]M[b] head, of the seven agreements of C, five are in company with Ald. The evidence for the close relationship between C and Ald. is farther increased by the CAld. list; while the C—Ald. list shows a certain amount of divergence. C and Ald. are evidently descended in this Book from a not remote common ascendant which resembled O[b] closely, but embodied certain corrections from a MS. or MSS. resembling M[b]. The C Ald. readings on the K[b]M[b] side of my first list are all, I think, explicable on the hypothesis of a MS. resembling O[b] having been corrected in these places from one resembling M[b].

D, though closely related to C and Ald., is not so closely related to them as they are to each other. The number and quality of its divergences in the C Ald. list must be set against the fact that in the K[b]M[b]—L[b]O[b] list its agreements are principally on the L[b]O[b] side, and in company with Ald. and C.

A in this Book belongs, with M[b], distinctly to the K[b] family. B[1] and B[2] belong as distinctly to the L[b] family.

BOOK II.

	K[b]M[b].	L[b]O[b].
1103 a 22	om. A.	αὐτόν CDAld.B[1]B[2].
32	τῶν ἄλλων τεχνῶν CB[1]B[2]DA Ald.	τῶν τεχνῶν τῶν ἄλλων.
b 15	γινόμεθα post ἀνθρώπους AB[1]B[2]DCAld.	γινόμεθα post ἄδικοι.
1104 a 25	τις ACAld.B[1]B[2]D.	om.
27	αἱ φθοραί Ald.AD.	φθοραί CB[1]B[2].
b 34	τε ACAld.B[1]B[2]D.	om.
1105 a 19	om. A.	τά post καί CB[1]B[2]DAld.
24	τι post γραμματικόν ACAld. D.	τι post ἐάν B[1] [ἐάν τι καὶ γραμματικόν τι ποιήσῃ B[2]].
27	γινόμενα ACB[1]B[2]DAld.	γενόμενα.
28	ταῦτα ACB[1]B[2]Ald.	αὐτά D.
29	ἐάν ACB[1]B[2]DAld.	ἄν.
32	καὶ προαιρούμενος CAld.	om. N[b]P[2]A.

1105 b 4	ἅπερ ἐκ AD.	ἅπερ καὶ ἐκ B¹B²CAld.
22	φιλίαν μῖσος ACB¹B²DAld.	μῖσος φιλίαν.
1106 a 28	πρός ACB¹B²AldD.	καθ'.
34	ἴσῳ A.	ἴσως CB¹B²DAld.
b 8	ἐπιτελεῖ B¹B²CDA (omitting εὖ).	ἀποτελεῖ.
27	ἄρα ἐστίν ACB¹B²DAld.	ἐστὶν ἄρα.
35	παντοδαπῶς δὲ κακοί ACAld. B¹B²D.	κακοὶ δὲ παντοδαπῶς.
1107 a 23	τὸ τό Ald.B¹B².	τό CD [A has a short lacuna here which is filled up on the margin, where τό stands only once].
b 3	δ' ἐν τῷ A.	δὲ τῷ B²Ald.DC [B¹ has a short lacuna here].
26	αὕτη.	αὐτή ACB¹B²Ald.D.
1108 a 2	ἐν D.	om. B¹B²CAldA (A also omits τοῖς before ἑξῆς).
28, 29	εἰ AD.	ὁ B¹B²CAld.
b 11	δί ACB¹B²DAld.	δή.
30	τόν.	μὲν τό ACB¹B²DAld.
1109 a 23	τοῖς πάθεσι καὶ (ἐν AK^b) ταῖς πράξεσιν ACB¹B²DAld.	ταῖς πράξεσι καὶ τοῖς πάθεσιν.
26	δί ACAld.	δή.
b 5	ἀπάγοντες AD.	ἀπαγαγόντες B¹B²CAld.
	K^bO^b.	L^bM^b.
1103 a 26	παραγίνεται ACB¹B²D.	περιγίνεται.
b 18	τά AC.	om. Ald.
1104 b 21	φαῦλαι CAld.	φαῦλοι AD.
1106 a 23	ἑαυτοῦ AC.	αὐτοῦ.
30	ἑκατέρου ACAld.	ἑκατέρων.
1108 b 35	ἀντίκειται CAld.	ἀντίκεινται A.

The following list contains the C readings which I have noted in the Second Book as agreeing with Ald. in other connexions than those recognised in the foregoing list. No inferences must be drawn from my silence regarding other MSS.

ENGLISH MANUSCRIPTS OF THE

CAld.
1103 b 10 οἱ ante οἰκοδόμοι, add. HᵃNᵇPᵃD [om. AB¹B²].
32 ὑπερκείσθω DNᵇP²B¹B² [ὑποκείσθω A].
33 ὁ ante ὀρθός add. MᵇNᵇA.
34 προδιωμολογίσθω C, προδιωμολογήσθω B¹B², προδιωμολογείσθω Ald. [προ-
ομαλογείσθω LᵇOᵇ, προδιομολογείσθω AD].
1104 b 14 πράξεις καὶ πάθη KᵇΓA et corr. P².
32 πάντα μὲν ταῦτα HᵃNᵇP² [πάντα μὲν δὴ ταῦτα D, ταῦτα μὲν πάντα A].
1105 a 7 ἢ LᵇDB¹B² [καί A].
b 6 ἢ ὁ Kᵇ [ἢ A].
8 οἱ post δίκαιοι καί LᵇA.
1106 a 8 πράττειν B¹B² [πάσχειν DA].
b 1 pro μναῖ, μνᾶς NᵇOᵇP²ΓB¹ ut videtur [μναῖ KᵇA, μναῖ BᵃD].
22 ἐπί B¹B²NᵇP² [ἐστί D, ἐστὶν ἐπί AKᵇ].
1107 b 24 δὲ λέγομεν NᵇP²Γ [δὲ ἐλέγομεν A].
1108 a 3 λέγομεν LᵇNᵇP²D [λέγωμεν A].

The following list contains the C readings which I have noted in Book ii. as differing from Ald. in other connexions than those recognised in the KᵇMᵇ—LᵇOᵇ, and KᵇOᵇ—LᵇMᵇ lists :—

C.	Ald.
1103 a 22 τό A.	om. Lᵇ.
b 18 τά prius A [τάς D].	om. Lᵇ.
18 om. Mᵇ.	τά alterum AD.
1104 a 1 πρακτέων KᵇLᵇMᵇAB¹B².	πρακτῶν OᵇD.
27 αὐξήσεις.	αἱ αὐξήσεις AMᵇP².
b 31 ὄντων τῶν MᵇNᵇP² [τῶν AD].	ὄντων LᵇOᵇ.
1105 a 11 ἀρετῇ AB¹B².	ἠθικῇ MᵇD, Par. 1417, pr. P², rec. Lᵇ.
b 2 πρὸς δὲ τό [πρὸς δέ KᵇA].	τὸ δὲ πρός.
19 μετὰ δὲ ταῦτα τί ἐστιν ἡ ἀρετὴ ἑξῆς.	μετὰ δὲ ταῦτα τί ἐστιν ἡ ἀρετή LᵇOᵇB¹B²Γ [τί δ' ἐστιν ἡ ἀρετὴ ἑξῆς KᵇAD].
1107 a 16 ἦν.	ἢ [ἢ A].
23 ἄκρον [lacuna in A, but margin has ἄκρον].	ἄκρων MᵇNᵇP².
28 om. A.	ἐν post καί add. LᵇΓ.
b 11 δὲ κατ' αὐτάς.	δὲ αὐτάς A pr. ut vid. sed man. rec. δ' ἑαυταῖς [δ' ἑαυτάς D].

NICOMACHEAN ETHICS.

1107 b 21   pro πῆ, ᾧ L^bO^bM^bN^bP^2 | δ.
        (corr. rec. πῆ C, πῆ AK^b).
    27   μικράν B^1B^2. | μικρά AK^bL^bN^b.
        σμικράν D.

Among the following quotations will be found all the cases which I have noted in Book ii, of agreement between C and K^b where the latter is unique in its reading among Bekker's MSS.—L^bM^bO^b. The only case of C=L^b unique which I have noted heads the list of quotations :—

    1103 b 29 ἀναγκαῖον ἐπισκέψασθαι L^bCB^1B^2, ἀναγκαῖόν ἐστι σκέψασθαι AD. See Rassow's Forsch. p. 55. He defends the reading of L^b on the ground that ἀναγκαῖον never occurs in the Ethics, and seldom in other Aristotelian writings, with the copula.   1105 a 21 τά ante μουσικά add. K^bAD om. C cum cet.   1105 a 26 τε add. K^bP^2ACD, om. Bek. cum cet.   1105 b 11 μελλήσεις K^bP^2AC, μελήσεις cet.   1107 b 7 οὐδ' ὀνόματος τετύχηκεν οὐδ' ὁ τοιοῦτος· ἔστω δὲ ἀναίσθητος D, A= Bekker, οὐδ' οὗτοι ὀνόματος τετυχήκασιν ἔστωσαν δ' ἀναίσθητοι B^1B^2.   1109 a 29 διόπερ K^bCB^1B^2Ald., post διόπερ add. ἐστί B^1B^2CL^bO^bM^bN^bP^2Ald., D reads ὅπερ ἐστὶ τί (sic) εὖ καὶ σπάνιον ὃ καὶ ἐπαινετὸν καὶ καλόν, A reads ὅπερ ἐστι τὸ εὖ καὶ σπάνιον καὶ ἐπαινετὸν καὶ καλόν.   1109 a 32 for τούτου B^1B^2C have ὡς τοῦ with L^bO^b, Ald. has τὸ ὡς τοῦ, A has τὸ τοῦ, and D τὸ μὲν τοῦ.   1109 b 15 καί πως K^bL^bCD A.   1109 b 24 δηλοῖ ACD.

The following list shows the extent of the agreement in Book ii. between A and K^b where the readings of the latter are unique among those of Bekker's MSS. :—

1103 b 7   καί ante γίνεται om. K^bA [habent B^1B^2C].
        9   οἱ ante κακοί om. K^b habent AC.
     15   γινόμενα K^b, γινόμεθα ACDB^1B^2.
     17   ᾖ AC om K^b.
     24   εὐθέως K^bA [εὐθύς B^1B^2CD].
     27   ἡ ἀρετή τί K^bA [τί ἐστιν ἡ ἀρετή C].
     29   ἐστι σκέψασθαι AD, ἣν σκέψασθαι K^b.
1104 a 3   ἀπαιτηταιοι K^b pr., ἀπαιτητέοι A, sed ἐ in ras. scripsit librarius ipse.
      8   πρός B^1B^2C] περί K^bA.
     10   τοῦ om. K^b, habent AC.
     19   ἄλλων om. K^b, habent AC.

1104 a 24 πᾶσαν K^b, πάσας AC.
   24 ἄγροι K^b, ἄγροικοι AD, ἀγρικοί (sic) C, ἀγροῖκοι B¹B².
   25 γάρ AC, δή K^b.
   32 δύναται ταῦτα ACD, ἅ δύναιτ' αὐτά K^bpr, ἄν δύναιτ' αὐτά γρ. mg² (rubr.) K^b.
  b 18 πρότερον AB¹B²C, πρώην K^b.
    29 ἔτι ACB¹B², ὅτι K^b.
    32 βλαβεροῦ K^bA [ἀσυμφόρου L^bM^bN^bO^bΓ^{Hα}P^aDB¹B²CAld.].
1105 a 3 συντετράφθαι K^b, συντέθραπται ACB¹B².
    21 τά ante μουσικά add. K^bAD, om. C.
    26 τε add. K^bP²ACD.
    32 διὰ ταῦτα ΓK^bA, δι' αὐτά C.
  b 21 ἄν τι ΓK^bAD, τι ἄν C.
    22 θάρσος post φθόνον K^bA.
    31 ἤ C] καί K^bA.
1106 a 9 καί om. K^b, habent AC.
  b 1 εἴ τῳ AC, ὧι K^b.
    1 μναῖ K^bA [μναῖ DB², μνᾶς B¹C pr.].
    13 εἰ δ' οἱ K^bA, οἱ δ' CΓL^bP²Ald.
    22 ἐστί D, ἐστὶν ἐπί K^bA, ἐπί CB¹B².
1107 a 26 οὔτε K^bAD, οὐδέ C.
  b 7, 8 διόπερ οὐδ' ὀνόματος τετυχήκασιν οὐδ' οἱ τοιοῦτοι K^bA, διόπερ οὐδ' οὗτοι ὀνόματος τετυχήκασιν C, διόπερ οὐδ' ὀνόματος τετύχηκεν οὐδ' ὁ τοιοῦτος D, mox ἔστω δὲ ἀναίσθητος,
    11 δ' ἑαυτάς A man. rec.] δὲ αὑτάς A pr. ut videtur, δ' ἑαυτάς D, κατ' αὑτάς C, δή K^b.
    20 διαφέρουσι δὲ αὗται τῶν περὶ τὴν ἐλευθεριότητα om. K^b, habent AC.
    32, 33 ἔστι μὲν ὅτε τὸν μέσον φιλότιμον καλοῦμεν ἔστι δ' ὅτι ἀφιλότιμον καί om. K^b, habent AC.
1108 a 1 ἔστι δ' ὅτε τὸν ἀφιλότιμον om. K^b, habent AC.
    8 δ' ἔλλειψις AC] δὲ κακία K^b.
    12 ἡ μὲν ὅτι ἔστιν K^bA, ὅτι ἡ μέν ἐστι C.
    35 ὁ post ἤ om. K^b, habent AC.
    35 μηδέν K^b, μηδέ AC.
1109 a 23 ἐν τοῖς πάθεσι καὶ ἐν ταῖς πράξεσιν K^bA.
    29 διόπερ K^bCB¹B², ὅπερ ἔστι AD.
    31 παραινεῖ K^bA, παρῄνει CDB¹B².
  b 18 ἀποκαλοῦντες K^b, ἀποκαλοῦμεν AC.
    25 ὅτε—ὅτε K^b, τότε—τότε ACD.

NICOMACHEAN ETHICS.

The results for Book ii. may be summed up. K^b and M^b agreeing in twenty-nine places against L^b and O^b, C sides with K^b and M^b in eighteen of them, and with L^b and O^b in eleven of them. Ald. sides with K^b and M^b in seventeen of these twenty-nine places, fifteen times in company with C, and in ten of these sides with L^b and O^b, nine times in company with C. In the small K^bO^b—L^bM^b list C sides with K^b and O^b in all six places, in three of them with Ald. The C Ald. and C—Ald. lists show considerable agreement and considerable divergence between C and Ald. Here again, as in Book i, C and Ald. are evidently descended from a not remote common ascendant, which, however, seems to have been related to M^b, and to have embodied very considerable corrections from a MS. or MSS. resembling O^b. The L^bO^b readings of C and Ald. can, I think, be explained without difficulty as the results of correction of this kind. 1103 a 22, the omission in K^bM^b is corrected by the insertion of αὐτόν; (1104 a 27, the omission with L^bO^b of αἱ by C may be explained by accident, καί preceding αἱ); 1105 a 19, τά inserted; 1105 b 4, καί inserted; 1106 a 34, a simple correction; 1107 a 23, the reading of C, may be explained by homœoteleuton; 1107 b 3, C and Ald. omit ἐν—a word which is omitted with extraordinary frequency by MSS.; 1107 b 26, a simple correction; 1108 a 2, the omission of ἐν puts C Ald. on the L^bO^b side; 1108 a 28, 29, a simple correction; 1108 b 30, if the common ascendant of C and Ald. read τόν it would be corrected, since all MSS., except apparently K^b and M^b, have μὲν τό; 1109 b 5, a simple correction. The K^bO^b—L^bM^b readings are not worth noticing specially. In 1103 b 29 and 1109 a 29, C, B^1 and B^2 preserve readings of L^b and K^b respectively, which have been lost by all other MSS. whose readings have been recorded (see p. 23).

In the following places D=C, no other MSS. being quoted, so far as I know, for the readings. 1103 b 5, διαμαρτάνουσι; 1103 b 6, ἔτι καί; 1106 a 23, ὁ ἄνθρωπος ἀγαθός; 1106 b 32, post ἐλλείπει add. τοῦ δέοντος.

B^1 and B^2, which are practically identical in this Book, belong with D to the same group as C and Ald., i. e. to a group which resembles M^b rather than O^b, and is somewhat distantly related to K^b.

A, as in the First Book, belongs distinctly to the K^b family.

BOOK III.

	K^bO^h.	L^bM^b.
1110a 14	ἑκούσιον δὴ καὶ (τὸ K^bB²D), ἀκούσιον ADB², lacuna in C.	ἀκούσιον δὴ καὶ τὸ ἑκούσιον B¹.
25	ὑπερτείνει post φύσιν ACB¹ B²DAld.	ὑπερτείνει ante ἵνα.
b 13	δί AD.	δή CB¹B²Ald.
23	ἔστω B¹B²CAld.A.	ἔσται [ἐστὶν D].
1111a 1	καί post γάρ CD.	om. AAld.B¹B².
6	ἂν A.	om. CB¹B²DAld.
25	om.	δι' CAB¹B²Ald.D.
1112a 1	δόξῃ O^bAB¹B²DAld.C, δόξει K^b.	καὶ δόξῃ.
7	add. ὡς N^b.	om. AB¹B²CDAld.
14	οὐθέν D.	οὐθέν ἐστιν AB¹B²C.
20	βουλεύσαιτ' ἄν τις A.	ἄν τις βουλεύσαιτο B¹B²DCAld.
b 15	τίνων ACB¹B²Ald.D.	τίνος.
1113a 33	ὤν O^bCDB¹B²Ald.	om. A.
	ὤν K^b.	
b 13	ἄρα.	ἔσται ACDB¹B²Ald.
20	ἐν A.	ἐφ' CDB¹B²Ald.
24	αὐτοὶ αἴτιοι ACB¹B²DAld.	αἴτιοι αὐτοί.
26	ὅσα A.	πρὸς ὅσα CB¹B²DAld.
29	ὁτιοῦν ἄλλο A.	ἀλλ' ὁτιοῦν B¹B²CDAld.
1114a 1	δί ACB¹B²DAld.	δή.
2	ὃν τὸ μὴ ἀγνοεῖν CAB¹B²D Ald.	τὸ μὴ ἀγνοεῖν ὄν.
12	τὸν ἀκολασταίνοντα ἀκώλαστον CADB¹B²Ald.	ἀκώλαστον τὸν ἀκολασταίνοντα.
21	ἔτι A.	om. B¹B²CDAld.
27	ἐλεῆσαι ACAld.	ἐλεήσει.
	ἐλεῆσαι B¹B²D.	
b 3	μὴ οὐθείς A.	μηδείς B¹B²CDAld.
10	καὶ τό ACB¹B²DAld.	τὸ δ'.
28	om. A.	καί CB¹B²DAld.
28	πρακτικαὶ καί CADB¹B²Ald. (καί om. K^b).	πρακτικοί.

1114 b 31	τοῦ A.		om. B¹B²CD.
1115 a 3	χρῆσθαι A.		χρήσασθαι CDB¹B²Ald.
	7	φανερὸν γεγένηται A.	καὶ πρότερον εἴρηται D (καὶ πρότερον εἴρηται· φανερὸν γὰρ γεγένηται CB¹B²Ald.).
	13	γάρ ADAld.	om. CB¹B².
	16	τι ὅμοιον A.	ὅμοιόν τι CB¹B²DAld.
	20	ἐν ACB¹B²Ald.	om.
	24	γ' οὖν.	οὖν ACB¹B²DAld.
	29	εἰ] om.	ἢ D (εἰ NᵇB¹B²Ald. and C in ras., ἢ in ras. A).
	29	om.	ἐν ante νόσοις CB¹B²AAld.
b	8	om. ACDB¹B²Ald.	γε.
	18	καί ante ὡς ACB¹B²DAld.	om.
	33	τούτοις AAld.CB¹B²D.	τούτῳ.
1116 a 21	καὶ οἱ C.		οἱ δέ AB¹B²DAld.
	31	ὅσοι (-οι in ras. C) A pr.	ὅσῳ B¹B²DAld.A corr.
	33	ὁ AC.	om. Ald.B¹B²D.
b	4	om. ACD.	τις Ald.B¹B².
	9	μή ACB¹B²DAld.	μηδέν.
	10	post ἐμπειρίας add. καὶ φυλάξασθαι καὶ πατάξαι CDB¹B²AAld.	om.
	32	διὰ τὸ φοβεῖσθαι C (διὰ φοβεῖσθαι A).	φοβεῖσθαι DB¹B²Ald.
	33	ἐν ACDAld.B¹B².	om.
	36	εἶεν AC.	ἂν εἶεν DB¹B²Ald.
1117 a 2,3	om. C.		οὐ δή—κίνδυνον ADB¹B²Ald.
	7	om. ACDB¹B²Ald.	add. μαχόμενοι.
	13	κράτιστοι ACD. κρατίστους Ald.	κρείττους B¹B².
	20	om. AC.	κμί B¹DAld.
b	26	ὁμοίως ACDAld.	ὁμοίως τῇ ἀνδρείᾳ.
1118 a 12	ἢ (καί in ras. C).		καί AB¹DAld.
	16	οὐδ' ἐν τοῖς C.	οὐδὲ τοῖς AB¹D.
	19	δ' αἴσθησιν ACAld.	αἴσθησιν δ'.
	23	δή ACAld.	δ'.
	32	φιλόξενος κ.τ.λ.[1] ACDAld.	om. B¹B².

[1] See details on p. 31.

28   ENGLISH MANUSCRIPTS OF THE

1118 b	10	ὁ ἐνδεής AC.	ὅταν ἐνδεὴς ᾖ B¹DAld.
	13	om. C.	καί AB¹Ald.
	17	ἕως πλησθῇ C.	ἕως ἂν ὑπερπλησθῇ AB¹B²Ald. (ἕως ἂν ὑπερπλησθείς D).
	26	εἰ C.	ἐπί AAld.
	30	οὐδ' ἀκόλαστος ACD (ὁ δ' ἀκόλαστος B¹Ald.).	ἀκόλαστος δέ.
	33	om. C.	καὶ τῷ ἀπέχεσθαι ADB¹Ald.
1119 a	5	δὲ τὰ περί AC.	τὰ περί B¹Ald.
	10	ὀνόματος ὁ τοιοῦτος C.	ὁ τοιοῦτος ὀνόματος Ald.A.
	16	ᾆ C.	ὅσα AB¹B²Ald.D.
	27	ἐπὶ δὲ τῶν φοβερῶν CA.	ἐπὶ τῶν φοβερῶν δ' D.
	34	καί AC.	om. Ald.
b	13	δί A (δή C).	γάρ B¹Ald.D.
	17	καὶ ὡς δεῖ ACAld.	om.

		K^bM^b.	L^bO^b.
1110 a	29	διακρῖναι.	τὸ κρῖναι AAld.
b	11	πάντες πάντα Ald.AD.	πάντα πάντες C.
1112 a	31	αἰτίαι.	αἴτια Ald.AC.
1113 a	10	ἐκ A.	om. CB¹B¹D.
1114 a	31	λόγοι C.	λέγει AD.
1115 a	1	πρόθεσις Ald.D.	πρόσθεσις AC.
	20	ἐλεύθεροι DAld.	ἐλευθέριοι ACB¹.
1116 a	35	ἐσεῖται DCB¹.	ἔσσειται A.
b	7	καινά ACB¹Ald.	κενά D.
1117 a	25	ὑποπτεύσωσιν K^bA. ὑποπτεύωσι M^b.	ὑποπτεύσωσι DO^bAld.C. ὑποπτεύσουσι L^b.
1119 b	4	τόν C.	τό DB¹AAld.
	6	om. AC.	καί ante μάλιστα Ald.D.

The following is a list of the C readings which I have noted as agreeing with Ald. in other connexions, up to the end of p. 1115 a. The divergence between C and Ald., which begins at this point and continues to the end of the Book, is so marked that it will not be necessary to go into details regarding their relationship in the latter part of the Book.

NICOMACHEAN ETHICS. 29

CAld.
1110 a 24   πράξειε MᵇNᵇOᵇP² [πράξῃ AD].
1111 a 13   λελογχευμένον [AD=Bek.].
        22 βιαίου NᵇOᵇDB¹B² [βίᾳ A].
      b 25 ἂν γενέσθαι LᵇD [γενέσθαι ἂν A].
1112 b 33   οὐκ ἂν οὖν LᵇMᵇCAB¹ [οὐκ ἂν εἴη D].
1113 a 15   τἀγαθοῦ ADΓ.
        20 τό ante βουλητόν add. HªNᵇAD.
      b 5   εἶεν ἂν KᵇNᵇAΓD.
        28 ὄντος NᵇOᵇD. [ὃν τό A.]
1114 a 25   post ἀσθένειαν add. καὶ αἶσχος LᵇNᵇAD.
      b 4   κακὰ ποιεῖν NᵇOᵇD [κακοποιεῖν A].
        15 τοῦτο Ald., τοῦτ' C [ταῦτ' AD].
        17 αὐτό [αὐτῷ D; and A, with ῷ however in ras.].
        28 καὶ καθ' OᵇΓAD.
1115 a 1   τῶν καθ' A [καθ' D].
        7   καὶ πρότερον εἴρηται· φανερὸν γὰρ γεγένηται B¹B² [D=Bek.; ἤδη φανερὸν γεγένηται A, instead of ἤδη καὶ πρότερον εἴρηται].

The following is a list of the C readings in Book iii. to the end of p. 1115 a which differ from Ald. in other connexions than those recognised in the KᵇOᵇ—LᵇMᵇ and KᵇMᵇ—LᵇOᵇ lists:—

	C.	Ald.
1109 b 30	δή.	δί D.
1110 a 6	πράξαντος.	πράξαντες MᵇNᵇP³AD.
27	ἀποθανετέον παθόντι A.	ἀποθανατέον παθόντα LᵇMᵇNᵇOᵇP²D.
32	ἃ δ' ἀναγκάζονται A.	τὰ δ' ἀναγκάζοντα MᵇNᵇD.
b 10	ἀναγκάζειν A.	ἀνάγκη.
10	οὕτω [αὐτῷ AD].	οὐ τῷ αὐτῷ.
12	τὸ ἡδὺ μεθ' ἡδονῆς.	τὸ ἡδὺ τὸ κακὸν μεθ' ἡδονῆς. [τὸ ἡδὺ καὶ καλὸν μεθ' ἡδονῆς A, τὸ ἡδὺ ἢ τὸ καλὸν μεθ' ἡδονῆς DP²].
1112 a 30	δι' ἡμῶν οὐδέν NᵇOᵇD. [οὐδὲν δι' ἡμῶν A.]	δ' ἡμῶν οὐδέν.
1113 a 17	τό ante βουλητόν prius A.	om. NᵇOᵇ.
21	ἄλλο δ' ἄλλῳ A.	ἄλλῳ δ' ἄλλως LᵇMᵇD.
31	om.	καὶ post ἐστι ANᵇΓ.
b 14	μακάριος ADB¹B².	μακάριον.

1114 a 18 λαβεῖν DB¹B². | βαλεῖν A and all Bekker's Codd.
b 21 εἰ μή. | om. K^bΓD [εἰ μὴ ἐν om. A].
1115 a 32 om. D. | αἱ ante ἐν add. N^bO^b.

As the agreement of C and K^b unique becomes very close after 1115 b 1, it will be well to note the cases of agreement in Book iii. before that point. I have found only the following (those cases having been excluded in which C=K^b Ald.), viz. 1112 a 31, add. καί K^bCΓ [om. D cum cet.], 1113 b 31, τά om. K^bC [habet D]; 1114 b 10, οἴονται K^bC. To these three cases may perhaps be added 1114 a 4, τοιοῦτον K^bN^bCD.

The results for iii^a, i.e. for 1109 b 30—1115 b 1, may be summed up as follow. There are thirty-six places in which K^b and O^b agree against L^b and M^b, and in twenty of them C sides with L^b and M^b, and in fourteen with K^b and O^b. Ald. sides with L^b and M^b in eighteen out of these thirty-six places, seventeen times in company with C; and in fourteen of them with K^b and O^b, thirteen times in company with C. Thus C and Ald. are evidently descended, in this part of the Third Book, from a not remote common source; but the cross-corrections have been so numerous that it is difficult to determine whether that source was genealogically related to M^b or O^b.

The same difficulty attaches to the question of the relationship of D, which is almost equally divided (both before and after 1115 b 1) between K^bO^b and L^bM^b.

With regard to B¹ and B² there can be little doubt that they are related to M^b rather than to O^b.

A again in this Book, as in Books i. and ii, belongs distinctly to the K^b family.

The following is a list, complete so far as I know, of the readings in which C agrees with K^b where the latter MS. is unique among Bekker's MSS. in the Third Book after 1115 b 1 :—

K^bC.

1115 b 23 om. τά ante κατά [habent DAB¹].
27 om. τά AAld.
31 om. οὗτος A [habent DB¹].
1116 a 23 ἀναθήσῃ [ἀναθήσει AB¹B¹D].
25 τρωίεσσι [τρώσσ' A].

1116 a 35 οὖ [οὗ D; and A with accent and breathing in ras.].
35 ἀρκείῶν [ἄρκιον AB¹D].
b 5 εἶναι post ἐπιστήμην MᵇOᵇA [add. ΓLᵇAld. DB¹Bª].
5 om. ἐν ante ἄλλοις D [habent AB¹].
8 ᾷ [οἷα AB¹BªD].
11 τὸ μὴ ποιῆσαι [τὸ ποιῆσαι ADB¹Bª].
24 φέρουσι A [ἀναφέρουσι D, marg. C, corr. A; ἐπιφέρουσι B¹Bª, corr. rec. C].
1117 a 8 om. τό ante πάθος [habent AD].
11 μέν [ἐν AB¹D].
12 πρότερον εἰρημένα A [προειρημένα DB¹Bª].
15 τὰ τοιαῦτα [τοιαῦτα AB¹BªD].
17 add. μή ante φαινόμενα ΓA [om. B¹D].
b 2 γίνεσθαι [γίνεται AB¹BªD].
7 εἰ δὲ δή A [εἰ δή B¹].
9 om. ἤ ante ὅτι [habent AB¹D].
10 ἔχει B¹ [ἔχῃ BªA].
11 λυπήσεται B¹BªAld. [λύπῃ ἔσται ADNᵇOᵇ].
13 τούτῳ [τοῦτο AB¹D].
24 om. αἱ ante ἀρεταί [habent AB¹D].
1118 a 13 ἐπιθυμημάτων [ἐπιθυμητῶν ΓOᵇA, ἐπιθυμῶν LᵇMᵇAld.DB¹B² etiam marg. C].
13 εἴδοι pr. Kᵇ, εἴδοι C [ἴδοι A et cet.].
32 post τις add. φιλόξεινος ὁ εὔξιος pr. KᵇC. [φιλόξεινος ὁ (ὁ om. NᵇAld.) ἐρύξιος AΓNᵇOᵇAld. corr.¹ Kᵇ ('ipse librarius'—Susemihl Eth. Nic. pref. xx); post ἂν add. φιλόξενος nec plura D; B¹=Bek., Bª=Bek. ñisi quod εὔξαιτο (Mᵇ) habeat.]
b 17 ἕως πλησθῇ ὑπερβολή [B¹Bª=Bek.; D=Bek. with ὑπερπλησθείς, A has ἕως ἂν ὑπερπλησθῇ ὑπερβολή].
24 ἡ μὴ ᾗ ὧδ (ἱ Kᵇ, εἱ C in ras.) [ἡ μὴ ὡς δεῖ ἡ ᾧ δεῖ LᵇD; ἡ μὴ ὡς δεῖ ἡ ὡς δεῖ B¹; ἡ μὴ ὡς δεῖ Bª with ἡ ὡς δεῖ in red ink on margin for insertion after δεῖ. A has a lacuna here].
27 καὶ ἡ ὡς A [ἡ καὶ ὡς B¹Ald.].
30,31 δὲ τῷ μὴ ἀλλ' ὁ μὲν ἀκόλαστος τῷ, om. Kᵇ.
δὲ τῷ μὴ ἀλλ' ὁ μὲν ἀκόλαστος om. C, habet A.
1119 a 3 λυπεῖσθαι Kᵇ, λυπεῖται AB¹DC—(τ in ras. C).
3 καί ante ἀποτυγχάνων om. [habent AB¹D].
15 post ἡ δεῖ add. οὐδ' ἐν A [add. οὐδενί DAld.B¹Bª].
15 ὅτι.

1119 a 20 οὐσίας [ἀξίας AB¹B²D].
   25 ἐπονείδιστον [ἐπονειδιστότερον L^{b}M^{b}N^{b}AO^{b}Ald.Γ].
   29 τά [ταῦτα AB¹D].
 b 4 πολλὴν ἔξιν αὔξησιν A [πολλὴν αὔξησιν DB¹].
    6 ἐν τούτοις γάρ (καὶ K^{b}A, om. C) ἡ A.
    8 πάντοθεν [πανταχόθεν DB¹, A has a lacuna here].
   12 καί post λέγομεν om. A.
   14, 15 κατὰ τὸν λόγον—ἐπιθυμητικόν om. [habet A].
   22 λέγωμεν δὲ καὶ ἑξῆς περὶ ἐλευθεριότητος bis in fine libri iii. et in initio libri iv; sic etiam A, καί et in lib. iii. et in lib. iv. omisso [om. in fine iii. DB¹B²].

As against the forty-three cases given in the foregoing list I have noted only the following seven unique K^b readings which C does not present, viz. 1117 b 4, αἱ ante τιμαί om. K^b. 21, ἰδέας. 1119 a 11, post μέσως add. μέν. 14, οὔτ' pro οὐδ' ante ἐπιθυμεῖ. 24, τοιοῦτο. b 6, post γάρ add. καί. 16 ante λόγῳ om. τῷ.

Reserving my remarks on K^{b}C till the Fourth and Fifth Books have been examined, I may sum up the results for Ald., D, B¹, and B² in the latter part of the Third Book. From 1115 b 1 to the end of the Book there are thirty-five places in which K^b and O^b agree against L^b and M^b and in nineteen of them Ald. sides with L^{b}M^b, and with K^{b}O^b in thirteen. Of these thirteen it will be observed that six are cases in which L^b and M^b have an omission. If the ascendants of Ald. were MSS. related to M^b they would naturally be corrected in these places, and Ald. would consequently exhibit so many K^{b}O^b readings.

In the thirty-five places in which K^b and O^b agree against L^b and M^b, D sides with L^{b}M^b in fourteen and with K^{b}O^b in twelve. B¹ and B² side distinctly with L^{b}M^b. Considering the close affinity between Ald.D, B¹ and B², throughout this whole book, we may, I venture to think, allow B¹ and B² to carry Ald. and D with them to the L^{b}M^b side.

BOOK IV.

[The readings of Par. 1853 (Par.) are given in the following list to show the relation of that MS. to D]:—

1119 b 22 K^{b}O^b. | L^{b}M^b.
1119 b 22 λέγωμεν Ald.AB¹Par. | λέγομεν CDB².
     34   om. AC. | τί DAld.Par.B¹B².

1120 a 4 χρεία C.   χρεία τις ADB¹B²Par.Ald.
     6 τοῦτο C.   ἕκαστον ADB¹B⁴Par.Ald.
    11 γὰρ ἀρετῆς AC.   ἀρετῆς γάρ DPar.Ald.B¹B².
    17 λαβεῖν AC.   λαμβάνειν DPar.Ald.B¹B².
    24 οὖν ACAld.B¹B²DPar.   δέ.
    30 ἴλοιτ' AAld.CB¹B²DPar.   αἱροῖτ'.
  b 2 ἰδίων ACB¹B²Ald.DPar.   οἰκείων.
     4 ὅπου C [ὅτε καὶ ὅπου A].   ὅτε καὶ οὗ Ald.DPar.B¹B².
     9 οὐδέν ACB¹B²DPar.   ὅθεν οὐδέν Ald.
    22 ταῦτα ACB¹B²Ald.   αὐτά DPar.
    26 ταῖς δόσεσι καὶ ταῖς δαπάναις   δαπάναις καὶ ταῖς δόσεσιν.
        ACB¹B²Ald.Par.D (omis-
        so altero ταῖς D).
    30 δ' add. C.   om. Ald.ADPar.B¹B².
1121 a 4 om. C.   καί Par.Ald.ADB¹B².
    11 om. AC.   ἐν δυσίν DB¹Ald.
    11 ἐν δόσει καὶ λήψει C.   ἐν λήψει καὶ ἐν δόσει B¹Ald.
        ἐν δόσει καὶ ἐν λήψει A.
    15 ἐπί ACB¹B²Ald.DPar.   ἐν.
    16 συνδυάζεται C.   συναύξεται M^bAB²DPar.Ald.
        συνδιάζεται B¹.   συναύξουσιν L^b.
    20 om. ACDAld.   inter ἀνελευθέρου et υίατος add. καὶ γὰρ
                       δίδωσι καὶ οὐ λαμβάνει Par.
    20 om. ADPar.   τε C, suppl. rc. K^b.
    25 om. C, and A which reads   οὐ ante λήψεται ΓDB¹B²Ald.Par.
        δώσει γὰρ οἷς δεῖ καὶ λήψεται
        ὅθεν δεῖ.
    28 om. C.   τε AAld.D.
    33 om. AC.   μὴ δύνασθαι Par.B¹B²DAld.
  b 4 om. C.   αὑτοῦ add. post τούτου ΓAld.AB¹B²DPar.
    28 ἂν ACB¹B²DPar.Ald.   om.
    33 ἐργαζόμενοι AC.   ἐργαζόμενοι καί ΓAld.B¹B²DPar.
1122 a 14 κακόν ἐστι AC.   ἐστὶ κακόν Par.ΓB¹B²DAld.
    23 γάρ ACB¹B²DPar.Ald.   om. Γ.
    34 δ' ὑπέρ AC.   δὲ περί H^aB¹B²Ald.DPar.
  b 18 ἔργον ἀρετὴ μεγαλοπρέπεια A   ἔργον μεγαλοπρέπεια ἀρετή.
        Cr.
        ἀρετὴ ἔργου μεγαλοπρέπεια B².

[I. I.]

1122 b 18 ἔργον μεγαλευπρέπεια Ald.B¹D Par.
20 περὶ θεούς ACAld.
21 καὶ περί.
30 om. C.

30 om. AC.
1123 a 2 ἡ πᾶσα AC.
3 om.

14 γὰρ ἡ καλλίστη AC.
14 μεγαλοπρέπειαν ἔχει ACH^a.
26 τὰ τοιαῦτα A.
τὰ τὸ ταῦτα C.
b 25 μεγαλοψύχου DB¹A.
26 om. C.
30 om. AC.
1124 a 1 μέν ante οὖν AΓC.
b 8 ἀφειδής ACB².
[ἀφειδεῖ DPar. et corr. C.]
14 εὖ τοῦ ACAld.
21 ἐπ' AC.
1125 a 1 om. C.
3 οὐ C.
20 ἄξιός ἐστιν CAAld.
24 διοπηροί DCAld.
34 χεῖρον AB¹B².
b 5 om. AC.
7 τε ACAld.
9 om. ACH^aN^b.
15 φάρομεν del ACH^aN^bΓ.
19 δὲ τῆς τιμῆς C.
25 τῷ CAld.
32 om. AC.
1126 a 10 θᾶττον ἢ καί AC.
16 ἀποδιδόασιν C.
20 ὀργίλοι AC.

περὶ τοὺς θεούς Par.H^aB¹B²D.
καὶ ὅσα περί ACB¹B²DPar., suppl. marg. rec. K^b.
τά ante τοιαῦτα add. B¹B²Ald.
[ταῦτα instead of τὰ τοιαῦτα ADPar.]
διά Ald.DB¹B²Par.
πᾶσα ἡ Par.Ald.DB¹B².
καὶ ἀντιδωρεάς AC, suppl. marg. rec. K^b.
γάρ Ald.DPar.
ἔχει μεγαλοπρέπειαν DAld.Par.
ταῦτα DAld.

μεγάλου C.
γε ADAld.
δ' D.
om. Ald.
ἀφειδήσει H^aB¹.

τοῦ εὖ D.
ἐν Par.H^aN^bDB¹B².
πρός ante φίλον ADB¹B²Par.Ald.
οὐδέ.
ἐστὶν ἄξιος.
νοεροί AB¹.
χείρων CDPar.
τά post καί B¹Ald.D.
om.
καί post ὡς B¹B¹DAld.Par.
ἀεὶ φέρομεν DPar.Ald.B¹B².
δὲ τιμῆς Par.H^aN^bAld.ADB¹B².
τό A.
add. καί ante ὡς B¹B²DPar.
θᾶττον καί DPar.Ald.B¹B⁴.
ἀνταποδιδόασιν AB¹B²DPar.Ald.
ὀργίζονται DB¹B²Par.Ald.

NICOMACHEAN ETHICS. 35

1127 a	8	τι ἄλλο AB¹B²CDPar.ΓH^aN^b Ald.	ἄλλο τι.
	8	τις ὠφέλεια AC.	ὠφέλειά τις DAld.
	14	αὐτή ΓC.	αὕτη.
	16	ἕκαστον ACAld.	ἕκαστα.
	21	δή AC.	δί Ald.
	27	λέγει καὶ πράττει AC.	πράττει καὶ λέγει Ald.
b	5	ὧς ACAld.	οὗ.
	21	ταῦτα AC.	τὰ τοιαῦτα Ald.
	26	om. AB² (spatio iii litt. relicto B¹).	add. τά ante φανερά CDAld.B¹Par.
	27	εὐκαταφρονητότεροι A. εὐκαταφρονητότερον C.	εὐκαταφρόνητοι DB¹B²Par.Ald. corr. C.
	31	καὶ ἀντικεῖσθαι ACB².	ἀντικεῖσθαι DPar.Ald.B¹.
	34	εἶναι ὁμιλία τις A (lacuna in C) B¹B¹DPar.	ὁμιλία τις εἶναι.
1128 a	16	καὶ ἐκ ACB².	ἐκ DAld.B¹Par.
	18	ἐλευθερίῳ C.	ἐλευθέρῳ H^aAld.
	26	ἐλευθερίῳ C.	ἐλευθέρῳ.
b	11	οὖν ΓCB².	γοῦν AB¹DPar.

		K^bM^b.	L^bO^b.
1120 a	21	om. AC.	σχεδόν B¹Ald.D.
1122 b	34	τοῖς ACAld.	om. H^aD.
1124 a	22	om. AC.	add. οἱ post ἤ H^aN^bDB¹Ald.
1127 a	32	τοῦ ACDAld.	om.
1128 a	3	om. C.	δ' ADAld.

Reserving my remarks on C to a future occasion, I may sum up the results for A, B¹, B², D and Ald. in Book iv.

K^bO^b stands against L^bM^b in seventy-eight places, in forty-three of which Ald. sides with L^bM^b, and with K^bO^b in nineteen. D sides with L^bM^b in forty-six of these places—thirty-seven times in company with Ald.—and with K^bO^b in fourteen. B¹ and B² occur together upwards of thirty times on the L^bM^b side and thirteen times on the K^bO^b side. As there is nothing in the quality of the agreements of D and Ald. on the L^bM^b side to suggest the opposite conclusion, we may, I think, give

ENGLISH MANUSCRIPTS OF THE

full weight to the quantitative test, and say that D and Ald. are both descended in this Book from a MS. related to M^b and therefore to L^b. The same may be said of B^1 and B^2. A, as in Books i, ii, and iii, belongs to the K^b family.

The following list gives the readings in Book iv in which C agrees with K^b where the latter MS. stands alone among Bekker's MSS. The readings of A, etc., have been appended for the sake of comparison:—

CK^b.

1119 b 22   δὲ καὶ ἑξῆς [δ' ἑξῆς ADB^1].
       22   ἡ post εἶναι add. A [om. D].
1120 a 22   τῶν ἀπ' ἀρετῆς om. A pr. [habet D].
       30   οὐδ' ὁ εἰδοὺς (sic) λυπηρῶς C, οὐδ' ὁ $\overset{διδούς}{λυπηρῶς}$ K^b (διδούς m. rec. quae eadem comma post οὐδ' addidit, as Professor Vitelli, who kindly examined certain places in K^b at my request, reports). [οὐδ' ὁ λυπηρός B^1B^2, οὐδ' ὁ λυπηρῶς AD.]
       32   οὐδέ] οὐ A.
           μή om. [habent ADB^1].
           τὰ χρήματα om. [habent AD].
   b 19   ἐπιμελόμενον [ἐπιμελόμενον pr. A].
       20   οὐδ'] οὔθ' A [οὐδ' D].
       29   δεῖ post ὅσα om. [habent AD].
1121 a 5, 6   ἠνάλωσεν [ἀνάλωσεν A].
       13–15 τῷ δὲ λαμβάνειν .... ὑπερβάλλει om. [habent AB^1].
       24, 25 δώσει γὰρ οὗ δεῖ καὶ λήψεται (λείψεται C) ὅθεν δεῖ [δώσει γὰρ οἷς δεῖ καὶ λήψεται ὅθεν δεῖ A ; B^1B^2=Bek.].
       26   τὸ ὑπερβάλλειν] τὸ μὴ ὑπερβάλλειν pr. K^bAC.
       33   μὴ τοῦτο ποιεῖν ταχύ [τοῦτο ποιεῖν ταχύ A ; DB^1B^2=Bekker].
   b 7   τήν [τινα AD].
       29   τό om. [habent AD].
1122 a 1   ὁπόσον] ὁπότε [ὁπόσον AD].
       8   εἰσίν om. A [habet D].
       34   καὶ ὡς οὐ δεῖ om. [habent ADB^1].
   b 22   οἷόν τε A.
1123 a 24   μέγαροι K^b, μεγαροί pr. C [Μεγαρεῖς ADB^1B^2].
   b 15   δί om. C, pr. K^b [suppl. rec. K^b, ADB^1].

NICOMACHEAN ETHICS. 37

1123 b 17 δεξιά pr. K^b, δ' αξία rec. K^b, δ' αξία C, the first a in ras. [δ' αξία A].
     24 δή post ό om. [habent DA].
     25 post χαῦνος add. μέν [om. AD].
1124 b 5 δέ] μὲν γάρ [δί AD].
     11 ante προσοφλήσει add. οἱ A [om. D].
     17 πεπόνθασιν A [πεπόνθεσαν D].
     18 μόλις [μόγις AD].
     24 προτέουσι [προτερεύουσιν A].
        μελλήσην.
1125 a 7 οὐθ'] οὐδ' A [οὐθ' D].
     14 ὁ om. [habent AD].
     24 δή] γε [δί AB¹D].
     28 ἠλίθιοι om. [habent AD].
        ὡς] οὐ [ὡς AD].
     31 post εὐτυχήματα add. καί [om. AD].
   b 7 ἐν τιμῇ καὶ ὀρέξει A inserting ἐν also before ὀρέξει [DB¹B² = Bekker].
     11 ἔτι δὲ τόν [ἔστι δ' ὅτε τόν ADB¹].
     23 ἀμφότερα δὲ ἢ ἀμφότερα, A reading ἤ.
     33 ἤπερ K^b, εἴπερ C, the εἰ on eras. [εἴπερ AD].
1126 a 5 οἱ om. [habent AD].
     10 καὶ ἐφ' οἷς οὐ δεῖ om. [habent AD].
     19 πικροί] μικροί K^b; π in ras. C [πικροί AD].
   b 1 παρεισβαίνων [παρεκβαίνων ADB¹B²].
      4 τοσοῦτον A [τοιοῦτον DB¹].
     18, 19 καὶ ὡς δεῖ ὁμοίως δέ om. [habent AD].
     24 ἐχθαίρειν [ἐχραίνειν pr. A, ἐχθραίνειν D et corr. A].
     26 καὶ ἀσυνήθεις om. [habent AD].
     36 διαφερόντως διαφόρως δ' A [διαφερόντως δ' DB¹].
1127 a 6 μεγάλης om. [habent AD].
     26 ἕκαστος [ἕκαστα AD].
   b 6 καθ' αὑτόν D [καθ' αὑτό A].
     15 τῷ] τό [τῷ AD].
     19 ἐν ἡδεῖ (ἡδεῖ pr. K^b) ἀπόλαυσις C: ἐν ἡδεῖα ἀπόλαυσις pr. A [DB¹ = Bekker].
        ἆ om. [habent AD, ἐν B¹].
     20 μάντιν σοφὸν ἰατρόν [μάντιν ἢ ἰητρικὸν σοφόν A pr. Post ἰητρικόν addidit man. rec. ἤ.—Habent DB¹B² ἰατρὸν ἢ μάντιν σοφόν].
     24 ὀχληρόν A in ras. [ὀγκηρόν DB¹].

1128 a 9 άγροικοι [άγριοι AD].
       21 αὖ τοῦ Hᵃ A [habet D].
       26 μὴ ἀπρεπῆ [μὴ ἃ πρέπει B²A, ἃ πρέπει DB¹].
           τῷ] τό [τῷ AD, τόν B²].
       28 post ἡδύ add. καί A.
       28 ἀκούεται [ἀκούσσται AD].
       35 καὶ τοιαῦτα] καὶ ταῦτα A [καὶ τοιαῦτα DB²].
    b   4 ἀναγκαία K^bH^e, ἀναγκαίον C, the final ν in ras., ἀναγκαία A.
        8 ἢ δ' ἐν ταῖς] αἱ δὲ [AD=Bekker].
       12 post ἀδοξίας add. καί [om. AD].
       26 ὥστε πράξαι K^bN^b, ὥστ' (erasure) πράξαι° (the ε by later hand) C.
           [ὥστ' (ει inserted by later hand) πράξ (εις later in ras.) A.]
       28 ἱκανσίοις] ἀκουσίοις K^bD, ἀκούοις (sic) C, ἑκουσίοις A.
       30 γάρ om. [habent AD].
       32 τὰ τοιαῦτα [τὸν τὰ τοιαῦτα A, τὸν ταῦτα L^bD et corr. C].

The following list contains the cases in which K^b has been corrected, and C follows the corrections. For the corrections in K^b I am mainly indebted to Susemihl's *Epistula Critica* appended to Ramsauer's edition:—

1119 b 27 ἢ alterum om. pr. K^b add. rec., habet C.   1120 a 16 μή om. Γ M^b pr. K^b, suppl. rc. K^b, ἢ C.   1121 a 20 τε om. pr. K^b add. rec. et C   b 22 αἰσχροί K^b pr., γλισχροί rc. et C.   25 ἢ om. pr. K^b, suppl. rc., habet C.   1122 a 2 αἰσχροκερδία pr. K^b, αἰσχροκέρδεια corr.² et C.   15 ταῦτα pr. K^b, ταύτην rec. et C.   15 post ἢ add. οἱ K^b pr., om. C.   21 χρήματι K^b pr., χρήμασι rc. et C.   22 δαπανηρὰς μόνον δ' ἐν pr. K^b, δαπανηρὰς μόνον ἐν rc. et C.   δ' ante ὑπερέχει om. pr. K^b, add. rec. et C.   b 15 κτῆμα μὲν γὰρ τὸ πλείστου ἄξιον pr. K^b; Prof. Vitelli writes to me—'al. m. non admodum rec. correxit—κτῆμα^ro (i. e. κτήματος) μὲν
                ἀρετῆς
γὰρ τὸ πλείστου ἄξιον ;' C has κτήματος μὲν γὰρ ἀρετῆς πλείστου ἄξιον καί.   21 ὅσα om. pr. K^b, add. rec. et C.   22 δεῖν add. rec. K^b habet C.   1123 a 3 καὶ ἀντι- δωρεὰς om. pr. K^bO^b, add. mg. rc. K^b et C.   b 1 τόν] τά rc. K^b et C.   11 ἔτι om. pr. K^b suppl. rc., habet C.   32 δσγ' pr. K^b, δγ' rec. et C.   1124 a 10 μικροῦ pr. K^b, μικροῖς rec. et C.   20 καὶ post διό add. rec. K^b et C.   Prof. Vitelli reports to me as follows on this passage as it occurs in K^b—'μικρόν ἐστι ° τούτοις καὶ τὰ ἄλλα. διὸ δ (sic) ὑ‖περόπται etc. ("lit. eras.; ‖ beginning of fol. 45^v).'   25 τιμητός M^b pr. K^b, τιμητέος corr. rec. K^b, τιμητ ὸς C, a letter having been erased before o.   b 7 οὐδὲ φιλοκίνδυνος om. pr. K^b, suppl. rec. K^b, habet C.   1127 b 6 εὐλαβεῖτο pr. K^b, εὐλαβεῖται corr.² et C.   19 ὧν ἡδεῖ ἀπόλαυσις pr. K^b, ὧν ἢ δεῖ ἀπόλαυσις corr.² et C.

NICOMACHEAN ETHICS. 39

The differences between C and K^b in the Fourth Book are exhibited in the following list:—

1120 b 5 post σφόδρα καί add. τοῦτο C. According to Prof. Vitelli K^b has no later addition here.   1120 b 6 τὸ γὰρ βλέπειν C, τὸ γὰρ μὴ βλέπειν K^bM^b apparently.   1121 b 12 post ἐπιμελείας add. καί K^b, om. C.   13 post ἀνίατος add. γε K^b; post ἀνίατος ras. C.   34 Prof. Vitelli reports as follows—'K^b τοιοῦταί κατὰ μικρὸν καὶ ἐπὶ πολλῶι pr.; sed eadem manus, ut vid., κατά in καὶ τά mutavit, ν καί erasit, et praecedens ὁ mutavit in ἀ.'   C has κατὰ μικρὰ ἐπὶ πολλῷ, above κατά standing καὶ τά in a later hand. [καὶ τὰ μικρὰ ἐπὶ πολλῷ DB¹B², καί (in ras.) μικρὰ καὶ ἐπὶ πολλῷ A.]   1122 a 7 ὁ ante λωποδύτης om. K^b, hab. C.   1124 b 27 καὶ ἀμελεῖν pr. K^b, καὶ μέλειν rec. K^b, καὶ μὴ μέλειν C.   1126 a 13 γίνηται K^b, γίνεται C.   1127 b 26 καί post δέ om. K^bΓAld., habet C.   1128 a 6 γέλωτας C, γέλωτα K^b, and no correction Vitelli reports. To this list may be added 1124 b 29, 30 where C varies from K^b pr. and corr. Pr. K^b reads (instead of παρρησιαστὴς—ἀληθευτικός of Bekker's text), καταφρονητικὸν γάρ. παρρησιαστὸν γάρ. διὸ παρρησιαστικὸς δὲ διὰ τὸ καταφρονητικὸς εἶναι καὶ ἀληθευτικός.   Rec. K^b has παρρησιαστὴς γὰρ διὰ τὸ καταφρονητικὸς εἶναι, καταφρονητικὸς δὲ διὰ παρρησιαστικός, παρρησιαστικὸς δὲ διὰ καταφρονητικὸς καὶ ἀληθευτικός.   C and D both read παρρησιαστὴς γὰρ διὰ τὸ καταφρονητικὸς εἶναι, καταφρονητικὸς δὲ διὰ παρρησιαστικὸς καὶ ἀληθευτικός. [φανερῶς· καταφρονητικοῦ γὰρ διὸ παρρησιαστικὸς καὶ ἀληθευτικός B², φανερῶς· παρρησιαστικὸς γάρ (two last words in ras.)
διὸ   ταφρονητικός (from φ to r in ras.)   ταφρονητικὸς δέ (last word in ras.) διὸ καταρρησιαστικός (whole word except ικός in ras.) καὶ ἀληθευτικός B¹, καταφρονητικοῦ δὲ διὸ παρρησιαστικὸς καὶ παρρησιαστικοῦ γὰρ διὸ καταφρονητικὸς καὶ ἀληθευτικὸς πλὴν ὅσα A.]

There are some other points of agreement and difference in Book iv between C and K^b which will be more conveniently noticed when I reach 1136 a 1, and am in a position to review the whole question of the relationship of C and K^b from 1115 a 1 to 1136 a 1.

BOOK V.

The following list contains all the agreements of C with K^b where the latter stands alone among Bekker's MSS:—

K^bC.

1129 a 11   οὔτε [οὐδέ D].
       33   καὶ ὁ ἄνισος] καὶ ἄδικος [καὶ ἄνισος D, καὶ ὁ ἄνισος B¹B²].
       34   ὁ ante ἴσος om. [habet D].

1129 b 1 δ' ante ἄδικον om. [habet D].
2 ἔσται om. D.
10 κοινόν. ἐπεὶ δ'. [Ad oram C manus, ut videtur, eadem suppl. καὶ παράνομος· τοῦτο γὰρ περιέχει πᾶσαν ἀδικίαν καὶ κοινόν ἐστι πάσης ἀδικίας. Post κοινόν habet D, καὶ παράνομος· τοῦτο γὰρ ἡ παρανομία ἤτοι ἡ ἀνισότης περιέχει πᾶσαν ἀδικίαν. Pro ἔστι δ' ἄνισος habet B¹ καὶ παράνομος, mox τοῦτο γὰρ ἡ παρανομία ἤτοι ἡ ἀνισότης περιέχει πᾶσαν ἀδικίαν καὶ κοινόν ἐστι πάσης ἀδικίας· ἐπεὶ κ.τ.λ. Post κοινόν habent B²A, καὶ παράνομος τοῦτο γὰρ ἡ παρανομία ἤτοι ἀνισότης περιέχει πᾶσαν ἀδικίαν καὶ κοινόν ἐστι πάσης ἀδικίας· ἐπεί.]
16 κατ' ἀρετήν om. [ἢ κατ' ἀρετήν DB¹B² rc. C].
32 ὅτι om. [ὁ om. D].
1130 a 17 ὁ ante ἐνεργῶν om.
22 ἄρα γε] γάρ [ἄρα γε DB¹].
24 ἔτι] ὅτι K^b, ὅτι ἔτι C.
25 προσλαμβάνων D.
26. μᾶλλον δόξει εἶναι [δόξειεν ἂν εἶναι μᾶλλον D].
b 10 μὲν οὖν om.
11 ἐπεὶ δὲ τὸ ἄνισον καὶ τὸ παράνομον πλέον οὐ ταὐτὸν ἀλλ' ἕτερον ὡς μέρος καὶ πρὸς ὅλον· τὸ μὲν γὰρ πλέον ἅπαν ἄνισον τὸ δ' ἄνισον οὐ πᾶν πλέον CK^b, i. e. K^b and C are the only MSS. which read καὶ πρός. P^bA have also παράνομον πλέον· [On the margin C has τὸ μὲν γὰρ ἄνισον ἅπαν παράνομον τὸ δὲ παράνομον οὐ πᾶν ἄνισον. D reads ἐπεὶ δὲ τὸ ἄνισον καὶ τὸ παράνομον οὐ ταὐτὸν ἀλλ' ἕτερον ὡς μέρος πρὸς ὅλον τὸ μὲν γὰρ ἄνισον ἅπαν παράνομον τὸ δὲ παράνομον οὐχ ἅπαν ἄνισον τὸ μὲν γὰρ πλέον ἅπαν ἄνισον τὸ δὲ ἄνισον οὐ πᾶν πλέον. B¹ reads ἐπεὶ δὲ τὸ ἄνισον καὶ τὸ παράνομον οὐ ταὐτὸν ἀλλ' ἕτερον ὡς μέρος πρὸς ὅλον τὸ μὲν γὰρ πλέον ἅπαν ἄνισον τὸ δὲ ἄνισον οὐ πᾶν πλέον.]
16 ὥστε καὶ περί] ὡς περί ὥστε καὶ περί D].
1131 a 7 δολοπατία.
16 καὶ πρός τι om. [D reads καὶ τισὶ καὶ πρός τι, B¹ καὶ πρός τι καὶ τισί.]
18 ἐστί om. D.
21 τὰ ἐν οἷς om. [habent DB¹ cum cet.].
23 ὅταν ᾖ ἴσοι μὴ ἴσα] ὅταν ᾖ μὴ ἴσα ἴσοι [D and B¹=Bek.].
27 ὑπάρχειν] κατ' ἀξίαν τινὰ θεῖν εἶναι [B¹D=Bek.].
b 2 ἡ τοῦ β τεθῇ δίς] τὸ δεύτερον δὶς τεθῇ.
5 ἔσται om.
16 ᾧ om.

NICOMACHEAN ETHICS.   41

1131 b 31 εἰς ἄλληλα προσενεχθέντα [DB¹=Bek.].
1132 a 6 ὁ μέν ante ἔβλαψεν om. [suppl. rec. K^b, habet D].
       21 ἰέναι (i.e. the second ἰέναι)—εἶναι om. pr. K^b, add. rc. K^b; ἰέναι (i.e. the
           second ἰέναι)—οἷον om. C, which reads ἐστί after the first ἰέναι [DB¹
           =Bek.].
       27 καί post ἀφεῖλε om.
           προσέθηκεν om.
       31 εἰ om.
     b 2 τε om.
        7 ἀφῃρῆσθω] ἀφῄρηται.
           προσκείσθω] πρόσκειται.
        8 ὅλην.
           ὑπερέχειν C, corr.^a K^b.
       15 ὅσοις] τοῖς.
       22 πυθαγόριοι B¹.
       30 καί ante κολασθῆναι om.
1133 a 7 οἷον om.
       16 καὶ τοιοῦτον om.
       22 ἄττα om.
       26 ἐστὶ τῇ] ὅτι.
     b 1 εἰς σχῆμα δ' οὐ διάγειν ἀναλογίας [οὐ διάγειν is crossed out, and δεῖ ἄγειν
           written on margin for insertion after ἀναλογίας C. Both D and B
           have Bekker's reading].
        2 ὑπερβολάς [ὑπεροχάς DB¹, etiam marg. C].
        9 τις om.
       12 δεῖ γὰρ τοῦτο φανερόν τι εἶναι λαβεῖν.
1134 a 13 τό ante ἀδικεῖσθαι om.
       20 διά ante προαιρέσεως om.
       22 οὐδέ ante κλέπτης] οὐ [οὐδέ DB¹].
       26 ἔστιν om.
     b 13 ἄδικον] ἀδικία ὄν.
       18 τοῦ δὲ πολιτικοῦ om.
           ante φυσικόν add. γάρ.
       20 νόμιμον.
       21 post διαφέρει alterum add. οὕτως ἢ ἄλλως [om. DB¹].
       29 οὐδαμῶς· παρ'. [Post οὐδαμῶς add. ἔχον L^bM^bN^bO^bP^bQD.]
       33 post ἄλλων add. καί.
1135 a 9 καὶ τὸ δικαίωμα καὶ τὸ δίκαιον om.

                                G   [I. 1.]

1135 a 12 post ἄδικον add. τι ὅταν πραχθῇ ἀδίκημά ἐστι [add. ὅτι ὅταν πραχθῇ ἀδίκημά ἐστι L^bN^bO^bP^b, om. D].
25 καὶ τίνι om.
26 ἕκαστον] ἑκάτερον.
b 5 ὃν add. [om. D et cet.].
11 ἀπροβούλευτα] προβούλευτα.
13 ὑπέλαβε πράξῃ [ὑπέλαβε ταῦτα πράξῃ H*L^bN^bO^bP^bM^bQDB¹Ald. rec. C].
14 βάλλειν [βαλεῖν D].
16 ᾧ [ὡς cet].
26 θυμοποιῶν [θυμῷ ποιῶν D corr. C].
29 ἐν om.
1136 a 8 δί om.
17 ἡ τὸ μὲν ἑκούσιον τὸ δ' ἀκούσιον om.
33 καί ante ἐνδέχοιτο] κἄν.

Here ends the agreement between C and K^b unique. From 1136 b 1 to the end of Book v C nowhere agrees with the unique readings of K^b, which are about forty-two in number. In the K^bO^b—L^bM^b list, given on pp. 45 and 46, C is on the K^bO^b side, except in two cases, up to 1136 b 1.

The following is a list of the cases in Book v up to 1136 b 1, which illustrate the relation of C to rec. K^b :—

1129 a 33 καὶ ὁ ἄνισος] καὶ ἄδικος pr. K^bC, crx. rec. K^b.
b 10 post ἄνισος add. καὶ παράνομος rec. K^b, om. C.
24 ὀρθῶς B²] ὀρθός CB¹M^bQAld.Dr and corr.² K^b.
25 χεῖρον B²] χείρων L^bM^bAld. B¹CD and corr.² K^b.
1131 b 16 ᾧ om. C et pr. K^b, suppl. corr.¹ K^b—i. e. ipse librarius according to Susemihl.
16 τοῦτο C, τούτῳ corr.¹ K^b.
1132 a 6 ὁ μέν om. C et pr. K^b, suppl. rec. K^b.
21 ἰέναι—εἶναι om. C et pr. K^b, suppl. rec. K^b.
b 8 ὑπάρχειν C et corr.² K^b.
10 πόσον pr. K^b, ὅσον C et rec. K^b.
24 νεμητικόν pr. K^b, διανεμητικόν C et rec. K^b. (C has τὸν διανεμητικόν.)
27 εἰ καί pr. K^b, εἴ τε C et rec. K^b.
1133 a 19 ταῦτα pr. K^b, πάντα C et rec. K^b.

NICOMACHEAN ETHICS.

1133 a 20   ὃ pr. K^{b}Ald.B^1, ᾧ CDL^{b}M^{b}N^{b}O^b and rec. K^b.
    23   τόσαδι pr. K^b, τοσαδί CD and rec. K^b, τόσα δή L^{b}B^1.
    27   ἤ om. pr. K^b, ἥτις C et rec. K^b.
  b 9   ἐξαγωγῆς pr. K^b, ἐξαγωγήν CD and rec. K^b.
    23   δή om. pr. K^b, suppl. C et rec. K^b.
1136 a 9   ἀνθρώπινον pr. K^b, ἀνθρωπικόν C et rec. K^b.
    12   τὸ πᾶς pr. K^b, ἀτόπως C et rec. K^b.

We are now in a position to sum up on the question of the relation of C to K^b from 1115 b 1 to 1136 b 1. The following table presents the relation in its quantitative aspect :—

Book III from 1115 b 1
K^b 50 — 43 C.[1]
K^{b}M^b 6 — 4 C.
L^{b}O^b 6 — 1 C.
K^{b}O^b 35 — 34 C.
L^{b}M^b 35 — 0 C.

IV.
K^b 80 — 73 C.
K^{b}M^b 5 — 5 C.
L^{b}O^b 5 — 0 C.
K^{b}O^b 78 — 69 C.
L^{b}M^b 78 — 7 C.

V to 1136 b 1.
K^b 92 — 71 C.
K^{b}M^b 6 — 4 C.
L^{b}O^b 6 — 2 C.
K^{b}O^b 16 — 14 C.
L^{b}M^b 16 — 2 C.
K^{b}L^b 31 — 26 C.

These figures show that C is more closely related than any MS. hitherto described to K^b from 1115 b 1 to 1136 b 1, although not closely related to it before, or, as will be seen, after. The nature of the agreements—many of them being omissions and other mere blunders—is such as to preclude the hypothesis that an ascendant of C belonging to the L^b family was corrected elaborately here by means of K^b or a MS. closely resembling K^b. The only tenable supposition is that C (from 1115 b 1 to 1136 b 1) was transcribed either from a MS. related collaterally to K^b, or from K^b itself. If C had been transcribed from a MS. collateral to K^b, it would not, as it does, agree with K^b in so many places where that MS. has been corrected by a later hand. Thus in Book iv, C agreeing largely with pr. K^b (which it would naturally do if descended from a common ascendant by a collateral line), also agrees with rec. K^b as against pr. K^b in twenty-four places—i. e. follows the corrections in K^b in almost all the cases in which that MS. has been corrected. This seems to point to the conclusion that C from 1115 b 1 to 1136 b 1 was copied (directly

[1] I. e. K^b is unique among Bekker's MSS. in fifty places, in forty-three of which C agrees with it.

or indirectly) from K^b itself. In the Fifth Book, C=rec. K^b fourteen times; in the latter part of Book iii the recorded corrections in K^b are not numerous, so the test cannot be applied as in Books iv and v; but the agreement with pr. K^b is so close that we should not be justified in refusing to be led by the analogy of Books iv and v. There are however a good many differences between C and both pr. K^b and rec. K^b which point to the conclusion that C was not copied directly from K^b as corrected, but indirectly through the intermediation of a MS. or MSS. which had additional marginal or other corrections which C embodies in its text. Thus 1120 b 5 C has καὶ τοῦτο τὸ ὑπερβάλλειν, while K^b has καὶ τὸ ὑπερβάλλειν, without later addition or correction, as Prof. Vitelli reports to me. 1123 a 6 πρέπουτα (sic) C, πρεπόντως K^b without correction (Vitelli), 1128 a 6 γέλωτας C, γέλωτα K^b without corr. (Vitelli), 1130 b 22 ἀπό K^b without corr. (Vitelli), ὑπό C, 1135 a 24 ὅταν C, ὃ ἄν K^b without corr. (Vitelli). See also list given on pp. 38, 39.

Although I think that C 1115 b 1—1136 b 1 was copied from K^b indirectly, I do not think that many intermediate links separate it from that MS. If there had been many intermediate links the agreement of C with both pr. and rec. K^b would not have been so close. Probably only one MS. intervened. Although the transcriber as a rule preferred corr. K^b to pr. K^b, there are a few cases in which C has the reading of pr. K^b, although corr. K^b exists. An examination of the list on p. 42 shows that in Book v there are six places in which C rejects corr. K^b for pr. K^b. In Book iii again, 1118 a 13, we have εἶδοι C, εἶδοι pr. K^b, and 1118 a 32 εὔξιος pr. K^b C, ἐρύξιος corr.[1] K^b. It may be thought that the corrections which C does not follow were made in K^b after the transcript from which C was copied had been made. In that case Susemihl is mistaken in ascribing ἐρύξιος to corr.[1]—ipse librarius. But I am inclined simply to suppose preference on the part of the transcriber for pr. K^b in these cases.

There is one other point which I must notice. At 1124 a 28 (i.e. iv. 3, § 20) C reads, μεγάλων ἀξιοῦσιν οὔτε ὀρθῶς μεγαλόψυχοι λέγονται ἄνευ γὰρ ἀρέσιν οὔτε ὀρθῶς μεγαλόψυχοι λέγονται ἄνευ γὰρ ἀρετῆς κ.τ.λ. In consequence of this blunder in C I asked Prof. Vitelli if -σιν οὔτε ὀρθῶς μεγαλόψυχοι λέγονται ἄνευ γὰρ ἀρε- constitutes a line in K^b, and he replied that it does. From this it might be inferred that C was copied directly from K^b; but the inference is not a necessary one. There is nothing improbable in the supposition that the MS. intervening between K^b and C adhered to the lines and pages of K^b; indeed, unless there were reasons for altering the whole scale of the transcript, it would be more convenient to adhere exactly to the scale of the original. K^b itself probably reproduces exactly the lines and pagination of its original. Prof. Vitelli, writing to me, says that, while each line in K^b contains on an average forty letters, the lines are either too long or too short for the space defined by the lineal; and his inference from this is that probably the writer of K^b adhered to the lines of his original.

The conclusion then which is forced upon me by the facts is that from 1115 b 1 to 1136 b 1 C is a transcript of a very faithful (slightly annotated) transcript of K^b. If I am mistaken in this conclusion, then C from 1115 b 1 to 1136 b 1 is collateral with K^b, and is a very important MS. I have stated the facts fully and leave it to scholars to estimate my conclusion.

As to how C happens to follow K^b in this particular mass of text I have nothing to say. The following facts however, which I have ascertained from Prof. Vitelli, may be stated here in case others should be able to make use of them. Fol. 33^r in K^b begins at 1115 b 9 with -θρωπον, fol. 33^v begins at 1115 b 32 with ἐν τούτοις, fol. 34^r begins at 1116 a 22 with ποιεῖ, fol. 34^v begins at 1116 b 12 with οὖν, fol. 35^r begins at 1116 b 35 with -τα, ἐπεί. Passing to the Fifth Book we find that fol. 63^r begins at 1136 a 29 with καὶ ἐπί. The beginning of fol. 33^r and the end of fol. 62^v thus mark very nearly the points at which the close agreement between K^b and C begins and ends, i.e. C agrees closely with K^b over thirty leaves of the latter. The points in C where this agreement begins and ends occur in the middle of pages, and show no changes in hand or ink.

The following list contains the K^{b}O^b—L^{b}M^b readings in Book v:—

K^{b}O^b.	L^{b}M^b.
1129 b 25. χεῖρον B².	χείρων corr.² K^{b}CB¹DAld.
29 θαυμαστὸς καὶ CDAld.	θαυμαστὸς διὸ καὶ.
1130 a 1 ἀρχή C.	ἀρχά DAld.
1131 a 21 om. C.	ἔσται B¹ [ἐστίν D].

46 ENGLISH MANUSCRIPTS OF THE

1131 a 23 ᾗ CB¹D.
       24 ἢ μὴ ἴσοι ἴσα CDB¹Ald.
       33 χρῆται CAld.
   b 1   οὕτως CAld.D.
       32 τούτῳ τὸ παρὰ τό CD.
1132 b 9 ἔστι δὲ τοῦτο καὶ CPᵇ.
       15 ὠνεῖσθαι καὶ πωλεῖν Bᵃ C.
1133 a 33 τό C.
   b 23   om.
1134 b 11 om. ΓNᵇPᵇC.
1136 a 17 πᾶν CAld.
1138 a 19 τὸ αὐτό CDAld.
   b 13   τῶν HᵃNᵘPᵇAld.

           KᵇMᵇ.
1130 b 8 δί C.
1132 b 27 ἔρεξε CAld.D.
1133 a 4 om. DAld.
       23 om. CD.
1134 a 31 κρίσις τοῦ CDAld.
   b 20   οὕτω [αὐτῷ D].
1137 a 13 γενόμενα Hᵃ.
1138 a 22 καὶ post ἅμα.

om. Ald.
om.
χρήσεται HᵃNᵇB¹D.
om.
τούτῳ παρὰ τό Ald.
ἔστι δὲ καὶ B¹Ald.D.
πωλεῖν καὶ ὠνεῖσθαι HᵃNᵇΓAld.B¹D.
om. D.
δή CDAld.Lᵇ and rec. Kᵇ, δί MᵇHᵃ.
μή HᵃAld. [οὐ D and rec. C].
ἅπαν HᵃNᵇQPᵇB¹ [D has a lacuna here].
τῷ αὐτῷ Hᵃ.
om. CD.

           LᵇOᵇ.
δή DAld.
ἔρρεξεν.
τε add. C.
ὁ ante οἰκοδόμος NᵇPᵇAld.
κρίσις ἐστί τοῦ.
οὐ τῷ C.
νεμόμενα LᵇCB¹D, διανεμόμενα OᵇBᵃ.
om. PᵇCD.

In the two foregoing lists D is about equally divided between Kᵇ and Lᵇ; and the same is true of Ald. If we take the cases of Ald. quoted by Susemihl—about eighty in all—we find that it agrees with KᵇLᵇ—either or both—in thirty-five, and with MᵇOᵇ or other inferior MSS. in thirty-three. D agrees with Ald. in some forty cases, and disagrees in about the same number. I find it impossible, on account of the great intermixture which has taken place, to assign either Ald. or D to any particular genealogical group. They are themselves not distantly related to each other, but show no preference for Kᵇ as against Lᵇ, or for KᵇLᵇ as against MᵇOᵇ, etc. B¹ and B² agree extensively with Ald. and D, as will be seen from the following list of the readings in Book v which D shares with Ald. :—

1129 b 8 μεῖον MᵇOᵇB¹Bᵃ.   18 τῆν ante εὐδαιμονίας [om. B¹Bᵃ].   24 ὀρθός ΓMᵇB¹.   25 χείρων ΓLᵇMᵇB¹.   1130 a 2 τόν add. NᵇOᵇB¹Bᵃ.   ἀρχά LᵇMᵘNᵇ.

NICOMACHEAN ETHICS. 47

5 κοινῷ ΓΒ¹ [Β²=Bek.]. 13 ἡ ante δικαιοσύνη ΚʰLʰHᵃNʰΒˢ [om. Β¹]. 22 τι post μέρος add. Β¹Β²ΓLʰMʰNʰΟʰ. b 11 παράνομον. 12 τὸ δὲ παράνομον οὐχ ἅπαν ἄνισον· τὸ μὲν γὰρ πλέον ἅπαν ἄνισον τὸ δ' ἄνισον οὐ πᾶν πλέον ΓMʰΟʰQPʰ. 16 καὶ post ὥστε add. Mʰ [om. B¹]. 23 προσταττόμενα B¹ΓΚʰPʰ. 1131 a 2 συναλλαγ- μάτων OʰNʰΒ¹. 31 λόγον ΓΚʰNʰPʰΒ¹C. 1132 b 15 πωλεῖν καὶ ὠνεῖσθαι B¹ΓLʰ MʰHᵃNʰ. 16 ἔδωκεν LʰMʰΒ¹ [δέδωκεν CΒˢ]. 27 κ'] γ'. 1133 b 15 ἔσται αἰεὶ MʰOʰHᵃNʰΒ¹Βˢ. 1134 b 7 ταῦτα ΓMʰOʰHᵃNʰ [C=Bek.]. 1135 a 4 αἱ om. ΓΚʰLʰNʰ. 12 τὸ κοινὸν μᾶλλον δικαιοπράγημα B¹ΓHᵃMʰNʰ [Βˢ=Bek.]. b 11 δὲ HᵃLʰPʰ. 13 ταῦτα ante πράξῃ add. ΓLʰMʰHᵃNʰOʰ. 18 ἐν ἑαυτῷ ἡ ἀρχή ΓMʰOʰHᵃNʰ [ὅτε ἐν ἑαυτῷ ἡ ἀρχή ᾖ τῆς κακίας Βˢ, ὅταν ἐν ἑαυτῷ ἡ ἀρχή ᾖ τῆς αἰτίας B¹]. 24 οὐδὲ B¹ΓHᵃMʰNʰ [Βˢ οὐ]. 1136 a 32 ᾦ LʰB¹ [δ Β¹]. 34 ἔν τι ΓHᵃNʰΟʰ. b 6 ἀλλὰ οὐδ'. 1137 a 13 νεμόμενα B¹LʰNʰ. 27 δὲ καὶ ΓHᵃMʰNʰPʰ. b 20 τούτοις NʰOʰC. 23 οὕτως CΓNʰPʰ. 24 ἂν LʰNʰC. 33 τί τό HᵃMʰNʰC. 1138 a 9 ὡς ΓHᵃMʰNʰPʰ. 10 νόμον ΓMʰΟ¹¹HᵃNʰ QB¹Β²C. 32 ἣν post ψεκτόν add. HᵃMʰNʰΒ¹ΒᵃC. b 6 οὐκ αὑτά.

From all the other Ald. readings quoted by Susemihl in this Book, D varies.

After ceasing at 1136 b 1 to follow Kʰ, C begins to resemble Oʰ, except in ch. 10 (on ἐπιείκεια). In ch. 9 from 1136 b 1 to the end of the chapter, and in ch. 11, i.e. the last chapter of the Book, Oʰ stands alone among Bekker's MSS. in nineteen places, in eleven of which C agrees with it. The unique Oʰ readings with which C agrees occur in the following places, 1136 b 8, 18, 18, 22, 31, 33, 1137 a 6, 8, 1138 a 5, 5, 33 (see Jackson's apparatus criticus). It will be seen that this agreement of C with Oʰ unique (curiously broken by the chapter on ἐπιείκεια which breaks the discussion of self-injury) is continued in the Sixth Book. Elsewhere (except in Book x) C, however closely it may agree with Oʰ in conjunction with other MSS, avoids its unique readings.

In chapter 10 (on ἐπιείκεια) Oʰ is unique in three readings, with none of which C agrees. At 1137 b 29 C and D have in common a curious blunder—ψηλαφίσματος for ψηφίσματος, and otherwise show themselves to be closely related in ch. 10, following the later MSS. in preference to Kʰ and Lʰ.

In Books i, ii, iii, and iv, we have seen that A is closely related to Kʰ. In Book v we have Mr. Jackson's collation of Pʰ (Vat. 1342), a MS. closely related to Kʰ; and A turns out to be practically identical with

P^b in this Book. That A and P^b agree almost *verbatim* throughout the whole of the Ethics is rendered probable by the fact that their readings are substantially the same in that part of the Tenth Book (1176 a 11—1177 a 30) where P^b has been collated by Wilamowitz; also by the fact that throughout the Eudemian Ethics (collated in P^b by Bekker) and the Mag. Mor. (collated by Susemihl in P^b) they present the same peculiarities; and lastly, by the important fact that they both have a long lacuna in common in Book viii Eth. Nic. from 1157 a 12 to 1161 b 19. From a peculiarity of this lacuna, Mr. Jackson (Journal of Philology, 1876, vi. 208 sqq.) infers that A is a transcript of P^b. The following are the facts concerning the lacuna in A. Fol. 85^v ends with θερα 1157 a 8. After fol. 85, four leaves of much coarser parchment have been inserted containing, in a fifteenth century hand, the omitted text. This later hand also occupies the four top lines of fol. 86^r and ends with ὄντα 1161 b 19. The old hand begins again at the beginning of the fifth line from the top of fol. 86^r with μᾶλλον (1161 b 19). As Mr. Jackson has pointed out, however, an examination of the four lines at the top of fol. 86^r shows that the first two lines and rather more than half of the third have been written in rasura, and that the last word erased is ἡδύ 1157 a 12. The line and a half intervening between ἡδύ (1157 a 12) and μᾶλλον (1161 b 19) had evidently been left blank by the old scribe, seeing a gap in his copy. The new scribe scraped out the two lines and a half at the top of fol. 86^r above the blank, and began the first of his inserted leaves with πενόμενος 1157 a 8, and having filled four such leaves, utilised the space for four lines at the top of fol. 86^r, thus getting the omitted text down to ὄντα 1161 b 19, exactly in. Now, as Mr. Jackson has pointed out, P^b has the same lacuna, except that the new hand begins after ἀντι not after ἡδύ 1157 a 12. The old hand in both MSS. begins again with μᾶλλον 1161 b 19. Thus P^b=A except that A has not ἀντι. Therefore, Mr. Jackson infers, P^b was not copied from A, and the probability is that A was copied from P^b. A, we know, was written in 1279; and according to Susemihl P^b belongs to the fourteenth century. Dr. Meyncke, who has examined P^b at my request, inclines to Susemihl's view, although he notes points which favour the view that it belongs to the end of the thirteenth century—e.g. the ancient forms of π and τ and of εἰ. The frequency of abbreviations weighs strongly with him in favour of assigning it to the fourteenth century; but A is also much abbreviated; and certain passages of P^b which Dr. Meyncke has copied out, reproducing the forms of the letters as they occur in the MS, impress me strongly with the conviction that it belongs to about the same date as A. The forms of the letters and the contractions are identical in the two MSS.

The following are the facts respecting the lacuna in P^b as they have been communicated to me by Dr. Meyncke. The fourth line from the top of fol. 76^v is:—

οὗτοι ἀλλ' ὁ μὲν ὁρῶν ἐκεῖνον ὁ δὲ θεραπευόμενος ὑπὸ τοῦ ἐραστοῦ λη
5. γούσης δὲ τῆς ὥρας ἐνιότι καὶ ἡ φιλία λήγει τῷ μὲν γὰρ οὐκ ἔστι ἡδεῖα ἡ ὃ
6. ψις τῷ δ' οὐ γίνεται ἡ θεραπεία πολλοὶ δ' αὖ διαμένουσιν ἐὰν ἐκ τῆς
7. συνηθείας τὰ ἤθη στέρξωσιν ὁμοήθεις ὄντας οἱ δὲ μὴ τὸ ἡδὺ ἀντι

Then begins the new fifteenth century hand with καταλλαττόμενοι in line 8, no blank being left. This new hand goes on through ff. 77, 78, 79, 80, 81^r and 81^v, in which page it occupies twelve lines. The old hand begins (μᾶλλον 1161 b 19) fol. 82^r. It would thus appear that the original scribe left the greater part of fol. 76^v blank—i.e. all after line 7—viz. twenty-six lines, P^b having thirty-three lines to the page. The scribe of A, we have seen, indicates the lacuna by a blank of one line and a half. It may be thought more probable that the MS. with the shorter was copied from that with the longer blank, if the one was copied from the other at all. But there is nothing in the facts hitherto adduced inconsistent with the view that A and P^b are copies of a common archetype in which the lacuna began with καταλλαττόμενοι. A might very well omit ἀντι as being merely part of a word, while P^b preferred to transcribe it as it stood.

For that part of the following notes which refers to P^b I am indebted to Dr. Meyncke. I give them in the hope that they may throw some light on the question of the relationship of P^b to A.

1147 b 21   P^b fol. 69^r reads ὅτι μὲν οὖν περὶ ἡδονὰς καὶ λύπας εἰσὶν οἵ τε ἐγκρατεῖς καὶ καρτερικοί καὶ οἱ ἀκρατεῖς καὶ καρτερικοί, καὶ οἱ ἀκρατεῖς καὶ μαλακοί, the words καὶ οἱ ἀκρατεῖς καὶ καρτερικοί being underlined by a later hand. These underlined words occur in A, but have been erased. They are perfectly legible under the erasure in the second line from the top of fol. 77ʳ.

1142 a 25 P^b has ἀντιληπτικοὶ μέν last words of fol. 64ᵛ. A has ἀντι[ληπτικὴ μέν by a later hand in ras.].

1145 a 24 P^b without correction or erasure reads θηριωδία. In A the original hand has converted into θηριωδία what was apparently θηριώδει.

1145 b 17 οἱ post συγκεχυμένως] ὁ P^bA pr.

1151 a 25 οὐδέ] ὁ δέ P^bA pr.

1096 b 20 πλήν] πλεῖ P^b at the end of a line: evidently, Dr. Meyncke remarks, carefully copied from the original: no later correction. A has πλήν, the ήν later in ras.

1103 b 7 καί ante γίνεται om. P^bA.

1107 b 11 δ' ἑαυτ' sic P^b without correction. A has δὲ αυτ in the original hand, the ὲ at the beginning having been inserted by a later hand.

1115 a 29 οἷον εἰ P^b without correction. οἷον ἤ A, ἤ being in ras.

1113 a 1 πέπεπται P^b, πεπ[αυ? in ras.]ται A.

     13 Here both P^b and A insert after τύπῳ—νῦν οὐχ ὡς εἰώθε λέγειν τὸ καθ' ὑπογραφὴν ἀλλὰ καθόλου. This insertion is by the original hand in both MSS.

1116 b 24 ἐπιφέρουσι] φέρουσι P^b (without correction) and A.

1118 b 17 ἕως ἂν ὑπερπλησθῇ ὑπερβολή P^bA.

1119 b 4 πολλὴν αὔξησιν] πολλὴν ἕξιν αὔξησιν P^bA.

      8 καὶ πανταχόθεν τῷ ἀνοήτῳ om. P^bA.

1127 b 20 μάντιν σοφὸν ἢ ἰατρόν] μάντιν ἢ ἰητρὸν σοφόν P^b, μάντιν ἢ ἰητρικὸν σοφόν A pr.

1145 b 24 P^b has ᾦετο καὶ ὥσπερ ἀνδράποδον, omitting Σωκράτης ἄλλο τι κρατεῖν καὶ περιέλκειν αὐτόν. A also omits these words, leaving a space of two or three letters between ᾦετο and ὥσπερ, where however an erased καί can be detected.

1185 a 33 Mor. Magn. i. 4 ἂν δὲ μὴ ἐμβάλῃς τροφὴν οὐκ ἔχει]. A has a space of twenty-seven letters erased between ἐμβάλῃς and τροφήν. P^b reads ἂν δὲ μὴ ἐμβάλῃς ἔχει ὁρμὴν τρέφειν ἐὰν δὲ μὴ ἐμβάλῃς τροφὴν οὐκ ἔχει κ.τ.λ. Most of these words interpolated by P^b are legible under the erasure in A.

So much for the information which I have obtained from Dr. Meyncke. It does not seem to me to prove that A is a transcript from P^b, or to be inconsistent with the hypothesis that both MSS. are derived from the same archetype independently.

In Book v, P^b (as collated by Jackson) and A agree in the following places where the readings of P^b are unique among those of Bekker's MSS :—

1129 a 15 δ' οὗ.   16 ὑπό.   26 δικαιοσύνη καὶ ἀδικία.   b 2 καὶ περί.   οὐ πάντα ἴσται.   23 ἄλλαι om.   1130 a 26 μᾶλλον δόξειεν εἶναι.   30 ἐγκατέλοιπε. b 10-13 ἐπεὶ δὲ τὸ ἄνισον καὶ τὸ παράνομον πλέον οὐ ταὐτὸν ἀλλ' ἕτερον ὡς μέρος πρὸς ὅλον· τὸ μὲν γὰρ ἄνισον ἅπαν παράνομον τὸ δὲ παράνομον οὐχ ἅπαν ἄνισον· τὸ μὲν γὰρ πλέον ἅπαν ἄνισον τὸ δ' ἄνισον οὐ πᾶν πλέον· καὶ τὸ ἄδικον κ.τ.λ.   1131 a 12 ἐστὶ πράξει. 20 ἰσότης ἔσται.   22 ἴσοι μὴ ἴσα om.   1132 b 8 αἱ P^b, εα A in ras.   15 ἀνείσθαι καὶ τῷ πωλεῖν.   23 ἀντιπεπονθὸς ἄλλω, τὸ δ' ἀντιπεπονθὸς οὐκ ἐφαρμόττει οὔτ' ἐπὶ τὸ νόμιμον οὔτ' ἐπὶ τὸ πολιτικόν, πολιτικὸν δὲ λέγω τὸ κοινωνικόν· τὸ δ' ἀντιπεπονθός.   29 οὐ δεῖ—ἐπάταξεν om.   1133 a 3 χάριτος.   ἕτερον.   21 post Γλαυκῷ add. μετρεῖ δηλονότι τὸ νόμισμα.   1133 b 1 οὐ δεῖ ἄγειν ἀναλογίας.   25 β. δῆλον] β. οἰκία ἐφ' ἧς ἁ. μνῶν ἅ. κλίνη ἐφ' ᾗ β. μνᾶς ἀξία. ἡ δὲ κλίνη πέμπτον μέρος τῆς οἰκίας ἂν εἴη. δῆλον. 1134 b 3 πλέον post νέμει om.   21 ὅταν δὲ θῶνται διαφέρει om.   1135 b 15 ἀλλὰ —ἀήθη om.   18 ἡ ἀρχὴ ἐν αὐτῷ.   1136 a 28 πράττειν om. (inter lineas πράττειν man. rec. A, add. marg. P^b ποιεῖν).   1136 b 15 τὸ πλέον.   30 κτήμη.   1137 a 3 ἐκεῖνο.   1138 a 25 τὴν ἑαυτοῦ γυναῖκα.

The present seems to be the best opportunity of indicating the relation of A and P^b in Eth. Nic. : 1176 a 11—1177 a 30 where P^b has been collated by Wilamowitz.

1176 a 11 λυπηρά ἐστι καὶ μισητά in ras. librarius ipse A.   15 τοῦτο post ἑτέρων. 17 καί ante ἑκάστου add. ΓΗ^{a}P^{b}Ald.ACD.   18 ὁ om. AP^b etc., add. Ald.C.   20 οὐδέ A.   22 ὁμολογουμένως P^{b}AC etc., ὁμολογουμένας D.   1176 b 5 post ἄλλο add. τι A.   7 περί ACD.   12 ἀγωγάς A pr.   15 τοιούτων A P^b etc., τούτων CL^{b}O^b Ald.   16 ταῦτα AP^b etc., τὰ τοιαῦτα D.   17 ταῖς δυναστείαις AD.   18 οὐδὲ νοῦς P^{b}A.   26 δὲ P^{b}AD etc.   27 ἡ om. ADC.   1177 a 4 τῶν ante μετά om. AC D, add. L^{b}P^b.   9 καί om. C, habet A.   19 τε add. L^{b}P^{b}Ald.AC.   25 σοφία AP^{b}Ald.C, φιλοσοφία D.   καθαριότητι P^{b}Ald.A.   27 διαγωγήν AP^b.   29 ὁ ante σοφός add. A.   Elsewhere, from 1176 a 11 to 1177 a 30, the readings of A are those of Bekker's text (Parker, 1871).

In order to present a connected view of the evidence for the relationship of P^b and A, I here add the more striking agreements of the two MSS. in the Eudemian Ethics, throughout which treatise P^b was collated by Bekker:—

1214 a 6 δ' om. P^bA.   ἐρᾶται P^bA, omisso τό.   24 διὰ τὴν τύχην P^bA.   30 συναγάγει P^bA.   b 23 περιπάτων] περὶ πάντων P^bA.   1215 a 4 βίον P^bA.   8 τὰ om. P^bA.   15 οὐδὲ διὰ τῆς P^b, οὐδὲ τῆς A.   19 τοῖς] ἃ τοῖς P^bA, ἐν τοῖς marg. P^b. 31 πρὸς ὃν AP^b.   b 9 ἐρώμενος P^bA.   19 δι' ἃ om. pr. P^bA.   24 ἐχόντων μὲν ἡδονήν P^bA.   29 οὐ om. P^bA.   33 αἰσθήσεων πορίζοι P^bA.   1218 b 32 ἐν om. P^bA.   35 ὃν ἡ P^bA.   1221 b 14 πλήκτης—15 ὀργῆς om. P^bA.   1224 a 4 προαιρεῖται—ἐξαίφνης om. P^bA.   11 ἀκούσιον καὶ—βίαιον om. P^bA.   31 χαίρων δέ om. P^bA.   b 39 pro δέ locum vacuum P^b; no space left in A.   1230 b 16 ἐπιπέδαιον] ἐπὶ πόλεως P^bA.   1234 b 14 περὶ—λεκτέον om. P^bA.   For the headings between Books iii and vii, see Bekker p. 1234; here P^b=A.   1235 a 37 post τῶν M^bP^bA litteris locum quinque vel sex.   1238 b 12 ἔτι] nescio quid corr. P^b, A has ἔτι distinctly.   ἡ ἐνί τι P^bA.   13 σπουδαίῳ AP^b.   1244 b 3 M^bP^bA leave a space after τούτῳ.   1245 a 1 συστοιχίας] εὐτυχίας A, εὐστοχίας M^b, συστοιχείας corr. P^b.   1246 a 23 οἰκεῖον om. P^bA.

Susemihl's publication De Magnorum Moralium Codice Vaticano 1342 (i. e. P^b), Berlin, 1881, enables me to add the following notes respecting the correspondence between P^b and A in the Magna Moralia:—

1181 a 24 ἠθῶν M^bP^bAAld.   26 δοκεῖ M^bP^bA.   27 γάρ] om. pr. P^b (γάρ suppl. eadem man. P^b) A.   b 25 τό] κατὰ τό M^bP^bA.   26 ἐστίν om. M^bP^bA.   26 ἆρα sed a in ras. P^b, ἀρετῆς A.   26 ὡς om. M^bP^bA.   28 ἔχειν in ras. et ἡ supra versum P^b, ἔχειν sine ras. A.   1182 a 3 ἐπαίειν] οἴεω pr. P^bA.   9 ἐστί om. M^b P^bA.   9 ἀγνοοῦσας τί M^bP^bA.   10 πρῶτον M^bP^bA.   11 εἰρήκεισαν M^bP^bA.   11 πρῶτον ΓM^bP^bK^b, πρῶτος A.   14 ἰσάκιος ἴσακις M^bP^b, ἰσάκιος ἴσως A.   15 ἐπιγινόμενος P^bA.   23 ὀρθῶς] εἰκότως M^bP^bA.   23 ταῦτα δέ AK^bM^bAld., δὲ ταῦτα P^bP^a. 24 τε om. M^bP^bA.   25 ἑκάστου τάς M^bP^b (attamen τάς in mg. P^b) A (attamen τας superscripsit man. haud scio an eadem A).   24 προσηκούσας] πρέπουσας M^b, πρέπουσας et προυσας in ras. P^b, πρ[ε in ras. spatio ii litt. relicto]πούσας A.   26 μέντοι τοῦτο] διὰ ταῦτα M^bP^bA.   27 κατέμιξε καὶ συνέζευξεν εἰς M^bP^bA.   28 οὐ δή] οὐδέν M^bP^bA.   b 4 ἄλλος ὁ P^bA.   5 ἡμῖν ἄρα ἀγαθοῦ λεκτέον P^bA.   8 ἐν] ὃν M^b P^bA.   9 μετέχοντα sed ἐχ in ras. a. pr. m. scr. P^b, sine ras. A.   25 ὅτι] εἰ M^b et fort. P^b (nisi potius om.) om. A.   33 δεῖ pr. P^b, δεῖξαι em. rec. (ut videtur) m. nigriore atramento P^b, δεῖξαι A.   33 τι] καί τι M^bP^bA.   34 ὅτι] ᾧ M^bP^bA.

NICOMACHEAN ETHICS. 53

36 ἡ om. M^b et corr. P^b (eras.) om. A. 1183 a 20 ἄλλας sequente ras. trium fere litt. P^b, ἄλλας ἀρετάς A, mox κατηγορίας. 26 ἀφανῶν bis pr. P^b (semel eras.) semel A. 38 ὑπὲρ τῶν in P^b evanuerunt, habet A. 39 ἐρῶ Ald.A, ἐρᾶ aut ἐρεῖ pr. P^b (ἐρεῖ mg. rc.). b 7, 8 διὰ—ἀγαθοῦ om. M^bP^bA. 1185 a 22 περί P^bA. b 9 τὰς τὸν λόγον ἐχούσας M^bP^b et οὐδεὶς τὰς τοῦ τοῦ τὸν λόγον ἔχοντος post haec verba add. pr. P^b, sed oblitt.; τὰς τὸν λόγον ἐχούσας τὰς τοῦ τὸν λόγον ἔχοντος οὐδεὶς ἐπαινεῖται κ.τ.λ. A. 39 λεγον' P^bA. 1186 a 20 ἔχον P^b pr. KA. b 17 δύο Ald. pr. P^bA. 20 πορρύτερον P^bA. 21 πορρότερον P^bA. 22 πορρότερον P^bA. 1187 a 21 οὐκ om. M^bP^bA. 21 ἱκουσίοις P^bA. b 7 ἂν om. pr. P^b (pallidius add. rc.), habet A. 1188 a 20 τό—ἀκούσιον om. M^bP^bA. 21 οὐ ante πράττει add. M^b et corr. (rc. ut videtur) P^b, om. A. 31 ὁ—32 βουλόμενος] ὁ δ' ἀκρατὴς τὰ κακὰ πράττει εἰδὼς (εἰδὼς πράττει P^bA) ὅτι κακά ἐστιν. εἰ δ' ὁ ἀκρατὴς τὰ κακὰ εἰδὼς ὅτι κακὰ πράττει βουλόμενος M^bP^bA. b 10 γὰρ φύσει P^bA. 32 ποιεῖν P^b, ποιῶν A. 34 οὐ ante οὐθέν add. pr. P^b A. 1189 a 23 δή post ἀναγκαῖον add. M^b et rc. P^b, om. A. 36 τὸ—διανοίας add. M^bP^bA. 1191 b 18 ἀνθρώπου om. pr. P^bA. 1192 a 37 σαλακωνείας P^bA. b 28 μέσος] μεσότης P^bAld.A. 1195 a 35 ὅσαι—δι'] haec in P^b paene tota evanuerunt. In A distincte leguntur. 1203 a 13 ὅσω (& rc.) γε ὅτι τιμὴ καὶ τιμὴ ἕτερον (τι μειότερον rc.) κακῶς pr. P^b, ὅγε ὅτι τιμῇ καὶ τιμιώτερον κακῶς A. 1209 a 7 τὸ M^bAld. rc. K^b, rc. P^b, rc. A, τῶι pr. K^b, pr. P^b, pr. A. 7 ἡδύ M^bAld. rc. P^b, rc. A, ἡδεῖ K^b, pr. P^b, pr. A. 7 τό M^bAld., rc. K^b, rc. P^b, rc. A, τῶι pr. K^b, pr. P^b, pr. A. 7 συμφέρον M^bAld., rc. P^b, rc. A, συμφέροντι K^b, pr. P^b, pr. A. b 16 μεταπίπτει K^bAld.P^2A, pr. P^b. 1212 a 19 οὐχ ἣ νοοῦσι A et Bekk. et, ut videtur, rc. P^b, οὐχὶ νοοῦσι M^b et, ut videtur, pr. P^b.

So much for the evidence bearing upon the relationship of P^b and A. It is not inconsistent with the view that both MSS. are copies of a common archetype; but more than this I will not venture to say.

BOOK VI.

	K^bM^b.	L^bO^b.
1138 b 33	τοῦτ' εἰρημένον DB^1Ald. [τοῦτο εἶναι εἰρημένον A].	τοῦτο τὸ εἰρημένον B^2C.
1139 a 3	om.	οὖν Ald.ACB^1B^2D.
4	εἶναι μέρη Ald.AB^1.	μέρη εἶναι D [δύο μέρη τῆς ψυχῆς εἶναι B^2 C].
12	λογικόν C sed crx. ead. ut vid. man.	λογιστικόν ADAld.B^1B^2.
b 13	ἀληθεύσει.	ἀληθεύει ACDB^1B^1Ald.

1139 b 15 om. A.
25 ἡ ἅπασα [ἅπασα ἡ A].

1140 a 5 διό C with καί above—by the same hand? διό AB².
14 ἡ AAld.B¹D.
18 ταῦτ'.
b 2 om. Ald.D.
7 αὕτη B².
10 τούς AAld.B².
11 ἔνθεν Ald.DB¹ [ἔνθα A].
12 om.
13 ἅπασαν A.
14 om. A.
18 om. A.
32 δ' αἱ ACB².
33 om. B².
1141 a 11 οὖν Ald.B¹.
19 ὥσπερ.
20 τὴν πολιτικήν.

23 καὶ εὐθύ AB¹DAld.
28 καί A [δ' εἴη ὅτι B²C].
b 1 ὁ κόσμος συνέστηκεν Ald.AD B¹.
30 καὶ φρόνησις ADAld.B¹.
1142 a 2 πολυπράγμονες AB¹B²DAld. πράγμονες C.
17 δή AAld.

20 om.
23 τοδὶ τὸ βαρύσταθμον B²C.
25 μέν CAld.
27 om. AAld. [οὐ—αἴσθησις om. B¹].
28 οἵᾳ ᾗ αἰσθανόμεθα B²C.
32 om. Ald.
b 9 ἡ εὐβουλία τις.

ἡ B¹B²CDAld.
πᾶσα B¹B²Ald.DC (but erasure after διδακ C).
καί Ald.B¹D.

om. B²C.
τὰ αὐτά ACAld.B¹B²D.
add. ἡ ACB¹B².
αὐτή ACAld.B¹D.
om. B¹CD.
ὅθεν B²C.
ὡς AAld.DCB¹B².
πᾶσαν Ald.CDB¹B².
τό B¹B²CDAld.
ἡ B¹B²CDAld.
δ' Ald.B¹D.
ἡ ACB¹Ald.D.
om. ACB²D.
καὶ ὥσπερ Ald.AB¹B²DC.
τὴν ἐπιστήμην πολιτικήν Ald.DCB¹B¹, τὴν πολιτικὴν ἐπιστήμην A.
καὶ τὸ εὐθύ B²C.
om. Ald.B¹D.
συνέστηκεν ὁ κόσμος B²C.

καὶ ἡ φρόνησις B²C.
φιλοπράγμονες.

δήποτε B² [δέ ποτε C; διὰ τί, omisso δή, B¹D].
οὐκ ACB¹B²DAld.
τοδὶ βαρύσταθμον AB¹DAld.
om.
οὗ B²CD.

οἵᾳ αἰσθανόμεθα AAld.B¹D.
καί ACDB¹B².
τις ἡ εὐβουλία ACB¹B²DAld.

1142 b 9 om. | δί ACB¹B²Ald.D.
15 τε καὶ κακῶς AB². | τε κακῶς Ald.B¹D.
21 om. ACAld.B¹B²D. | add. εἶναι.
23 δι' ACB¹B². | τούτου δι' Ald.D.
25 αὕτη CD. | αὐτή AAld.B¹B².
30 τίς δί [ἡ τὶς δί A]. | ἡ δί τις B¹B²CDAld.
1143 a 5 ὁτουοῦν. | ὁτιοῦν AAld.B¹B²D corr. C.
19 συγγνώμονας. | εὐγνώμονας AAld.B¹B²CD.
31 ἁπάντων AAld.B¹B²DC. | πάντων.
b 1 καί B². | om. B¹CDAld. [om. A in ras.].
14 ἀρχάς [τὰς ἀρχάς AB¹B²DC Ald.]. | ὀρθῶς.
16 τί A. | τίνα B¹B²CDAld.
19 θεωρήσει A. | θεωρεῖ CAld.B¹B²D.
28 ῥητέον A. | θετέον CDAld.B¹B².
30 αὑτοῖς (nescio quid corr. A). | αὑτούς CAld.
1144 a 2 τοῦ B². | om. ACB¹Ald.D.
14 λέγομεν ACB¹B²DAld. | om.
23 om. A. | τις B¹B²CDAld.
b 1 καὶ γὰρ ἡ ἀρετὴ παραπλησίως ACAld.B¹B². | παραπλησίως γάρ D.
1145 a 2 ὑπάρξουσι ACB¹B²DAld. | ὑπάρχουσι.
3 om. | ἄν ACB¹Ald.D.
8 om. B¹. | ἡ ACDAld.

K^bO^b. | L^bM^b.
1138 b 19 μηδί AC. | μήτε Ald.
21 ἐν AAld. | om. C.
1139 a 7 ὅσων ACB². | ὧν Ald.B¹D.
1140 b 32 ἀποδεικτῶν Ald.ADB¹. | ἀποδεικτικῶν C.
1141 a 9 τε C [om. AAld.]. | γε.
10 ἀποδίδομεν AAld. | ἀποδιδόαμεν C.
b 34 τό ACD. | τὸ τά [ὡς τό Ald.].
1143 a 11 τό ACAld. | τῷ.
12 τό ACAld. | τῷ.
36 ἀμφότερα ACAld. | ἀμφότερον.

In the following list, which contains all the recorded cases of O^b

unique in Book vi, asterisks have been prefixed where C agrees with
O^b unique—viz. in eleven places out of the thirty-two.

O^b unique in vi.

1138 b 19   μηδέ O^b, μήτε Ald.ΓM^b, μή AC cum cet.
     *21   καί om. O^bC, habet A.
     34   τίς ὁ ὅρος O^b, τίς ὅρος AC.
*1139 b 30   ἆρα αἱ ἀρχαί O^b, ἆρα καὶ ἀρχαί C, ADB¹=Bek.
*1140 a 7   ἔστι om. O^bC (sed correx. man. ead. ut vid. C), habet A.
     *12   γίνηται O^bC, γένηται A.
     18   τέχνη καὶ ἡ τύχη O^b, AC=Bek.
     *28   ζῆν] ζῆν ὅλον·O^bCD, ζῆν ὅλως L^bM^bAld., ζῆν ὅλ (ras.) A, ὅλως om. K^b.
1141 a 12   ἐστίν om. O^b, habent AC.
*1142 a 1   τό om. O^bC, τό pr. K^bD, τά A cet.
     2   διὸ καί O^bAld., διό C with καί above later, διό A.
     *11   λεγομένου O^bCB², εἰρημένου AB¹.
?*17   διά om. O^b, C? (διά at the end of a line on the immediate margin; but I am not sure whether by a later hand or not C), habet A.
     *19   αἱ om. O^bC, habent AD.
     32   διαλαβεῖν O^bAB¹Ald., λαβεῖν D et pr. C (corr. man. rec. διαλαβεῖν C).
     33   ἡ post δόξα om. O^b, habent AC.
     b 16   τίς om. O^b, habent AC.
     *20   ὑπειληφώς O^bCDB¹, εἰληφώς A.
     24   ὥστε O^b, ἀλλά AC cum cet.
1143 a 3   ἐπιστημῶν κατὰ μέρος O^b, τῶν κατὰ μέρος τῶν ἐπιστημῶν C, τῶν κατὰ μέρος ἐπιστημῶν A.
     3   οἷον] οἷον ἡ O^b, οἷον ἡ CAK^bM^b, om. ἡ D.
     12   ἡ om. O^b, habent AC.
     32   ἔστι] εἰ O^b, ἔστι AC.
     *33   ἅπαντα O^bC, πάντα L^b, ἁπάντων K^bM^bΓAld.DA pr.
*b 27   καί] ἡ O^bC, καί AD.
1144 a 2   γ'] τι O^b, δί CAld., om. D, γ' A.
     6   τῷ ἐνεργεῖν] ἐνεργεῖ O^b, τῷ ἐνεργεῖν AC.
     b 3   καί om. O^b, habent AC.
     24   τήν om. O^b, habent AC.
     29   γὰρ εἶναι] γὰρ ὥστε O^b, γὰρ εἶναι AC.
1145 a 2   ἅπασαι O^b, πᾶσαι AC.
     2   καί O^b, κἄν AC.

The results for Book vi may be summed up as follow.

The agreement between C and O^b unique is greater in the earlier than in the latter part of the Book, 1143 a 1 marking approximately the place at which the correspondence ceases to be at all striking. We may say that a marked agreement between C and O^b unique extends (with the interruption of the chapter on ἐπιείκεια) from 1136 b 1 to 1143 a 1.

On the other hand, the agreement between C and Ald. is greater after than before 1143 a 1. Out of twenty-nine places referred to by Susemihl, and not included in the K^bM^b—L^bO^b and K^bO^b—L^bM^b lists, C and Ald. agree in eleven, and differ in eighteen. The following are these eleven cases of agreement, eight of which occur after 1143 a 1 :—1139 a 3 λέγωμεν, 36 αὕτη, 1139 b 1 γὰρ τούτου, 1143 a 10 γὰρ οἱ ante συνετοί add., b 5 ἔχειν post δεῖ, 29 χρήσιμος, 1144 a 2 δέ, ἑκατέρας, 7 κατά τε, b 7 εἶναι ἄλλως, 17 τινές om. Again, in the K^bM^b—L^bO^b list C and Ald. always agree after 1143 a 1; whereas before that point they differ in sixteen places.

If we turn from O^b unique to O^b with K^b or L^b, we find that the agreement of C and O^b extends throughout the whole Book, all parts of which contribute about equally to the following figures :—

C 38 — L^bO^b 58 K^bM^b — 14 C[1].
C 7 — K^bO^b 10 L^bM^b — 3 C.

C thus follows K^b or L^b where O^b happens to follow the one or the other. O^b of course belongs in this Book distinctly to the L^b variety.

The relationship of Ald. is exhibited in the following table :—

Ald. 37 — L^bO^b 58 K^bM^b — 21 Ald.
Ald. 6 — K^bO^b 10 L^bM^b — 3 Ald.

Of the thirty-seven Ald.L^bO^b readings twenty-seven are given by C; of the twenty-one Ald.K^bM^b readings seven are given by C; of the six Ald.K^bO^b readings three are given by C. Ald. and C are thus closely related. Although Ald. inclines somewhat towards M^b, yet C and Ald. are both more nearly related to O^b in this Book than to any

---

[1] I e. there being fifty-eight cases of L^bO^b *versus* K^bM^b, C sides with L^bO^b in thirty-eight of them, and with K^bM^b in fourteen.

58   ENGLISH MANUSCRIPTS OF THE

other MS. Several of the cases of Ald.=K^{b}M^b will be found to be cases in which L^b and O^b (with C it may be) have an omission, and may consequently be easily explained by correction.

D is in this Book a member of the group to which O^{b}C and Ald. belong.

A is still of the K^b family, but shows a considerable L^b admixture, as may be seen from the following table:—

A 29 — K^{b}M^b 58 L^{b}O^b — 20 A.
A 9 — K^{b}O^b 10 L^{b}M^b — 0 A.

It will be seen from the list of O^b unique, that A does not present any of the peculiarities of that MS; while the following list of the principal cases of K^b unique in Book vi will show that it does not present many of the peculiarities of K^b either.

K^b unique in vi.

1138 b 18   καί om. K^{b}AAld.
       21   πράξεσι K^{b}A.
       31   ὡς K^b, ὅσα A.
       34   τε om. K^b, habet A.
1139 a 3   λέγωμεν K^{b}AAld.
       4, 5 καὶ ἔχοντος om. K^b, habet A.
        8   τῶν δ ἐνδέχονται K^b, A=Bek.
       12   βούλεσθαι K^b, βουλεύεσθαι A.
       23   διά A, δί K^b.
       23   ταῦτα μὲν K^b, μὲν ταῦτα A.
       36   δ' om. K^b, habet A.
     b 11   πεπραγμένα om. K^b, habet A.
       14   ἄλλοθεν K^b, ἄνωθεν A.
       30   om. ὁ K^b, habet A.
1140 a 16   ταῦτα τήν A, ταύτην K^b.
     b 15   δύο ὀρθάς K^b, δύο ὀρθαῖς A.
       24   ἥττων K^b, ἧττον A.
1141 a 1   οὐδ' ἡ σοφία K^b, οὐδὲ δὴ σοφία A.
        7   νοῦν A, γοῦν νοῦν pr. K^b, οὖν νοῦν corr.
1142 a 1   διατρίβων φρόνιμος om. K^b, habet A.
     b 28   οὐ δεῖ καὶ ὡς A, οὐ δικαίως pr. K^b.
1144 a 6   τῷ ἐνεργεῖν εὐδαίμονα A, ἐνέργεια εὐδαιμονία K^b.

NICOMACHEAN ETHICS. 59

B¹ and B² belong in this Book to the L^b family, being closely related to Ald. and C, and presenting considerable agreement with O^b. The relationship of B¹ and B² is shown in the following table:—

$$\left.\begin{array}{l} B^1\ 37 \\ B^2\ 35 \end{array}\right\} L^bO^b\ 58\ K^bM^b \left\{\begin{array}{l} 17\ B^1. \\ 19\ B^2. \end{array}\right.$$

As C seems to possess some independent authority in this Book, I here append all my notes of its readings, occasionally inserting the readings of other MSS:—

1138 b 18 ὅτι] ε in ras. C.   19 μηδέ pr. C, corr. rec. μήτε, μηδέ A.   20 ἐν om. C, habet A.   21 καί om. C, habet A.   23 καί A] τε καί C.   24 τῆς ante ὑπερβολῆς om. C.   26 ἀληθές] -έ in ras. C.   29 ἄν τις om. pr. C.   30 ἄν om. C, δεῖ] -εῖ in ras. C.   31 εἴποιεν C, εἶποι A, ἡ om. C, habet A.   32 τάς] -άς in ras. C.   33 ἀληθές] ε in ras. C.   τοῦτ'] τοῦτο τό C.   34 ἐστίν in ras. C, ὁ om. pr. C. 1139 a 3 δύο μέρη τῆς ψυχῆς εἶναι C, A = Bek.   7 τοιαῦτα] αι in ras. C, ὅσων AC] ἐν D.   8 ἐν δέ γε AD et rec. C.   9-10 ἕτερα—γίνει bis C.   10 τὸ πεφυκὸς πρὸς ἑκάτερον C, AD = Bek.   12 post ἐπιστημονικόν add. C τὸ δὲ λογίεσθω δὲ τούτων τὸ μὲν ἐπιστημονικὴ. λογιστικόν A] λογικόν C sed correx. eadem, ut vid., manus.   16 ἡ ἀρετή C.   18 κύρια add. man. rec. in spatio a librario vacuo relicto C.   21 καὶ ἀπόφασις om. pr. C.   23 διὰ μὲν ταῦτα δεῖ C, δεῖ διὰ μὲν ταῦτα AD.   25 σπουδαῖα C.   28 ἐστι om. pr. C, τὸ ψεῦδος C.   29 διανοητικοῦ] οὗ in ras. C.   30 ἡ om. C.   34 ἀπραξία pr. C.   36 αὕτη C.   τοῦ om. pr. C.   36 καὶ πρακτική—1139 b 1 ποιητικῆς om. C sed suppl. ad oram man., ut videtur, eadem.   1139 b 1 τοῦ] τούτου pr. C.   2 οὐ] οὔτε C.   3 ἀλλ' οὐ τὸ πρακτόν AD, rec. C.   ἀπραξία pr. C.   7 βουλεύεται] -εύεται in ras. C.   13 ἀληθεύει CADB¹.   15 ἔστω pr. C ut vid., rec. ἔσται.   17 post ὑπολήψει add. καί C sed correx.   18 post φανερόν add. C ἠδία (sic).   24 πάντα δίδια C.   25 διδακτή] τή in ras. C.   26 δέ] ἐ in ras. C.   27 ἐν om. C.   ὀλίγομεν C, λέγωμεν D.   28 ἀρχή ἐστι τοῦ pr. C, ἀρχῆς ἐστί καὶ τοῦ rec. C, AD = Bek.   30 post ἄρα add. καί C, om. AB¹D.   31 ἐπιστήμη ἄρα C, B¹ = Bek.   33 πως om. C sed suppl. librarius, ut vid., ipse.   36 τούτων τὸν τρόπον C, A = Bekker. 1140 a 1 ἔχον pr. C.   2 ποίησις] alterum ι in ras. C.   καί om. pr. C.   3 καί post αὐτῶν in ras. C.   ὥστε καί] ε καί in ras. C.   4 μετὰ λόγου bis C.   5 διό C, καί sup. vers., καί D.   περιέχεται CAB¹B²D.   6 post οὔτε add. C ησις πράξις (sic).   πρᾶξις C littera inter ξ et ι erasa.   9 τὸ αὐτό C.   12 γίνηται C.   τι om. pr. C.   14 ἡ om. C.   22 ἀτεχνία] ί in ras. C.   25 post τίνας add. δή B¹ et rec. C.   27 ποῖα om. pr. C, habet D.   28 ante ἰσχύν add. πρός C, om. D.   ποῖα om. D.   περί (πρός corr. man. rec. C) τὸ εὖ ζῆν ὅλον CD, ὅλως pro ὅλον B¹.   29 τι om. pr. C.   31 inter εἴη

I 2

et φρόνιμος unius litterae rasura C. 32 μή om. pr. C. 33 μετά] τά pr. C, suppl. μ< man. rec. 1140 b 1 τῶν om. C. 3 πρακτικόν pr. C. γένος ACD, τέλος B¹ et rec. C. 4 post λείπεται add. τούς pr. C. 5 καί ante ἕξιν pr. C. 7 ούκ ἄν είη CADB¹. 10 οίκουμενικούς pr. C, AD=Bek., οίκο[νομικούς in ras.] B². τούς om. C. 11 ἔνθεν DB¹, ὅθεν B²C, sed in marg. γρ. ἔνθεν C, ἔνθα A. 12 ὡς τὴν σωφρόνησιν σώζουσαν pr. C, man. rec.=Bek., A=Bekker. 13 πᾶσαν CB¹, ἅπασαν A. 15 δύο B²C sed in marg. γρ. δυσίν C. ὀρθαῖς B²] αἴς in ras. C, δυσὶν ὀρθαῖς B¹. 16 al—πρακτῶν in marg. C. Ante τό ras. C. 18 φανεῖται CAB¹B². ἕνεκα C. 19 καί add. man. rec. C. 21 μήν] ἡ in ras. C. 26 τῶν] τόν C. 27 post ἔχειν add. ἐστί D, rec. C. 28-30 ἀλλά—ἐστιν om. C, sed ad oram. 32 post δ' add. al ACB², om. DB¹. ἀποδεικτικῶν pr. CA, ἀποδεικτῶν B¹D, corr. C. 34 εἴη D] τῆς ἀρχῆς pr. C, εἴη corr. C. 1141 a 4 περὶ τὰ ἐνδεχόμενα ἢ καὶ μὴ ἐνδεχόμενα C, DB¹= Bek. 5 ἐπιστήμην·pr. C. καί post ἐπιστήμη om. pr. C. 6 δέ post τούτων om. pr. C. 7 post σοφίαν add. δί pr. C. 9 τε eras. man. rec. C, om. A, ταῖς τέχναις om. pr. C, sed sup. vers. suppl. man. rec. 10 ἀποδιδόαμεν C, ἀποδίδομεν A. 11 πολύκλειτον] λ in ras. C. ἀνδριαντοποιόν] ε post ρ in ras. C. οὖν om. C. 12 σημαίνοντες] ση in ras. C. τήν om. pr. C. ἐστὶ τέχνης C. 14 ante σοφούς add. ἢ C D, om. A. μαρ pr. C; sup. vers. γείτη addidit man. rec. μαργείτη D, μαργίτη A. 16 τι om. pr. C. 17 ἡ post ὅτι om. C, habet D. ἡ ante σοφία om. D. 18 τὸν σοφόν post εἰδέναι C. τὰ ἐκ τῶν ἀρχῶν μή μόνον C, D=Bek. 20 ante ὥσπερ add. καί ACD. ἔχουσαν ἐπιστήμην D. 21 post γάρ add. εἰδέναι D. τὴν πολιτικήν] τὴν ἐπιστήμην πολιτικήν CDB¹, τὴν πολιτικὴν ἐπιστήμην A. 24 τὸ εὐθύ C, εὐθύ AD. τὸ αὐτό C. 24 καὶ τὸ σοφόν—26 ἕκαστα om. C, sed ad oram suppl. man., ut vid., eadem. 26 τὸ εὖ C. ἄν om. DC. 29 δὲ καὶ ὅτι A] δ' εἴη ὅτι C, δὲ ὅτι D corr. C. ἄν εἴη] ἐστί pr. C, ἄν εἴη D corr. C. 1141 b 1 γε A] τε D. συνέστηκεν ὁ κόσμος C, in rasura autem κόσμος. Scripsit, ut mihi videtur, prima manus νόμος. ADB¹= Bek. 2 δέ D. 3 καί ante ἐπιστήμη om. CD. 6 αὑτοῖς C. 10 βουλεύεται om. pr. C. 14 οὐδ'] δ in ras. C. 17 ἑτέραν A et pr. C, ἐνίων suppl. rec., ut videtur, manus. ἐνίων D. 19 ἀγνοεῖ B¹B²CD. 21 δεῖν DC. 24 τὸ αὐτό CD. 25 ἡ δὲ ὡς—27 πρακτική καί om. D. 27 καί ante βουλευτική om. ACB², habet B¹. 30 ἡ φρόνησις C, φρόνησιν D, φρόνησις A. 34 τὸ αὑτῷ A et pr. C, τὰ αὑτῷ man. alt. 1142 a 1 τά om. pr. C, τό D. 2 πράγμονες C, πολυ sup. vers. suppl. man. alt., πολυπράγμονες A. καί ante εὐριπίδης add. man. rec. C, om. A. 4 ἠριθμημένῳ] φ in ras. C, ῳ D. 6 καί τί] καίτοι D. Post πλέον add. οὐκ ᾤετο φρονίμους C, om. AD B¹B². 9 τὸ αὑτοῦ εὖ A] τὸ αὑτοῖς ἀγαθόν C. εὖ om. D. 10 ὅτι τὸ αὑτοῦ pr. C, ὅτι δὲ τὸ αὑτοῦ D et rec. C. 11 εἰρημένου ADB¹, λεγομένου B²C. 14 post ὅτι add. καί CD; post ἕκαστα unius litterae ras. C. σοφρόνησις pr. C. 15 τὰ γνώριμα pr. C. 16 ποιεῖ C, ποιήσει D. 17 διά ad finem versus om. C sed ad oram suppl. man., ut vid., rec.; habet A. δή] δέ ποτε C, om. δή DB¹. μαθηματικήν pr. C. 19 al om. C, habet D. καί in ras C. 21 βουλεύσασθαι D, βουλεύεσθαι C. 23 τοδὶ τό C, om. τό D. 25 αντίκειται] αντική CB¹, αντι[ληπτική μέν corr. man. rec. in ras.] A, αντικοί B¹D. 28 οίᾳ ῇ C, οίᾳ A. 29 στήσωνται C. 30 ἡ] ἡ AC, ἡ D. εκείη C, εκείης AD. 32 λαμβείν (sic) pr. C, διαλαβείν corr. man. rec., διαλαβείν A, λαβείν D. εύβουλίας] εύλαβοίας pr. C. b 1 post τις add. C καί ταχύτης; post τις add. D εστίν. 6 αγχοινία C. 7 κακώς—9 ορθότης om. C, sed ad oram suppl. manus eadem, ut videtur. 9 επιστήμης Β¹. 10 επιστήμη pr. C, επιστήμης D. αμαρτία] αμαρτάνει D. 11 ante αλήθεια add. ή man. rec. C. καί in ras. C. διώρισται DC. 14, 15 εάν τε εὖ κακώς καί κακώς βουλεύηται C. εάν τε εὖ εάν τε καί κακώς A, D=Bek. 17 τί καί] ί καί in ras. C. 18 καί om. pr. C. 19 ιδείν A] καί σκέψασθαι δείν D. 20 μέγα AB¹D, μέσα C. υπειληφώς CDB¹, ειληφώς A. 21 post τι om. είναι C. βεβουλεύσθαι C, βουλεύεσθαι D. βουλής εύ-] om. C; suppl. in marg. man. rec. 25 πως CD. 26 έστι δέ πολύν pr. C; έτι έστι πολύν corr. C et D. 29 βεβουλεύσθαι CD. τι D, om. pr. C. 30 τό ante απλώς om. pr. C, habet D. 31 βουλεύεσθαι CD. 33 τι pr. CD, τό corr. C. 34 καί post δεί om. C, habent DB¹. 1143 a 3 τών επιστημών C, επιστημών A. οίον in ras. C. ή ιατρική CA, ιατρική D; post υγιεινών suppl. in marg. manus, ut videtur, recentior γάρ άν ῇν C, quod in textu habet D, om. A. ῇ in ras. C. 4 μεγέθη CDB¹. 5 post υγειομένων add. C ά ή ιατρική περί υγιεινών ή γεωμετρία. ότωούν (sic) C, sed ω in ras. et ούν addidit man. rec. spatio sex litterarum inter ούν et αλλά relicto. ότωούν D. 8 επιτακτή C, επιτακτική D. δεί γάρ C. 9 post εστίν add. C ή μέν γάρ φρόνη. ξύνεσις CD. 10 ταύτον] ταυτά AC; ante ξύνεσις (sic) habet C καί, om. D. καί post ξύνεσις om. pr. C. εύξυνεσία C. 10, 11 καί συνετοί καί ευσύνετοι] καί γάρ οι συνετοί καί ευσύνετοι ACD. 12 ξύνεσις C. 13 ξυνιέναι. 15 εὖ om. pr. C. 16 ταυτό DC. 17 τής] τών pr. C, corr. man. rec. 19 δέ om. pr. C; post καλουμένη add. C άνω, om. D. 25 πάσαι αί έξεις εύλόγως DC. 30 post είναι add. καί C, om. D. 33 άπαντα C et rec. A, απάντων pr. A et D. γάρ om. C, habet D. 35 τών om. pr. C, habet D. b 1 καί ante ό om. CD. 2 τοίς πρακτικοίς pr. C, ut videtur; τοίς πρακτικαίς corr. C, τοίς πρακτοίς D. 3 ante ετέρας habet C αρετής. 5 δεί έχειν DC. 10 αρχήν pr. C ut videtur, αρχή AD; post εκ add. τε D. αί om. pr. C, habet D. 12 αναποδείκτως pr. C. 14 ορθώς] τάς αρχάς ACDB¹B². 15 ή σοφία καί ή φρόνησις CB¹, D=Bek. 16 τυγχάνει εκατέρα DCB¹. 21 μέν] -ίν in ras. C. 23 ανδρός εστι C, D=Bek. 27 τήν ante ιατρικήν om. pr. C, habent AD. καί] ῇ C, καί AD. 29 γενέσθαι DC. 31 ήμίν] ίν in ras. C. 36 νῦν—1144 a 1 καθ' αύτάς om. D. 36 γάρ om. C. 1144 a 1 αιρετάς] αρετάς D. 2 γ' A] δί C, om. D. του om. AC. 4 ή ιατρική C. 5 άλης] η in ras. C. 7 post κατά add. τε CA. 13 ταύτην] accent. et ην in ras. C. 26 ό om. C, habet D. 28 καί ού πανούργους C, καί πανούργους AD. 29 δεινότης] δύναμις CADB¹B². 32 τοιόνδε] -δε in ras. C.   b 6 inter ὅμως et ζητοῦμεν unius litterae rasura C.   7 post ἀγαθόν add. εἶναι DC.   ἄλλον τρόπον] ἄλλως C, ἄλλον τρόπον D.   10 ἐν σώματι DC.   15 οὕτω καὶ ἐπί] οὕτως ἐπί CD.   17 τινές om. DC.   23 inter δ et ἐστί spatium unius litterae et rasura C.   27 ἀλλ' ἡ μετά DC. ὀρθός] ὅς in rasura litterae, ut videtur, ἡ C.   30 πάντας pr. C.   οὖν] τοίνυν CD. 34 αἱ om. pr. C, habet D.   1145 a 1 post λέγεται add. pr. C τοῦτο γάρ.   2 οὔσῃ] ὑπαρχούσῃ A.   3 ἦν AD, ἢ C.   4 inter ὀρθή et ἄνευ unius litterae rasura C. 6 τά om. pr. C.   7 γ'] τε C.   ὥσπερ om. pr. C.   9 post οὖν add. ἐστί D.   10 τήν om. pr. C.   πολιτικήν] -ήν in ras. C.   ἄρχεων] εἰ in ras. C.   11 περί om. D, habet C. [Except in the variants given in the foregoing list, C agrees with Bekker's text (Parker's reprint, Oxford, 1871).]

BOOK VII.

K^bM^b.

1145 a 33 τῆς διαθέσεως τῆς τοιαύτης A.
  b 6 τε CAld.
    8 δ' ἡ ἐγκράτεια AB² [δὴ ἡ ἐγκ. B¹].
    9 τῶν ACB¹B²Ald.
    10 om.
    17 οἱ Ald. pr. A, D.
    17 ὅτι ACB¹B²Ald.D.
    22 om.
1146 a 8 τῶν γὰρ ἐσχάτων AD.
    11 ἔσται AB¹B²CAld.
    14 μή ACDAld.B¹B².
  b 1 om.
    3 πάντα ACB¹B²Ald.
    4 ἁπάσας ACB¹B²DAld.
    14 δ' B¹CDAld.
    15 ὁ post καί.
    17 ἢ οὐ ἀλλ' ἐξ ἀμφοῖν.

L^bO^b.

τῆς τοιαύτης διαθέσεως CAld.B¹B²D.
om. B¹B²DA (sed post λύπται ras. A).
δὴ ἢ τε ἐγκράτεια DCAld.

om. D.
τε ACB¹B²DAld.
ὅτι C, corr. A, B¹B².
τοτί.
μέν ACAld.
τῶν ἐσχάτων γάρ B¹B²CAld.
ἔστιν D.
om.
μή ACAld.
ἅπαντα D.
πάσας.
δ' ἡ AB².
om. DCAld.
om. [CA have μόνον (ὁ A) ἀκρατὴς ἢ οὐ ἀλλὰ τῷ ἐξ ἀμφοῖν. D has Bekker's reading from μόνον to ἀμφοῖν, adding τῷ before ἐξ. B¹ and Ald. omit ἀλλὰ τῷ ὡς ἢ οὐ, reading ἀλλὰ τῷ ἐξ ἀμφοῖν. Ald.B¹ and C thus agree, except that

NICOMACHEAN ETHICS. 63

			C omits ἀκρατὴς ὁ. Β² has μόνον ὁ ἐγκρατὴς ἢ οὐ ἀλλὰ τῷ ἐξ ἀμφοῖν.]
1146 b	19	om. ACDAld.	ἀλλ' ἐξ ἀμφοῖν post οὔ.
	21	ἂν CB¹B².	om. Ald.AD.
	29	ἔνιοι γάρ ACB²B²DAld.	ἔνιοί τε γάρ.
1147 a	6	ὁ αὐτός.	αὐτὸς οὗτος [οὗτος B¹BᵀDCΓNᵇAld., ὁ οὗτος A].
	7	om.	ἢ post τοιόνδε B¹B²CDAld.
	9	εἰδέναι ACB¹Ald.	εἶναι B² [εἶναι εἰδέναι D].
	14	οἱ ἐν AB².	οἵ γε ἐν B¹CDAld.
	19	om. ACB¹B².	τοῦ ἐνεργεῖν κατὰ τὴν ἐπιστήμην post σημεῖον add. DAld.
	21	πρῶτοι μαθόντες A.	πρῶτον μαθόντες CB¹B²DAld.
	21	συνέργουσι.	συνείρουσι ADB¹B²CAld.
	22	τοῦτο ACDB¹Ald.	τούτῳ B².
	32	om. A.	τό B¹B²CDAld.
	34	μὲν οὖν λέγει AB²DAld.	μὲν λέγει B¹C.
b	4	om. ACB¹B².	τῶν DAld.
	16	αὕτη A.	αὑτή DCAld.B¹.
	18	εἰδότα ἐνδέχεται ACAld.B¹.	ἐνδέχεται εἰδότα.
	29	οὐχί.	οὗ ACB¹B²Ald.
	31	om.	οὖν ACB¹B²Ald.D.
1148 a	13	τόν post καί AB².	om. B¹CDAld.
	25	διειλάμην.	διείλομεν CAld.A.
	28	πῶς.	πῶς καί ACDB¹B²Ald.
	34	om. CDAld.B¹.	καί AB².
b	22	ἀνδρῶν A.	ἀνθρώπων DB² [CB¹ and Ald. have κρέασιν ἀνθρωπείοις].
	23	δανείζειν ἀλλήλοις ACAld.B¹ B².	ἄλλοις δανείζειν [ἀλλήλοις δανείζειν D].
	30	γυμναζομένοις A.	ὑβριζομένοις CAld. ἐθιζομένοις B¹B²D.
	33	om. A.	δί B¹B²CDAld.
1149 a	13	μὲν μόνον.	μόνον ACAld.B¹B²D.
	13	λέγω δί ACAld.B¹B²D.	om.
	25	om. B¹C.	ἢ post ἤ Ald.AB²D.
	29	ἂν ACAld.	ἐάν.
	30	om.	ὁ ACB¹B²Ald.

1150a 2 βέλτιον D. | βέλτιστον ACB¹B²Ald.
3 συμβάλλειν DB². | συμβαλεῖν ACB¹Ald.
15 κἂν ACAld.B¹B²D. | καί.
25 διὰ τὴν ἡδονήν ACAld.B¹B². | δι' ἡδονήν D.
28 τις μή ACAld.B¹B². | μή τις D.
b 17 δί ACB¹B²Ald. | γάρ.
17 εἴπερ οὖν ἀνάπαυσις AB¹B²D CAld. | εἴπερ ἀνάπαυσις.
23 προαισθανόμενοι A. | προαισθόμενοι B¹B²CDAld.
24 ἑαυτούς ACAld. | αὑτούς.
31 καί ACAld.B¹D. | om. B².
1151a 2 ἔχοντες μέν ACB¹B²DAld. | μὲν ἔχοντες.
9 μιλήσιοι ἀξύνετοι ACD. | μιλήσιοι γὰρ ἀξύνετοι B¹B²Ald.
15 om. AB¹CAld. | ἡ ante μοχθηρία B²D.
17 ὁ AB¹B²CDAld. | om.
34 δὲ ὁ τῷ AAld. | δί τῷ CB¹B²D.
b 7 οἷον ACAld.B¹B². | ὥσπερ D.
21 τι ACAld. | om.
31 ἐναντίον εἶναι ACB¹B²DAld. | εἶναι ἐναντίον.
1152a 19 οὐδέ AB²DAld. | οὐ CB¹.
21 ὥσπερ AB¹B²CAld. | καθάπερ D.
23 ἐβούλεθ' CAld. (ἐβούλετο A pr.). | ἐβουλεύετο.
28 βουλευσαμένων ACB¹B²Ald. | βουλευομένων D.
b 21 ὅτι ACB¹B²DAld. | ἔτι.
1153b 1 om. | καί ante ἡ ACAld.
25 ἅπαντα ACB¹Ald. | πάντα D.
30 πάντες ACB¹B²DAld. | ἅπαντες.
1154b 3 αὑτοῖς ACAld. | ἑαυτοῖς.
5 βλαβεράς ACB¹B²DAld. | βλαβεραί.
10 ὥσπερ οἱ οἰνόμενοι διάκεινται ACB¹B²DAld. | διάκεινται ὥσπερ οἱ οἰνόμενοι.
11 δέονται δεῖ A. | δεῖ δέονται B¹B²CDAld.
12 ἰατρείας ACB¹B²Ald. | θεραπείας.
30 ἡ post καί ACAld. | om.
34 ἐροῦμεν ACB¹B²DAld. | ἐστὶν εἰπεῖν καὶ ποῖόν τε καὶ τίς ὁ φίλος.

NICOMACHEAN ETHICS. 65

		K^{b}O^b.	L^{b}M^b.
1145 a	23	θιοί AD.	θείοι CAld.
	26	τιμιώτερον ACAld.	τιμιωτέρα.
	29	σείος C.	θείος ADAld.
b	31	δή.	δί CAld.
1148 a	1	μικρῷ ACAld.	μικρόν.
	29	κρατοῦνται ACAld.	ἀκρατυῦνται.
1149 a	2	καρτερεῖν.	κρατεῖν CAAld.
b	4	ἀκολουθεῖν ACAld.	ἀκολουθεῖ.
	9	τύπτοι CAld.	τύπτει A.
1150 a	28	πράττοι CAld.	πράττει.
	29	τύπτοι [om. CA].	τύπτει Ald.
b	22	προγαργαλίσαντες AAld.B².	προγαργαλισθέντες B¹CD.
1153 a	12	τήν CAld.	om. A.
b	23	αὐτή CAld.	αὕτη A.
1154 a	27	οὖν ACAld.	om. D.
b	17	λέγω δὲ κατὰ συμβεβηκὸς AC Ald.	om.
	19	ἡδὺ δοκεῖ ACAld.	δοκεῖ ἡδύ.

The following tables, summing up the results of the foregoing lists, are here appended :—

I.
$$\left.\begin{array}{ll} A & 58 \\ D & 27 \\ C & 48 \\ Ald. & 46 \\ B^1 & 36 \\ B^2 & 35 \end{array}\right\} K^bM^b\ 80\ L^bO^b \left\{\begin{array}{ll} 18\ A. \\ 35\ D. \\ 28\ C. \\ 31\ Ald. \\ 27\ B^1. \\ 28\ B^2. \end{array}\right.$$

In table I, C and Ald. differ in only seven places (see K^{b}M^b—L^{b}O^b list).

II.
$$\left.\begin{array}{ll} D & 1 \\ C & 12 \\ Ald. & 12 \\ A & 9 \end{array}\right\} K^bO^b\ 17\ L^bM^b \left\{\begin{array}{ll} 3\ D. \\ 4\ C. \\ 5\ Ald. \\ 5\ A. \end{array}\right.$$

In the K^{b}O^b—L^{b}M^b list C and Ald. differ in only two places. They seem to be descended from a not remote common ascendant which belonged to the K^b variety. Many of the L^bO^b readings in this Book were, it seems to me, shared by a near ascendant of K^b, although lost by that MS. itself: and I think it is probable that these readings are marked by the agreement of C and Ald. with L^b and O^b.

While differing from all the other Ald. readings quoted by Susemihl C agrees with the following:—

1145 a 24 θηριωδία.   1146 b 18 ἡ ante ἐγκράτεια om. AD.   19 ἅπαντα D [πάντ' A].   1147 a 22 συμφυῆ εἶναι [συμφῦναι AD].   1148 a 12 ἀκόλαστοι [μαλακοί AD].   b 4 καὶ ἁμαρτήματα om. post φευκταί [om. A].   13 θυμοῦ K^b [θυμόν A].   22 κρίασιν ἀνθρωπείοις.   1149 a 5 κακία ante καὶ ἀφροσύνη add. AB^1B^2D.   28 πράξεως B^1 [προστάξεως AB^2D].   b 25 ἡ ante ἀκρασία om. [habent AD].   33 σινομωρία K^bL^bD [συνομωρία A].   1150 a 3 ἡμάρτηται καί ante οὐκ add. $B^1ΓO^b$ [ἔφθαρται καί add. A., om. B^2].   7 μυριαπλάσια K^bL^b [μυριοπλάσια A].   1151 a 7 τήν om. M^b [habet A].   27 τούτου $ΓM^b$ [τούτων AD].   33 μέν om. $ΓM^bDB^1B^2$ [habet A].   b 7 τῷ om. pr. K^b [τό A].   15 ἄν AM^bD.   1152 a 11 μέν om. $ΓM^b$ [habet A].   34 τί ante καρτερία et τί ante μαλακία om. $ΓM^b$ [habet A, alterum om. D].   5 τήν $ΓO^b$ pr. L^b [τῇ A].   28 post γενέσεις add. ἀκολουθήσουσι AD.   35 ὑπολύσου AM^b [ὑπολοίπου DK^b].   1153 a 1 ἐνδεούσης $DAB^1B^2K^b$.   12 τελείωσιν A.   24 ἡδονῇ post μηδεμίαν DrL^b [A=Bek.].   b 7 δ' ΓAD.   27 λαοί Ar [om. B^2D].   28 πολλοὶ φημίζωσιν B^1Dr [πολλοί AB^2].   33 γε post εἰλήφασι om. AK^bL^b.   1154 b 5 ἑτέραν K^bAld.   ἕτερα rec. C, sed post a unius litt. atque paroxyt. rasura [ἕτερα A].   15 λύπης DrM^bO^b [λυπῶν A].

In addition to the agreements in the foregoing list I have noted the following between D and Ald.:—

1145 b 30 ὅτι μέν [ὅτι AC].   1146 a 35 τὸν φάρυγγα πνίγῃ τί δεῖ ἔτι πίνειν (Ald. has τόν not τήν) [AB^1B^2C = Bek., A reading ἔτι πίνειν].   1150 b 14 ὥσπερ [οἷον AC].   31 πως [πᾶς A, om. C].   1151 a 23 ἀναίδην A [ἀνέδην B^1B^2C].

D agrees with K^b unique in the following places:—

1145 b 24 αὐτήν.   1148 a 6 δέ.   1152 b 35 ὑπολοίπου.

In 1150 a 29 C agrees with K^bA and N^b in omitting τύπτοι ἢ εἰ ὀργιζόμενος; but the homoeoteleuton makes the agreement of little consequence.

While C and Ald. are very closely related, being descended from a MS. not distantly related to K^b, but corrected by means of one resembling O^b, D is also descended, in this Book, from a MS. related to K^b, but very considerably corrected by means of a MS. or MSS. of the L^b variety. This conclusion respecting D I rest principally on the ground that D has considerable affinity to Ald., which distinctly, although not so distinctly as C, belongs to the K^b variety. To the omission in 1150 a 29, common to C with K^bA and N^b, may be added 1151 a 19 ἐθιστή ΓK^bL^bAC, and 1152 a 22 οὐδέν K^bAC [οὐδενί D].

C or D agrees with the following Ald. readings not quoted by Susemihl:—

1145 a 30   post θηριώδης add. φησίν CAld., om. AD.
1146 a 34   παρανομία DCAld. [παροιμία A].
1147 a 32   ἡ κωλύουσα CAld. [κωλύουσα A].
      34   ἰνοῦσα A] οὖσα CAld., ἰροῦσα D.
   b 21   ἐφεξῆς ACAld. cum. cet., ἀπ' ἀρχῆς D.
1149 b 2   γὰρ τοῦ om. CAld., habent AD.
      30   ἀκολασία AD, ἀκρασία C, ἡ ἀκρασία Ald.
1150 a 15   ἕξεις B¹B²CAld. [μεταξὺ δὲ τῶν πλείστων ἕξεις B¹B²].
      15   κἂν εἰ ῥίπωσι AAld., κἂν ῥίπωσι B¹C, B²D=Bek.
      20   post προαίρεσιν add. καί CAld., om. AD.
      22   ἀμεταμέλητος] μὴ μεταμελητικός DAld., ὁ γὰρ ἀμεταμέλητος ἀνίατος om. AC.

A, in this Book belongs distinctly to the K^b family.

BOOK VIII.

K^bM^b. L^bO^b.

1155 a 12   δί ACAld.   δεῖ.
      29   δ' ACAld.   τε.
   b 15   τό ante ἧττον, καί post ἧττον   om. [τό om. B², habet καί].
          ACB¹DAld.
      27   ἐν ACDAld.B¹B².   ἐπί.
      32   ἂν ACAld.B¹B²D.   ἐάν.
1156 a 24   δοκεῖ φιλία C.   φιλία δοκεῖ ΛDAld.B¹B².
      27   οὐδέ ACAld.B¹B²D.   om.
   b 9   ἀγαθοὶ δ' ACAld.   om.
      23   ἡδὺ ἁπλῶς ACAld.B¹B²D.   ἁπλῶς ἡδύ.

K 2

68   ENGLISH MANUSCRIPTS OF THE

1157 a 17	ἀλλήλοις εἶναι CAld.DB¹B².	εἶναι ἀλλήλοις A*¹.
32	ὁμοιόν τι ταύτῃ Ald.B¹.	ὅμοιον ταύτῃ A*CD.
b 5	τῷ CAld. [om. A*].	τό.
1158 a 19	ἀπ'.	ὑπ' A*CDAld.B¹B².
24	αὐτὸ ἀγαθόν C. αὐτὸ τὸ ἀγαθόν ΓK^bM^bB².	αὖ τὸ ἀγαθόν A*Ald.DB¹.
33	om. D.	ὅτι B¹B²CAld.A*.
1159 a 7	οὐ.	οὐδὲ CAld.A*.
1161 a 27	δεῖ Ald.	δὴ A* [δὴ δεῖ C].
28	βούλονται καὶ ἐπιεικεῖς CB¹D Ald.	καὶ ἐπιεικεῖς βούλονται A*.
b 8	δή C.	δεῖ A* [δεῖ τό Ald.].
17	καὶ ἠρτῆσθαι B¹CAld.	ἠρτῆσθαι δεῖ A*.
23	ὀδοὺς (ἢ M^bAld.) θρίξ ACB¹ B²Ald.	θρὶξ ὀδούς.
1162 a 2	συνῳκείωνται ACAld.B¹.	συνοικειοῦνται.
b 16	συνημερεύειν ACB¹B²Ald.	συνδιημερεύειν.
1163 a 28	om. Ald.	ὁ AC.
31	πλεῖον [om. C].	πλείω AAld.B¹.
b 10	τιμὴν ἀπονέμουσιν ACB¹Ald.	ἀπονέμουσι τιμήν.
17	τὴν ἀξίαν ποτ' ἄν ACB¹B²Ald.	ἄν ποτε τὴν ἀξίαν.
20	ὀφείλοντα [τὸν ὀφείλοντα υἱόν Ald.].	ὀφείλοντι AC.
22	ἀφιέναι B¹B² (Α ἐφιέναι).	ἀφεῖναι CAld.

	K^bO^b.	L^bM^b.
1155 b 4	εἰς AAld.	ἐς.
1156 b 5	κατὰ τὴν φιλίαν ACB¹B².	κατὰ φιλίαν DAld.
27	συναναλῶσαι ACB²Ald.D.	συναλῶσαι B¹.
28	δή K^bAld., δὲ O^b, om. C.	δεῖ A.
34	om.	ταὐτά] ταῦτα ACDAld.
1157 a 2	οὗτοι A.	τοιοῦτοι CAld.
4	μένουσιν.	διαμένουσιν ACAld.
1158 a 13	πολλούς CAld.A*.	πολλοῖς.
27	ὑπάρξει αὐτοῖς.	αὐτοῖς ὑπάρξει CDA*Ald.
b 5	om.	καί post δεῖ CAld.A*.

¹ An asterisk is attached to A throughout the lacuna supplied by pages in a later hand. See p. 48.

NICOMACHEAN ETHICS. 69

1158 b 33	γίνηται.	γίγνηται CAld.A*.
1159 a 23	ἐφίενται περὶ αὑτῶν.	περὶ αὐτῶν ἐφίενται A*CB¹B²DAld.
32	μηδὲν ὧν μητρὶ προσήκει ἀπονέμωσι.	μὴ δύνωνται τῇ μητρὶ ἃ προσήκει ἀπονέμειν B¹B²CDAld.A*.
b 1	τούτων.	τῶν τοιούτων A*CB¹B²Ald.D.
7	om. C.	post ἐπιτρέπειν add. ὑπηρετεῖ L^b, ὑπηρετεῖν M^bAld.A*B¹B²D.
20	τοῦ CAld.	om. A*.
21	ὑγρῷ οὐ ξηρῷ.	ξηρῷ οὐχ ὑγρῷ B¹B²CA*Ald. ξηρῷ οὐχ ὑγρόν D.
21	γενέσθαι B¹B²CAld.	γίνεσθαι A*D.
1160 a 24	αὑτοῖς.	ἑαυτοῖς CAld.DA*.
1161 a 18	τε.	τε γάρ A*CD (τε omisso D) Ald.
33	om. Ald.	τῷ post καί CA*.
b 3	οὐδέ.	ἢ CA*Ald.
1162 a 11	ἐν A.	om. CAld.
1163 a 2	om. A.	καὶ ἑκόντι B¹B²CAld.
b 23	δοκεῖ CA.	δοκῇ Ald.

The following tables sum up the results of the foregoing lists :—

$$\left.\begin{array}{rl} 20 & \text{Ald.} \\ 13 & B^1 \\ 20 & C \\ 0 & A^* \\ 8 & D \\ 11 & B^2 \\ 13 & A \end{array}\right\} K^bM^b \; 29 \; L^bO^b \left\{\begin{array}{rl} 7 & \text{Ald.} \\ 5 & B^1. \\ 6 & C. \\ 10 & A^*. \\ 4 & D. \\ 3 & B^2. \\ 4 & A. \end{array}\right.$$

Out of the twenty agreements of Ald. with K^bM^b, seventeen are in company with C ; and out of the seven agreements of Ald. with L^bO^b, four are in company with C.

$$\left.\begin{array}{rl} B^1 & 2 \\ \text{Ald.} & 7 \\ C & 8 \\ B^2 & 3 \\ D & 1 \\ A & 7 \\ A^* & 1 \end{array}\right\} K^bO^b \; 25 \; L^bM^b \left\{\begin{array}{rl} 7 & B^1. \\ 18 & \text{Ald.} \\ 16 & C. \\ 5 & B^2. \\ 11 & D. \\ 3 & A. \\ 13 & A^*. \end{array}\right.$$

Out of the eighteen agreements of Ald. with L^bM^b, fifteen are in company with C; and out of the seven agreements of Ald. with K^bO^b, five are in company with C.

The following list contains the agreements which I have noted in this Book between C and Ald. in other connexions than those recognised in the K^bO^b—L^bM^b and K^bM^b—L^bO^b lists:—

1155 a 31   ἔτι καὶ ἔνιοι [καὶ ἔνιοι ΑΓM^bD].
     35   ὅσα ΓM^b [τά A].
1156 a 7   γάρ ἐστι B^1 [γάρ D omisso ἐστιν, δέ A, δή B^2].
      7   εἴδη τῆς φιλίας DB^1 [τὰ τῆς φιλίας εἴδη A, εἴδη τὰ τῆς φιλίας B^2].
     22   ἄλλο post γίγνεται B^1B^2ΓM^b [A=Bek.].
   b 8   ὁμοίως ἀλλήλοις βούλονται ΓM^bDAB^1B^2.
     19   τοῖς φίλοις post δεῖ ΓM^b [D has τοῖς φίλοις ὑπάρχειν δεῖ, A=Bek.].
1157 a 3   οἱ $H^aM^bN^b$ [om. K^bO^bA].
      4   ἴσον ΓM^bD [αὐτό A].
      9   ἡδεῖα post ἡ ὄψις B^1B^2ΓM^bD [A^*=Bek.].
     33   τι post ἀγαθόν add. ΓM^bD [om. A^*].
   b 17   μέν ΓM^bH^a [om. A^*].
1158 a 14   ἀγαθόν Γ [ἀγαθούς D, ἀγαθοῖς A^*].
   b 3   ἀντικαταλλάττονται $A^*B^1B^2$.
      4   δὲ καὶ L^bA^* [δ' D].
      9   εἶναι καὶ μόνιμον M^bB^1 [A^*B^2D=Bek.].
1159 b 28   οὖν ΓAld. [γοῦν D, γάρ L^bA^*].
1160 b 16   δὲ δή M^bΓ [δέ A^*].
1161 a 22   γὰρ ἂν καὶ ΓM^bD [γὰρ καί A^*].
   b 23, 24   ἐκείνων δ' οὐθενὶ ἀφ' οὗ B^1 [A=Bek., ἐκείνων δ' οὐθενὶ τῷ ἀφ' οὗ B^2].
     32   διά M^bB^1 [ὅθεν A].
1162 a 36   γίνονται φίλοι ΓM^b [φίλοι γίνονται A].
   b 12   ἐφίεται ΓM^b [ὀρέγεται AB^1B^2].
     29   τούτων οὐκ εἰσί Γ$M^bB^1B^2$ [οὐκ εἰσὶ τούτων A].
1163 a 32   πλείω ΓO^b [πλεῖον A].

The foregoing list does not pretend to exhaust the agreements between C and Ald.; but it is large enough, taken in connexion with the K^bM^b—L^bO^b and K^bO^b—L^bM^b lists, to show that in this Book again C and Ald. are closely related. They are related through common descent from a MS. resembling M^b. This common ascendant had a text in which, as in that of M^b, extensive intermixture of K^b and L^b readings had taken place.

D seems to be related to M^b, although more distantly than C and Ald. B¹ and B² are also related to M^b. A belongs to the K^b family, and A* to the L^b family.

BOOK IX.

	K^bM^b.	L^bO^b.
1163 b 32	πάσαις AB².	ἀπάσαις B¹CAld.
1164 a 25	μαθόντα ACB¹B²Ald.	μανθάνοντα.
28	τό ACB¹B²Ald.	om.
34	γίγνεται B².	γίγνηται ACB¹Ald.
b 9	τάττειν AC.	τάσσειν.
1165 a 17	ἁρμόττοντα ACB¹B²Ald.	ἁρμόζοντα.
24	θεοῖς ACB²Ald.	καὶ θεοῖς [B¹ reads here καὶ τιμὴν καὶ καθάπερ θεοῖς οὐ πᾶσαν δὲ γονεῦσιν οὐδὲ γάρ].
30	ἁπάντων ACB¹B²Ald.	πάντων.
31	ἀεὶ πειρατέον ACB¹B²Ald.	πειρατέον ἀεί.
b 21	τούτῳ ἢ B²ΓAld. [τούτῳ ἢ A].	τῷ C, τό B¹.
22	οὖν (γοῦν ACB¹B²Ald.).	δέ.
23	γίνοιτο AB².	γένοιτο CB¹Ald.
35	προγενομένην B². (προγινομένην A, προσγινομένην B¹CAld.).	προγεγενημένην.
1166 a 23	om.	ἢ ACAld.
25	μνεῖαι AB².	μνῆμαι B¹CAld.
35	εἶναι φιλία.	εἶπει ἡ φιλία CAld.B¹B².
b 12	καὶ διά B¹CAld.	διά B².
12	μισοῦνται (καὶ K^bB¹) φεύγουσι ACB¹Ald.	μισοῦσί τε καὶ φεύγουσι, B² omisso τε.
19	οἱ τοιοῦτοι ἑαυτοῖς ACB¹Ald.	ἑαυτοῖς οἱ τοιοῦτοι.
20	τό A.	τοτί B¹CAld.
29	om. B¹C.	καί ante πρός AAld.
32	τοιαῦτ' A.	ταῦτ' B¹CAld.
1167 a 16	ἐλπίδα ἔχων εὐπορίας ACB¹Ald.	εὐπορίας ἐλπίδα ἔχων.

1167 a 18 om. A. | ἡ B¹CAld.
24 ὁτουοῦν ACB¹ (ὁτοοῦν Ald.). | ὁτιοῦν.
29 om. ACB¹Ald. | τά post καί add.
b 18 om. | οἱ ACB¹Ald.
22 οἱ δανείσαντες δὲ καὶ ἐπιμελοῦν- | οἱ δὲ δανείσαντες καὶ ἐπιμέλονται B¹CAld.
ται A.
29 οὐδ' A. | οὐχ B¹CAld.
32 πεπονθότας C (εὖ πεποιθότας | εὐεργετηθέντας.
ΑΓΝʰAld.B¹).
1168 a 1 τοῦτο περὶ τοὺς ποιητάς ACB¹ | περὶ τοὺς ποιητὰς τοῦτο.
Ald.
19 ἔχειν A (ἔχειν post ἔοικεν B¹ | om. C.
Ald. et corr. C).
20 ἤν ACB¹. | om.
21 τό ACB¹. | καὶ δὴ τό.
b 4 μάλιστ' αὐτῷ ACB¹Ald. | αὐτῷ μάλιστα.
7 τὸ μία ψυχὴ καὶ κοινὰ τὰ φίλων | τὸ κοινὰ τὰ φίλων καὶ μία ψυχή.
B¹CAld., A with τῶν after
τά.
9 μάλιστ' ἂν ὑπάρχοι A. | μάλισθ' ὑπάρχει B¹CΓAld.
11 χρεὼν ἕπεσθαι ACB¹Ald. | χρεὼν δὴ ἕπεσθαι.
15 om. A. | οὖν B¹CAld.
27 ἑαυτῷ ACAld. | αὐτῷ.
1169 a 6 ᾗ τοῦ καλοῦ ᾗ ACAld. | τοῦ καλοῦ ᾗ.
11 ἐστίν ACB¹Ald. | om.
15 om. | πράττειν ACAld.
16 ταῦτα ἃ δεῖ A. | ἃ δεῖ ταῦτα B¹CAld.
25 δ' AC. | δή.
29 περὶ τιμάς A. | περὶ τὰς τιμάς B¹CAld.
b 6 οὐδενός ACB¹Ald. | μηδενός.
10 εἴ τε ACAld. | εἰ δέ.
13 ἐπιζητεῖται ACB¹Ald. | ζητεῖται.
17 αὐτὸν τὰ πάντ' ἔχειν ἀγαθά A | αὐτὸν πάντ' ἔχειν τἀγαθά.
CB¹Ald.
21 om. | τῶν ACAld.
22 εὐδαίμονι καὶ τῶν φίλων A. | εὐδαίμονι φίλων B¹CAld.
31 τοῦ δ' ἀγαθοῦ A. | τοῦ ἀγαθοῦ δ' B¹CAld.
1170 a 6 ῥᾷον ACAld. | ῥαίδιον B¹.

1170 a 19	εἶναι κυρίως ACB¹Ald.	κυρίως εἶναι.
25	αὐτῆς.	λύπης ACAld.
29	αἰσθάνεται post ὁρᾷ B¹CA, (with καί after ὁρᾷ A.)	post ἀκούει.
b 2	ζωή A.	ἡ ζωή CAld.
8	om.	ἡ ACAld.
10	ἑαυτήν AC.	αὐτήν Ald.
11	γίνοιτ' ACAld.	γένοιτ'.
16	κἂν ὁ.	καὶ ὁ ACΓAld.
16	om. ACB¹.	ἂν Ald.
22	om. ACB¹.	ante καί add. καλεοίμην Ald.
1171 a 6	ὑπάρχειν AAld.	ὑπάρχει B¹C.
10	οὐ.	οὐδέ ACB¹.
10	ἐνδέχεσθαι δόξειεν ἂν ACB¹ Ald.	δόξειεν ἂν ἐνδέχεσθαι.

	KᵇOᵇ.	LᵇMᵇ.
1163 b 32	ἀνομοιοειδέσι B².	ἀνομοειδέσι ACB¹Ald.
1164 a 27	om. CAld.	post ἀνδρί add. ἄρκιος ἔστω A in ras.
b 10	γὰρ ἂν ACB¹B²Ald.	γάρ.
1166 a 5	τῶν φίλων A.	τὸν φίλον CAld.
1167 a 7	ἐπιθυμεῖ A.	ἐπιθυμῇ C.
b 33	γένοιτ' C.	γένοιτ' AAld.
1169 a 29	δή A.	δέ CAld.
1170 a 16	δυνάμει ACAld.	δύναμιν Nᵇ.

The following are the numerical results for Book ix:—

$$\left.\begin{array}{rl} A & 55 \\ B^1 & 30 \\ B^2 & 13 \\ C & 37 \\ Ald. & 31 \end{array}\right\} K^bM^b\ 67\ L^bO^b \left\{\begin{array}{ll} 10 & A. \\ 21 & B^1. \\ 3 & B^2 \text{ up to } 1166\ b\ 12. \\ 28 & C. \\ 29 & Ald. \end{array}\right.$$

Thirty of the thirty-one Ald.KᵇMᵇ readings are shared by C; and twenty-four of the twenty-nine Ald.LᵇOᵇ readings.

$$\left.\begin{array}{rl} 5 & A \\ 4 & C \\ 3 & Ald. \end{array}\right\} K^1O^b\ 8\ L^bM^b \left\{\begin{array}{ll} 3 & A. \\ 4 & C. \\ 4 & Ald. \end{array}\right.$$

L   [I. I.]

All the three Ald.K^{b}O^b readings are shared by C; and three of the four Ald.L^{b}M^b readings.

It would be difficult, on the evidence afforded by the foregoing lists, to determine whether B^{1}C and Ald. belong to the K^b or L^b variety; but the following list of the agreements between C and L^b, where the latter MS. differs from K^b, M^b, and O^b, enables us to decide in favour of the view that C and Ald. (together with B^1) belong to the K^b family, because more than half of the L^{b}B^{1}CAld. peculiarities are shared by A, and A is distinctly of the K^b family. The large admixture of L^b readings therefore in B^{1}C and Ald. may be explained by the correction of a common ascendant belonging to the K^b variety by means of a MS. of the L^b variety. B^2 in this Book seems to belong to the K^b family more distinctly than B^{1}C or Ald. The whole of this Book up to 1171 b 35 is omitted by D.

1165 b 5   ἤ] ἢ διά L^{b}CAld.Γ [ἤ A].
   26   διαμένοι] διαμένει L^{b}CA.
   36   ὅταν] ὅτε L^{b}C [ὅταν A].
1166 a 6   οἱ προσκεκρουκότες] οἱ μὴ π. L^{b}B^1 et C marg. [A οἱ προσ.].
  b 20   ἀπεχόμενον] ἀπεχόμενος L^{b}B^{1}C [ἀπεχόμενον A].
1167 a 10   ἂν οὐθέν] οὐθέν ἂν L^{b}CAld.Γ [ἂν οὐθέν A].
1168 a 28   καί] om. L^{b}CAld. ΓA.
  b 2   ᾧ] ᾧ μάλιστα L^{b}B^{1}CAld. [ἢ ᾧ A].
   11   ἐχόντων] ἐχόντων L^{b}C (ἐχόντων manus, ut videtur, eadem C), ἐχόντοιν Ald.
   29   γοῦν] γάρ L^{b}B^{1}CAld.A.
1169 a 18   δὲ περί] δὲ τὸ περί L^{b}CΓAld.AB^1.
   28   δή] δέ L^{b}CAld.ΓA.
  b 1   φίλαυτον εἶναι δεῖ A] δεῖ φίλαυτον εἶναι L^{b}CB^{1}Ald.
1170 a 11   γίνοιτο] γίνοιτο L^{b}CAld.A.
1171 b 10   συστένουσι] συστενάζουσι L^{b}CAAld.B^1.
1172 a 4   δέ] δὲ καί L^{b}CDAld.

BOOK X.

K^{b}M^b.	L^{b}O^b.
1172 a 19 ἴσως ACDB^{1}B^{2}Ald.	om.
22 ἀρχήν N^b, ἀρ(ετήν in ras. man. rec.) A.	ἀρετήν CDAld.B^{1}B^2.

1172 a	26	τῶν τοιούτων CAld.ADB¹B².	τούτων.
b	12	ὃν A.	om. CDAld.B¹B².
1173 a	1	ἅ.	ὃ ACDAld.
	1	ταῦτ'.	τοῦτ' ACD, τοῦτο Ald.
	10	om. Γ.	μέν ACDAld.
b	11	ἡ ἀναπλήρωσις ἡδονή A (ἡ ἀναπλήρωσις ἡ ἡδονή D).	ἀναπλήρωσις ἡ ἡδονή B¹B²CAld.
	23	ἐστίν.	ταῦτ' ἐστίν ACDAld.ΓB¹B².
	23	πλήν.	ἁπλῶς πλήν ACDB¹B²NᵇAld.Γ.
	34	τῷ.	τό ACAld.D.
1174 a	1	τ' CDAld.	δ' A.
	20	om. D.	ἡ ACAld.
	31	om.	καί ACDAld.
b	16	αἴσθησιν.	αἴσθησιν κειμένων ACB¹B²Ald.D.
	17	μή A.	μηθέν B¹CAld.D [μηδέ B²].
1175 a	25	om.	τάς ACAld.D.
b	4	κατακούωσιν.	κατακούσωσιν ACDB¹B²Ald.
	11	ἀρεσκόμενοι καί.	ἀρεσκόμενοι οἷον καί ACDB¹B²Ald.
1177 b	23	τὰ κατά.	κατά ACDAld.
	31	οὐ χρὴ δέ A.	χρὴ δὲ οὐ B¹B²CDAld.
1178 a	2	om.	δ' ACAld.D.
	9	κατὰ ταύτην AB¹.	κατ' αὐτήν CAld.D [κατὰ τήν B²].
	21	κατὰ ταύτας A.	κατ' αὐτάς CAld.DB¹B².
	24	ἡ ἐπί ACB¹B²Ald. [ἡ D sine ἐπί].	ἐπί.
	34	τε [δὲ τί B¹B²].	δέ AAld.CD.
1178 b	20	ἀφαιρουμένου (ἀφαιρουμένῳ A).	ἀφῃρημένῳ B¹B²CAld.D.
	21	θεωρία A.	θεωρίας B¹B²CAld.D.
1179 a	4	ἄρχοντα A.	ἄρχοντας B¹B²CAld.
	21	φέροντας.	ἐπιφέροντας ACB¹B²Ald.D.
	33	περί ΓA.	περί τε B¹B²CAld.D.
b	15	ἔννοιαν A.	ἐννοίας B¹B²CAld.D.
	22	τινας (A has a lacuna here; with τινός marg. rec.).	τινος B¹B²CAld.D.
	27	αὖ CAld.	ἂν ADB¹B².
1180 a	8	ἐπιεικῶς D.	ἐπιεικῶν ACB¹B²Ald.
	10	om. [C has a lacuna here].	καί AAld.D.
	29	τό ACAld.D.	om.

76   ENGLISH MANUSCRIPTS OF THE

1180 a 32	μᾶλλον A.	μάλιστα B¹B²CDAld.
b 5	ἴθη CAld.	ἤθη AD.
1181 a 11	συνηθείας πολιτικοί A.	συνηθείας μᾶλλον πολιτικοί CDAld. rec. A.
18	τοῦ.	τό ACDAld.
22	om. AD.	τό ante μή CAld.
b 15	ἀνθρώπεια.	ἀνθρώπινα ACAld.D.

	K^bO^b.	L^bM^b.
1173 a 10	ὄντων κακῶν ADB².	ὄντοιν κακοῖν [ὄντοιν κακῶν B¹CAld.].
1174 a 21	om. AB².	δή B¹CDAld.
21	ἤ ACDB¹B².	om. Ald.
29	ἅπαντι AD.	παντί B¹B²CAld.
b 29	ἤ A.	εἴη B¹B²CDAld.
32	ἤ ACD.	om. Ald.
1175 a 7	ταὐτό A.	ταῦτα CAld.D.
b 17	φθείρουσι—λῦσαι B¹CAld.	om. ADB².
29	αἰσχρῶν δί A.	δ' αἰσχρῶν D¹B²CAld.D.
1176 b 17	ἀπασχολάζειν Ald.AB¹B².	ἀπασχολάζειν H²CD.
27	ἤ B².	om. ACDAld.B¹.
1177 b 3	παρά CAld.A.	περί D.
9	παρασκευάζει.	παρασκευάζειν ACAld.D.
1179 a 16	μόνον ACAld.D.	μόνων.
26	om.	τῷ post καί ACDAld.
29	πάντα ταῦτα [πάντα om. D].	ταῦτα πάντα AC.
33	om. AD.	καί post δί CAld.

The following tables sum up the numerical results of the foregoing lists:—

$$\left.\begin{array}{ll} A & 18 \\ C & 6 \\ B^1 & 4 \\ D & 7 \\ Ald. & 7 \\ B^2 & 3 \end{array}\right\} K^bM^b \ 43 \ L^bO^b \left\{\begin{array}{ll} 23 & A. \\ 35 & C. \\ 20 & B^1. \\ 33 & D. \\ 36 & Ald. \\ 22 & B^2. \end{array}\right.$$

CDAld.=K^bM^b five times: CDAld.=L^bO^b thirty times.

NICOMACHEAN ETHICS. 77

$$\left.\begin{array}{l}B^1 \quad 3 \\ B^2 \quad 5 \\ C \quad 5 \\ D \quad 6 \\ \text{Ald.} \quad 4 \\ A \quad 12 \end{array}\right\} K^bO^b \ 17 \ L^bM^b \left\{\begin{array}{l} B^1 \quad 6. \\ B^2 \quad 4. \\ C \quad 11. \\ D \quad 11. \\ \text{Ald.} \ 11. \\ A \quad 5. \end{array}\right.$$

CDAld. = L^{b}M^b seven times.

CD and Ald. are thus very closely related to one another, being descended from a common ascendant nearly related to L^b. That their relationship to this ascendant is not through the intermediation of a MS. of the O^b branch of the L^b family is, I think, shown by the following list, which contains the agreements of CD and Ald. with L^b where that MS. differs from K^b, M^b, and O^b. [Where A, C, or D is not specified in the following list, its reading is that of Bekker: no inferences must be drawn from silence regarding B^{1}B^2]:—

1172 b 1 ὀφθεὶς ποτ'] αὐτῆς τ' L^b, B^{1}B^2=Bekker.
  8 τῆς om. L^b.
  12 φέρεσθαι ὡς πᾶσιν ἄριστον μηνύειν L^b; sic etiam B^{1}B^{2}CDAld., nisi quod μηνύει habeant; φέρεσθαι μηνύει ὡς πᾶσι τοῦτο ἄριστον ὃν A.
  30 μετὰ φρονήσεως τὸν ἡδὺν βίον L^{b}B^{1}B^{2}CD [A=Bek.].
1173 a 2 αὐτῶν] αὐτῆς L^{b}A, B^{1}B^2=Bekker.
  2 ὀρέγετο L^{b}D, ὀρέγεται ACB^{1}B^2 cum cet.
  8 καὶ post γάρ add. L^{b}B^{1}CD, om. AAld. cum cet.
  17 τό post καί om. L^{b}CA.
  21 καὶ σωφρονεῖν] om. L^b.
  23 τί γὰρ κωλύει] τί κωλύει δή L^{b}ACAld.DB^{1}B^2.
  28 τοιοῦτον] τοιοῦτο L^{b}CAld.
  28 τό] om. L^{b}CDAld.
  34 ἡσθῆναι] κινηθῆναι L^b et rec. B^1; B^1 pr. et B^2=Bekker.
 b 4 οὐκ ἔστι ταχέως] ταχέως οὐκ ἔστι L^{b}CDB^{1}B^{2}Ald.
  7 τοῦ κατὰ φύσιν εἶναι] εἶναι τοῦ κατὰ φύσιν L^{b}CDB^{1}B^{2}Ald.
  10 ᾧ B^1] ᾧ ἡ L^{b}AB^2.
  11 οὐδ'] οὐκ L^{b}AAld.D.
  20 ἔνδειαι γεγένηνται CDAld.L^{b}B^2, ἔνδειαι γεγένηται B^1.
  20 οὐ γένοιτ' ἂν ἀναπληρώσεις L^{b}Ald.; pro γένοιτ' habet D λέγοιντ'.
  21 λέγοι τις ἄν] λέγοιτ' ἄν τις L^b.

1173 b 24   πικρὰ ἢ γλυκεῖα L^b.
       25   οὕτω] οὕτω δή L^bCAld.D.
1174 a 28   λαβεῖν κίνησιν τελείαν] κίνησιν τελείαν λαβεῖν L^b.
       33   ἐν secundum om. L^bCDAld. (ἐν τῷ σταδίῳ καὶ τῷ μέρει καὶ ἐν ἑτέρῳ καὶ ἑτέρῳ μέρει L^bDAld.C; ἐν autem ante alterum ἑτέρῳ addit C cum Kb; B² habet ἐν τῷ σταδίῳ καὶ ἐν τῷ μέρει καὶ ἐν ἑτέρῳ καὶ ἑτέρῳ μέρει οὐδέ: A habet ἐν τῷ σταδίῳ καὶ ἐν τῷ μέρει καὶ ἐν ἑτέρῳ οὐδέ κ.τ.λ.; B¹ habet ἐν τῷ σταδίῳ καὶ τῷ μέρει καὶ ἐν ἑτέρῳ μέρει οὐδέ).
     b 26   ὁμοίως om. L^bD; add. CAB¹B² et rec. L^b.
       26   αἰτιά εἰσιν L^b.
       28   δέ] γὰρ δή L^bCDAld.
       31   γε τοῦ] γε τοῦ γε L^b.
       33   ἕως οὖν ἂν ᾖ τὸ αἰσθητὸν ἢ νοητὸν ἢ οἷον δεῖ καὶ τό L^b; ἕως δ' οὗ ἄν ποτε τὸ αἰσθητὸν ἢ νοητόν κ.τ.λ. B¹B²CDAld.; ἕως ἂν τό τε νοητὸν ἢ αἰσθητὸν κ.τ.λ. A.
1175 a 8   περὶ αὐτά] περὶ τὰ αὐτά L^b (ἐνεργεῖ περὶ αὐτοῦ D).
        9   post οὐ add. γίνεται L^bCAld.DA.
       34   οἱ om. L^bCD.
     b 2   τοῦτ'] ταῦτ' L^b.
        8   κἄν] καὶ ἐάν L^bCDAld.AB¹B².
       19   γάρ om. L^bCDAld.
       20   συμβαίνει δὴ περὶ τὰς ἐνεργείας om. L^b.
       22   εἴρηται L^b solus, εἴρηνται ACD cet.
1176 a 1   καὶ ἡ ἀκοὴ καὶ ἡ ὄσφρησις L^b.
        4   καί ante ἡδονή om. L^b.
       11   ἐστί post λυπηρά L^bA (λυπηρὰ ἔστι καὶ μισητά librarius, ut vid., ipse in rasura scripsit A).
       30   τε om. L^b.
     b 8   καλὰ καί om. L^b, καὶ καλά post σπουδαῖα D.
       23   φαίνεται] φαίνονται L^b.
       33   σπουδάζῃ] σπουδάζειν L^b.
1177 a 4   τῶν add. L^bP^b, om. ACDAld.B¹B².
        5   σπουδαιοτέραν] σπουδαιοτάτην L^b, σπουδαιοτέρου D.
       26   δέ] τε L^b.
       27   διαγωγήν] ἀγωγήν L^bCAld.
       30   τοῖς δὲ τοιούτοις] τῶν δὲ τοιούτων L^b.
       33   αὑτόν] ἑαυτόν L^b.
     b 7   ἐν om. L^bCD.

NICOMACHEAN ETHICS. 79

1177 b 7 αἱ ἐνέργειαι L^bCDAld.
15 καί om. L^bD.
18 αἱρεταί εἰσιν] εἰσὶν αἱρεταί L^bCD.
26 ἂν εἴη βίος κρείττων] εἴη ἂν κρείττων βίος L^b, ἂν εἴη κρείττων βίος B¹B²C DAld.
33 ἀποθανατίζειν L^bB², ἀπαθανατίζειν ACB¹N^bAld., ἀπαναθανατίζειν D.
33 πάντα] ἅπαντα L^bCD.
1178 a 2 πάντων om. L^bC, post ὑπερέχει A.
2 ἕκαστος εἶναι L^bAld.A, ἕκαστος om. C, ἕκαστος τοῦτο εἶναι D.
6 ἐστίν] ἔσθ' L^bCAld., ἔσται D.
7 μάλιστα τοῦτο L^bCAld.D.
10 καὶ ἄλλα τά] καὶ τὰ ἄλλα τά L^bACDAld.
13 διατηροῦντες post ἑκάστῳ L^bCD [Ald. διαιροῦντες].
34 ἀμφισβητεῖται] ζητεῖται L^bCB¹B²Ald.D.
b 3 τῷ δὲ θεωροῦντι] τῶν δὲ θεωρούντων L^b.
5 συζῇ] συζῆν L^bD.
12 post ὅσα add. ἄλλα L^bCDAld.
12 ἀνδρείους] ἀνδρείας L^b.
15 αἱ L^bA, εἱ CD cum cet.
28 οὐδαμῇ] οὐδαμῶς L^b, οὐδαμοῦ O^bCDB¹B²Ald.
1179 a 3 ἡ πρᾶξις K^bAld.] ἡ κρίσις οὐδ' ἡ πρᾶξις L^bACDB¹B², ἡ κρίσις οὐδ' αἱ πράξεις M^bO^b.
b 7 προτρέψαι L^bN^bB¹CDAld., ἀποτρέψαι B².
24 δίῃ ACD, δίει L^b, δεῖ ΓM^b.
25 ἔθεσι] ἤθεσι L^bAld.
27 συνείη] συνίη L^bACDAld.B¹B¹.
1180 a 2 ἐπειδή] ἐπεί L^bC, B¹B²=Bek.
3 ἂν om. L^bB²D, habet B¹.
16 ἐν om. L^b.
19 οὐδέ B¹B¹CDAld.Γ, οὔτε δή L^b, οὐδὲ δή A cet.
b 3 ἐπιτηδευμάτων] παιδευμάτων L^bB¹B²CD, ἐπιτηδευμάτων AAld.
9 ἡσυχία καὶ ἀσιτία] ἀσιτία καὶ ἡσυχία L^bCDAld.
11 δή] δέ L^bCDAld.
30 παρά] περί L^b.
1181 a 10 πολιτικῆς om. L^bCD, del. K^b, habent Ald.A.
20 ἐπιτελεῖται] τελεῖται L^b.
b 12 παραλιπόντων] παραλειπόντων L^b.
19 ἑκάστας] ἑκάσταις L^b.

In the foregoing list, which contains all, or nearly all, the recorded readings of L^b where that MS. differs from K^b, M^b, and O^b, eighty-seven in number, the agreements of C are thirty-seven in number, of D thirty-eight, of A thirteen, and of Ald. twenty-eight. In thirty-one readings C and D agree with L^b in company; and of the twenty-eight agreements of Ald. with L^b, twenty-four are in company with C or D, or both. CD and Ald. are thus much more closely related to L^b than O^b is in this book. We may assume, I think, that some of the numerous readings in which CD and Ald. agree against L^b and other MSS, or L^b alone, are readings which existed in an ascendant of L^b. Some of these readings in which C and D or C or D=Ald. have been given in the foregoing lists; others are given in the following list, which contains some Ald. readings not recorded by Susemihl:—

CD and C or D=Ald. versus $K^bL^bM^bO^b$.

1172 b 2 ὡς οὐ τοιαύτην DAld. [om. οὐ CA].
10 [ἄλογα CD, ἄλογα AAld.]
28 μόνον μόνον Ald. pr. C [DA=Bek.].
1173 a 11 ἢ ἕτερον ACB¹B²Ald. [μηδέτερον D].
20 καὶ κατά ADAld., καί, omisso κατά, C.
26 αἰεί CDAld., δεί A.
1174 a 3 ὡς οἷονται ACDAld.
b 21 ἡ ἡδονή DAld., ἡδονή CA.
1175 a 26 τῷ ante alterum εἴδει add. DAld., om. AC.
30 συνάξει CAld., συναύξει D, lacunam hic habet A.
b 8 κἄν] καὶ ἐάν ACDAld.B¹B².
1176 a 18 ὁ add. CDAld., om. H⁰L⁵M⁵O⁵A, hic est lacuna apud K^b.
b 31 ἕνεκα] χάριν B¹CAld., ἕνεκα ADB².
1177 a 2 μετὰ σπουδῆς B¹B²AD] σπουδαῖος CAld.
25 φιλοσοφία D cum cet.] σοφία AP⁵CAld.B¹B².
33 σοφώτερος] σοφός CAld., σοφώτερος ADB¹B².
1178 a 1 ἀλλά ante δυνάμει add. B¹CAld., om. ADB².
b 19 δή] δεῖ CDAld., δή A.
31 αὕτη CAld., αὕτη AD cum cet.
1181 a 20 συνιᾶσιν] ἃ δεῖ συνίσασι Ald.; συνιᾶσιν ἃ δεῖ, omissis καὶ ποῖα ποίοις συνᾴδει, B¹C; συνίασιν ἃ δεῖ καὶ ποῖα ποίοις συνᾴδει D, B²A=Bek.

The following list contains K^b readings (not quoted in other lists)

NICOMACHEAN ETHICS. 81

which agree with CD and Ald.—all three or two of them, or one of them.

1173 a 9 οὐ] δ' οὐ K^{b}CDAld.Γ.
       33 τῇ τοῦ K^{b}CAld., τὰ τοῦ D.
1176 a 7 ὅνον B^2] ὅνους K^{b}B^{1}CDAld.A.
1179 b 9 κατοκώχιμον K^{b}Ald., κατακώχιμον AC.
       22 ὡς om. K^{b}CAld., add. D cum cet.

B^1 and B^2 in this Book belong to the CDAld. group, i.e. are closely related to L^b. A, although still of the K^b family, contains a large number of readings which occur in L^b. Some of them probably existed in an ascendant of K^b, although lost by K^b itself.

The Table on pages 82 and 83 sums up the numerical results obtained in this work, so far as K^{b}O^b—L^{b}M^b and K^{b}M^b—L^{b}O^b are concerned. In Book i, e.g. K^b and M^b agree against L^b and O^b in thirty-eight places, in twenty-six of which A sides with K^b and M^b, and in ten with L^b and O^b; and so on with the other MSS, B^{1}B^2, etc., along the line:—

ENGLISH MANUSCRIPTS OF THE

			A.	B¹.	B².	C.	D.	Ald.
Book I.	38	KbMb	26	8	8	8	10	6
		LbOb	10	29	29	29	27	29
	7	KbOb	4	1	1	3	3	3
		LbMb	2	0	0	4	3	3
Book II.	29	KbMb	24	15	15	17	19	17
		LbOb	4	11	10	12	8	10
	6	KbOb	4	1	1	6	1	3
		LbMb	2	0	0	0	1	1
Book III.	12	KbMb	5	2	0	1	4	3
		LbOb	7	3	1	5	5	5
	71	KbOb	52	20	21	12	28	27
		LbMb	18	40	32	21	31	35
Book IV.	5	KbMb	4	0	0	5	1	2
		LbOb	1	2	0	0	4	3
	78	KbOb	56	14	16	69	14	19
		LbMb	13	37	29	7	46	43
Book V.	8	KbMb	A	0	0	4	4	3
		LbOb		1	1	4	3	2
	18	KbOb	A	2	3	15	6	7
		LbMb		7	0	3	9	9
	19	Ob (from 1136 b 1)............... 11						
	31	KbLb 26						

NICOMACHEAN ETHICS.

			A.	B¹.	B².	C.	D.	Ald.
Book VI.	58	K^{b}M^b / L^{b}O^b	29 / 23	17 / 37	19 / 34	14 / 38	14 / 41	21 / 37
	10	K^{b}O^b / L^{b}M^b	9 / 0	1 / 1	1 / 0	7 / 3	2 / 1	6 / 2
	32	O^b				... 11		
Book VII.	80	K^{b}M^b / L^{b}O^b	58 / 18	36 / 27	35 / 28	48 / 28	27 / 35	46 / 31
	17	K^{b}O^b / L^{b}M^b	10 / 5			12 / 4	1 / 3	12 / 5
Book VIII.	29	K^{b}M^b / L^{b}O^b	13 / 4	13 / 5	11 / 3	20 / 6	8 / 4	20 / 7	A*(1157a8–1161b19). 0 / 10
	25	K^{b}O^b / L^{b}M^b	7 / 3	2 / 7	3 / 5	8 / 16	1 / 11	7 / 18	1 / 13
Book IX.	67	K^{b}M^b / L^{b}O^b	55 / 10	30 / 21	13 / 3	37 / 28		31 / 29
	8	K^{b}O^b / L^{b}M^b	5 / 3			4 / 4		3 / 4
Book X.	43	K^{b}M^b / L^{b}O^b	18 / 23	4 / 20	3 / 22	6 / 35	7 / 33	7 / 36
	17	K^{b}O^b / L^{b}M^b	12 / 5	3 / 6	5 / 4	5 / 11	6 / 11	4 / 11
	12	K^{b}L^b				... 11	12	

[The C figures in Book iii. refer to the first part of the Book only, up to 1115 b 1, after which to the end of the Book C never occurs on the L^{b}M^b side, and only once on the L^{b}O^b side.]

The following Table gives the number (approximately) of the readings of K^b where that MS. is unique among Bekker's MSS. in certain books of the Ethics,—the right hand column gives the number of times in the various books that C agrees with K^b unique:—

	K^b unique.	C.
Book I.	87	2.
Book II.	95	2.
Book III to 1115 b 1.	76	4.
Book III from 1115 b 1.	50	43.
Book IV.	80	73.
Book V to 1136 b 1.	92	71.
Book V from 1136 b 1.	42	0.
Book VI.	61	2.
Book VII.	94	6.

NICOMACHEAN ETHICS.

The following Table gives the number of the unique readings of L^b in Book x, with the agreements of ACDAld.:—

	L^b unique.	A.	C.	D.	Ald.
Book X.	87	13	37	38	28.

The following Table indicates the family—K or L—to which the five English MSS. and the Aldine edition seem to belong in the various books. Books iii. and v. have been divided into iii¹, iii², and v¹, v², on account of the peculiar character of C between 1115 b 1 and 1136 b 1. An *italic* K or L indicates the fact that the relationship is not very marked; (M) or (O), that the relationship is not independent of that of one or other of these two later MSS. or of its near ascendant; and a point of interrogation, that I am unable, on account of deficiency of data, or for other reasons, to determine the relationship at all:—

Affinities of M^b and O^b.	Book I K^bM^b—L^bO^b.	II K^bM^b—L^bO^b.	III¹ K^bO^b—L^bM^b.	III² K^bO^b—L^bM^b.	IV K^bO^b—L^bM^b.	V¹ K^bO^b—L^bM^b.	V² K^bO^b—L^bM^b.	VI K^bO^b—L^bM^b.	VII K^bM^b—L^bO^b.	VIII ?	IX K^bM^b—L^bO^b.	X K^bM^b—L^bO^b.
A.	K	K	K	K	K	K	K	*K*	K	K	K	*K*
B¹.	L	*K*	L	L	L	L	L	L	*K*	(M)	*K*	L
B².	L	*K*	L	L	L	?	?	L	*K*	(M)	K	L
C.	L	*K*	*L*	K	K	K	(O)	(O)	K	(M)	*K*	L
D.	L	*K*	*L*	*L*	L	?	?	L	*K*	(M)	lacuna	L
Ald.	L	*K*	*L*	*L*	L	?	?	(O)	K	(M)	*K*	L

APPENDIX.

I HAVE reserved for an Appendix my remarks upon a sixth English MS. which, on account of its lateness, could not properly be placed on an equal footing with the other five for the purposes of description and comparison. The MS. in question is Brit. Mus. Royal MS. 16. C. xxi (I call it B^2), written on paper in the sixteenth century. It contains ff. 131, and has twenty-three lines to the page, and between forty and fifty letters to the line. There are numerous Latin notes on the margin.

Although late, it was possible that this MS. might be found to have been transcribed from a MS. of mark; but this possibility was not realised. My examination, which covered nearly all the K^bM^b—L^bO^b and K^bO^b—L^bM^b readings in the Ethics, and many others of importance, shows that its text is essentially that of B^1 and the Aldine Edition. In the following list (covering the whole Ethics) the readings not within square brackets [ ] are those of B^2. To these readings of B^2 I have appended the symbols of other English MSS. where their readings had not been recorded in the body of this work; in cases of their agreement with B^2 their symbols have been simply appended to the readings of that MS; where they differ, their readings have always been enclosed within square brackets. Thus, ' 1095 b 6 ἀρχή B^2D [ἀρκεῖ B^1] ' means that B^2 has ἀρχή, and that B^2 and D agree with it; while B^1 reads ἀρκεῖ.

B^2.

1094 a 8 καί. 10 ἀρετήν. 13 τόν. δί. b 8 γε. 23 ἕκαστον. 1095 a 3 πράξεων. 13 πεφροιμιάσθω. 27 τοίσδε πᾶσιν αἴτιόν ἐστι τοῦ εἶναι ἀγαθά. 32 πλάτων. 1095 b 6 ἀρχή B^2D [ἀρκεῖ B^1]. 10 add. φρασσόμενος κ.τ.λ. 23 τοῦτο τό. 27 ἀγαθοὺς εἶναι. 1096 a 9 καίτοι. 23 τούτων. b 1 ἀνθρώπῳ. 8 ἔστω. 10 εἰρῆσθαι. 26 γε. 32 καὶ ἔστω] ἔστιν. τό. 33 τι αὐτό. 1097 a 4 ἔχει τινά. 7 ἅπαντας τοὺς τεχνίτας. 26 ἕτερα. b 10 γυναικί. 11 πολιτικόν B^1B^2D. 1198 a 11 τό ante κιθαρίζειν om. 22 ἀναγράφειν. 1099 a 10 φιλοθεώρῳ. 13 τοιαῦται δὴ αἱ. 28 ἥδιστον δὴ τυχεῖν οὗ τις ἕκαστος ἐρᾷ. 30 τὴν ἀρίστην. b 9 ἢ ἄλλως. 20 ἢ διά. 1100 a 8 ἡρωικοῖς. 17 τῶν post καί om. 32 τό post δή om. b 35 καὶ φαῦλα. 1101 a 20 μακαρίους δ' ἀνθρώπους. 21 μέν. b 2 ἀφαυρόν. 12 δή.

APPENDIX.

29 κρεῖττον. 34 ψυχικῶν CD [ψυχικωτέρων L^bB¹B²]. 1102 a 5 ἐπεί. 6 ἐπισκεπτέον τάχα. 12 ἡ σκέψις αὕτη. 25 πλεῖστον [πλεῖον B¹B²]. b 13 τῆς. 14 ἐγκρατοῦς καὶ ἀκρατοῦς. 17 τε. 1103 a 22 αὑτόν. 26 παραγίνεται. 32 τῶν ἄλλων τεχνῶν. b 7 καὶ γίνεται D. 10 οἱ οἰκοδόμοι. 15 ἀνθρώποις γινόμεθα. 24 εὐθύς. 29 ἀναγκαῖον ἐπισκέψασθαι περί. 32 ὑπερκείσθω. 34 προδιωμογείσθω. 1104 a 1 πρακτῶν. πρὸς D. 25 τις. 27 αἱ φθοραί. b 18 πρότερον. 29 ἔτι. 32 ἀσυμφόρου. 34 τε. 1105 a 7 καί] ἤ. 11 ἡδικῇ. 19 τὰ σώφρονα. 24 ἐὰν καὶ γραμματικόν τι ποιήσῃ. 27 γινόμενα. 28 ταῦτα. 29 ἐάν. b 4 ἄπερ καὶ ἐκ. 19 μετὰ δὲ ταῦτα τί ἐστιν ἡ ἀρετὴ σκεπτέον. 21-23 ἐπιθυμίαν—ἥλεον] B²=Bek. nisi quod θυμόν post ὀργήν addat. 1106 a 8 πράττειν ἁπλῶς. 28 πρός. b 1 μυᾶς. 8 εὖ ἐπιτελεῖ. 13 ὥς δὴ λέγομεν. 22 ἐπί. 27 ἄρα ἐστίν. 35 παντοδαπῶς δὲ κακοί. 1107 a 12 ψέγεται] λέγεται B¹B²D. 23 τὸ τό] τό. b 3 δὲ τῷ. 7 διόπερ οὐδ' οὗτοι ὀνόματος τετυχήκασιν ἕστωσαν δὲ ἀναίσθητοι. 26 αὑτή. 27 μικρά. 1108 a 2 ἐν om. 28, 29 ὁ. b 11 δέ. 30 μὲν τό. 1109 a 23 τοῖς πάθεσι καὶ ταῖς πράξεσιν. 29 διόπερ ἐστὶ τὸ εὖ καὶ σπάνιον καὶ ἐπαινετὸν ὃ καὶ καλόν. 31 ἡ καλυψὼ παρῄνει. 32 τούτου] τὸ ὥς τοῦ. b 5 ἀπαγαγόντες. 1110 a 14 ἑκούσιον δὴ καὶ τὸ ἀκούσιον. 25 ὑπερτείνει post φύσιν. b 13 δή. 23 ἔστω. 1111 a 1 καί post γάρ. 6 ἄν om. 22 βιαίου. 25 δι'. 28 ἢ θυμόν. b 18 διὰ B¹B²D. 1112 a 1 δόξῃ. 7 ὥς om. 14 οὐδέν ἐστιν. 20 ἄν τις βουλεύσαιτο. b 15 τίνων. 21 εἰρημένον B¹B²D. 1113 a 1 τοῦτο ἢ πέττεται ἢ πεποίηται ὡς δεῖ. [τοῦτο ἢ πέπεσται ὡς δεῖ B¹B²L^b, ἢ πέπ(ras. au?)ται ὡς δεῖ A]. 9 προείλοιντο B¹B²C [προείλοιντο D]. 10 ἐκ om. 33 ἄν. b 13 ἄρα] ἔσται. 14 μακάριον. 20 ἐφ'. 24 αὐτοὶ αἴτιοι. 26 πρὸς ὅσα. 29 ἀλλ' ὁτιοῦν. 1114 a 2 ὃν τὸ μὴ ἀγνοεῖν. 12 τὸν ἀκολασταίνοντα ἀκόλαστον. 18 βαλεῖν A. 21 οὐκέτι] οὐκ. 27 ἐλεῆσαι. b 3 μηδείς. 4 inter τοῦ et τέλους habet B² τῆς ἀρετῆς 1115 b 13—οὗ ἕνεκα 1115 b 17, quae quidem verba iterum apud 1115 b 13 praebet. 28 καί. πρακτικαὶ καί. 31 τοῦ om. 1115 a 3 χρήσασθαι. 13 γάρ. 16 ὁμοίῳ τι. 20 ἐν. 24 οὖν. b 18 καί ante ὥς. 33 τούτοις. 1116 a 21 οἱ δέ. 33 ὁ om. b 19 post Ἑρμαίῳ add. τῷ ἐν Κορώνῃ τῆς Βοιωτίας [om. C]. 26 θυμοειδεῖς· τὸ ὁρμητικώτατον ἰτηκώτατον (sic). 33 ἐν post ἤ. 36 ἄν εἶεν. 1118 b 15 ἕως ἂν ὑπερπλησθῇ ὑπερβάλλειν 1119 b 22 λέγωμεν δὲ καὶ ἐξῆς περὶ ἐλευθεριότητος om. in fine libri iii. λέγωμεν. b post εἶναι om. 34 τι. 1120 a 4 χρεία τις. 6 ἕκαστον. 11 ἀρετῆς γάρ. 17 λαμβάνειν. 22 τῶν ἀπ' ἀρετῆς. 24 οὖν. 30 οὐδ' ὁ λυπηρός. ἔλοιτ'. b 2 ἰδίων. 4 ὅτε καὶ οὗ. 9 ὅθεν οὐθέν. 19 ἐπιμελόμενον. 22 ταῦτα. 26 ταῖς δόσεσι καὶ ταῖς δαπάναις. 30 δ' om. 1121 a 4 καί. 15 ἐπί. 16 συναύξεται. 18 διδόντας ἰδιώτας B¹B²CA. 20 τε om. 25 οὐ ante λήψεται. 33 τοῦτο ποιεῖν μὴ δύνασθαι. b 4 αὐτοῦ add. 28 ἄν. 33 ἐργαζόμενοι καί. 34 καὶ τοκισταὶ καὶ τὰ μικρὰ (sic) ἐπὶ πολλῷ. 1122 a 14 ἐστι κακόν. 23 γάρ. 34 δὲ περί. b 15 κτῆμα μὲν γὰρ τὸ πλεῖστον ἄξιον καὶ τιμιώτατον. 18

APPENDIX.

ἔργου μεγαλοπρέπεια, omisso ἀρετή. 20 περὶ τοὺς θεούς. 21 καὶ ὅσα περί. 30 τὰ τοιαῦτα. διά. 1123 a 2 πᾶσα ἡ. 1124 b 8 ἀφειδής. 21 ἐν. 26 φανερόμισον. 29 φανερῶς· καταφρονητικοῦ γὰρ διὸ παρρησιαστικὸς παρρησιαστικοῦ διὸ διὰ καταφρονητικὸς καὶ ἀληθευτικός. 1125 a 1 πρὸς ante φίλον. 34 χεῖρον. b 7 ἐν τιμῆς ὀρέξει. 9 καί post ὡς. 15 δεῖ φέρομεν. 19 δὲ τιμῆς. 32 add. καί ante ὡς. 1126 a 10 θᾶττον καί. 16 ἀνταποδιδόασιν. 20 ὀργίζονται. 1127 a 8 διά τι ἄλλο. b 26 add. τά ante φανερά. 27 εὐκαταφρόνητοι. 31 καί ante ὠνεῖσθαι om. 34 εἶναι ὁμιλία τις. 1128 a 16 μικρὸν ἐκ. b 11 γοῦν. 18 δὲ κεκωλύσθαι. 1129 a 33 καὶ ὁ ἄνισος. b 1 ἐπεὶ γὰρ καί. 8 μεῖον. 18 τῆς εὐδαιμονίας. 24 ὀρθός [ὀρθῶς B²]. 25 χείρων [χεῖρον B²]. 1130 a 2 τὸν ἄνδρα. 5 κοινῷ. 13 ἡ δικαιοσύνη. 22 μέρος τι. 25 μοιχεύοι καὶ προσλαμβάνοι. b 10-13 ἐπεὶ δὲ τὸ ἄνισον καὶ τὸ παράνομον οὐ ταὐτὸν ἀλλ' ἕτερον ὡς μέρος πρὸς ὅλον τὸ μὲν γὰρ ἄνισον ἅπαν παράνομον τὸ δὲ παράνομον οὐχ ἅπαν ἄνισον τὸ μὲν γὰρ πλέον ἅπαν ἄνισον τὸ δ' ἄνισον οὐ πᾶν πλέον. 23 προσταττόμενα. 1132 b 15 πωλεῖν καὶ ὠνεῖσθαι. 16 ἔδωκεν. 23 ἀντιπεπονθὸς ἄλλῳ B² [ἀντιπεπυνθὸς ἄλλων B¹, ἀντιπεπονθός D]. 1133 a 15 ἂν om. cum B¹B²CDAld. (non add., ut dicit Susem., Ald.). b 15 ἔσται ἀεί. 1134 b 29 οὐδαμῶς ἔχον B¹D Par 1853 H^aM^bQN^bO^bP^bL^b. ἔστι μὲν τι (ε in ras.) καὶ φυσικὸν κινητὸν οὐ μέντοι πᾶν B¹ [ἔστι μέντοι καὶ φύσει κινητὸν μέντοι πᾶν D, ἔστι μέντοι καὶ φύσει κινητὸν οὐ μέντοι γε πᾶν B²]. 1135 a 12 καὶ τὸ κοινὸν μᾶλλον δικαιοπράγημα. b 18 ὅταν ἐν ἑαυτῷ ἡ ἀρχὴ ᾖ τῆς αἰτίας. 24 οὐδέ. 1136 a 32 ᾧ. b 6 ἀλλὰ οὐδ' [οὐδ' B¹B²]. 1137 a 13 νεμόμενα. b 29 ψηφίσματος B¹. 1138 a 10 νόμον. 14 ἔτι B¹ [ἔστι B²]. 32 ψεκτὸν ἦν. 1138 b 33 ἀληθῶς K^bΓAld. τοῦτ' εἰρημένον. 1139 a 3 οὖν. 4 δι' εἶναι μέρη τῆς ψυχῆς. 12 λογιστικόν. b 13 ἕξεις μάλιστα. ἀληθεύει. 15 ἡ. 25 πᾶσα. 1140 a 5 καί περιέχεται. 14 ἡ. 18 τὰ αὐτά. b 2 ἡ om. 7 αὐτή. 10 οἰκονομικούς. τούς om. 11 ἔνθεν. 12 ὡς. 13 πᾶσαν. 14 τό post καί. 15 δυσὶν ὀρθαῖς. 18 φανεῖται. ἡ. 32 δ' ἀρχαί. 33 ἡ. 1141 a 11 οὖν. 20 καὶ ὥσπερ. 21 τὴν ἐπιστήμην πολιτικήν. 24 καὶ εὐθύ. 29 δ' ὅτι. b 1 ὁ κόσμος συνέστηκεν. 17 ἐνίων B¹ [ἑτέρων B²]. 19 ἀγνοεῖ. 30 ἡ φρόνησις. 1142 a 2 πολυπράγμονες. 6 nil post πλέον add. 11 εἰρημένον. 17 διὰ τί, omisso δή. 20 οὐκ. 23 τοδὶ βαρύστατμον. 25 ἀπτικοί. 27 οὖ om. 28 οἷς αἰσθανόμεθα. 32 διαλαβεῖν καί. b 9 τις ἡ εὐβουλία. δί. 15 τε κακῶς. 19 ἰδεῖν. 21 εἶναι om. 23 τούτου δί. 30 ἡ δέ τις. 31 βουλεύεσθαι B¹B². 1143 a 5 ὁτωοῦν. 19 εὐγνώμονες. 31 ἁπάντων. b 1 καί ante ὁ om. 14 τὰς ἀρχάς. 19 θεωρεῖ. 28 θεῖον. 1144 a 2 τοῦ ante μορίου om. 14 λέγομεν. 23 τις. 29 δύναμις. b 1 καὶ γὰρ ἡ ἀρετὴ παραπλησίως. 1145 a 2 ὑπάρξουσιν. 3 ἰδεῖτο ἄν. 8 ἡ. 33 τῆς τοιαύτης διαθέσεως. b 6 τε om. 8 δὴ ᾖ τε ἐγκράτεια. 9 τῶν. 10 τε. 17 οἱ. ὅτι. 1146 a 8 τῶν ἐσχάτων γάρ. 11 ἔσται. 14 μή. 34, 35 ἐν ᾗ φαμὲν ὅταν τὸ ὕδωρ τὸν φάρυγγα (sic) πνίγῃ τί δεῖ ἔτι πίνειν. b 3 πάντα. 4 ἁπάσας. 14 δ'. 16 ταδὶ B¹

APPENDIX.

[τὰ δίκαια B²]. 17 μόνον ἀκρατὴς ὁ ἀκρατὴς ἢ οὐ ἀλλὰ τῷ ἐξ ἀμφοῖν ἔπειτ'. 21 ἂν om. 1147 a 6 οὗτος. 7 ἦ. 9 δοκεῖν μὲν οὕτως εἰδέναι. 14 οἵ γε. 19 σημεῖον τοῦ ἐνεργεῖν κατὰ τὴν ἐπιστήμην. 21 πρῶτον. συνείρουσι. 22 συμφυῆ εἶναι. τοῦτο. 32 τὸ γλυκύ. 34 οὖσα. μὲν οὖν λέγει. b 4 τῶν. 16 αὐτή. 18 εἰδότα ἐνδέχεται. 29 οὔ. 31 οὖν. 1148 a 13 τόν post καί om. 28 πως καί. 34 καί om. b 21 φασὶ χαίρειν. 22 μερῶν post ἀπηγριωμένων add. cum Ald. κρέασιν ἀνθρωπείοις. 23 δανείζειν ἀλλήλοις. 28 τράξεις. 30 ἐθιζομένοις. 33 δέ. 1149 a 5 κακία καὶ ἀφροσύνη. 13 ἐνίοτε μόνον. λέγω δὲ οἷον. 25 ἢ ἤ. 28 πράξεως. 29 οὕτως ὁ B² [οὗτος ὁ B¹, οὕτω καὶ θυμός D]. b 30 ἀκρασία CB¹ [ἀκολασία B²DA]. 1150 a 2 βέλτιστον. 3 post ἀλλ' add. ἡμάρτηται καί. συμβαλεῖν. 15 μεταξὺ δὲ τῶν πλείστων ἕξεις κἂν εἰ ῥέπωσι [D=Bek.]. 25 διὰ τὴν ἡδονήν. 28 τις μή. b 17 δέ. εἴπερ οὖν. 22 προγαργαλίσαντες. 23 προαισθόμενοι. 31 οὕτω καί. 1151 a 2 ἔχοντες μέν. 9 μιλήσιοι γὰρ ἀξύνετοι. 15 ἤ ante μοχθηρία om. 17 ὁ λόγος. 23 ἀναιδήν. 33 μέν om. 34 δὲ ὁ τῷ. b 7 οἷον. 31 ἐναντίον εἶναι. 1152 a 19 οὐδέ. 21 ὥσπερ. 28 βουλευσαμένων. b 21 ὅτι. 1153 a 1 ἐνθεούσης. b 25 ἄπαντες. 27 τινα λαοὶ πολλοὶ φημίξωσιν. 30 πάντες. 1154 b 34 ἐροῦμεν. 1155 a 14 βοηθείας B¹DCA [βοήθεια B²]. 18 ὁρνίοις CDB¹B² [ὄρνεσι (sic) A]. b 15 τὸ ἧττον καί. 17 φανερὸν περὶ αὐτῶν CMᵇAld. 27 ἐν. 32 ἄν. 1156 a 7 τρία γάρ ἐστιν εἴδη τῆς φιλίας. 22 ἀλλὰ ἄλλοτε γίγνεται ἄλλο B¹B²DC [A=Bek.]. 24 φιλία δοκεῖ. 27 οὐδέ. b 5 κατὰ φιλίαν. 8 ἀλλήλοις βούλονται. 22 ὅμοια CD [ὅμοιοι pr. A]. 23 ἡδὺ ἁπλῶς. 27 συνεναλῶσαι. 1157 a 9 ἡ ὄψις ἡδεῖα. 17 ἀλλήλοις εἶναι. 32 ὅμοιόν τι ταύτῃ. 1158 a 24 αὐτὸ ἀγαθόν. 33 ὅτι. b 3 ἀντικαταλλάττονται. 9 εἶναι καὶ μόνιμον. 13 παντὶ ἄρχοντι. 1159 a 23 περὶ αὐτῶν ἐφίενται B¹B²CDMᵇAld. 32 μὴ δύνωνται τῇ μητρὶ ἡ προσήκει ἀπονέμειν. b 1 τῶν τοιούτων. 7 post ἐπιτρέπειν add. ὑπηρετεῖν. 21 ξηρῷ οὐχ ὑγρῷ γενέσθαι. 1160 a 36 δ' ἡ τιμοκρατία. 1161 a 13 πράττωσιν. 26 ὁμοήθεις καὶ ὁμοπαθεῖς. 28 βούλονται καὶ ἐπιεικεῖς. b 23, 24 ἐκείνων δ' οὐθενὶ ἀφ' οὗ. 39 διό. 1162 a 2 συνεπιέσπαται. b 12 ἑκάτερος B¹B²C [ἕκαστος AKᵇLᵇ]. ἐφίεται. 16 συνημερεύειν. 29 διόπερ ἐνίοις τούτων οὐκ εἰσὶν (δίκαι B², δίκαιοι B¹, δίκαιον B²) B¹B². 1163 a 2 καὶ ἔκοντι. b 10 τιμὴν ἀπονέμουσι. 17 τὴν ἀξίαν ποτ' ἄν. 22 ἀφιέναι. 32 ἀπάσαις. ἀνομοειδέσι. 1164 a 25 μαθόντα. 27 ἀρκεῖ B¹B²CA. 28 ἐν. 34 γίγνηται. b 10 γὰρ ἄν. 20 λαβόντες B¹Mᵇ Ald. [λαμβάνοντες B²CALᵇOᵇKᵇ]. 1165 a 17 ἁρμόττοντα. 24, 25 καὶ τιμὴν δὲ γονεῦσι καθάπερ θεοῖς οὐ πᾶσαν δὲ γονεῦσιν οὐδὲ γάρ [καὶ τιμὴν δὲ καθάπερ θεοῖς οὐ πᾶσαν δὲ γονεῦσιν οὐδὲ γάρ C; AB¹=Bek.]. 30 ἀπάντων. 31 δεῖ πειρατέον. b 21 γὰρ τούτῳ ἢ τοιούτῳ. 22 γοῦν. 23 γένοιτο. 35 προσγενομένην. 1166 a 6 οἱ προσπεκρουκότες. 25 μνῆμαι. 35 εἶναι ἡ φιλία. b 12 καὶ διά. μισοῦνται καί. 14 συνημερεύσουσι B¹B²AKᵇAld. [συνημερεύουσι C.] 19 οἱ τοιοῦτοι ἑαυτοῖς. 20 τότε. ἀσχολούμενος. 29 καί ante πρός om. 1167 a 16 ἐλπίδα ἔχων εὐπορίας. 18 ἡ. 24

APPENDIX. 91

ὁτουοῦν. b 22 οἱ δὲ δανείσαντες καὶ ἐπιμέλονται. 29 οὐχ. 32 τοὺς εὖ πεπονθότας.
1172 a 19 ἴσως. 22 ἀρετήν. 26 τῶν τοιούτων. b 1 ὀφθείς ποτ'. 2 ὡς οὐ τοιαύτην. 12 δή B¹B²CD Par. 1853 [δή AKᵇ]. 12 φέρεσθαι ὡς πᾶσιν ἄριστον μηνύει ἕκαστον. 30 μετὰ φρονήσεως τὸν ἡδὺν βίον. 1173 a 2 ὀρέγεται. αὐτῶν. 8 μηδέτερα AC [μηδέτερα (sic) B¹, μηδ' ἕτερον (sic) B², μηδ' ἕτερα D]. 10 ὄντων κακῶν. 11 ἡ ἕτερον. 23 τί κωλύει δέ. 34 ἡσθῆναι. b 4 ταχέως οὐκ ἔστιν. 7 εἶναι τοῦ κατὰ φύσιν. 11 ἀναπλήρωσις ἡ ἡδονή. 18 πολλαὶ δὲ καί AB¹B²D, et C omisso δέ. 23 ἡδέα ταῦτ' ἐστίν. ἁπλῶς πλήν. 1174 a 21 ἅπαντι δὴ τῷ χρόνῳ τούτῳ [ἅπαντι δὴ τῷ χρόνῳ ἢ τοιούτῳ D, CB¹=Bek.]. b 17 μηθέν. 26 ὁμοίως, 29 εἴη. 33 ἕως δ' οὗ ἄν ποτε τὸ αἰσθητὸν ἢ νοητόν κ.τ.λ. 1175 b 4 κατακούσωσιν. 8 καὶ ἐάν. 11 ἀρεσκόμενοι οἶον καί. 29 τῶν δ' αἰσχρῶν. 1176 a 7 ὄνους AB¹CD [ὄνον B²]. b 12 διαγωγάς B¹B²CD [ἀγωγάς pr. A]. 17 ἀποσχολάζειν. 31 χάριν. 1177 a 2 σπουδαῖος. 4 τῶν om. 33 σοφός. b 26 ἂν εἴη κρείττων βίος. 31 χρὴ δὲ οὐ. 33 ἀπαθανατίζειν. 1178 a 34 ζητεῖται. b 20 ἀφῃρημένῳ. 21 θεωρίας. 28 οὐδαμοῦ. 1179 a 3 αὐτάρκες οὐδ' ἡ πρᾶξις δυνατόν. 4 ἄρχοντας. 33 τι. 1180 b 3 ἐπιτηδευμάτων.

Anecdota Oxoniensia

TEXTS, DOCUMENTS, AND EXTRACTS

CHIEFLY FROM

MANUSCRIPTS IN THE BODLEIAN

AND OTHER

OXFORD LIBRARIES

CLASSICAL SERIES. VOL. I—PART II

NONIUS MARCELLUS, HARLEIAN MS. 2719

COLLATED BY

J. H. ONIONS, M.A.

Oxford
AT THE CLARENDON PRESS
1882

[*All rights reserved*]

London

HENRY FROWDE

OXFORD UNIVERSITY PRESS WAREHOUSE

7 PATERNOSTER ROW

NONIUS MARCELLUS

DE COMPENDIOSA DOCTRINA

HARLEIAN MS. 2719

COLLATED BY

J. H. ONIONS, M.A.

SENIOR STUDENT OF CHRIST CHURCH

Oxford
AT THE CLARENDON PRESS
1882

[*All rights reserved*]

London
HENRY FROWDE

OXFORD UNIVERSITY PRESS WAREHOUSE
7 PATERNOSTER ROW

NONIUS MARCELLUS,

HARLEIAN MS. 2719.

THIS is the oldest known MS. of Nonius in existence, and has never been collated throughout, though the Editors of the Fragments have consulted it here and there for their own special purposes. Quicherat, in his edition of Nonius (Paris, 1872), professes to give a complete collation, which is however quite untrustworthy. The readings he has are nearly always those of the second hand; and even where he cites the original reading, his quotations are often incorrect. The MS. is referred by Mr. Bond, of the British Museum, to the end of the ninth or the beginning of the tenth century, and is in three hands. The first ends abruptly in the middle of a page with the words 'ovum inspexerant' (117, 9). The second begins on the top of the following page with the words 'quae gallina peperisset,' and continues to the end of the treatise 'De indiscretis generibus.' The third begins with the 'De uaria significatione sermonum,' and goes on to the end of the work. All three hands are, according to Mr. Bond, of nearly the same date, but the first two are much more careful than the third, who frequently omits syllables, words, and whole examples, which are however generally supplied by a later hand in the margin. The MS. is annotated throughout in three hands, which either correct the text, or give epitomes or explanations of the glosses. Two of these hands are referred by Mr. Bond to the same date as the MS.; the third, though later than the other two, is still old. The Paris MS. 7667 (P), of which Quicherat gives a collation, seems to have been copied from the Harleian, after it had been corrected by the first two hands. It has generally the second reading of the Harleian, sometimes however the original reading, and sometimes a combination of the two. I have given a considerable number of the marginal notes, as they have often been introduced into the text of the Paris MS., and serve to show how the original text of

NONIUS MARCELLUS.

Nonius may have been corrupted in many cases by the insertion of glosses from the margin. The collation has been made from Quicherat's edition of Nonius, adding the readings that he omits, and correcting him when wrong; when the reading given by him is correct, it is not mentioned here. The Harleian gives no new glosses or examples, its value depending chiefly on the following considerations:—

I. That it gives new readings which have never previously been suggested; e.g. Non. 67, 17, in the example from Varro, the Harleian reads 'parentacte,' though in lines 12, 14, and 16 it has respectively 'parectatum,' 'parectato' and 'parectaton.' In line 17 the Leyden MS. has 'praeutactae,' and 'praeutacton' in line 16, on the authority of Lucian Mueller in his edition of the fragments of Lucilius. Quicherat, however, does not mention these readings. 'Parentactoe' should apparently be restored throughout this gloss. It completes the metre in line 14, which should run, 'Unde parentactoe chlamydes ac barbula prima,' while line 16 should be altered to 'Ephebum quemdam quem parentacton vocant.' Παρένταξις is quoted by Suidas, where we find παρένταξις, ἡ τῶν ἀνομοίων παρένθεσις, οἷον ὁπλιτῶν πρὸς ψιλοὺς ἢ ψιλῶν πρὸς ὁπλίτας: thus παρένταπτοι might naturally be used of young men admitted for the first time to the society of their seniors. Παρέκτατοι, on the other hand, seems never to occur, and it is difficult to see what sense it could bear. Again 78, 30: for 'Quid est istuc,' &c., the first reading of the Harleian gives, 'Quid prodest istuc te blaterare atque obloqui,' which completes both sense and metre. So 79, 1: 'Caecilius Hymnide,' &c., the Harleian first reading gives, 'Cecilius imnide; Sine blanditie nil agit'... which seems clearly right. I suspect that 'blandities' has dropped out after 'blateres,' and that we should read, inserting a new gloss, 'Blandities, Caecilius, Hymnide; Sine blanditie nil agit In amore inermus.' So 124, 29: 'Liberne es,' &c., the Harleian gives as the first reading, 'Liberne es? non sum liber verum inibi est quasi,' which is no doubt right, as it completes the iambic line. So again 178, 22: 'Iam istam colaphis comminuissem [testam] testatim tibi,' Quicherat conjectured 'testam,' which is adopted by Ribbeck. The Harleian, however, preserves the original reading, the first hand giving, 'Iam istam calvam colafis comminuissem testatim tibi.' Besides these there are also many other similar instances.

II. That it supplies manuscript authority for conjectures already

NONIUS MARCELLUS. 95

made, as instances of which may be cited 18, 21 : 'atque rutellum Una affert.' For 'una' Scaliger conjectured 'unum,' which is the first reading of the Harleian. 108, 3 : 'Ebriulare ebrium facere, et ebriacus;' ib. 7, 'Homo ebriacus somno sanari solet;' in line 7 Ribbeck conjectures 'ebriatus' for 'ebriacus,' to restore the metre, and this is in both places the first reading of the Harleian. Ib. 14: 'Excissatum... Plaut. Cist.; Capillo scisso atque excissatis auribus.' For 'excissatis' Meursius conjectured 'excisatis,' and the Harleian actually gives as the first readings, respectively, 'excisatum,' and 'excisatis.' 124, 31 : 'Profecto aut inibi est aut iam potiuntur Phrygum.' For 'aut iam' the other MSS. seem to give 'tam iam:' 'aut iam' is a conjecture of Lipsius; it is, however, given as the first reading by the Harleian. 126, 8 : 'Ientare, Afranius; Ientare nulla invitat. Plaut. Curc.; Quid? antepones Veneri te ientaculo? Afranius; Haec ieiuna ientauit.' The first hand of the Harleian runs 'Ieientare, Afranius; Ieientare nulla invitat. Plaut. Curc.; Quid antepones Veneri ieientaculi. Afranius; Haec ieiuna ieientauit,' and these readings are clearly right, as in each case they restore the metre. Ribbeck has already made the same correction from the Bamberg MS. In the passage from Varro, line 15, the Harleian gives 'pulli ientent,' from which I conjecture that the gloss may originally have run, 'Ieientare et ientare,' one of the verbs having dropped out. 146, 29 : 'Extinctas [et] iam oblitteratas memoria;' here Ribbeck reads, 'Extinctas pausa oblitteratas memoria;' Iunius conjectured, 'Extinctas iam atque oblitteratas memoria,' which is the first reading of the Harleian. 110, 18: 'Fulguriuit, fulgorem fecit uel fumine afflauit. Naeuius, Danae; Suo sonitu claro fulguriuit Iupiter;' the Harleian gives 'Fulgorauit.... Naeuius, Danae; Suo sonitu claro fulgorauit Iupiter,' which should be right, 'fulgorauit' corresponding to 'fulgorem fecit;' Ib. 20, 'Lucil. lib. 26, Luporum exactorem maluanum et fulguratorem arborum,' for 'fulguratorem' Lipsius conjectured 'fulguritarum,' which is the first reading of the Harleian. For 'exactorem' the MSS. give 'exauctorem,' from which I conjecture that the original reading may have run, 'Lucorum exauctorem Albanum et fulguritarum arborum,' which would restore the metre; cf. Verg. Georg. i. 27, 'Auctorem frugum tempestatumque potentem.' There are also very many other similar instances of greater or less importance.

(3) B 2

III. That even where the reading of the Harleian is not absolutely correct it is still of great importance, as in the case of fragments, many of which are extremely corrupt, the change of one or two letters will often decide against or in favour of a reading, or throw an entirely new light upon the passage. As instances of this may be mentioned 12, 18: 'Noui non inscitulam ancillulam Uespere et uestispicam;' Ribbeck reads, 'Noui non inscitulam Ancillulam uestrae hic erae uestispicam;' the first hand of the Harleian gives, 'Noui non instituram ancillunam uespere et vestispicam,' from which I conjecture that the true reading may be, 'Noui non inscitulam Ancillulam unam uestrae erae,' &c., where 'ancillulam unam' would account for the corruption to 'ancillunam.' 49, 1: 'Trossuli dicti sunt torosuli,' here the Harleian, first hand, gives 'Trossuli, equites Romani dicti trossuli dicti sunt torosuli,' for which I propose, 'Trossuli, equites Romani, dicti sunt torosuli.' The 'dicti trossuli' represents, I believe, part of a gloss, 'Equites Romani dicti trossuli,' which has crept into the text from the margin. Again, 84, 6: 'Colustra,' &c., the Harleian, first hand, reads 'Columnum lacconere giumere mammis. Lucilius lib. 8; Beram insulam fomento omnicolore. Colustra,' beginning a new gloss at '.Colustra.' This I believe to be right, and suggest as the first gloss, 'Columna . . . . Lucilius, Beram (?) insulam (?) fomento omnicolore [columna].' Then follows 'Colustra, Laberius in Virgine, Si quidem mea colustra,' &c. After this came, I believe, a third gloss on 'creterra' to which the words 'terris studere . . . sumere aquam ex fonte' belong; Nonius 547, 23 has a gloss on 'creterra' illustrated from Naeuius Lycurgus: 'Nam ut ludere laetantes inter se uidimus, Praeter amnem creterris sumere aquam ex fonte.' We should read then, 'Creterra . . . . Naeuius Lycurgo, Creterris . . . . ludere . . . . sumere aquam ex fonte.' The three glosses have been confused, as frequently happens in glossaries. Glosses on 'columna' occur in Paulus and Isidore, while 'creterra' is found in Paulus. The number of instances where the reading of the Harleian has been misquoted is very large; in many cases no doubt the correction is of slight importance, in others it will probably be found of value. The spelling of the MS. is good on the whole. It gives, for instance, 'cum' invariably, so generally 'ecum,' 'relincunt,' 'locuntur,' &c. In the accusative plural of nouns with 'i' stems, it almost invariably writes 'is,' sometimes, however, in the nominative as well. It distinguishes between ae, oe, and e, though not always correctly, giving, for instance, 'proelium,' 'caelum,' 'caena,' I believe without exception. In proper names and Greek words, on the other hand, it varies very much. As to the relation of the Harleian to the other MSS. of Nonius it is very difficult to speak. If the apparatus criticus in Quicherat's edition may be trusted, the Harleian is certainly much superior to any other existing MS. On the other hand, the readings given by Quicherat differ so widely from those quoted by the editors of the Fragments that it may fairly be doubted whether he is not as inaccurate in the case of the other MSS. as in that of the Harleian; and the Leyden MS., at any rate, would probably repay a careful and accurate collation.

1,	9	mala est mers, mala est ergo.		27	lurcando lurchare M¹, l. lurcare M².
2,	16	emigrarent M¹, emigrarunt M².			
3,	9	comparce M¹, comperce M². velitare, so 12.	11,	2	carnalia M¹, carnaria M². fartim M¹, parum M².
4,	14	equis edoceat M¹, equiso doceat M².		5	lurchabar M¹, lurcabat M².
				20	ero M¹, ero om. M².
	16	ibi tolutim.		25	eius regi M¹, e. rei M².
		mg. cocleatum cocleis asperatum.			sum factus finitor.
		mg. cocleae scilicet in mari.	12,	18	instituram ancillunam M¹, inscituram ancillulam M².
5,	22	libro primo.		21	ut vestispicam M¹, ut om. M².
6,	20	significantiam.			inspiciat M¹, spiciat M².
		infixam M¹, inflexam M².	13,	27	ducit et M¹, ductitet M².
7,	9	exitare M¹, exilire M².	14,	18	decoratis M¹, decoratus M².
	19	habebit tibi amillic M¹, habebit iamillic M².	15,	13	pater M¹, patri M².
				15	sint M¹, sunt M².
	26	sartor satorque.		20	torrus M¹, torris M², and 22 and 26.
	29	sarriunt M¹, sariunt M², so 8, 2.			
8,	5	nauciis, *et in mg.*		21	Melanippo.
	6	odor.	16,	8	aspiciunt M¹, spiciant M².
	10	intricenare M¹, intricare M².		13	mulgere M¹, mulcere M².
	22	tricas tellanas.		17	scipobolimea M¹, hipobolimea M².
9,	6	haec amusim.			
10,	11	popli M¹, populi M².		26	succusare M¹, succussare M².

16,	28	lib. iii M¹, lib. iiii M².	25,	1	coponem M¹, cuponem M².
17,	11	pinnata M¹, pennata M².		4	eaque dissensione.
	12	qui manduci.			alias M¹, alios M².
	19	senica, and 22.		10	mg. v. et v. intortis pedibus
	20	seneca.			araneae vocabulo quae grece
	30	potest M¹, potes M².			votrax dicitur.
	31	Lira est autem, f. r. q. c. agros		16	perniciem M¹, permiciem M².
		t. d. e. i. q. uligo terrae		26	xvii M¹, xvi M².
		decurrat.	26,	6	neunum M¹, neuum M².
18,	21	unum affert.		17	aitarum M¹, aitharum M².
	24	a mendaciis M¹, a om. M².		21	vestrae hae voluptates M¹,
19,	19	magnum M¹, magnus M², mag-			hae om. M².
		num M².	27,	1	mg. qui oblicum habent as-
	22	prima valva est M¹, in prima M².			pectum "guelchi."
20,	9	causa ut M¹, c. aut M¹.		8	ni M¹, ne M².
	13-16	idem—regia om.		14	exodium M¹, in exodio M².
	19	opificio M¹, opifico M².		19	mg. putus purgatus.
	25	goerus M¹, girus M².	28,	9	corrigiis.
	28	dicimus et venenum.		11	diana retae.
21,	16	crebrae scintillae M¹, crebrae		13	quoque M¹, quocum M².
		ut s. M².		16	fulget et tonitrum.
	20	rudite M¹, rudete M².		18	coangulum M¹, coagulum M²,
		heiulitavit M¹, heiulavit M².			and 23.
	21	anxarius M¹, ancarius M².		26	subjecti sint.
	27	non M¹, num M².	29,	4	pedetemtim M¹, and 6, 7, 9,
		illum illa ec pudet.			11, pedetemptim M².
23,	2	canes dicuntur.		12	c. a. c. q. e. nitendo dictae
	9	largiatia.			sunt n. a. c. nam et.
	11	que M¹, quae M¹.		18	arrecto M¹, arrectum M².
	12	multis ignota.		22	ut scenam M¹, ut in schenam
	24	magistas M¹, maiestas M².			M².
24,	5	damnato offerent nisi M¹, offe-		24	mediocritas.
		rent om. M².		30	haec M¹, hae M².
	6	tantum modo in.	30,	10	immune.
	13	teloniarii M¹, telonearii M².		14	mg. dirum quasi deorum ira
	14	ut M¹, et M², ut M².			missum.
	23	allatam esse delatam M¹, a. m.		27	xxviiii.
		e.a.portitorem esse M², in mg.		29	difficillimum M¹, dicit facilli-

		mum M², difficillimum M², autem est.	3	caecutis M¹, caecuttis M².
			23	*mg.* nugas turbans aliquam rem.
31,	9	defrudare.	31	capillos M¹, capillo M².
	11	defraudans ingenium M¹, defrudans genium M².	36, 2	dictum est pedem supponere M¹, supra ponere M².
		confersit M¹, conspersit M². *mg.* dissipavit in quibusdam cod. legitur consparsit.	18	agglomerare M¹, adglomerare M¹, implicare.
			37, 1	aqua intercus est, M², est om. M².
	13	defrude tenego M¹, tenego defraude M².		
			18	portitorium M¹, portorium M².
		defrudaveris M¹, defraudaveris M².	38, 7	Tricolius M², Tricorius M². sirus ipse ad mestitias M¹, mastitias M².
	16	*mg.* sudus quasi subudus.		
	20	sudum M¹, sudus M², est sol et Lucilius.	11	convivones M¹, conbiviones M². dicit M¹, dicti M².
	21	xxviiii.	24	quidni idem M¹, q. et tu idem M².
	22	suda secundet M¹, s. secundent M².	39, 6	tum ut deliminor M¹, tum ut eliminor M².
	25	inritata (*irritare* alibi).	21	anplicare M¹, amplificare M².
32,	5	arcis.	22	ordiri M¹, ordire M², ordiri M².
	11	*mg.* tormines sic solent ponere qui minus considerate locuntur.	31	potuerunt M¹, poterunt M².
			40, 5	supersidere M¹, supersedere M², and 7, 9, 11.
		torqueant M¹, torqueat M², torqueant M³.	9	faces M¹, face M².
			12	tintinire M¹, tintinnire M².
	14	gravidinosos quosdam torminosos.	14	tintinire.
			15	xviii aptanus M¹, adtanus M². tintinat.
33,	10	pedetemtim, and 11.		
34,	2	immitere M¹, intermitere M².	24	cuossim dictum quasi quoxim M¹, cossim d. q. coxim M². procaria M¹, porcaria M².
	5	veterem M¹, vetera M². quasi novam M¹, q. in novam M².		
			25	quossim M¹, cossim M².
	12	divarricari M¹, divaricari M².	41, 5	sticmatios M¹, sticmatias M².
	15	divarricari.	7	quam conjugem M¹, om. M².
	17	vaccillare M¹, vacillare M².	13	reserat.
	18	defessi atque ad.	16	fretis M¹, foetis M².
	20	vaccillante M¹, vacillante M².	42, 5	*mg.* adpendix quasi ex alio pendens.
35,	1	inimica est mentis.		

NONIUS MARCELLUS.

42, 9 accumbitionem M¹, accubitionem M².
quae M¹, quia M².
12 semen cohibet M¹, accipit M².
18 coaugmentavit M¹, augmentavit M², coaugmentavit M².
23 locupletium.
25 ditione M¹, dicione M².
43, 18 concinare M¹, concinnare M².
23 recte a. concinare M¹, concinere M².
26 reconcinnebatur his M¹, re concinebatur verbis M².
27 quae cum s. v. concinnare M¹, concinere M², sibi maxime.
44, 9 a blatu M¹, a balatu M².
10 naugias M¹, nugas M².
18 adindigenda M¹, adigenda M².
27 aut larvatus aut cerritus M¹, aut larvatus es aut c. M².
28 infestent M¹, infestant M².
45, 3 religione aliqua.
mg. votitum religiosum.
6 sed et a verbis.
14 crocchitum M¹, crochitum M², mg. grocire.
16 croccibat M¹, crocibat M².
46, 6 has nos.
8 frigido sabase M¹, sabaxe M².
13 veneri vaga.
19 fervitate M¹, feritate M².
mg. febris a feritate quidam a fervore.
20 calorem vel candorem M¹, vel caldorem M².
48, 10 menippu antiqui M¹, m. tantiqui M².
nostriin M¹, nostrum M².

11 lapidibus.
14 ΕΙΑΠΑΑΑΝΤΟΙ cocedenes M¹, cocedones M².
17 dequoquitur M¹, decoquitur M².
nam lixam aquam ad castra M¹, lixam aquam veteres dixerunt &c. M².
23 erit M¹, erat M².
49, 1 Trossuli equites Romani dicti trossuli dicti sunt torosuli M¹, equites Romani dicti trossuli om. M².
4 mg. proboscis quod inde pascatur a greco qui boscen pascere dicunt.
13 animaceterarios M¹, animadvertis cetarios M².
20 crucifixi M¹, crucefixi M².
24 veterina M¹, vetera M², veterina mg.
tuta vita M¹, vita om. M².
50, 2 rustici utuntur cum tritas f. a. v. i. a erigunt M¹, tritae eriguntur M².
9 a furu M¹, furuo M².
R. v. atrum appellaverint M¹, R. v. furum atrum a. M².
12 rerum divinarum.
quod furum atrum.
13 facilius furentur.
19 notos dicitur M¹, dictus M², dicitur M¹.
20 quod notos graece.
23 ac vertigine.
51, 3 PENI (*graecis litteris*) velnoris M¹, peni vel penoris M².
5 recordantur M¹, recondantur M¹.

NONIUS MARCELLUS.

    mg. quare pietas dicatur quod pietas intus animo condita sit.
7 veteres putant.
15 rudere M¹, ludere M².
52, 6 lavadire luantar maluae M¹, lavandi reluant arma lue M².
21 antiquitatis M¹, antiquitas M².
53, 6 non abhorret a vocabuli.
8 significantiam dictam M¹, dicta M².
9 venissent M¹, venisset M², venissent M³.
12 faciam M¹, faciem M².
13 dictos M¹, dictas M².
15 et hoc quidem et genus.
16 auctoritatem M¹, auctoritate M².
54, 3 fetura quadam M¹, foeturam quandam M².
4 ceteros sine a M¹, ceteros antiquiores sine a M².
5 fetus et fecunditas.
6 recepticium, and 17.
7 venundatus.
17 cum reliqua M¹, cum om. M².
20 obum M¹, solum M².
55, 4 vectari solent.
13 culinam M¹, colinam M², and 15, 16, 19.
19 erat M¹, erant M².
23 optume dixisse M¹, dixe M², q. d. vixissent.
56, 3 quod aut dici.
15 infortis facinus oli culi vesciuntur M¹, infantis f. oculi v. M².
17 quicquam somniat an quicquam somniat.

21 subpedit M¹, subpediat M², subpedita M³.
27 schemis M¹, schenis M².
    mg. quod nos dicimus laubias laop dicitur germanice folium inde laubia facta tecta ex foliis.
57, 2 lib. ii.
4 dilectu M¹, delectu M², and 5.
8 defelicis m. e. intellectu M¹, difficilis intellectus M², ut uero.
15 ex hoc dictae.
17 nexum M¹, enixum M².
    actum M¹, artum M², in Amph. id probat dicens.
19 ut M¹, uno M².
58, 12 Tintinius M¹, Titinius M².
14 constituit M¹, constitit M².
27 adolet cum M¹, que M².
59, 3 velut accensiti M¹, accersiti M².
5 adoreum est quo M¹, in quo M'.
10 prorsuspicium M¹. prorsus pium M².
20 quasi mansuetum M¹, manu assuetum M².
21 permultione.
25 manu patiens.
29 in hos M¹, inter hos M².
60, 3 testis M¹, testi M².
8 angulis M¹, anguli M².
19 patefecit.
61, 5 scenis M¹, schenis M².
9 quiare M¹, quare M².
13 sequentur.
14 non quod secentur.
18 istriam.
29 potui? M¹, potus M².

(9)   C   [I. 2.]

NONIUS MARCELLUS.

62, 2 fricari M¹, friari M², *in mg.*
8 lexivum.
11 haec habetur. sumministret.
12 greci dicunt M¹, grece dicuntur M², greci dicunt M³.
16 confluges M¹, confluge M².
63, 4 fixae M¹, fixa M². *mg.* qua posita.
5 ad lineam diriguntur.
11 Cornicula.
13 a graeco sermone dicta M¹, vel dicta M².
20 feratrina aut M¹, ut M².
23 pastillas M¹, pastillos M².
64, 3 vitiis M¹, vicis M².
5 *mg.* patentem amicitiam potius immunditias. Profluvium a fluendo proluvies a lubidine lucus veneris libentina.
15 lib. iiii.
20 excrescebat.
26 contextum M¹, contextus M².
27 continua vel longe ducta.
28 propagare genus.
65, 2 promicare est M¹, est om. M².
7 Alcion ut genuit cladis M¹, hunc g. claudis M².
17 ego M¹, equo M².
66, 1 pisciculas quae M¹, pisculasque M².
4 concordesvae M¹, ve M². *mg.* excordes concordesve a corde.
5 dissentio.
6 excordes concordesque M¹, excordes vecordes c. M².
10 deos manes manes appellari M¹, deos manes appellari M².

11 sapientoribus quam vitam M¹, q. vita M².
67, 1 argutando praeficasque alios M¹, Idem Truculento praeficas M², *in mg.*
9 iii M¹, iiii M².
12 parectatum M¹, parectaton M², parectato *mg.*
14 unde M¹, inde M², parectato et calumiac M¹, calumiades ac M².
17 parentacte M¹, parectate M².
19 proletarii M¹, proletari M².
20 ex atque proletarium pedito M¹, corr. M².
29 et M¹, ut M².
68, 2 appellatos referentur centurionibus et decurionibus M¹, et decurionibus om. M².
12 hostium jam clientium.
17 deligato siguium M¹, siguuium M².
18 leporem teneat. *mg.* abstemius de vino abstinens.
19 Apuleius in se fuisti q. a. paucius a. a. in libro ludicrorum lucilius.
69, 4 tamquam adipatae.
5 *mg.* adamare obligare inherere ab hamo tractum.
8 assentire M¹, assentiri M².
15 Diogenis.
18 admissum.
70, 3 quo prino M¹, co prino M².
71, 1 portatum.

(10)

NONIUS MARCELLUS. 103

20 pro Callio M¹, Gallio M², mg.
   aboriatur pro abortet.
23 mg. adulescentioris luxuriaris.
72, 10 subdealbet M¹, subdeabbet M².
11 non tam M¹, nantam M², nam tam M².
25 assint illae M¹, adsint illae M², ascintille M².
33 fortitudine sit M¹, fortune sic M².
73, 6 affigere M¹, affligere M².
7 amolimini est recedite vel tollite.
17 fieri ingenii M¹, feri ingeni M².
30 mg. atri dies nefasti posteri.
32 atridies M¹, ater dies M².
74, 2 adjutamini M¹, ajutamini M².
3 notam M¹, nota M², xxviiii.
5 appectones M¹, apetones M², apeditones M², mg. apetones adpetentes.
7 mg. advocavit i. e. provocavit adversarium.
13 mg. adulescenturire nugari.
19 miserinum M¹, miserrimum M².
21 diminuerint M¹, dimonuerint M².
23 possum ego.
28 ut et ego M¹, et om. M².
29 accepso accipio.
75, 1 auxit M¹, ausit M².
3 adanxunt (?) igant M¹, adanxint adigant M².
9 anima mater M¹, animam aer M².
15 nec mortalibus n. m. ullo M¹, n. mortalis n. m. ullum M².
26 attigat M¹, attiga M².
76, 4 exta M¹, extra M².
14 pro praesentibus et absentibus nobis.

18 venerit M¹, venierit M².
77, 5 organicum M¹, organicon M².
15 baetere.
16 sanos multos baretere M¹, betere M².
17 niptrabos h. d. p. i. p. idem bibite medo.
22 ad adulterum M¹, ad ad alterum M².
78, 6 lavat.
7 seti homibus bulga M¹, s. hominibus b. M².
25 et quicquid M¹, nam et q. M².
28 bacchato nemens M¹, bacchatur nemes M².
30 quid prodest M¹, q. est M².
79, 1 imnide sine M¹, imnis desine M².
9 exeunt citis trepunt exeunt bount.
11 dolonum M¹, dolonem M².
12 manifestum est id dici.
14 pinnaria M¹, pinnari M².
15 et levis M¹, ut l. M².
17 dunnos M¹, unnos M², c. naufragii ut cicero nec quarum bipennis.
20 ad parmenonem M¹, parmenone M², ad om.
80, 5 uterique M¹, utrimque M².
7 scriptum espectare M¹, spectare, M².
10 discripseris M¹, descripseris M².
32 conari adversarios contra bellosum.
81, 11 farris in farris trite M¹, farris intrite M².
15 rem disperdit.
19 comes.

(11)   C 2

NONIUS MARCELLUS.

81, 33 comestque.
82, 4 paretur M¹, paratur M².
7 turba et colluvione M¹, turbae colluvione M².
10 dedi umquam.
11 cupiditas non imposui M¹, imposuit M².
12 *mg.* cetram obstaculum scutum.
13 quis re tunc dum M¹, rutundam M².
24 conscripsi varro columna M¹, varro om. M².
83, 10 plauda u. e. p. c. mensu iabino M¹, libano M².
20 sirpare adde M¹, s. noli a. M². in uxorculem opocillum M¹, opicillum M².
26 ne ego te M¹, te om. M².
84, 6 columnum lacconere giumere mammis M¹, columnam lacchonere iunmi mammis M¹, colustra lumnam etc. M².
7 beram M¹, hiberam M².
14 idem et dolosi conquinis cesi istic.
22 collutulet, and 24.
23 haec famieratiae t. h. et me c. etsi sine dgte M¹, famigeratio . . . dote M².
25 fidinisque ueat graio M¹, fidinisque at grafo M².
29 proin dustriant teregem.
85, 9 liguratio M¹, ligurritio M².
21 non ita Telamonis patris atque faciet proavi.
26 consistit cibi M¹, consistit ibi M².
86, 2 que M¹, qui M¹.

4 de uita p. r. libro i.
5 toribi M¹, toris M², toribus *in mg.*
8 citrus et faces cingit fores M¹, citrus fasces c. M².
9 *mg.* cecutiunt lippiunt. utrum cecuttiunt lippiunt oculi mei cecuttiunt M¹, utrum oculi mei cecuttiunt M², oculi mihi M².
12 succussatoris M¹, succusatori M².
18 carnales sedulas M¹, setdules M².
21 ebet et stulto M¹, ebeti et M².
87, 14 reddidimus M¹, reddimus M⁷.
15 mercenari M¹, mercennari M².
20 *mg.* clipeat operit.
21 c. liquit c. c. a. c. operit clipeat et accium M¹, operit clipeat om. M².
22 *mg.* galeare operire.
23 m. a. g. p. galeare operire M¹, galeare operire om. M².
26 me coicerem M¹, me ego c. M².
88, 4 est haec M¹, sed haec M².
6 dicorporeis M¹, dicorporois M².
8 *mg.* tibicidas tibicinas.
10 contenturi contenturi M¹, contenturum contenturum M², *mg.*contenturum contentum.
11 tu lucilium credis contenturum cummercum perint summa omnia fecerim M¹, cum me ruperint M².
17 magconis M¹, magonis M².

(12)

21	mg. commentum pro commonitum.	
23	commentus sies.	
89, 11	his M¹, is M².	
19	dum abeam quodam et ubi nihil coepiam.	
21	unde certissent.	
90, 1	mg. concaluit incaluit.	
11	exemplo M¹, extemplo M².	
15	consortiare M¹, consociari M².	
18	congerminati tenuere M¹, congerminata t. M².	
19	Collabella Laberius annalium, mg. collabella adjunge labra.	
23	mg. concinnare hic dissipare alibi componere.	
28	lacu balerna.	
29	exculeto inpatienti catulientem M¹, excoleto M².	
91, 16	mg. conjecturarium a conjectura suspicacem.	
92, 7	atque inter mare nostrum.	
17	calfacimur M¹, calficimur M².	
20	castus M¹, catus M², so 21, sed homo.	
93, 1	tamen haec M¹, et M². relincuntur M¹, relinquentur M².	
2	ita haec.	
5	cicures M¹, cicuras M².	
11	in cubiculo dormire.	
22	primum ac secundum.	
94, 1	figuratio et M¹, ut M².	
4	caput colos temtatur cocsendicibus.	
8	oleam M¹, oleo M².	
23	edent M¹, edint M².	
95, 2	ne quod M¹, quo M², iret.	

5	caenae M¹, caena M².	
6	devitant M¹, divitant M², and 7, and 10.	
19	deuniatus' M¹, deunciatus M².	
26	divides M¹, dividos M².	
96, 1	mg. domutionem domo itionem.	
2	dalanaps M¹, danaps M².	
5	dissinnare M¹, dissignare M².	
8	dissignavit M¹, dissingnavit M².	
10	c plennus M¹, plennus M².	
19	dicit.	
29	conspiritum M¹, conspiratum M².	
33	dulcedine M¹, dulcitudine M².	
97, 1	ex corditate.	
4	depoculassere M¹, depeculassere M², mg. quasi pecus auferre.	
6	depoculassere M¹, depeculassere M².	
20	atiere M¹, patiere M².	
98, 1	delatere M¹, delectare M².	
22	noctuque nec M¹, et M².	
24	eram M¹, eam M².	
99, 2	discesset M¹, discessisset M².	
8	favitores.	
9	depserere M¹, depsere M².	
20	denthaspagae M², dentarpagae M².	
21	sacciis M¹, saucciis M².	
23	spectare M¹, exspectare M².	
26	bonam.	
100, 7	decidua quae cadant.	
13	fodere M¹, foedere M².	
22	mg. duritas saevitia.	
23	disrississimum M¹, dirississimum M², and 24. mg. dirissimum severum.	

100, 26 quem nobilem d. lyras M¹, quam mobilem M².
101, 11 lib. iiii M¹, iii M².
  19 mg. dividae dissensiones dividiae dissensiones.
  27 unianimitatem.
  29 et M¹, ea M².
  32 mg. evirescat pallescat. exsanguinibus M¹, exsanguibus M²; dolere M¹, dolore M².
102, 1 evallere M¹, evallare M². e. vallum mittam. mg. evallare eicere.
  2 pilia M¹, prilia M².
  10 exigno M¹, exigo M².
  18 Ut varias.
  32 urundinis M¹, hirudines M².
103, 14 autem est.
  16 emungere M¹, emulgere M², emungere M³. mg. emungere per fallaciam tollere.
  23 maulta M¹, mata M².
  24 elevavit M¹, elevit M². mg. elevit perleniit polluit.
  25 sibi vestimenta M¹, si hic v. M².
  26 magnum ad cacinnum imprudens.
104, 17 extemplo excite vadit qua M¹, exemplo M².
  27 seraperrectae M¹, seraparectae M².
  28 quam videbis.
  30 genus adverbiorum adverbii motu quae venit.
105, 9 exhibetis M¹, exhibebis M².

  10 educatum quam.
  11 culenarum M¹, culeratum M².
  14 ita nimis.
  15 si nemini M¹, si menti M².
  16 dominatur in suos M¹, in suos om. M².
  17 ut dejurare.
  28 equito M¹, equite M².
  30 quam nauticiiae quisones per viam qua ducerent lora M¹, nautici equisones M².
106, 2 equiso M¹, quis M².
  6 aut aliqua liberos M¹, aliqui M².
  7 mg. equilam equam.
  9 esurigo fames.
  10 strennosus silimus, quostas M¹, costas M².
  15 sicito fulgenti splendore. mg. elucificare lucidare.
  27 cum sit hominis secum insidentis M¹, ecum M².
107, 4 liberti semiatrati.
  14 donare M¹, donari M².
  18 mg. exinanita vacuata.
  19 quae c. seculo sepatuerat M¹, qui c. se loco potuerant M².
  23 incideret quae in mortis M¹, quae om M².
  25 naturalia muliebria.
  27 sene eugio ac destina M¹, sine M².
108, 3 ebriatus M¹, ebriacus M², so 7.
  5 hilariam.
  10 externavit ut conternavit M¹, exterminavit ut consternavit M².
  mg. exterminavit finibus suis evertit.

NONIUS MARCELLUS.

13 in pectoras M¹, in pectora curas M².
14 excisatum M¹, excissatum M². *mg.* excissatum scissum.
15 excisatis M¹, excissatis M².
18 aeduse a potinam pontine nutrici M¹, a potina M².
21 fortunas se illos non nature M¹, fortuna s. i. n. natura M².
28 albetis M¹, albeus M².

109, 5 quam hi servitutis famulatus et servientis voluntati.
13 de fortunabunt vestra M¹, dei f. vostra M².
31 fidelitatem ob fidam naturam M¹, fidelitate M².

110, 3 meaeactio M¹, meaeaaio M².
8 summa M¹, summum M².
18 fulgoravit M¹, fulgurivit M², and 19.
21 fulguritarum M¹, fulguritatem M².
30 fligi affligi.

111, 1 frangescere M¹, fragescere M².
3 persenserim imperii M¹, persenserint M².
5 cum ea M¹, cum mea M².
6 quiqui M¹, qui M².
11 tibi M¹, tiberi M².
14 obsecrate M¹, obsecro te M².
19 exposco hoc M¹, ut hoc M².
25 propitiares M¹, propitiaturos M².

112, 1 ea mihi raliquae f. r. vobisqui e quiritis se M¹, reliquae f. r. vobisque q. M².
4 frustri (*duobus vel tribus litteris erasis*) tim M¹, frustatim M².
7 frustratim M¹, frustatim M².
9 minutatim M¹, minutim M².
10 fastidiligenter f. v. c. credo h. n. q. i. a. a. mutabiliter habere et non habere fastidiligenter habet habere fastidiligenter M¹, fastidiliter M², *passim.*
25 foco M¹, fuco M²; ejus sumptus fax ex pinalba M¹, e. s. cum fax ex pinu alba M².
29 diceret M¹, dicere M².

113, 1 priscos latinos M¹, latine M².
2 esset flata signa atque M¹, sed flata signataque M².
3 formidolosum eo quod ipsum et formidet quod sit M¹, formidulosum et q. i. f. et q. s. M¹.
4 formidolosus M¹, formidulosus M².
6 aequa M¹, aequae M².
8 parco M¹, pareo M².
10 varro manio M¹, varro om. M².
11 hospitium M¹, hospicium M².
14 ex ea difficultate.
17 fabellarumque.
19 paratim ferabite M¹, et partim ferabite M²; arbusto ac muta M¹, arbuto ac multa M².

114, 1 pro frode M¹, fronde M². *mg.* quia frons et frondis dicunt veteres.
2 praecipuae cum M¹, om. M².
21 grunire M¹, grunnire M².
26 grundulsis M¹, grundulis M².

(15)

mg. Aeneas cum venit in
Italiam habebat porcam ex
qua divinationem solebat
capere quae elapsa peperit
xxx porcellos in ejus honorem erant ista sacra quae
istic dicuntur.
115, 1 divinarum lib. ii M¹, lib. i M².
2 seminare incipere M¹, semi-
nari i. M².
18 gladitores s. colobathatrari
gralare e. s. f. qui mituntur
M¹, gladratores... mittun-
tur M². *mg.* forsitan gladia-
tores qui certabant gladiis,
mg. illi fustes qui in cer-
tamine mittebantur sic dicuntur mataras materellos
quos dicimus.
20 ut gladatores qui graduntur
M¹, gladratores qui gradi-
untur M², p. s. lignae finare
molet M¹, inolet M², a. h. e.
quiinistatagitantur M¹, an-
gitantur M².
sicilianiminri.
22 galea M¹, galae M².
116, 1 vi dehinc lacrimae M¹, v. d.
meae inquam l. M².
8 Protesilatidamia M¹, Protesi-
laodemia M².
28 cujus jam ramus roborascit.
117, 4 gragadiare M¹, gragaliare M¹,
gargaridiare M².
mg. quod nos dicimus gar-
garzare.
13 ospitialis M¹, ospitalis M².
20 lib. iiii M¹, lib. iii M².

24 defraudans M¹, defrudans M²,
and 27.
118, 1 laminae M¹, lamia M².
5 aris tamquam M¹, arista quae
M².
9 *mg.* gerdius textor.
11 probro M¹, probo M².
22 regratum M¹, se gratum M²,
se om. M².
29 credo congerrae omnia ejus
ut collusor M¹, c. congerrae
congerio meus ut M².
119, 2 quidum esse na hora M¹,
essena h. M².
n. a. i. aedilis signosiae et
deum M¹, deam M².
11 *mg.* glubere destringere.
12 reliquit.
15 grammonsis M¹, grammosis M².
16 gigerica M¹, gigeria M².
24 genius generis laberius.
mg. genius naturalis deus qui
ortum nostrum excipit.
27 habentia industria M¹, ut industria M².
120, 8 Halofantam aut, and 11.
23 productaest M¹, productae M².
121, 3 culpas M¹, culpes M².
5 quodsi sisyfius M¹, quod sisyfius M².
11 *mg.* hilaresco hilaris fio.
13 recedere ab hostia M¹, r.
dictum ab hostia M².
15 cohercuero M¹, coercuero M².
hostiaero M¹, hostio M².
24 *mg.* hilariter jucunde.
122, 3 et innullis M¹, et mulis M².
5 hillas M¹, hilla M², Bobilla

mg. hilla intestina unde
Bohilla dicta.
7 fragilis M¹, flagris M².
10 hillam M¹, hilla M².
11 Claudius annalibus.
14 mg. incurviscere incurvare.
17 popularis et s. s. n. p. his enim.
22 quae esset insania.
25 mg. infractionem torporem.
29 instituit ut M¹, i. que ut M².
123, 5 quadere liquit M¹, liquid M².
10 ignauuum fecit.
21 ad incitam M¹, incita M², so 23.
124, 11 animam M¹, animum M².
17 quae quondam M¹, quandam M².
24 quod agitur M¹, quod num a. M².
25 mg. inibi sic mox.
29 non sum liber verum inibi est quasi M¹, liber and quasi om. M².
31 aut jam M¹, tam jam M².
125, 11 pro mare latrocinando.
29 mg. forsitan conscindere.
126, 4 scabie summa in re summa.
8 jejentare M¹, jentare M², so 9.
11 jejentaculi M¹, jentaculi M².
13 jejentavit M¹, jentavit M².
26 mg. infelicitent felicem faciant.
31 indignat M¹, indignanti M².
127, 8 etacrista M¹, etarista M².
17 nausimacho M¹, epinausimacho M².
19 si ston habuissem ingenio M¹, habuissem ingenio siston M².

24 indiscrimatim M¹, indiscriminatim M², lib. xviii.
128, 2 vitam hominum tuendam.
6 de officiis ut ii qui M¹, de off. ii ut qui M².
7 rem expetendam.
15 sin aliter essent.
16 oppugnatus se oppidum.
20 ista prudentia doctrinaeque.
26 mg. impedio, impendio.
28 pertire M¹, impertire M².
129, 8 mg. inaudita auditu carentia.
9 alio carent aut a natura aut.
11 infestim M¹, infestum M², aliud aliud sit infestum. mg. infestum aliud et aliud infensum.
15 nesciat ut sit M¹, nesciat cura ut M², nesciatur aut.
21 at inermes M¹, atque inhermis M².
29 incursionem.
130, 2 indictum M¹, inductum M².
6 intonso M¹, intonsa M².
8 lib. iiii.
9 sentis c. M¹, senati M². jussum M¹, jussu M².
12 inhisim M¹, incisim M². bonis M¹, binis M², mg. inhisim simul.
13 inhisim M¹, incisim M².
14 exportatum ablatum.
131, 1 quam M¹, quem M¹, impudentius.
3 mg. inextinguibilis quod extingui non possit.
4 est inextinguibilis.
6 non esse una sine numero

NONIUS MARCELLUS.

magis innumera M¹, una se numero M².
131, 17 ΠΕΡΙ ΦΙΛΟCΟΦΙΑC.
23 scribitario M¹, scribilitario M².
24 luculentulus.
28 fiet cular M¹, fiet et c. M².
132, 6 ea sibi bona ducens.
8 laenitudine M¹, laetitudine M².
18 praeclaro M¹, claro M².
19 lactuose M¹, jactuose M².
20 *mg.* laxitas laxitudo.
23 cujusmodi M¹, cujusquemodi M².
133, 8 progredere.
9 atta atqui scalis.
14 tunc M¹, tune M².
16 nundinam M¹, nundina M².
21 *mg.* lutescit lutea fit.
134, 4 lenitudinem.
22 faciunt M¹, facient M².
23 unde alligurrire.
mg. adligurrire vorare.
27 priopo demio M¹, de meo M².
31 stipendium acceptitasti.
35 lavernea cui M¹, laverna ea cui M².
36 furti scelebrassit M¹, furtis celebrassit M².
135, 1 Simesses facis musas.
4 Thucca M¹, Tucca M².
11 vespere M¹, vesperi M².
23 lenitatis M¹, levitatis M².
24 subsilis M¹, non subsilis M², ac plaudis et ab aratro posces oronum.
136, 1 macritudinem.
11 constat M¹, constet M².

16 et amiseritudo eorum nulla est M¹, ulla est M².
18 ubi aspexi.
24 ne dici M¹, neque dici M².
26 nausutus M¹, nasutus M².
137, 3 attius M¹, atticus M².
5 matris similis. *mg.* matrisca matri similis.
6 ut meum patrem ulscisci queam.
15 sere id Caelius M¹, id om. M².
24 pro mestifices.
26 myctiris paupercula pulmenta M¹, pulmentaria M², lib. xx.
mg. myctilis pauper apparatus.
28 se mictyris haec est M¹, haec est meri M².
138, 1 atrenavis M¹, etre n. M².
2 *mg.* madore infusione.
4 madore infirmarentur.
6 mercantibus M¹, mercatibus M².
9 maceries M¹, maceria est M².
mg. maceries maceratio.
15 et si maxime id quod.
16 *mg.* mordicus a mordendo.
17 et flamma M¹, e f. M².
21 *mg.* quod mortem ferat.
22 mendicaries M¹, mendicarier M².
25 niministrantur illumnunc M¹, boniministrantur i. M².
28 mertare mergere M¹, mertaret mergeret M².
29 fortassean sit quod M¹, quos M².
139, 5 subdicimur M¹, subducimur M².

NONIUS MARCELLUS.

7 atque ego occulsero fonteme M¹, fontem M².
   mg. oculsero occuluero.
11 pl. Tr. o. s. m. m. aquiloniam i. s. f. M¹, pl. Tr. o. s. m. m. infidelem etc. M².
18 magnificio M¹, facio M².
23 peragant M¹, peragrant M².
25 dicitis sevius M¹, dictis sevis M².
26 *mg.* morsicatim a morsu.
28 mutatiliter, and 29.
30 *mg.* mordicibus mordisicus.
32 asinis M¹, asini M².
140, 2 labyrinthorum claviculis M¹, lab. hortum cl. M².
   mg. sic fingebatur quasi essent claviculi in parietibus aut in veste.
4 facias M¹, facies M².
9 dein certuali fluctu ut sicut pareret M¹, d. certe alii f. ut sicum M².
14 proferre posset et mansu M¹, proferro posset mansu M².
26 canis.
29 id bellum.
141, 1 invenerit M¹, inveniat M².
4 medie M¹, medio M², acutum modo varro modo.
5 canat.
19 *mg.* maceries parietes.
26 et quo M¹, ex quo M².
142, 1 marsyppii.
3 galli M¹, om. M².
5 *mg.* modiperatores moderata imperantes.
8 *mg.* magniloquentia eloquentia.

13 *mg.* male audiam maledicta feram.
17 sacrorum M¹, saccorum M².
18 voluerint M¹, voluerunt M².
143, 4 medias trinos.
   mg. quasi medias partes tenentes quos nos corrupte mastinos dicimus. mediastrinos non solum balneatores sed et curatores.
6 viculum aristocratem M¹, vilicum aristocratem M².
13 novicium.
14 neminisitum pro nullalius M¹, nullius M².
15 meminis miseret M¹, neminis me miseret M².
   mg. nullius misereor quia nullus miseretur mei.
28 formae figurae.
144, 7 nisi tu nevis.
12 albunt M¹, abluunt M².
   mg. nitidant albent.
16 advenient.
17 quapripedantur sonipedum.
24 nervos M¹, nervus M².
145, 2 clancula M¹, e lacuna M².
4 *mg.* nidulantur nidum faciunt.
11 quidam cancrum.
14 aut cum nepa esset dubium.
17 angulos M¹, anguigulos M².
24 iis quibus.
25 exhiberetur M¹, exhiberet M².
26 obtutum avoce.
27 solitu M¹, solita M², at tibiis M¹, at tibias M².
28 obscelavit M¹, obscevavit M², and 146. 2.

NONIUS MARCELLUS.

146, 6 *mg.* obscevavit scevum fecit, scevum sinistrum malum.
oppirasque offert M¹, oppiparas M².
7 *mg.* quidam existimant id dici obbam quod nos nunc cuppam dicimus.
8 triclinearis.
12 plotio M¹, potio M².
25 in tutum in totum M¹, in totum om. M².
26 obscurare facere M¹, obscure f. M².
29 exstinctas jam atque o. M¹, exstincta tam o. M².

147, 2 qui inillas tacta M¹, quin illa tacta M².
7 *mg.* obstigillare obstare.
11 qui quod invidis tanto scriptori obstrigilandi M¹, obstringillandi M², causa ut cum praeclara quaedam quae laudes.
15 decerneretur aut ne iterum fieret consul.

148, 1 *mg.* olivitatem oleae nimietatem.
2 omnes cum lucernae M¹, lucerna M².
mg. inlucubrare est ad lucem lucernae degere.
5 esui ut optume M¹, ut om. M².
10 *mg.* orbitum ab orbe dictum.
11 motu M¹, motur M².
12 opulescere, *mg.* opuliscere ditescere.
13 opulescere M¹, opuliscere M².
23 absedet.

25 *mg.* psilotrum est confectio quaedam ex calce et auripigmento qui pili adimuntur.
149, 7 habeat M¹, habet M².
11 quam fidem et justitiam M¹, qua fide et justitia M².
13 octingentum, *mg.* octingentum octingenta.
14 lib. iii M¹, iiii M², auri pondo mille octingentum.
15 hieronimole M¹, heronamole M².
16 *mg.* panus panucla.
18 subteminis M¹, subteminus M².
21 inquam M¹, inquem M².
29 Lucilius.
30 penulamento.
150, 2 penulamentum M¹, peniculamentum M².
6 scio haercle utrum bella te indie ac prognariter M¹, belle a te indica p. M².
17 *mg.* ducibilitate facilitate.
22 annicula M¹, anicula M².
30 populacia aut nugalia vel puerilia M¹, populatia ut M².
31 et dum M¹, e dum M².
35 tontrix M¹, tonstrix M².
impultrix M¹, impulsatrix M².
37 *mg.* perpetuitassent perpetuam fecissent.
151, 3 omasum pernam gallus.
5 praeciso.
8 fluvius hiberus oritur M¹, fluvium hiberum is o. M².
13 alutamenicato M¹, alutamen cato M².

16 pientolam M¹, piencolam M².
18 est hortator.
19 que M¹, qua M², excursum et exhortamenta.
29 *mg.* perplexabile perplexum.
32 ea dici voluit.
152, 1 quin ipse quidem t.
6 *mg.* picos grypas.
13 pristino M¹, pistrino M².
14 nepistoris M¹, necpistoris M². nomen erat qui nisi ejus ru M¹, ruri M², far pinsebat nominativa M¹, nominata M², quod eo pinsunt.
17 proinde ut.
22 putridam.
29 praebitio nimia? nuam.
153, 4 dicitur M¹, dicatur M².
7 die proximi.
9 dictum est M¹, est om. M².
10 properatim dictum est M¹, p. id est M².
12 xxviiii M¹, xxviii M², *mg.* permities pernicies.
14 permitiae.
23 perbiteris, and 26, and 29.
29 quos quis.
31 pateor M¹, fateor M². proferre (?) M¹, proterre M².
154, 5 evirescere M¹, revirescere M², revirdiscere M², *mg.* puellascere revirdiscere.
9 m manum pape palestrios M¹, mi m. p. palestricos M².
11 ergo perdidi.
13 praesente coram vel praesentibus.

mg. praesente coram.
18 munia M¹, mania M².
19 dono donare.
25 protulim M¹, protuli M², item p. i. adprimitus.
155, 1 et consules M¹, eo c. M².
14 praefracte M¹, praefractum M².
23 fierique M¹, ferique M².
28 polentia p. a pollendo M¹, polendo M².
29 polentia.
30 pollere.
33 adolabilis M¹, adulabilis M².
mg. adolabilis sine dolore.
34 pauxillo M¹, pausillo M².
156, 1 decem M¹, plus decem M². pauxillis M¹, pausillisper M².
6 *mg.* pueritia innocentia.
11 qua sinit M¹, quas s. M².
17 pupam M¹, pupum M².
25 ineridebo M¹, in eiybo M².
26 trocto medicarios M¹, toctro m. M².
157, 3 fecit M¹, facit M².
4 pretium M¹, pretio M².
8 feci te M¹, fecit te M².
14 pauciens.
17 paucies, and 19, and 20.
19 tis M¹, tus M², acini quiinurbem p. v. s.
21 pollictores M¹, pollectores M², pollinctores M².
mg. pollictores funeratores.
22 medicis M¹, medicos M².
23 pollictores M¹, pollectores M², aestate videas.
25 pollictori M¹, pollinctori M².

(21)

158, 13 *mg.* prosperari M¹, prosferari M², impetrari.
27 se vel vivum M¹, seu eluvium M², dummadore addere puellum sexagesimos ultra nutri.
32 quadrupedes M¹, quadrupes M².
36 lascivum.
159, 1 nisi nostrique M¹, niri n. M².
3 dilarat M¹, delirat M².
mg. ut nostra colera.
14 quis M¹, qui M².
22 *mg.* putret putridum est.
23 hoc corpus.
27 iustrum.
32 invadi vermibus e. p. in eorum posse.
36 peculantia.
37 *mg.* procet prohibet.
160, 2 egones M¹, eligones M².
10 Pac. doloremtes oromin efflectas M¹, dulorestes oromine flectas M², *mg.* prolixitudinem a prolixo.
12 *mg.* perfica perfice.
16 adeo nolo nudo.
20 morbi genus.
23 internicionem M¹, interitionem M².
29 in ea provincia.
161, 1 adfecta sunt perfecta sunt perfecta M¹, perfecta sunt om. M².
3 mitescere M¹, mitiscere M².
4 commoti M¹, commoto M².
mg. patritum patrium quod nos paternum dicimus.

5 avito M¹, abito M².
8 percidere vel decidere M¹, percedere v. decedere M², percidere v. decidere M³.
mg. percedere ut decedere.
9 concisum non concesum et quod quidam percisum M¹, percesum M².
12 qui M¹, quis M².
15 *mg.* animam aebeti corpori pro sale dari ciceronem dixisse, *mg.* putidum putens non putre.
18 *mg.* percursionem excursum.
19 brevi tempore percursiones.
20 *mg.* praefestinatim festine.
24 libro iiii M¹, iii M².
162, 3 mitterent M¹, permitterent M².
4 *mg.* proicere effundere.
15 animadvertere M¹, animo advertere M².
17 *mg.* paupertina paupera.
20 *mg.* plumarium a plumando.
23 *mg.* purpurascit purpureum fit.
24 ceruleum aut M¹, c. at M².
26 *mg.* perpendiculi a perpendendo.
163, 7 tam variae multa M¹, t. varia et tam multa M².
15 pristino.
17 libro iiii M¹, iii M².
19 terentes M¹, teretes M².
25 varro de vita M¹, varro sepe de v. M².
26 Apolloni.
164, 4 rotunde M¹, rutunde M².

(22)

NONIUS MARCELLUS.

165, 9 recipocra,*mg*. reciproca recipe.
10 andromedarus sus M¹, andromeda riscus M².
12 *mg*. repedare pede iterare reverti.
13 ut Roma vitet.
22 redostit viam cometem obtet M¹, obbiet M².
23 vel in M¹, velint M². assit M¹, ac sit M². redostire M¹, redhostire M², sponsum.
25 repuerascere in puerum redire M¹, in puerum redire om. M². *mg*. repuerascere in puerum redire.
166, 1 *mg*. rhetorissat rhetorice loquitur.
2 dolasti M¹, dalasti M².
4 pamones M¹, pulmones M². *mg*. ramites pulmones.
11 pythaulesymflet M¹, p. inflet M². tibi has M¹, tibias M².
13 apptitus M¹, apθpiticus M². aspotagrosus M¹, ac podagrosus M².
14 ramite M¹, ramice M².
29 at ego M¹, ad e. M².
167, 3 redurare a. c. i. q. dicitur obdurare M¹, obturare M², *mg*. redurare aperire.
18 reda vehiculum M¹, vehiculum om. M². *mg*. reda vehiculum.
20 recentiorum novorum M¹, novorum om. M². *mg*. recentiorum novorum.

22 illo M¹, ullo M².
168, 2 *mg*. reiculas oves debiles.
4 saepe enim.
5 inquid M¹, inquit M².
6 *mg*. saltuatim bellicatim. *mg*. vellicatim avulsis sententiis a loco in locum.
7 *mg*. una estate forsitan debet esse quia tunc fiunt bella vel una etate uno seculo.
9 vellicatim M¹, bellicatim M².
11 mihique dividum s. n. papiri nolevi? M¹, nolevii? nolevu? M², *mg*. scapum dividum.
13 qui M¹, quid M².
19 libro xvii censores inquit p. scipio &c.
20 et cum M¹, ecum M². n. strigosum M¹, stricosum M², e. m. h. s. equitum.
26 *mg*. ab altitudine.
169, 4 georgicorum libro iiii M¹, in bucolicis M².
8 es crate M¹, es crapte M², crupede strictibilesordide.
16 aequoretto totras M¹, ae. toto troas M².
20 sic ille manus.
21 scapres pro scabres.
22 quam excrabrent.
30 simat deprimit.
31 si movet amaximadnares M¹, s. m. aximadnares M².
32 varro M¹, cicero M², de or.
170, 4 cum manus M¹, cui M².
13 quod consectura M¹, consecutura M².

NONIUS MARCELLUS.

170, 14 mg. sempiterne semper.
15 med populoque M¹, medo puloque M².
16 sata M¹, santra M².
20 exossabo illum M¹, e. ego illum M².
21 mg. scriptat cunctatur et est rarum.
24 succidam M¹, succidiam M². mg. succidiam successionem.
25 ipsius agricole M¹, ipsi a. M².
171, 1 suicidia M¹, succidia M². mg. succidiam laridum.
2 signatam integram M¹, integram om. M². mg. signatam integram.
4 redere.
9 abibis M¹, abiis M².
10 sugillare M¹, suggillare M². mg. sugillare claudere.
14 satullem M¹, satulem M².
16 etad singulum.
18 cingulum M¹, singulum M².
20 singulum esset M¹, s. esse M².
22 veteres spem.
25 jactato nominatuo voluntatis M¹, volitantis M².
28 habitatem M¹, habitantem M².
29 scalpurrire scalpere M¹, scalpere om. M², mg. scalpurrire scalpere.
30 obscepit M¹, obcepit M², ibi scalpurire ungulis.
172, 1 somnurnas, and 3.
9 termeextrimorum ame externorum agros M¹, tamen etiam externorum a. M².
11 xxviii M¹, xxviiii M².

12 satias te jam M¹, te om. M².
14 ut M¹, ubi M².
18 terrae M¹, terra M².
21 theobogenes.
23 a somno si jacet M¹, ad somnos vacet M².
173, 10 ut mihi hi a. M¹, hi om. M².
13 libro iiii M¹, iii M².
20 sodalis M¹, sodales M², cicero. mg. sodales socii.
25 qui subiti M¹, quid s. M², mg. escivit commovit.
174, 2 dulebra M¹, delubra M². coeli maris M¹, c. tu maris M².
5 scopulis M¹, scopuli M².
14 aiumquamquam M¹, haudquaquam M².
19 philosophae scriptiones.
20 aeneidis aut decio.
23 dicam te metu a. s. addubitare M¹, aut dubitare M².
24 et quoniam—Satyrarum lib. i om. M¹, add. M².
27 nam tamen ae. t. hanc.
31 mg. speratus sponsus.
33 adducere M¹, adduce M².
34 ad puellam M¹, at p. M².
36 odit M¹, odi M².
175, 5 fluctifrago M¹, fluctivago M².
6 umescunt M¹, uvescunt M².
14 hinc M¹, hic M².
20 una hoc ceperis.
22 propterea M¹, preterea M². subsicuia M¹, subsiciva M².
23 succidaneum M¹, succedaneum M².
31 sarcinator Lucilius, mg. sarcinatorem sutorem.

(24)

176, 14 scenatilis v. scenaticus pro
scenico M¹, schenatilis v.
schenaticus pro schenico
M², and 16, and 18, and *mg.*
20 tum simus M¹, cum s. M².
26 *mg.* unde simphonia dicitur
concentus vocum diversa-
rum.
27 gallinacius.
177, 2 salabras M¹, salebras M², m.
Tullius. *mg.* salebrae a saltu
dictae, salebrae ab exili-
endo compas solent vul-
gares dicere.
3 devidere M¹, dividere M².
mg. devidere bene videre.
6 in salebra cupit enim dicere.
8 sublestum M¹, subletum M².
frivolum M¹, fribolum M².
9 infamam M¹, infamiam M².
12 oratori et quasi superlectiles
suppellex M¹, suplex M².
16 nec inprobum M¹, ne i. M².
17 sportas Sallustius. *mg.* sportas
aut ab sportu M¹, spartu
M², quasi sparteas aut ab
sportanda, sunt vasa quaedam ex sparto facta in illis
etiam positus fuit sanctus
Paullus.
20 acris rebus M¹, varis r. M².
22 *mg.* sodes socius unde sodalis.
178, 5 necteret M¹, ne tetret M².
6 tentinnerit M¹, tetinerit M².
21 *mg.* testatim minutim.
22 istam calvam colafis.
26 haeccine M¹, hecine M², nobis
terne.

179, 3 subi sumat M¹, sibi s. M².
5 area M¹, aerea M².
7 mangonis M¹, magonis M²,
esse v. s.
9 quaeso tae utrum.
17 funestatu este et tonsu M¹,
funestat veste tonsu M².
20 Pl. Pers. tuburcinari s. m. v.
reliquias M¹, corr. M².
23 cessas M¹, cessat M².
25 tibificabile M¹, tabificabile M².
mg. tibificabile, tabificum.
26 parneti M¹, parneci M².
32 tertritudo M¹, tetritudo M².
180, 2 te temnere M¹, te om. M².
9 levis tippula M¹, ut levis t. M².
11 leviores quam.
17 uno in loco.
19 transsennam M¹, transsenna
M².
20 strepitu coronam.
24 *mg.* trutina a trutinando.
26 trutinare M¹, trutina M².
181, 7 et sunt M¹, ut s. M².
8 trucenus M¹, tricinus M².
11 *mg.* tristis mulier.
18 eccos signis M¹, segnis M².
23 tenta dictum pro.
28 deucaligine M¹, deucalione M².
30 ordine M¹, ordines M².
32 tenta atque M¹, tentae aque M².
34 *mg.* trititiae tristitia.
182, 1 quid istic e. u. alligataeque.
3 tristia ante M¹, tristitia a. M².
14 insilui.
15 ubi M¹, ibi M².
16 ille lanigeras M¹, hec l. M².
19 intitione.

NONIUS MARCELLUS.

22 pro vile habuit M¹, pro om. M².
24 ut corpus vulgata sum M¹, corpus vulgavit suum M², ut om.
28 vulgare decoepit M¹, v. coepit M².

183, 1 vegeat M¹, vegetat M².
5 veget M¹, viget M², veget.
7 movile M¹, mobile M².
9 est audax M¹, est om. M².
12 simulaturus M², insimulaturus M¹.
18 v. per viscera M¹, per viscera om. M², *mg.* visceratim per viscera.

184, 1 frustando M¹, frustrando M².
14 capere M¹, captare M².
19 vargitus M¹, vagitus M².
20 ite miscetur.
21 vetustas et antiquitas. *mg.* vetustas sapientia.

185, 7 desiderantur M¹, deserantur M².
15 vastatus a natura et M¹, vastus ab natura et M², vastus et humano M², ab natura om.
21 venerans M¹, verans M².

186, 4 horpinos.
7 huic M¹, hic M².
vilicar M¹, vilicabar M².
9 huic M¹, hic M².
16 tracto pedes quas M¹, quasi M². g. e. inter inolem quae insulamari v. c. honestium M¹, hostium M².
19 *mg.* volentia a voluntate.
28 vici M¹, vinci M².

31 vescum fastidio vivere M¹, v. cum fastidio v. M².

187, 4 imbecillis M¹, imbecillus M².
6 quiddam M¹, quid clam M². facit M¹, fecit M². voluptare M¹, volup M².
7 *mg.* virgindemiam a virgis ut vindemiam.
8 vel demtionem vel deceptionem M¹, decreptionem M².
9 agit hanc M¹, angit hanc M².
18 addere in b.
20 verruncam M¹, verrucam M².

188, 4 rexamanius M¹, rex an manius M².
7 crescent M¹, crescunt M².
15 vicatim Sisenna conplures. *mg.* vicatim per vices M¹, vicos M².
18 vultuosum cicero M¹, v. tristem c. M², *mg.* vultuosum tristem.
24 cornelia M¹, corneliana M².

189, 3 dicundi.
7 versutiloqux M¹, versutiloquax M², *mg.* versutiloquax versutus.
8 et conjunctione M¹, ex c. M².
16 vincere M¹, vincire M².
19 quibus M¹, quibusdam M²; adeo M¹, abeo M².
20 toxis M¹, togis M², olim non reges nostri.
22 *mg.* vervecem.

190, 27 medeom M¹, medico mi M².
29 rubor M¹, robur M².
34 aut acrius M¹, ut a. M².

191, 11 aen lib. ii om.
22 dua evarro M¹, duo varro M².

NONIUS MARCELLUS. 119

24 ut aspexit M¹, cujus ut a. M².
34 emnis M¹, amnis M², nec mons.
192, 4 alta in omni.
9 genere verrite M¹, gemina everrite M².
10 abstergete.
13 buxis M¹, buxus M².
18 jus incolomem M¹, j. incolumem M².
20 mala est ergo, cf. 1. 9.
27 usaeque volantes M¹, visaeque v. M².
28 neutri sunt generis.
31 l. libro ii quaquae M¹, quaque M².
193, 3 infracta M¹, anfracta M².
7 attigit meam M¹, meta M², aevitas.
8 umquam M¹, inquam M².
13 acili M¹, acini M².
14 ardebat M¹, arebat M².
15 sarrano M¹, serrano M².
23 alvo sed alius auctoritatis.
26 majores accubitionem aepularum M¹, aepularem M².
quasi vitae M¹, quia v. M².
habent M¹, haberet M².
194, 10 infoebis M¹, in imbris M².
25 saepe neutri M¹, feminini M².
31 fortunae scendere.
195, 17 libro xii M¹, xiii M².
23 cupressos.
28 gallia post carrus M¹, carros M².
adcurat M¹, ac curat M², u. polytos.
196, 2 saepe quaestus masculini M¹, quaestus om. M².

197, 4 atheriis M¹, atheris M².
6 hi sunt caelis M¹, caelus M².
8 caelis M¹, caelus M².
16 generis masculini M¹, genere masculino M².
24 corbes corbulas varro.
28 quis et g.
34 quisquis tu es.
198, 3 ego vero confiteor.
4 hyporisticos.
5 caniculam M¹, canaliculam M².
10 immundam M¹, immundum M².
12 vaccillat.
13 fueris M¹, fuerit M².
28 accubitarum M¹, accubituram M².
m. magis s. exercitata M¹, exercitare M².
30 ratione M¹, rare M².
35 quale qui M¹, cul est qui M².
199, 10 neutrum catellis M¹, n. a catellis M².
22 disperavit M¹, disperivit M².
quaerit M¹, civerit M².
25 subit M¹, sibit M².
28 superius M¹, supernus M².
29 q. et arborum M¹, et om. M².
31 relinquit.
200, 5 neviri Plautus M¹, neviri om. M².
11 veniense caseum.
20 plena iasolorum M¹, plenai i. M².
27 si vultis hoc onus.
36 meritus a nobis.
38 suppa tortas copulas.
201, 3 caepae? taepae? talpae?

NONIUS MARCELLUS.

201, 6 avi et avi M¹, et atavi M², n.
c. alium ac cepe.
9 cepe f.
10 acris M¹, acri M².
assiduae M¹, assiduo M².
13 acria est M¹, est om. M², ut est.
sinapi M¹, sinape M².
20 lib. xx.
27 andealbueibus M¹, cibus M².
31 lib. iii M¹, iiii M².
202, 5 ad eandem voluptatem.
7 iter M¹, inter M².
19 graus M¹, graius M².
26 gerundum morem senseo M¹, censeo M².
203, 4 masculini Plautus, om. nam.
6 genere masculino M¹, generis masculini M².
masculini decentiam M¹, m. nam decentiam M².
11 animi despicientia M¹, animi om. M².
12 lib. iiii omnium M¹, lib. ii in omnium M².
15 feminini M. Tullius M¹, f. ut plerumque masculini M².
16 quid tunc M¹, tum M², cum es.
17 lib. ii M¹, lib. i M².
20 ut manifestum est n.
21 debitio pecuniae.
30 cultus M¹, cultis M².
204, 1 horum inventa M¹, eventa M².
7 pondens M¹, pendens M².
11 errantia M¹, errantiae M².
morigebor M¹, morigerabor M².
22 ut hiserat M¹, uti serat M².

23 ervi illam M¹, ervil!am M².
28 fimbriatum frontem.
30 innata M¹, innato M².
205, 2 quis M¹, quos M².
ut vitare M¹, ut om. M².
4 petilis M¹, petulis M².
17 huminitasque a.
29 animi M¹, anni M².
35 seranaecae M¹, seranacae M².
ci li nomina M¹, nomine M².
206, 2 augustam M¹, agustam M².
22 cras credo.
26 fulmentum M¹, fulmenta M².
28 aeis M¹, aeneis M², atque aeneis.
30 sucit huic suldum M¹, sulcum M².
32 foco M¹, fico M².
35 generis famulatu M¹, g. in famulatu M².
207, 4 Vesuvium M¹, Vessuvium M².
16 militem M¹, gutturem M².
32 gelu sed multo otius M¹, ocius M².
vento M¹, venio M².
208, 3 lib. ii qui aquantum M¹, lib. ii libyi qui aquatum M².
10 implicatus M¹, implicatur M².
12 herebat mucro gladium.
28 munera ulla horrea.
209, 3 et id genus herbae M¹, herba M².
11 cum M¹, tum M², aratorum.
18 portae verro M¹, verre M².
21 oratore perfecto M¹, perfectum M², hac M¹, om. M², video hanc primum.
22 de media M¹, e m. M².

NONIUS MARCELLUS. 121

25 deserendus M¹, disserendus M².
26 protheosilao dam ineunt M¹, protesilao dam iniunt M²; cachinnos M¹, cacinnos M².
210, 6 lenti calido elvella trapula romicae.
10 luce M¹, luci M², diripiamus M¹, disripiamus M².
11 lucanas M¹, lucanam M², lucaniam M². luciclaro latam non latam M¹, non latam om. M².
19 per sane M¹, persa nunc M².
21 neutri generis M¹, n. est generis M².
22 labium M¹, lavium M².
36 generis sunt neutri.
211, 8 uni rebus ipsis alteri assumptis.
9 et feminino genere.
16 lusus vel ludus.
20 artificio proprioe M¹, a. e proprio M².
29 ad dextera M¹, ad dextra M².
212, 6 latrinas g. f. et est latrina M¹, lavatrina M².
8 latrina lan quae neutro.
10 gustus M¹, gustes M².
14 agerebant M¹, aggerebant M².
15 lib. iiii om.
16 laum genere masculino M¹, lanitium genere neutro M², lib. iii.
25 habebant ibi nunc.
29 spero rem M¹, perjorem M².
30 lib. vi M¹, lib. viii M².

213, 13 acri crepitantes M¹, a. crepantes M².
21 se meminis M¹, se minis M².
32 magnum esse (me est *in mg.*) non proba vindemia M¹, vindemedia M².
214, 7 masculino feminino nevius M¹, feminino om. M².
11 acciti M¹, iacciti M². depontaremur murfitverus M¹, depontare murmur fit verus M².
13 muliebris M¹, mulieris M². generis est M¹, est om. M².
14 xvi M¹, xvii M².
18 miserii M¹, miserie M², munium.
20 neutri M¹, om. M². majus M¹, majores M¹, sunt.
21 expectant M¹, spectant M².
23 nundinum M¹, nundino M².
24 ac rusticus romanus.
27 rerum humanarum.
215, 5 surene M¹, serene M². pedes dici M¹, dici om. M².
8 alia denepos M¹, ilia danepos M².
10 lectum sed doctos M¹, lectum est sed M².
15 tracitare M¹, traitare M².
19 alternis tonsas M¹, a. idem tonsas M².
22 odium parit.
23 obsequela M¹, obsequila M², *passim.*
31 fimbriana M¹, fimbriane M².
32 grave scarique M¹, grave om. M².

NONIUS MARCELLUS.

216, 8 ex salo? M¹, sala M².
12 concas quod ethinos M¹, c. echinos M², om. quod.
13 sollertiamque eam.
25 rerum humanarum xxij M¹, xxiii M².
26 Homerum secutos.
37 ad puteos greges M¹, a. p. aut alta g. M².
38 currentem ilignis M¹, elignis M².

217, 2 stagnae M¹, stagna M².
6 cocis M¹, cogis M².
13 lib. iiii M¹, iii M².
14 protundit M¹, profundit M².
25 cibi quae M¹, qua M².
29 paritudo et partitio M¹, paritio M².
32 prope adest.
34 partitionis M¹, partionis M².

218, 5 praesepium M¹, praesepim M².
8 ab illis his M¹, is M², habebat.
9 unam M¹, vinam M².
18 veocios M¹, veotios M².
32 creto? M¹, cretum M², purpurissum.
34 Manlius novis M¹, novius M².

219, 1 Melanippo.
16 potestate M¹, post aetate M².
19 masculino M¹, feminino M².
23 adstuc periculum fieri in filia.
31 varro M¹, parvo M², spatio.
32 penemque o. ceterum aliam praebere penum.
35 meam in p. M¹, in om. M².

220, 9 noprandis M¹, adnoprandis M².
11 papaveram M¹, papaverem M².

15 obsecro lide.
18 lucinius M¹, licinius M².
19 vulgani.
27 pedis unus ingens.
29 supfurabatur M¹, suffurabatur M².
31 tum c. p. pluiam.

221, 4 cantent M¹, cantant M².
5 munatius M¹, oratius M².
10 boni secunde M¹, bonis unde M².
11 Lucinius M¹, Licinius M².
12 deligata M¹, deligat M², a. p. deligantur.
17 rictus rideat? M¹, r. ricta M².
19 nudantia M¹, nudantes M².
20 ut signum M¹, rictum M², m. q. e. paulo sit attritus M¹, attritius M².
26 sepeliet M¹, sepelicet M².
31 in verrinarum siciliemsi M¹, siciriemsi M².
33 plenum M¹, pleno M², plenum M².

222, 1 auctoribus M¹, actoribus M².
11 affuisse.
16 Tarquilinios M¹, Tarquinios M².
nec quam redditionis M¹, reditionis M².
20 sexus (x *in rasura*), and 23, and 25.
27 admissam.

223, 1 patebat M¹, petebat M².
4 femini varro M¹, femini neutro v. M².
18 sordidum siistum (ii *in ras.*).
36 spari quod est genus teli.

224, 9 eheu eheu me M¹, heu me M².
  lambere M¹, labere M².
 17 vepatrum.
 20 Aeneae M¹, Aenea M².
 24 subcuboneum M¹, subcuboneam M².
 25 abirer M¹, arbitrer M², subcuboneam.
 32 prometinensibus M¹, pometinensibus M².
 36 quod ego huc praecessi M¹, processi M².
  scema M¹, schema M², *et pass.*
225, 4 antiqua est peccatores M¹, antiquo et spectatores M².
 8 haec M¹, ec M², fodiebam.
 10 quoddam M¹, quod dum M², fodiendo.
 15 feminino genere appellatur M¹, f. appellatur genere M².
 23 si canis M¹, sic c. M².
 26 camo M¹, culmo M².
 27 et quibus M¹, e q.M².
 30 non aliquo M¹, aliquod M², om. est.
226, 3 luctusque horrificiali M¹, luctuque horrificali M².
 7 suasiones M¹, suasione M².
 10 ibam M¹, scibam M².
 16 hedycis M¹, hedycus M².
 18 nostrae essent seplesiae.
 23 prostratura M¹, pro statura M².
 26 vii M¹, viii M².
 34 ad stirpem M¹, a s. M².
227, 9 aurium tactus M¹, tactus om. M².
 10 et actionum M¹, et tactionum M².

 12 talis etiam est? M¹, t. eti e M².
 13 tonitus M¹, tonitrus M².
 20 masculini est.
 24 nyctegresias scendit M¹, nyctegresi ascendit M².
 26 feminini accius M¹, f. neutri a. M².
228, 7 torqueas aureas et scuta M¹, torques aureae scuta M².
 11 sacris et M¹, et om. M².
 12 et torques.
 16 terret et.
 25 infectori M¹, inpectori M².
 28 trabeaeque.
229, 2 torpore M¹, torpor M².
 4 obprepsit M¹, obpressit M².
 13 pleni M¹, pledi M².
  conta M¹, contra M¹, caudes audes.
 14 cum in M¹, cum i in M².
  e. l. ac purpure operis toro M¹, purpureo peris toro M².
 18 nepraenettarte.
 25 tartaris.
 26 tantum t. q. s. M¹, t. q. s. om. M².
 30 ut eorum M¹, uterum M².
230, 1 diisperi.
 26 discicit M¹, dissicit M².
 28 vel levi vulgum.
 29 in orono M¹, cycno M².
 30 praecepit M¹, praecipit M².
 31 ut in melle c. si centum M¹, sic centum M².
231, 12 portoperipocori vepra est veprecula M¹. sma decaelo M¹, decaedo M², cacatum, M², *in mg.*

(31)

231, 25 ad mani M¹, a m. M².
27 aethera.
232, 3 operam superet.
4 adminicultarem M¹, amminicularem M².
qui videt alium M¹, quid vidit aliud M².
6 pro victa M¹, vita M².
7 persecutus aristoteles, om. est.
17 illa M¹, illum M².
23 fabulare M¹, fabulavere M².
24 dominum suum.
26 egone ut ea.
28 haec pietas M¹, haec vero p. M², nequa isti gratia.
29 expiatione.
30 anima est s.
32 vulnere M¹, vulnera M².
233, 8 anfetet animae M¹, anima M².
10 animam faetidat M¹, fetidat M².
13 adsedit M¹, assedi M².
16 hoc cepsitio M¹, h. cepsio M².
18 frios M¹, frigios M².
19 vel furorem M¹, v. furiosum M².
23 auxilium M¹, auxilio M².
27 pericli.
30 libidines innumerabiles M¹, l. quae sunt i. M².
31 terrent M¹, tenerent M².
33 quaereretur.
36 quos animosi.
41 tessalia indolita M¹, thessalia indomita M², subigantque domemque.
234, 7 sudes vadem M¹, sudo sualem M².
13 lib. iiii ea denique.

16 ut pulcritudo M¹, ut enim p. M².
26 xxviiii.
27 si id quod.
35 convivium M¹, conviviam M².
235, 2 demer hic M¹, hinc M², colomen ala M¹, ale M².
4 funibus.
7 hoc seherere.
8 pericula M¹, pellicula M².
13 ullam inesse.
15 obcere M¹, obcepere M².
17 rebus M¹, prestibus M², et mg.
25 rursus M¹, rursum M².
26 mimanta M¹, minanta M².
29 cecidisset amesenem M¹, cecidisse tamen s. M².
30 constet M¹, constat M².
32 aequalem eum.
34 fidi aequales M¹, fide requales M².
36 aequalemte marcidemiden M¹, aequalem timarcidem M².
38 fili qui M¹, filium qui M².
236, 1 qui primo.
5 sed tum vestram etiam aetatem M¹, s. cum vestra etiam aetate M².
6 senum M¹, serenum M².
11 perstrenue M¹, praestrenue M².
14 *mg.* nudatum, latus haurit apertum.
18 invictariam M¹, invictaria M². dictatorem sibi munia M¹, d. uni sibi M².
20 nisi quod causu M¹, casu M².
26 de vita p. r. lib. i.

(32)

	33	natibus apertibus M¹, apertis M².	241,	11 filisto? M¹, filippo M².
237,	5	patri M¹, patris M².		17 acvim M¹, actum M².
	7	socratum M¹, socratium M², mississe tipum M¹, mississe aristippum M².		25 Aen. lib. v M¹, Georg. lib. ii M².
				29 pertuleris? perculeris? M¹, pertuderis M².
	10	verum qui insimiles M¹, quin simules M².	242,	1 admonere est.
				9 ambit M¹, ambiit M².
	14	ab alimento M¹, ab alendo M².		28 melivem M¹, me bilem M².
	15	magnum vel gloriosum.		30 vel qui M¹, vel eos qui M².
	20	fatum M¹, factum M².		36 ubi quod.
	36	placito M¹, placo M².	243,	7 vastitatudine M¹, vastitudine M².
238,	6	turpidinem M¹, turpitudinem M².		13 actum r. M¹, adductum r. M².
	15	sed cum animo a.		20 quam procul.
	20	concedetibi M¹, conceditibi M².		23 profugos.
				34 augebes sed conpron.
	28	agere M¹, agerem M². in j. si quod M¹, quid M², quo M².		36 vulsci M¹, volsci M².
				38 si quo stu vinis actus M¹, actis M², opost.
239,	2	imitatione M¹, imitatore M².		43 impellare M¹, impellere M².
	15	mendaci.		47 umquam memiseriis M¹, u. emiseriis M².
	18	exiberes M¹, exibes M².		
	19	ac lectum M¹, ac laetum M².		48 ardifet alampade M¹, ardifeta lampade M².
	23	habonium M¹, abonium M².		
	34	Varro de r. r. — delectatus esset om.		aridat M¹, arida M², agat a. a.
			244,	13 laborum M¹, laborem M².
240,	2	accipite nunc, mg. accipite ergo animis audite.		29 actione tunc tertia M¹, a. tertia tunc M¹.
	8	prosus M¹, prorsus M², atque prolixius. mg. pascere, rex accipiebat in amplis.		30 quieti prope praeter.
				31 grecorum otium. accommodatum M¹, accommodati M².
	13	autumus tu M¹, optumus t. M².		
	25	fulgere M¹, fulgorem M². emitere M¹, emittere M².	245,	8 auritopet M¹, auris et M², sonus.
	42	quod altius M¹, q. alterius M². acceptum M¹, acetum M², alterius sic acre ut melymetium.		11 anceps dubium M¹, a. est dubium M².
				17 cessare versione M¹, cessar reversione M².

245, 34 venit cum M¹, v. alii cum M².
36 sublire M¹, sussilire M².
37 nonaqua M¹, novaqua M².
246, 5 neve qui adtingat.
9 optantibus.
10 austare, *mg.* auscultare.
14 sembono M¹, embono M².
17 ne ego vel tantis M¹, ne ego illos v. M².
25 cicero de senectute cogi M¹, m. tullius de senectute M².
29 a. excutere producere M¹, excutere om. M².
31 aequor mare campus M¹, mare om. M².
247, 7 morbo jube M¹, jure M².
19 acerbo M¹, acerbum M².
21 acerbo et in multis ita M¹, et in multis ita om. M².
25 voluerunt M¹, noluerunt M².
37 ut magi M¹, macte M², magis aucte.
248, 1 unde adulescentem dicimi M¹, dicit M².
4 laus nomine agendi nomine gloria M¹, nomi gloria M¹, agendi nomi om. M².
alescit M¹, adolescit M².
11 cartao M¹, carteo M², epitafio nago.
aqua M¹, aquo M².
14 socis M¹, socius M², est hostibus socius bellum ita.
19 barricam M¹, barbaricam M².
249, 6 d. multitudo minus M¹, multi dominus M².
16 muttires.
20 et num M¹, aenum M².

21 c. oprimere vicere M¹, obprimere convincere M².
27 honore M¹, onere M².
250, 2 potire M¹, potiri M².
6 primo M¹, primi M².
15 colunae M¹, colonae M², colenae M².
19 colunum M¹, colonum M².
33 vitam illam colet.
35 cedere secundum M¹, c. significat secundum M².
41 pudore excessit M¹, p. ex pectore cessit M².
42 cui quidam.
251, 11 imo M¹, im M², hosce.
23 lib. iii quae cursu.
32 virtutis probare M¹, rubore M².
252, 33 differre M¹, deferre M².
34 qui nobis.
38 capiendos M¹, capiundos M².
253, 3 nate pus M¹, pius M².
13 carmine quod M¹, quo M².
16 adduci et suscipere.
18 istidem M¹, itidem M².
19 volumus M¹, voluimus M².
28 xxvi M¹, xxvii M².
30 me fortasse inquit.
35 abduxerunt.
36 coenator M¹, venator M².
254, 8 malis necesse iautume M¹, lutume M².
m. purae c. cibus M¹, cibum M².
20 achillidone M¹, achelidone M².
26 torquere M¹, contorquere M².
32 signis M¹, cignis M².
255, 10 prope M¹, propter M², percrepis vocibus.
12 concrepare M¹, crepare M².

	14	molliciam.		37	armenia M¹, tormenta M².
	17	libucius M¹, lucilius M².		43	eximone salcolocheo M¹, ixi-
	20	increpe M¹, increpa M².			ones alcholocheo M².
	24	crepere M¹, crepare M².	259,	2	cu isti M¹, c. istac M².
	28	increpere M¹, inrepere M².		3	lucilius M¹, licinius M².
256,	14	sua comparent M¹, sua ut c. M².		13	bonorumque.
				17	iterum significat.
	20	substat M¹, subsistat M².		19	hoc ait ita contendo.
	33	consistit M¹, constitit M².		22	hinc comportet. Salaminam M¹, Salaminem M².
	35, 36, 37, om.				
	38	dicubia M¹, discubia M².		24	habet potestatem senis M¹, ha-
	43	lib. iiii, sit comparant.			bet ubi potestatem p. s. M².
257,	14	tutam possit M¹, possis M².	260,	1	aequalitatem M¹, aequitatem M².
	18	quid componere M¹, quid est cur c. M².			
				16	deinde inde Romam.
	30	componere simulare.	261,	4	seducere M¹, educere M².
	40	cum ploco M¹, poclo M².			decrevi M¹, decrevit M².
		e. obvicam plector M¹, e. obvio amplector M².		17	cernet M¹, cernat M².
				24	quis ee M¹, qui sese M², ad finem e. ad causandam.
	44	lib. iii M¹, iiii M².			
	47	cum M¹, quin M¹, lenones.		31	omnia sunt.
	52	calx est finis lucil. sat. lib. vii, hoc est cum ad Verg. aen. lib. v, etc.	262,	3	duratia M¹, duritia M².
				12	perdunt M¹, perduint M².
				13	terentius M¹, idem terentius M².
	59	numero meo M¹, numeri mei M², melius calli rem.			hetera quidnam *in mg.*
258,	3	callet M¹, callent M².		14	qui in illo homine.
	7	saginastu M¹, satin astu M².		32	confidenter consternari sig- nificat deici pro se et.
	8	lib. iii lucilium.			
	10	*mg.* a collo calliscere firmum esse.		36	ex pectore hanc et M¹, hac et M².
	14	aprunum M¹, aprinum M².		38	offeras M¹, efferas M².
	25	si legas M¹, si leges M².	263,	1	fert curri M¹, a curru M¹, dimminutio.
	27	ut honera c. c. feruntur M¹, facilius feruntur M².			
		pessimos M¹, pessimis M².		5	extemplo M¹, exemplo M².
	32	contentiones vocis et remis- siones.		13	*mg.* melius exemplum vergili calidumque animis et cur- sibus acrem.

264, 8 quid contendi M¹,q.contentus M².
sum diliges M¹, diligens M¹, diliges M².
21 faceret.
26 numte emere M¹, nimium temere M².
265, 1 apud conium.
5 contentionem M¹, contionem M².
12 coaptare M¹, coartare M².
22 nostri M¹, nostris M².
25 citum incitatum divisum v. s. M¹, incitatum om. M².
27 at M¹, aut M².
266, 15 quo magis te in altum.
22 bis quin actogena.
267, 2 cadens M¹, candens M².
18 arbitrare M¹, arbitrari M².
19 nam mea M¹, n. ea M².
20 altero M¹, alteros M².
22 censet M¹, censent M².
35 non sine novis M¹, nonvis M².
36 coicere agere Afranius incendio M¹, Afranius Matertera —auferre M², *in mg*.
268, 3 nicasio s. curiosis cum M¹, curiosus is cum M².
4 filio coicere M¹,filio ei coicere M².
7 quo coicis istuc.
12 contigit M¹, contingit M².
28 dici a lectoribus M¹, lictoribus M², tuis p. r. ante oculos tuos concidisse.
34 dedidi.
269, 13 quod non M¹, quos non M².
14 honestatis M¹,honestitatis M².

22 confessio M¹, confectio M².
35 credere vel cedere M¹, vel consentire M², terentius in hecyra M¹, terentius formione—cedere M², *in mg*.
270, 10 medicae M¹, medicinae M².
15 lib. iii.
33 quid inter M¹, qui i. M².
271, 1 et ipse conscripsi.
6 die pac M¹, epc M², *in mg*. conveniens M¹, convenimus M².
convenire similem esse M¹, convenire constare — debuit M², *in mg*.
10 forti secus M¹, fortis secus M².
21 posse M¹, possit M².
23 cedere est.
29 xxviii.
273, 5 constet M¹, constat M².
8 constent M¹, constet M².
9 componere M¹, disponere M².
13 exgregenda M¹,exercenda M².
14 ponere M¹, proponere M².
15 lib. iii M¹, lib. i M².
18 parere M¹, parare M².
28 sed manifesto furto.
36 quin ipse.
274, 4 ita M¹, iter M², faciet.
26 cuiquam ubi M¹, c. ibi M².
275, 6 jusso M¹, jussu M².
9 credere servandum M¹, c. est servandum M².
20 cognoscat M¹, cognoscas M².
21 pappipole M¹, papipole M².
27 non M¹, ni M².
33 omnis disciplina M¹, omnes disciplinae M².

NONIUS MARCELLUS. 129

276, 18 damnare est.
22 sectorem M¹, sextorem M².
277, 20 defendere vindicare verg. M¹, vindicare depellere verg. M².
23 defendere debellare M¹, depellere M².
veri M¹, tueri M², Ennius.
28 nego M¹, neco M²
mediam quem M¹, quam M².
32 satis te qui.
278, 21 degitur M¹, deagitur M².
25 jejunam M¹, ei unam M².
279, 15 nisi si M¹, nisi M².
17 depositam M¹, deposita M².
38 actione itaque M¹, a. prima i. M².
280, 4 dicare m̄ accius M¹, m̄ tullius accius M².
10 hinc M¹, hunc M².
25 lib. ii.
26 darniam M¹, dardaniam M².
27 pecunias appia dictas M¹, appia om. M².
281, 4 dignatus rursum qui ab alio h. d.—superbo. dignatus significat d. habitus virg. lib. iii—superbo.
8 dignabonatibi M¹, dignabor dari M², in mg.
18 dominia ad convivia M¹, ad om. M².
23 sodalicia.
28 convenerat M¹, cum venerat M².
30 exira M¹, extra M².
32 alteri M¹, alter M².
282, 15 a media fronte.
19 fortis turba.

(37)

27 omnes ut M¹, omnes nam ut M².
30 pistrix M¹, pristis M².
34 aquiaetes M¹, alaetes M².
283, 10 magnopere M¹, magno opere M².
20 tantome M¹, tanton me M².
21 dixisti M¹, duxisti M².
35 police vestrae quas erifice. trahere ferre M¹, t. differre M².
284, 14 mortem. diffamare divulgare, M¹, differre M², in mg.
37 popule M¹, papule M².
285, 7 aut duro M¹, ut d. M².
21 decernendi fortitudo M¹, oratio quam decertandi M², in mg.
25 praeterisset M¹, peperisset M².
29 decerne ut est dicere.
286, 1 perspicuum est enim.
4 dimissa M¹, demissa M².
287, 10 dissupent M¹, dissipent M².
288, 4 nido inplumis M¹, nido et i. M².
8 adtraxerit M¹, detraxerit M².
11 detrahant M¹, detrahunt M².
16 Alexi M¹, Alexin M².
19 super M¹, desuper M².
26 adest ad abnescio M¹, adest at banescio M².
32 et fenestris M¹, et fenestras M², i. c.
deiciam M¹, deiciunt M².
289, 6 evocare M¹, vocare M².
7 deduc orationem M¹, deduce rationem M².
12 retrahere M¹, trahere M².
18 deinfinitam M¹, definitam M².

289, 22 religio M¹, relligio M².
28 xxviiii M¹, xxviii M², and 32.
290, 7 eligantu bimacera.
14 secundo deprecor,om. 15, 16,
17.
mollissima quam multorum *in mg.*
20 graeci M¹, gracci M².
erepiteo M¹, eripiteo M².
24 sint M¹, sunt M².
32 perdiscernere M¹, perdiscere M².
291, 5 pregnantem M¹, pregnatem M².
31 aetas M¹, aestas M².
36 miser, *cum signo compendii* i. e. miserrimus.
38 e. oculos elidere et sicum M¹, e. oculos et et sicum M².
40 jube M¹, jubeo M², o. idem ut s. f. ut coqui M¹, faciunt quoqui M², ut om.
43 elise M¹, elisisse M².
292, 8 edo pol v.p. exanclavit plautus in penulo s. e. merum. s.
11 Melanippe.
12 endrus M¹, ennus M².
14 torquantis M¹, torquentis M². i.e. eum diem M¹, eum om. M².
18 amfitrasone M¹, amfitrione M².
26 antiqua aedilis.
33 deo ex oraculo M¹, deo ostendo ex M².
293, 2 evadit M¹, evadat M².
10 propter valuisset M¹, properavisset M², *in mg.*
17 concitat aquam unus M¹, murus M².

19 lib. ii ut tandem M¹, evado—lib. ii M², *in mg.*
27 nec partem.
28 cujus est M¹, cuivis e. M².
32 filiorum postremum M¹, f. suorum p. M².
45 innotescentes M¹, innocentes M².
50 exacuta M¹, ex hac vita M².
294, 20 exsuspensa M¹, et suspensa M².
24 lib. iii M¹, lib. v M².
295, 8 exercere imercere M¹, e. imperare imponere M², *in mg.*
11 Pl. in Amph. exerciturus M¹, si in me M², *in mg.*, imparietem.
21 equitem equum M¹, equites equos M².
25 pinnis M¹, pennis M².
296, 24 exit.
297, 24 medecoris M¹, medecordis M².
38 praeter ceteros nostra, om. hunc.
298, 10 velit eve M¹, evel M², grandi.
11 eplere M¹, explere M².
15 lib. vi aramque sepulchri M¹, Discedam—lib. vi M², *in mg.*
22 educere educare ducare M¹, ducare om. M².
28 mittere M¹, emittere M².
299, 4 exponere est deponere.
10 dedie M¹, dedi M².
18 ornat ample.
24 orationem M¹, et rationem M².
26 explicare de off. M¹, ex. idem de off. M².
300, 3 firma notio.
14 excidit M¹, excidant M².

15 in oblivionem virg. M¹, i. o.
    venire v. M², oblivisci M², *in
    mg.*
18 After servitutem excluserit
    (301, 15), excidere est in
    oblivionem venire, virg.—
    animo, is repeated a second
    time.
20 ego vivo ab arciloco excidere
    M¹, ergo quo ab arciloco
    excido M².
21 ejectum dictum.
25 ibi erat scopiose M¹, scopios
    M².
26 eicere M¹, ejecere M².
34 delellas me.
301, 20 quia M¹, qui M², ad id quod s.
    24 expectare M¹, expetere M², *in
    mg.*
302, 9 f. item M¹, ima M², altitudo.
    13 q. caelo M¹, q. e caelo M².
    22 amoris filium, *cum signo la-
    cunae.*
    28 fero M¹, fere M².
    fortiter varro M¹, f. animo M².
    29 non posses se amplius M¹,
    non posses eam amplius M².
    30 suadet notat M¹, ut notat M².
303, 7 ferebant.
    9 de oratione lib. M¹, de oratore
    lib. ii M².
    est autem v. verbum verbum
    M¹, verbum om. M², sic
    quod.
    13 prohiberentur M¹, prohibetur
    M².
    17 hic M¹, hinc M², *in mg.*
    27 referri Virg. G. lib. ii M¹, spes

(39)

304, 12 ex longe M¹, ex longo M².
    27 movemetuo M¹, me metuo M².
    34 trasileone fretus M¹, t. novili-
    tate factione f. M².
    40 at M¹, ac M².
305, 2 simillare M¹, sum i. r. M².
    7 ut domatum mecum M¹,
    ˜equum M².
    14 animo eam M¹, eram M².
    19 nummis M¹, numinis M².
    29 meum laborem.
306, 10 ea quivis M¹, equivis M².
    17 familiam tuam M¹, tuam om.
    M².
    29 molesta potin M¹, molesta es
    p. M².
    31 justa.
    39 dico facessite hinc M¹, d. fa-
    cessti item facessite h. M².
307, 23 in stabulae.
    24 iterum M¹, item M².
    26 citos cursus M¹, citus c. M².
    29 virg. lib. ii.
    33 nisi M¹, nixi M².
308, 10 oculis fun fungens M¹, o. ful-
    gens M².
    11 frigutare M¹, friguttire M².
    mg. al. ecfriguttire cum
    sono exilire.
    13 nam quid istud.
    19 c. proclo M¹, ploclo M².
    abra M¹, labra M².
    compone M¹, compono M².
    h. e. c. uia M¹, uia om. M².
    ΟΚΟΠΟΥΜΗ M¹, ΟΛΟΚΟΠΟΥ-
    ΜΗ M².

danaum—excrescere M², *in
mg.*

NONIUS MARCELLUS.

308, 27 imperati M¹, impertit M².
     31 tumido M¹, timido M².
309, 2 sibi ipse fingit.
      3 et vocem M¹, ea v. M².
      7 fingit M¹, finget M².
     16 non M¹, nunc M².
310, 1 quod M¹, ad quod M².
     20 purgationes M¹, purgatiores M¹.
     26 virg. aen. M¹, georg. M¹, lib. i
        frigusque M¹, virg. aen. lib. i
        —ut M², *in mg.*
311, 10 movens M¹, vovens M².
     17 tui nominum.
     30 mestum fovere M¹, est tum
        f. M².
     31 aspargere M¹, aspergere M².
312, 6 videas M¹, videtis M².
     14 mense a. ponebatur e. c. cuno
        M¹, acuno M².
        i. q. v. adfertam M¹, ad fetam
        M².
     28 georg. lib. v M¹, lib. iiii M².
     35 fusis sisine mente.
     37 ullo jacerent M¹, u. sub-
        jacerent M².
     43 fundere virg. M¹, fundere di-
        cere v. M¹.
     45 talia fundebat lacrimas funde-
        bat M¹, t. f. lacrimans M².
313, 16 mores M¹, ores M².
     17 ducte M¹, ducite M².
     18 *mg.* flagitium quasi flagrans
        vitium.
     25 et plerumque M¹, ut p. M².
314, 3 g. f. f. consuetudine pondero-
        sum.
     14 absentium M¹, absinthium M².

        castoreum l. q. r. grave multum
        M¹, amarum uirg. et g. o. c.
        M², *in mg.*
     21 procilio M¹, plocio M².
     22 emortua M¹, est mortua M².
     25 hosti hostis M¹, hosti om. M².
     26 eis M¹, his M².
        vitiis M¹, vitiosis M².
315, 3 facilius m. i. g. M¹, f. in m. i.
        adulescentes g. M².
      8 humum M¹, hominum M².
        e. grave a. imperium M¹,
        imperii M².
     11 atquem Orestes. adtituere M¹,
        astituere M².
        sistit M¹, sistit om. M².
     12 virg. georg. lib. xii M¹, virg.
        lib. viii M².
316, 3 confingere M¹, cum fingere M².
      5 errat anus M¹, cretanus M².
        deploida M¹, deploidia M².
      7 haec eadem sum.
     11 via quibus M¹, v. a quibus M².
     14 suspendat M¹, suspendit M².
     39 gradientum M¹, grassantium
        M², *in mg.*
317, 9 incassum videas.
     20 conectat M¹, constat M².
     22 herbam det.
318, 1 malos et bonis M¹, m. a b. M².
     17 impulsum M¹, impulsus M².
     22 habet M¹, habes M².
     26 m. epicrocum M¹, m. et epi-
        crocum M².
     29 habere est M¹, hiare e. M².
319, 1 evidenter et M¹, et om. M².
        hiantes videor hidentes M¹,
        hiantes M².

NONIUS MARCELLUS. 133

	non audeo M¹, audio M².	324, 5	saltem est M¹, salutem est M².
15	juvat M¹, levat M².	21	oportere M¹, oportet M².
18	ea M¹, et M², fontia.	25	facta M¹, fata M².
21	hauriet M¹, hauriret M².	29	imbuta et ero M¹, i. est et ero M².
31	haud mollia M¹, haud haec m. M².	325, 1	regrediendum M¹, regrediundum M².
320, 1	summo honore M¹, s. cum h. M².	6	iii M¹, vi M².
8	delectatione M¹, delectatio M².	10	et tunc M¹, et tum M².
27	ipso M¹, ipsos M², ipsis M².		nesciebat M¹, nesciebant M².
321, 8	retardat M¹, retrahat M², *in mg.*	14	ignoscite est.
9	invitari est.	19	conconcurristis M¹, concurristis M².
10	curaque M¹, curasque M².		
26	invitavit viri M¹, viri om. M².	20	adeste est amer q. f. ignoscite, i *in rasura scriptum.*
30	cito bene enim.		
32	audivi non M¹, audi vino M².	25	emtu M¹, aintu M².
322, 6	commotus saepe.	26	parmeno.
	furacesemus M¹, furaces essemus M².	28	innocens *in mg.*
		33	accepit M¹, acceptis M².
	nequissimus M¹, ac n. M².	326, 5	iii M¹, iiii M².
	ibis ac M¹, i. juxta ac M².	17	et perindulgens M¹, et qui p. M².
8	juxta mecum rem.		
12	aut insolens aut.	33	patris M¹, patres M².
18	occepi M¹, occepit M².	327, 5	qua M¹, quia M², imprudentissimum.
323, 1	regari M¹, regalis M².		
2	agitatis M¹, agitis M².	15	quanto vehementius M¹, blandior h. t. M², *in mg.*
	frondiferos M¹, frundiferos M².		
	arbusta M¹, arbusto M².	29	si quost v. a. opus est.
	obsitu M¹, obstutas M², *in mg.*	30	jacere M¹, jactare M².
6	hinc M¹, nunc M².		virg. lib. vii M¹, virg. georg. lib. iii M².
9	templi M¹, templa M².		
12	bonum nocens M¹, et nocens M².	328, 12	emittere *in mg.*
		15	jactantibus M¹, jactant tibi M².
17	miti more M¹, minore M², esse saninmani M¹, esses anima ni M².	31	tuque mearum.
		329, 19	increpat et i. M¹, increpitat et i. M²; *mg.* alter non habuit.
26	intestatus est rursum.		
28	ipsius M¹, ipsus M².	330, 9	ighymnis M¹, hymnis M².

(41)   G   [I. 2.]

330, 11 et utile M¹, et ut ille M².
16 cantus totidum M¹, cantu sto-
tidum M², custoditum M²,
in mg.
29 nego interpellare dicere M¹,
interpellare adire c. M², *in
mg.*
31 xxviii M¹, xxviiii M².
331, 1 interpellam ut M¹, interpella
me ut M².
4 xxviii M¹, xxviiii M².
10 claudus M¹, caudam M², *in
mg.*
insignam M¹, insignem M².
11 parasti M¹, parasiti M².
16 inme M¹, inmo M², impediunt.
28 farticula.
332, 11 in jugurte M¹, in gurgite M².
27 *mg.* eligere virg. praestantes
virtute legit.
40 postes? portes? M¹, pestes
M², arscedat.
45 sermone aius M¹, sermones
atus M².
333, 18 is apud M¹, is om. M².
23 quibus rem rebus.
27 omnes in pudica in domo M¹,
omnes impuritates in M².
31 liquimus.
36 linquat M¹, linquit M².
37 defluxere M¹, defluere M².
38 licuntur M¹, linquuntur M²,
and 41.
42 deterere *in mg.*
334, 3 salio mercedem.
4 nisi ab sese M¹, missi abesse
M².
quiquam M¹, quicquam M².

8 cum illos solim ex M¹, soli
mea M², volutate.
12 cum meo M¹, c. eo M².
14 limassit M¹, limassis M².
19 vocasset M¹, vocasse et M².
29 c. a. f. cum h. i. hista M¹,
hasta M².
vicunea M¹, ut vinea M².
fulmine ita e. i. vista M¹, ut
ista M².
34 *mg.* nec tantum dulcia quantum et liquida.
335, 1 subidaeloidelore M¹, sibidae-
deloidelore M²
3 aenas M¹, enas M².
4 liquerit M¹, reliquerit M².
15 lib. v M¹, lib. ii M².
25 nereissimum.
26 cantem M¹, cantum M².
classem M¹, classum M².
32 postea M¹, postera M².
35 comedant M¹, comedunt M².
38 perspicere M¹, praespicere
M², prospicere M², *in mg.*
336, 9 volucri sventi ut illos M¹,
volucris venti M².
17 jubet primus.
18 eligere M¹, erigere M².
33 illos vate M¹, illo suapte M².
337, 7 absentium M¹, absinthium M².
10 et aenea sembolum M¹, te ne
asembolum M².
25 et lautum et convivium.
27 redi M¹, redii M².
29 ac victime legentem M¹, ac
victum eligentem M².
30 diceret M¹, deceret M².
instituisset M¹, instituissent M².

338, 11 pacem M¹, paceni M².
25 dat M¹, dedat M².
339, 15 cui derim in vita mea epitag-
ma appelli M¹, cui ubi
derim in utia mea e epi-
tegma appepelli M².
24 exiit M¹, exit M².
26 longe ut a p. abessces M¹,
longe te a p. abesse M².
30 et supra modum.
340, 3 luxuriae M¹, luxuria M².
19 xoenonis M¹, senonis M².
30 sicuti consuetudine.
341, 2 lentum M¹, plenum M².
11 in significatione manifesta M¹,
significationis manifestae
M².
39 armis M¹, armisque M², macte
virtutem.
41 hic versibus.
342, 6 modo a. M¹, malo a. M².
9 mactabo mastigia M¹, m. exuo
m. M².
11 dodate M¹, dotate M².
mactant et M¹, mactantem M².
13 hisce verbenis M¹, h. virgl
verbenis M².
23 commodum M¹, cum modo
M².
moderatum commodum *in mg.*
25 ubile M¹, utibile M².
38 statu M¹, statue M².
343, 2 modice Sallustius ambust in
M¹, m. ambis S. in M².
10 eoforo M¹, teoforo M².
11 audientiam M¹, audientia M².
diserti s (*sic*) sermonibus coacta M¹, coacta om. M².

24 illi mitem M¹, i. limitem M².
344, 21 si quid de te.
26 merui quoque saepe M¹, et
saepe M².
29 habera M¹, hibera M².
terras ac meretersa M¹, ac
meret tersa M².
32 annos incerrat M¹, a. hic errat
M², hiberna.
36 qui in excitu M¹, exercitu
M², ex aequo.
345, 3 unde et mercennarii.
4 ordine ratis est M¹, es M².
8 iste M¹, primum iste M².
26 minutum obscuros scrupulum
M¹, obscurum et scrupulo-
rum M².
346, 1 iter in silvis.
13 retinere ac repigrare M¹, r.
morari ac r. M².
26 tonsoribus M¹, censoribus M².
in aera M¹, in area M².
28 valitudo M¹, altitudo M².
347, 12 tenrenos M¹, teneros M².
in canendi M¹, in om. M².
13 absterserit M, absterseris M².
22 laborem.
25 miseratus M¹, miratus M².
27 mirari venerari M¹, m. metu-
ere M², munerare *in mg.*
29 custos admirantur M¹, c. illum
a. M².
quo optant M¹, circumstant M².
32 dicunt M¹, ducunt M².
348, 6 muoco M¹, muco M².
11 ut virg.
24 obstitisse M¹, exstitisse M².
28 exusta M¹, exausta M².

348,	30	metuere M¹, me utere M².	24	neque sat M¹, neques ad M².
	31	missum facit.	32	praemoniebant M¹, praemu-
	41	dein M¹, deinde M².		niebant M².
		tertius M¹, terentius M².	33	qui M¹, quis M², sine.
349,	3	maturare M¹, mature M².	34	indigitare M¹, indigetare M².
	5	nullum M¹, nalum M², vide.	353, 6	propter M¹, post M², *in mg.*
	13	muscati M¹, mussati M².	13	virg. lib. vi.
		acaenam M¹, adcaenam M².	16	agrestia ac.
	24	gursilum M¹, cirsilum M².	21	latratu M¹, latrato M².
	28	me aliud fatum M¹, factum M².	22	nitens humo M¹, nitens om.
	32	decet M¹, condecet M².		M².
350,	10	turpitudo M¹, turpido M².	31	natare iterum.
	27	jubet primus, cf. 336. 17.	354, 2	aurigatur M¹, arrigatur M².
	31	expromere.	12	cui nomina.
	33	cohibet et omnia aestus M¹,	22	continuoque M¹, que om. M².
		cohibet domina maestus M².	355, 8	erga M¹, ergo M².
	35	injectum M¹, enectum M².		foris ut praessit M¹, foras ut
351,	1	virg lib. xxiiii M¹, xxvi M².		praesit M².
	2	pulices M¹, publices M².	14	per eos et n. clam egem M¹,
	4	ceteris issa M¹, isasa M².		clamoris regem M².
		mittis m. a. t. satrafa acutia		regna M¹, regina M².
		M¹, satrafacta vitia M².	22	qui tunc si illum occupas.
	14	si hoc M¹, sic hoc M².	25	comedisset non nugas M¹,
	19	lucilius M¹, lucius M².		et non nugasset M².
	23	improbius quam M¹, quem M².	27	necsio quid M¹, nescio quis M².
	25	reluces M¹, relucens M².	36	scola M¹, sola M².
	26	agro referam M¹, me agros	356, 5	agriculani M¹, a. lucani M².
		referam M².	6	angelli M¹, macelli M².
352,	4	notifacerent M¹, notificarent	7	occupare est M¹, est om. M².
		M².	18	mebimatrem M¹, mebimatram
		praelia M¹, prilia M².		M².
	5	magisque M¹, quae M².	19	confirmant M¹, confirmam M².
		f. o. accius M¹, ne e. m. f. n.	21	stirpem medocabant M¹, s.
		M², *in mg.*		educabant M², uteremur.
	7	telefona is denum.	26	unicam M¹, vincam M².
	11	hic in eis M¹, hecine is M², est.		opinionem adferunt M¹, tuam
	12	numero M¹, numerum M².		—opinionem M², *in mg.*
	15	degerit M¹, digerit M².	27	eorum sit M¹, se M².

NONIUS MARCELLUS.

	30	popinius? M¹, popedius M².
		opinio M¹, opinione M².
357,	1	redurant M¹, restaurant M².
	9	astianactet M¹, astianacte M².
		hunc aicais panem M¹, pinem M².
		regione M¹, regionum M².
	11	domuictonem arcere M¹, domuitione marcere M².
		tuo bsceno homine.
	13	actum M¹, actum tum M².
	15	fautis.
	16	faventius M¹, faventiam M².
		dictis egregent M¹, dicta segregent M².
	18	rixa vertat verba M¹, r. vertat vertat verba M².
358,	3	si tu M¹, sic tu M².
		olim defensorem ut per eum M¹, olim quis uti possis M².
	8	amatorum M¹, amatorem M².
	11	quid mens M¹, q. veri mens M².
	12	xviiii M¹, xxviiii M².
	15	atque cupio M¹, a. cum c. M².
	16	spe M¹, spes M².
		quibus M¹, quibuscum M².
	29	nihil est M¹, nihil em M², *in mg.*
	30	dein mittit.
359,	2	incolumitas M¹, incolumis M².
	18	omore M¹, eo more M², factum.
	19	nil M¹, nihil M².
	23	comprehenderit M¹, comprenderit M².
	30	intes M¹, intus M².
	32	ubi obit M¹, u. is o. M².
360,	9	lib. iii M¹, lib. iiii M².
	26	lib. xxvii M¹, xxvi M².
	30	acrem M¹, ac rem M², ihi.

	33	apere M¹, aperire M².
	36	obducet M¹, obducat M².
361,	10	oppetas obesum gracile M¹, obesum — terga M², *in mg.*
	20	atquem metu.
	29	ullamque addicere M¹, u. queat dicere M².
362,	6	vita ulli.
	13	datum M¹, datum est M².
	21	inclama M¹, inclamar M², a. amea M¹, mea M².
		affiter illis M¹, affileberis M².
		praeberet M¹, praevertitur M².
	24	ultrorem M¹, ultorem M².
	28	incipiantque M¹, incipiamque M².
	31	gratia M¹, graecia M².
363,	2	sejudiciis M¹, sevidicis M².
	13	ac minus M¹, nimis M².
	14	protelo ad discendunt M¹, discedunt M².
	32	regeret genus M¹, r. et genus M².
		alto sanguine M¹, a. a sanguine M².
	34	proderat M¹, proderet M².
	35	jussi magnis M¹, jus imaginis M².
364,	1	est sallustius M¹, salutis M².
	8	ut ipsis M¹, ipsi M².
	13	quorum utilitates.
	19	naius est vehemens M¹, majus et v. M², *mg.* vehementius.
	21	adire M¹, adigere M².
	22	aī, *i. e. aler*, M¹, autem M².
		stutum quam in pariendis M¹, fuit umquam in partiundis M².

364, 29 sulcum quaesivi.
35 vergere M¹, urgere M².
365, 3 pedere M¹, pondere M².
8 levem M¹, levo M².
p. pedem M¹, pede M².
pondere M¹, pondera M².
18 premimus et lib. xi quos Simois premat ille viros.
20 capitis.
22 excidere M¹, excindere M².
25 premis M¹, premes M².
48 nec parvo catullo pretio M¹, n. par vocat ullo M².
366, 12 lib. iii M¹, iiii M².
17 si q. et h. M¹, et om. M².
27 spargat M¹, spargit M².
34 recum expilatorem M¹, rerum expiratorem M¹.
367, 14 s. et petant M¹, putant M².
25 ea hostia M¹, eha h. M¹.
28 propter intuens M¹, p. enectum est M².
29 delectatur etiam M¹, etiam om. M².
(367, 17 (*magna lemmatis perturbatio*) propter s. eius causa — odere. varro sesqueulysse. (*omisso exemplo*). propter juxta—propter aquam. adtestatas e. f. p. c. a. e. h. e. c. varro cato v. d. l. e. i. q. p. virum e. Terentius—assidere. varro sesqueulisse q. m. p. est et id s. e. p. d.)
368, 4 committere M¹, conterere M².
5 eame tantum M¹, eam etiam tum M².
24 novellae v. g. lib. iii ne maculis

M¹, v. g.—non album M², *in mg*.
29 propure M¹, purpurea M².
369, 8 uno illo ietulo plagas M¹, u. i. ictu loquebantur p. M².
12 lege aeniados M¹, l. maeniados M².
adminiandos M¹, adminianos M², admirantes.
20 plaut. tur putatur M¹, plaut. in aul. cur putatur M², *in mg*.
27 miletur M¹, multetur M².
31 cogitat M¹, cogitet M².
33 versantur ti.
35 putat M¹, putet M².
370, 11 passus sit lautilior M¹, passo sithia utilior M², psthitia *in mg*.
17 h. v. p. eum expassum.
33 cui possit.
37 *mg*. virg. oremus pacem.
371, 19 si facies praestat, om. facie.
24 pontificem turini viri M¹, ponti centurionis viris M².
26 praestat utile esse M¹, utile est M².
27 Trinacria.
29 ut dentique.
372, 12 fuisset in Hortensio.
31 completo M¹, complecto M².
35 nec tua M¹, n. te tua M².
373, 5 producere ducere M¹, p. foras ducere M².
19 inmundis M¹, inmunda M².
27 longe actum M¹, jactum M².
28 ejusmodi atque M¹, e. loco a. M².
32 spectat M¹, expetat M².

NONIUS MARCELLUS. 139

	36	q. h. sunt facit M¹, senatus consultum M², *in mg*.
	39	ingere M¹, attingere M².
374,	5	parmam M¹, palmam M².
	23	jubet opes M¹, j. proferre opes M².
	29	si tris mens se simine deut.
375,	1	bona. Pariter convenienter.
	20	sistuc more moratam M¹, si istuc memoratam M².
	21	postulam M¹, postulem M². placere martem M¹, placerem artem M². tibi quoque M¹, quo M².
	30	negotii M¹, negoti M².
376,	5	comisatum M¹, comisa tum, M².
	12	tamedus M¹, timidus M².
	13	i. e. pedibus longius.
	14	continuationem.
	34	antiquae.
377,	1	hic M¹, huic M².
	3	terenum M¹, tenorem M², *in mg*.
	28	aegro M¹, aeger M².
	29	ut si M¹, sit M². ipsum actenus M¹, hactenus M, tenus M², hucusque *in mg*. positionem M¹, praepositionem M².
	45	virg. in georg. lib. iiii M¹, virg. lib. vii M².
378,	5	massyli querunt.
	8	pietate M¹, picta de M².
	9	quae M¹, quam M².
	11	demet et plagilam M¹, demea et plagulam M².
	16	terrae aennius.

	19	cognota M¹, cognita M².
	33	quatere *passim*.
379,	3	diem M¹, viam M². aliensis M¹, alienis M².
	4	orbis M¹, urbis M².
	9	non fit thens (*litteris graecis*) auris M¹, non fit thesauris M², *in mg*.
	24	modo ne nefarium M¹, ne om. M².
	32	tamen et M¹, et om. M². indolis M¹, in dulis M².
380,	1	quin M¹, qui M².
	4	idem virg. in georg. lib. iii ruit arduus, om. ruit—lib. i.
	20	conminus.
	22	ciceros M¹, ceteros M².
381,	7	si quis quid.
	15	remus regis M¹, remos remiges M².
	20	referre censere M¹, recensere M².
	28	lib. xxxvi.
	31	qui M¹, quis M².
	38	ut in eo M¹, in om. M².
382,	12	rimare M¹, inrimare M².
	14	loco M¹, loca M².
	22	rimatur M¹, rimantur M².
	25	vincla M¹, vincula M².
	30	miser M¹, misera M².
	35	contentum M¹, contemptum M². cum eruperint M¹, c. me ruperint M².
	42	Ter. Eun. cesso huc M¹, Ter. Eun.—introire M², *in mg*.

(After 383, 1 Plaut. in As., the passage from quo magis, 381, 39—

(47)

NONIUS MARCELLUS.

Plaut. in As. spectandum,
383, 1, is repeated with the
following alterations:)

382, 1 refferre.
8 lib. vi.
12 rimare.
14 loco.
25 tua vincula.
30 miser.
35 contentum cum eruperint.
43 jamne rumpere h. m. jacet g. r. introire.

383, 3 roget. Rogare dicitur deprecare M^1, deprecari M^2, poscere.
4 asperneret M^1, aspernarer M^2. lib. i M^1, lib. vii M^2.
7 scitari.
8 acciperem M^1, acceperim M^2.
15 oriundis M^1, oriundus M^2, progator *in mg*.
26 sed qui M^1, quibus M^2.
29 recedere M^1, recipere M^2.
30 rumeari M^1, ruminari M^2. c. peri tropon M^1, perit ropon M^2.
31 s. teseiore caeperis M^1, te seio receperis M^2.

384, 5 primo M^1, primum M^2.
8 sic fata M^1, effata M^2.
10 recipisset ad iratum M^1, r. et admiratum M^2.
16 in putes M^1, im rutis M^2. caesi solum M^1, caesis solum M^2.
21 redundant M^1, redundat M^2.
32 rursus retro, virg. in georg.

385, 7 Cato M^1, C. Cato M^2.

9 plemeo simul jam M^1, tholomeo qui s. j. M^2.
17 oblatum M^1, sublatum M^2.
23 referuntur M^1, refertur M^2.
28 paulum.
31 ut M^1, hic ut M^2.
33 caelum M^1, caelo M^2.

386, 15 combibi M^1, convivi M^2. p. sufficit unt M^1, p. tuo sufficiunt M^2. sane medicantis M^1, medicamentis M^2.
28 in fil. lib. vii.
40 tenebris M^1, teneris M^2.

387, 36 quid adtinet M^1, quid id a. M^2.

388, 4 supremum M^1, suppremum M^2, and 6.
15 Achillem M^1, Achillen M^2.
21 q. te inte in tranquillum.
30 aquae M^1, idque M^2. t. factis saevus M^1, saevis M^2.

389, 12 sternitur infelix M^1, s. i. Acron. M^2.

390, 3 lib. xxviii M^1, xxviiii M^2.
16 orientis M^1, orantis M^2. rumpes M^1, rupes M^2.
22 in quo filium M^1, inquit in f. M^2.
23 usu significat.

391, 17 virg. lib. viiii, quos illi M^1, simul ense — lib. viii M^2, *in mg*.
39 adstare c. M^1, astare M^2.
41 mea heredibus meis.

392, 6 lib. viiii.
9 cui stet M^1, cui si stet M^2.
11 sese et ipse M^1, et om. M^2.
20 n. rei e. c. M^1, n. e. spei c. M^2.
31 quia qui M^1, q. quid M^2.

perspessoevit M¹, perspisso evenit M².
36 ubi si ita M¹, u. spissa M².
37 miseria mysteriis, om. varro.
393, 1 extropas M¹, exstrophas M².
3 pigra est ita M¹, est ipsa M².
18 achibidis M¹, achivis M².
394, 8 facerem ad M¹, at M².
13 quod pueras M¹, quot puras M².
18 nec isto.
26 quem M¹, quam M².
395, 6 espuerentur M¹, spuerentur M².
8 corporis siccitatem.
21 ardentem.
22 summo M¹, somno M².
28 solem auram.
396, 4 omnia crede, om. sumet.
5 prae se M¹, praesse M².
26 nitorem M¹, monitorem M².
27 dare mihi desunt M¹, Luculle —mihi M², *in mg.*
32 sustinere est s. M¹, sufferre est s. M², *in mg.*
397, 2 sufferam et quae M¹, sufferamque et M².
6 nam me pudet ubi.
9 qui sine.
16 lib. viiii M¹, lib. viii M².
20 virg. lib. vi sceptrumque M¹, caererique—lib. vii M², *in mg.*
25 s. succurram M¹, succuram M².
33 colfo saxirofenix.
36 set M¹, sed M², jam me inridens.
398, 1 sicuti vult.
6 patrocinatem M¹, patrocinantem M².

audiverit Sallustius M¹, a. saucius S. M².
14 multis civibus fugatis M¹, ex utraque—occisis M², *in mg.*
30 simpuia M¹, simpuvia M².
31 gratas instamiae M¹, grata sint samiae M², u. hi s. cappudines.
34 lucilius M¹, ulcisci M², pro cele.
399, 9 subdere M¹, subducere M².
15 amori M¹, amore M², praeceperit.
400, 9 subducemus stupidus M¹, corbulis M², *in mg.*
12 expuere M¹, spuere M².
15 offensum M¹, offensant M².
16 museos M¹, musteos M².
24 gratis M¹, grata M².
30 ducione M¹, dicione M².
34 subigere est superare M¹, s. exarare M².
35 Lysander proceritatem.
401, 1 hominum M¹, humum M², et s. a. p.
9 patris M¹, aratris M².
15 subigitque fateri Lucil. amantis et lib. vi M², decernere amantes M², *in mg.*
17 castigatque M¹, que om. M².
19 jugans M¹, jungas M².
27 a. t. in s. h. fulit s. extra v. c. M¹, a. t. incita s. h. t. s. q. ex M¹, exti M², v. c. M¹, *in mg.*
30 enectus.
35 summam aerumna M¹, s. in ae. M².

402, 9 respectabit M¹, respectavit M².
24 spectandae an exigendae M¹, spectandi an exigendi M², sunt.
34 exercere M¹, exerere M², lib. x.
403, 10 vacam M¹, vacant M².
29 Ascaniusq. omnisq. domos M¹, om. M².
31 haec inquit.
404, 5 dato M¹, doto M².
7 sectatores bonorum sectatores M¹, b. sectoris M².
18 possimus M¹, possumus M².
29 sustuleris M¹, sustulerit M².
405, 2 xxviiii M¹, xviiii M².
12 si socrates i. a. et in a.
13 signant M¹, signat M².
22 duodecim dum.
24 enisum *in mg.*
28 e Latini M¹, ea L. M².
406, 1 atinius geminas in foma odio M¹, titinius in gemina sin fonia odio M².
4 canutinam M¹, anutinam M².
11 adflicti a suis.
12 postremum M¹, postremo M², interent.
13 tegendo.
14 habetur.
17 quae inter.
23 *legi non potest.*
24 febris atque una.
25 vini, *cetera legi non possunt.*
35 virg. aen. i, mulcere M¹, et lib. xii et M², *in mg.*
40 arectum M¹, adrectum M².
407, 1 potierit M¹, potuerit M².

2 montes et faetera.
16 frementem.
18 menses tuli.
20 m. in inpunitates scelera M¹, m. inpunitates scelerum M², tulissem.
408, 1 naturae quae M¹, n. eaque M². s. c. partis aetatis M¹, s. c. parcitatis M².
2 celulam M¹, cenulam M².
10 trepidanti M¹, trepidante M².
35 hoc q. ig. i. s. neas mi noxas M¹, noxias M², erum, *cetera legi non possunt.*
409, 18 c. ne tristem M¹, c. ne te t. M².
19 exiluisse vere tristes M¹, ex silvis severe tristis M².
20 C. Af. pr. de off. lib. i, ad in ejus M¹, ac dein ejus M².
32 principium M¹, principum M².
is vocis M¹, vocibus M².
34 incidunt gravius M¹, i. adulescentes g. M².
410, 4 quodam M¹, quondam M². pamem? M¹, fulmen M², *in mg.*
5 dici quaero M¹, d. non q. M².
9 huc M¹, huic M².
31 decerpere M¹, decipere M².
411, 16 scabiemquae M¹, optuma torvae M².
20 gracile lentum M¹, gracilentum M².
412, 2 hunc M¹, huc M², liber.
6 tenens.
23 miseri M¹, miserum M².
26 sudat quid tremit.

413, 4 eiam.
16 studio se ab omnis M¹, hominis M².
21 faciendum M¹, faciundum M².
25 ityreos M¹, ituree M², in mg.
27 i. videos ut M², i. vide os M¹, ut om.
30 torqueat ingens M¹, torquet agens M².
33 servare m. tull. M¹, custodire M², in mg.
38 plauso M¹, plausu M².
414, 7 hinc raptas.
10 potes M¹, potest M².
11 et tergino M¹, et in t. M².
17 scolem M¹, scotlem M².
24 si quae M¹, sic q. M².
25 cannabolino M¹, cannabilino M².
26 quaeque f. s. n. poterunt M¹, potuerunt M².
29 aequaliter M¹, aequabiliter M².
415, 4 turrimus M¹, curribus M².
7 venire possunt M¹, v. non possint M².
17 c. virtus. virtus etiam significat auxilium.
30 virum si aura M¹, servant si vescitur M², in mg.
36 arte haec M¹, hac M².
416, 4 cur istuc M¹, c. is istuc M².
vadimonia sum M¹, suum M².
18 mane ante peti M¹, maneant te piti M².
20 videret sciret M¹, viderit sciet M².
417, 8 picturam.
12 vastitatis M¹, vastitas M².

18 patiatur M¹, patitur M².
balbarum M¹, beluarum M².
efferarum M¹, efferari M².
19 asperitates altari M¹, valtari M².
27 q. p. ultimum.
418, 5 inertis. et versaque.
32 affatur. vertere fallere M¹, vertere—collo M², in mg.
419, 3 v. libera trahere M¹, t. libera M².
10 vindicassent M¹, vindicavissent M².
epistolis latiniae.
13 vindicassent.
14 videatur M¹, videtur M².
28 significantiam M¹, significationem M².
420, 7 geminae verrite.
9 lib. xxvii.
12 strepitum et strata M¹, strepitumque strata M².
27 quid tuis tunc M¹, q. tu istuc M².
421, 7 furgarum M¹, furiarum M².
19 amabit M¹, ambit M².
26 pauzillus M¹, pausillus M².
422, 1 habebam M¹, habeam M².
7 perit at.
14 levare et erigere.
19 tulit M¹, tolit M².
25 et teres M¹, terens M², tum.
423, 1 et id M¹, hii M², quos.
10 meretricem et prostibulam M¹, menetricem et prostibulum M².
meretrix M¹, menetrix M².
11 meretrices M¹, menetrices M², a manendo.

423, 12 stabula M¹, stabulum M².
15 intro bonam M¹, i. ad bonam M², i. abonam M².
16 prostibula sana M¹, sane M².
424, 11 quae fecerat M¹, q. te fecerit M².
26 saciari M¹, satiari M².
30 satiari M¹, satiare M².
425, 6 dea ipsa est.
8 est quem M¹, quam M².
20 est saevum.
22 nova M¹, novo M².
25 fusum numidam M¹, fusam numidiam M².
30 mandit M¹, mandet M².
426, 6 quantu M¹, quam tu M².
10 continet. Faustum et festum M¹, patria — lucrum M², *in mg.*
19 phoebi cuus M¹, et Ter.—diem M², *in mg.*
24 multae animus M¹, multa a. M², ergitantes disciscere M¹, isciscere M², *in mg.*
28 teliquo M¹, reliquo M², diffusus.
427, 4 citera morbus.
5 aequalitas M¹, aequabilitas M².
28 digitis M¹, digitibus M².
30 carpurni M¹, calpurni M².
428, 1 edepol M¹, etpol M².
8 quid valeat.
10 parva poesis M¹, poema M².
12 stoc unum est hoc majus M¹, hoc om. M².
16 entymemate malo cumque M¹, entymematima locum M².
19 et rythmis. fora et fori—sedes masculino M¹, sedes est m.

M²,—ludis. minutilias—en M¹, enni M², —earum M¹, earum rerum M².
429, 1 aedificatio M¹, aedificia M².
12 civitas quae M¹, qua M².
430, 1 monstrant et ostentant M¹, ostendant M².
3 recte velint.
5 in auspiciis ostenduntur M¹, auguriis extispiciis M², *in mg.*
6 semper pessimum est.
10 hoc distat.
14 aerumnam f. possunt.
15 nisi M¹, misi M².
constat M¹, constant M².
16 fulmen et fulgur et fulguritum M¹, fulmen et fulguritum M², fulmen et fulgur M², *in mg.*
20 unde et fulgor M¹, fulgur M², fulgurae M², fulgere M⁴.
dicitur M¹, dicuntur M².
et fulgur M¹, et fulgor M².
28 lib. iiii.
431, 3 putet inter se vicinos.
25 tota die, sibi sui.
432, 3 per culturam M¹, prae cultura M².
15 rotunda M¹, rutunda M², and 16.
31 pervicacia et.
433, 1 pertinatia M¹, pertinacia M².
22 juventa M¹, juventas M².
26 quod morosa est contrariis.
434, 7 quae festis M¹, festi M².
8 primoscit omnino M¹, promiscit omnia M².

NONIUS MARCELLUS.   145

16 in proelia M¹, proelia M².
20 simus M¹, simis M², atque in.
25 honestius profiteri.
435, 8 a. e. quarto et a. quartum p.
f. M¹, a. e. quarto p. f. a.
quartum et M².
quartum l. s. t. a. f. M¹, et tres
M², quarto t. s. et t. a.
factum.
11 quintum M¹, quintus M².
12 habeat M¹, habeant M².
24 ducere M¹, dicere M².
436, 10 q. est celere M¹, celare M².
21 distent M¹, distant M².
437, 1 temperatior M¹, temperatio M².
3 leviorem M¹, livorem M².
9 imitatoriae M¹, imitatore M².
23 vet. et veterascere M¹, vetustascere M².
438, 3 item esse habendum.
7 Ad. annuere qui in pugnus.
9 verrem M¹, verum M².
10 peccato tamen. flagrare—discretio. annuere &c., *permixtis duobus lemmatibus sed transponenda indicantur*.
a. est cedere M¹, a. concedere M².
16 nictet M¹, nictes M².
17 flagrare M¹, fraglare M², *bis*.
26 inscii M¹, insci M², innat attingunt.
439, 2 quod plus M¹, plures M².
4 in ampitrione uxorem.
19 affectu, tum M¹, tuum M².
28 neque illa M¹, ulla M².
440, 9 pars sit, ceteriis M¹, ceteris M².

11 auctoritate varro g. M¹, varro g. *post* saginare M².
16 neutrum genus tangitur.
17 nostra M¹, rostra M², *in mg.*
441, 6 die quarta et die quarto.
14 judicet M¹, incidit M², *in mg.*
17 quidquid mutare transigit M¹, quid mature transit M².
442, 5 futura M¹, futurae M², spe m̄t nomine.
10 delectatione.
17 ut sall. audacia, om. Catilinae bello.
24 ut virg.
31 prospicere distant M¹, pros. et respicere M².
443, 2 non esse M¹, est M².
12 qui autem est confidens.
13 a timendo fidens.
16 non dixi in invidentiam.
17 potest et ut fugiamus.
24 nominavit M¹, nominatur M².
444, 6 distant.
12 p. et prestantiam c. d.
mg. pernicitatem velocitatem virg., pernicibus insignem plantis, pernix patiens perdurans, pernicitatem cicero discrevit et virg.
15 ut virg.
17 dura M¹, duro M².
29 n. s. legitur s. e. eligitur ad vivendum ut sit l. M¹, ad bibendum, eligitur ad edendum ut sit l. M².
445, 1 c. ut p. legitur M¹, eligitur M², m. q. &c.

445, 3 veteres M¹, ceteri M².
8 luctum dedit M¹, addit M².
12 et m. mei M¹, et m. talia M²,
et aliquando.
14 farre M¹, ferre M².
purgato M¹, purgatio M².
20 tunc graeci.
21 lateraris M¹, laterariis M².
25 parcis seu.
27 satis esse potis esse potuisset
M¹, satis esse potisset M².
29 posse M¹, potisse M².
30 lib. xviiii.
446, 18 ut totas integras sint M¹, ut
sit t. i. M².
19 niti inniti et obniti M¹, niti et
obniti M², niti et obniti et
enixae M³, in mg.
20 eniti M¹, niti M².
23 defuncti.
25 innititur M¹, nititur M².
447, 4 ergastylum M¹, ergastulum M²,
et ergastylus, and 7.
9 possit.
10 hujus M¹, hoc M².
15 et forsi M¹, ecfossi M².
18 perpessarum M¹, perpessa
sum M².
22 fruges M¹, fruge M².
solas ac sic probo rem M¹, re M².
448, 1 hoc est m. M¹, hoc et m. M².
4 factum M¹, factus M².
5 quid M¹, quod M².
18 ora M¹, ore M².
21 reliquum penula M¹, r. pede
p. M².
449, 3 Sisenna de contiario h. lib. iiii
oriri de contrario s.

16 repente M¹, repetente M².
450, 3 neque M¹, ne qui M², casum.
5 gannire M¹, garrire M².
12 eodem pacto logannis.
15 videris M¹, videres M².
20 dicimus M¹, discimus M².
451, 3 palustrem M¹, plustrem M¹.
8 repente M¹, repetente M².
12 et vigilia igitur.
13 torpidinem M¹, torpitudinem
M².
14 dixere gimedeam.
17 libis sacraturus M¹, sacratury
M².
frontem M¹, forem M², in mg.
22 nexile at avis M¹, nec sileat
avis M².
26 ebrius M¹, ebrios M².
et ticinius M¹, ticinos M², je-
junos M².
sino civo M¹, sine cibo M².
452, 3 gibero M¹, libero M², in mg.
7 operto M¹, aperto M².
8 ejecit M¹, eicit M².
17 mg. squalere non solum sordidum sed et plenum dici.
18 sed et honesta.
21 congeries quae M¹, qua M².
23 et tunicam M¹, per tunicam
M².
453, 1 desertio M¹, de sertorio M¹.
4 praeceptus M¹, praecepturus
M².
7 vox M¹, vos M², f. s.
f. quae M¹, que M², aspera.
16 et appetitum.
23 te tu M¹, tu te M².
24 ablatas M¹, ablata M².

454,	4	minorem M¹, minores M², m. e. s. et minoribus.	467,	3	urbs.
	11	idem homini versuto.		31	tumultu vecordi v. v. i. turp. leuc. vultu v. v. i.
	23	ut vinum sine fecibus.	469,	6	augurem M¹, augurer M².
	28	proposuerit M¹, praeposuerit M².		8	nulla M¹, nullum M².
				19	rationem et quam.
455,	9	dici debere M¹, d. non d. M².		22	pappipol.
	18	arripio rostrum M¹, a. et r. M².		30	ut ipse cunctet M¹, cunctent M².
	25	indagationis M¹, indagantes M².		32	accingere.
456,	21	mala M¹, malo M².	470,	17	amplexare M¹, amplexari M².
	30	suboles M¹, sub sole M².		35	proficisceret proficisceretur M¹, proficisceret pro proficisceretur M².
	33	neutiquam ab ingenio.			
457,	4	sine alacritate ulla lubidine.			
	23	non ex ope M¹, mg. non ex ope sed ex opere.	471,	21	populabundos.
			473,	1	soror M¹, soro M².
458,	4	maneat sucusque lacerto M¹, maneatque s. l. M².		6	pro labo M¹, lavo M².
				7	nullum e. i., om. nam.
	15	i. s. vere volitantibus a.		24	consolare M¹, consolaret M².
459,	6	sed de facie M¹, sed om. M².		26	minitaris M¹, minaris M², livius.
460,	2	virgilio auctore.	474,	1	mutum et m. s. M¹, mutuet m. s. M².
	10	lib. iiii, Hic Helenus M¹, tum —aen. lib. iii M², in mg.		6	aeneidos M¹, aennius M².
	18	inimum altum.		16	luctatium M¹, lutatium M², reconciliant captivos plurimos idem sicilienses.
	21	solum a precando praecando et poscendo.			
	26	rancidum emputidum M¹, seu p. M², est M², in mg.		25	fatues istudium M¹, fatue si studium M².
461,	21	sed et incestare.	475,	7	inter me M¹, mea M².
462,	14	habebamus.		8	promeres pro promereris M¹, pro om. M².
463,	7	sunt vi d. M¹, s. di d. M².			
465,	6	his quae M¹, qui M².		19	partire M¹, partiret M².
	9	de elegantia.		27	eandem me suspicionem M¹, me in s. M².
	14	cato M², in mg.			
	17	impensum M¹, imfensum M².		31	usione recredo M¹, usi honere credo M², patienter.
	25	c. est M¹, potest esse M².			
466,	5	dolentis personat M¹, persona M², eos.	476,	15	tota M¹, tuta M².
				27	tibi ut M¹, t. ita ut M².

476, 28 ludificata e. h. pro ludificata lepido ero culpam.
477, 4 fac mihi M¹, f. tum m. M².
7 opertis oculis M¹, ita o. o. M¹. manducantur M¹, manducatur M².
10 ipsum con con manducatur M¹, i. conmanducatum M².
15 misere pro miseret M¹, miseretur pro M¹, and *mg.*
16 matris M¹, maris M².
23 vigilat M¹, vigilant M². calant M¹, calent M².
478, 5 meo loco M¹, in eo l. M².
11 sed M¹, et M², quae.
21 num M¹, nam M², nutricator oliva.
25 sane caput.
27 et dola a. acomus M¹, atomus M².
479, 4 maiestrinum M¹, meiastrinum M².
12 altera ita altera M¹, ita et a. M².
18 evulsa.
21 jam atque ego.
29 antiquitatum rerum divinarum.
480, 1 cubiculo M¹, in c. M².
9 spolor pro spolior M¹, pro spolio M².
12 expoliabatur M¹, expolabatur M².
13 verecundantur M¹, verecundatur M².
17 ruminatur *in mg.*
481, 10 speetent M¹, spectant M².
28 sceptra M¹, escreptra M².

482, 15 ab eo quod est iter iteris M¹, itiner itineris M², *in mg.*
22 gladiis.
24 c. tisia p. e. t. itiner ingressum via M¹, tendere i. m. mi l. a. m. i. M¹, *in mg.*
483, 36 deridebant M¹, deribant M².
484, 9 accie M¹, acie M², rimer.
17 m. tullius c. i. a. quicumque M¹, circumque M².
22 iii M¹, i M².
485, 14 spesque summas.
19 quod M¹, quodquod M², quotquot M².
30 intra M¹, inter M².
486, 9 luctos M¹, lutos M².
17 noluisti.
21 c. ego i. istasime.
487, 7 lib. vi.
16 advorabili M¹, vorabili M².
488, 9 volverentur M¹, volverunt M².
13 interea loco.
19 tumeor at M¹, tum erat M².
489, 8 sublime volat M¹, sublima evolat M².
17 ego inquit etiam M¹, eam M².
19 gracila est pro gracilis M¹, g. est pro g. est M².
25 vulcanaliorum d. i. moratur M¹, moratus M².
490, 2 hem q. tumulti exaudii M¹, hoc p. p. q. M², *in mg.*
17 ferocitate M¹, fericitate M².
20 puellari M¹, puellitari M².
491, 22 soniti et sonu M¹, soni et sonus M¹.
29 glutinato glutino M¹, glutinator glutinor M².

492,	8	superciliam i cerstis M¹, supercilia mi cestis M².		circumlabit M², austri vis circumlavit M², *in mg.*
493,	5	intemperantias M¹, intemperias M².	7	lavere sanguinem M¹, l. sanguen sanguinem M².
	19	verborum M¹, morborum M².	17	levere etiam.
	23	maxima fiunt M¹, maximi sunt M².	21	sono M¹, seno M².
			25	mulieres M¹, mulieris M².
496,	37	in ea mancipato M¹, idem in emancipato M².	505, 22	sed qui M¹, se qui M².
			28	aut qua M¹, quae M², e. a.
497,	14	laevius M¹, laelius M².		velaxime verruncen.
	16	sed volo.	506, 3	molarium.
	27	dicis esse M¹, esse om. M².	8	et furnacium.
498,	10	lib. viii.	15	correpte fulgere M¹, c. prof. M².
	30	haec M¹, hae M².	27	ac bono.
	31	et prudentiaeque M¹, p. quae M².	33	vermionibus M¹, vernionibus M².
499,	4	m. a. vivunt plaut. M¹, pro m. a. vivunt M², *in mg.*	34	non possum patior cus est.
			37	profringe M¹, perfringe M².
	37	cum illos M¹, illo M².	508, 19	qui in f. M¹, quin f. M².
500,	10	ipsa mens.	509, 2	videbo M¹, vivebo M², and M².
	12	epigrammata M¹, epigrammatia M².	4	deplorabundus deplorans M¹, d. pro d. M².
	14	menalippo.	6	Plaut. in Aul. qui ossa M¹, solet ire—Plaut. in Aul. M², *in mg.*
	35	lecte ne M¹, lecnete M², duo.		
501,	9	amori M¹, amari M².		
502,	2	adulescentia sermone fautorum s. f.	26	tuque M¹, tuquae M².
			510, 9	censoriae M¹, censorie M².
	7	videat M¹, vivat M².	15	pulchrae familiae.
	17	orant ut.	28	prohibiter M¹, probiter M².
	23	lib. iii alii M¹, ali M².	29	rapere a M¹, ac M².
	27	qui sit secundus.		concedere, strepere? M¹, sapere M².
503,	6	aula M¹, paula M².		
	20	*mg.* aptius virg. fervere leucanten M¹, leucaten M².	511, 1	penulo tam seviter (*tribus literis erasis post penulo*) M¹, aha M², *in mg.*
	29	aere M¹, rere M².		
	31	desultoribus M¹, desultorio M².	9	similet gnatam ab illo.
			15	propritim proprie M¹, p. pro p. M².
504,	1	astrici s. f. circumlabitur M¹,		

NONIUS MARCELLUS.

511, 26 aliquantisper tantisper M¹, tantisper om. M².
31 paulisper *in mg*.
34 quantisper *in mg*.
512, 25 haeret.
30 fluxam referas M¹, feras M².
35 referunt dum.
513, 24 aspiter, and 25, and *mg*.
514, 7 pro pugnus M¹, pugnis M².
16 humanitas M¹, humanitus M².
20 memomore M¹, memore M².
515, 5 verre salbeolo M¹, verres albeolo M².
8 superbiter M¹, superviter M², and 9, and 11.
17 leto M¹, lecto M².
18 perplexim lacessam M¹, pro perplexe—lacessam M², *in mg*.
23 adorate M¹, adorare M², ac s.
516, 4 esse M¹, es M², ratus.
5 restrictim *in mg*.
6 ferme M , firme M².
15 furiter M¹, puriter M².
18 accipere.
19 verecunditer, and *mg*.
518, 26 thespiadum M¹, tespiadum M².
519, 12 mella M¹, male M².
ac si sap. M¹, ac si a sap. M².
19 civis M¹, cibis M².
22 de re rustica.
520, 6 quide ascriptivis M¹, quidea scriptivis M².
10 non quae t.
16 hunc habent.
19 in factis sunt et M¹, factis sunt om. M².

521, 11 quae cum.
23 mala rei M¹, re M².
25 me M¹, meae M², miseram.
26 m. et vel m. M¹, et om. M², mira vel miracula M², *in mg*. ponebant.
28 telefantes M¹, telefantas M².
522, 4 et quidem M¹, equidem M².
21 forum fuisse M¹, f. fuisse se M².
523, 14 operam M¹, operatam M². digerem M¹, degerem M².
19 laetis M¹, laetus M².
27 id est quod suffragium.
524, 9 promuntoriis M¹, promunturiis M².
525, 17 tampio sedissent' autdividi gn. M¹, autdividi centum gn. M².
21 dixerunt M¹, dixerint M².
526, 6 illos M¹, illum M².
29 eam fatum M¹, jam f. M².
33 iniqui M¹, iniqua M².
527, 10 enim M¹, etiam M².
16 aut ut mutatos.
26 hujus M¹, hoc M², invenisset.
28 fidelis ad M¹, f. vel ad M².
528, 4 H. athlaetae M¹, H. atla a. M².
11 picumnus M², picuminus M².
18 mercurii M¹, mercuri M².
529, 1 vel labor M¹, labore M².
16 oculos solis M¹, loli M².
20 pignere facto foedera M¹, pignera f. foedere M².
21 priusquam quid.
25 bellum his M¹, is M².
530, 20 antiqui romani lydios M¹, lidios M².
531, 2 evitantis M¹, vitantis M².

NONIUS MARCELLUS.

    10 daret M¹, darent M².
    11 tertium in s., om. quem.
    29 vocabulum forno M¹, a forno M².
532, 1 ignomiam, so 5.
     4 annuum M¹, annum M².
    12 credit M¹, crevit M².
    14 statilinum M¹, and *mg.*, statillinum M², fabulinum *in mg.*
    16 pontificis M¹, pontifices M².
533, 8 hercules M¹, hercles M².
    17 versificta M¹, versificata M².
    21 hori M¹, horia M².
        piscatori M¹, piscatoria M².
    24 me apperam M¹, mea opera M².
        recte M¹, rete M².
    27 fortiores M¹, portitiores M².
    31 at utique M¹, uti atque M².
534, 12 remigiis M¹, remigis M².
    24 tons illitore M¹, illitorem M².
    28 gantes M¹, grandes M².
    30 in lenunculo.
535, 4 lib. ii M¹, lib. i M².
    14 quamquam ad naves, om. id.
    20 navium M¹, navigium M².
536, 21 candendis M¹, candidis M².
    25 adde M¹, addit M².
    30 etiam aliis M¹, alis M².
537, 1 clautice M¹, clautica M², caulatica *in mg.*
     3 vincerentur M¹,vincirentur M².
        caulaticam M¹, calauticam M².
    16 pallae Pallae M¹, Pallae om. M².
        auleae M¹, aureae M².
    20 symdonem M¹, syndonem M².
        plagae M¹, plagula M².

    21 plagae.
    26 medi M¹, medici M².
    28 olorfyro.
    29 partim.
    30 honesti M¹, honeste M².
        mulieres M¹, mulieris M².
538, 26 consulares M¹, consularis M².
    30 paludamentum vestis M¹, p. est v. M².
539, 2 astari M¹, ostari M².
     8 clamidas et M¹, ed M².
    25 auraticae mitrae *in mg.*
    30 aliae mitrant M¹, mitram M².
540, 5 indusiatapatagiata.
     7 malacis M¹, malicis M².
    10 ritam M¹, ricam M².
    14 te M¹, tace M², tace om. M².
    17 hinc indutus.
    21 *mg.* plumatile virg. in plumam squamis auro conserta tegebat.
    24 novius epidico.
    26 amphytapae M¹, amfytapae M², amfytape M², *in mg.* hillos M¹, billos M², villos M².
    28 amfyta M¹, amfytape M².
    30 amfytapoe M¹, amfytapi M².
    31 amfytabo.
541, 1 intellecto M¹, in lecto M².
    11 fluii M¹, fluvii M².
    20 tegerentur togae. Praetexta insigne.
    27 limbo lari M¹, larii M², alcularii.
    28 *mg.* flammeum ut Lucanus velabant flammea vultus.
    30 cararii M¹, carari M².

NONIUS MARCELLUS.

542, 1 ricinium M¹, ricinum M², and *mg.*
2 dicere muliebre.
4 rebus ac luctibus.
23 lib. i.
25 adorbita M¹, ab orbita M².
institutio M¹, instituti M².
26 ac lacertis.
28 *mg.* combomata et parnacidis.
543, 2 pernacidas.
5 sed est M¹, et est M².
10 figura ter M¹, figuratur M².
544, 3 cuppas M¹, cupas M², and *mg.*
4 in conviis.
5 ponebant id est in M¹, in om. M², mori longi cum operculo ad cupas.
12 quae deinde M¹, inde M².
19 *mg.* polybruin grece cerniba aqua manale antiqui trullum.
23 simpuum M¹, simpuium M², and *mg.*
545, 3 calitias M¹, calicis M². *mg.* matula dolia apothecas melicas calenas calices.
6 cantharus M¹, cantarus M².
7 gravi M¹, gravis M².
11 carnalia M¹, and *mg.,* carnaria M².
16 bacyola M¹, batyola M².
23 argento atque aspera M¹, atque om. M².
25 aquiline pater aeguti M¹, paterae guti M².
28 crateras vasa M¹, and *mg.,* crateres M².

29 statuam M¹, tantum M².
546, 3 arcas M¹, orcas M², and *mg.*
8 ex sese M¹, exsesse M².
11 *mg.* patellae patinae salinum saliniacae.
19 tertius hinc M¹, hic M².
547, 5 massiternam M¹, nassiternam M².
6 parata jus M¹, ejus M².
18 sinu M¹, sinum M².
19 lepiste, *mg.* lapiste.
21 finis M¹, fanis M².
pauperibus M¹, pauperioribus M².
files M¹, fictiles M².
22 haenae M¹, haeneae M².
24 in se M¹, inter se M².
25 fonte M¹, ponte M².
548, 2 creterrae lucis.
15 molochina M¹, molichina M². amperinata M¹, amperina M².
16 institutores M¹, and *mg.,* institores M².
colores M¹, coloris M².
19 quem nunc dicimus.
20 impluiata M¹, impluviata M².
23 pinguia lateola M¹, luteola M², vacchinia.
29 malitiis, *mg.* malachium.
30 cartulam?
31 cartula est.
549, 2 plumatile aut cumatile.
3 volunt fere M¹, vere M².
7 habes M¹, habeas M².
17 ardebant m. lenae M¹, ardebat m. lena M².
23 non sunt aequae ut lutea.
28 *mg.* violacia.

NONIUS MARCELLUS.

	29	violarii cariarii M¹, cariari M².	23	nacti.
	30	mg. pullus fuscus ut virg. infuscet vellera pullis.	26	tracula M¹, tragula M².and mg.
550,	12	lapadium, mg. lapatium.	554, 1	vulcioque M¹, vulscioque M².
	21	nascitur cium M¹, nasturcium M².	8	mg. sparos lancea rustica de qua virg. agrestisque sparos.
551,	3	ocinum M¹, ocimum M².	10	ut quemque.
	8	Loram dicebant, *tanquam novum lemma*.	12	mg. falerae ornamenta bellica.
			13	si restitui et M¹, restui et M².
			18	uminibus M¹, viminibus M².
		mg. loram vinaciam aqua dilutam.	19	fuere ad ea M¹, fuerat ea M².
			20	parmae equestri M¹, equestris M².
	12	into M¹, cito M².		
	15	defretum M¹, defritum M².	27	verrutum M¹, verutum M².
		mg. samiam, defritum, passum, murmurinam.	28	ingentia turbae saxae.
			555, 1	eminebant M¹, minebant M².
	20	redigerant M¹, redegerant M².		erigi M¹, and mg., hirci M².
	24	moriolam, mg. muriolam.	4	verrutus ab artem.
	25	muriolam, ex uvi M¹, ex uvis M².	9	mg. gesa M¹, cesa M².
			14	falerica M¹, falarica M².
552,	11	inmittier M¹, inmitter M².	18	q. validae v. fallarica M¹, falarica M², missa.
	12	revortit quoniam.		
	16	cebro M¹, crebro M².	20	sparum, mg. sparus.
	20	vigisti plautras corris M¹, viginti plautra coriis M².	35	suis silvaticos.
			556, 5	mater et a M¹, matereta M¹ gravia b., om. tela.
	28	velitis M¹, velites M².		
	30	quem rutundis M¹, cum r. M².	6	alii M¹, ali M².
553,	6	rorari, mg. rorarii.	8	manipulis parte M¹, manipuli spartei M².
	8	antesignorum M¹, antesignanorum M¹.		
			11—13	*legi non potest.*
		proprietates M¹, proprietas M².	14	catafracti.
	12	fundis magis.	26	qui a cesa M¹, qui cesa M².
	17	est plumbi M¹, plumbum M², mg. plumbum in formam gladis.	27	agrippae quae M¹, qui M².
			557, 5	*legi non potest.*
			7	fratrum matris.

Anecdota Oxoniensia.

Lately published.

ARYAN SERIES. Vol. I. Part I.—*Buddhist Texts from Japan. I.*
Edited by F. MAX MÜLLER, M.A., Fellow of All Souls' College, Oxford. Small 4to., paper cover, price 3s. 6d.

CLASSICAL SERIES. Vol. I. Part I.—*The English Manuscripts of the Nicomachean Ethics, described in relation to Bekker's Manuscripts and other sources.*
By J. A. STEWART, M.A., Classical Lecturer, Christ Church. Small 4to., paper cover, price 3s. 6d.

Nearly ready.

SEMITIC SERIES. Vol. I. Part I.—*Commentary on Ezra and Nehemiah.*
By RABBI SAADIAH. Edited from Manuscripts in the Bodleian Library by H. J. MATHEWS, M.A., Exeter College, Oxford.

MEDIÆVAL AND MODERN SERIES. Vol. I. Part I.—*Sinonoma Bartholomei.*
A Glossary from a Fifteenth-Century MS. in the Library of Pembroke College, Oxford. Edited by J. L. G. MOWAT, M.A., Fellow of Pembroke College.

Lately published, uniform with the above.

Olaf. Passio et Miracula Beati Olavi.
Edited from a Twelfth-Century MS. in the Library of Corpus Christi College, Oxford, with an Introduction and Notes, by FREDERICK METCALFE, M.A. Small 4to., stiff cover, 6s.

Gascoigne's Theological Dictionary: 'Liber Veritatum.'
Selected Passages, from the MS. in the Library of Lincoln College, Oxford, illustrating the Condition of Church and State, 1403-1458. With an Introduction by JAMES E. THOROLD ROGERS, M.P. Small 4to., cloth, 10s. 6d.

CLARENDON PRESS, OXFORD.

RECENT PUBLICATIONS.

A Practical Introduction to Greek Accentuation.
By HENRY W. CHANDLER, M.A., Waynflete Professor of Moral and Metaphysical Philosophy, Fellow of Pembroke College, Oxford. Second Edition, revised. Demy 8vo., cloth, price 10s. 6d.

A Manual of Greek Historical Inscriptions.
By E. L. HICKS, M.A., formerly Fellow and Tutor of Corpus Christi College, Oxford. Demy 8vo., cloth, price 10s. 6d.

A Treatise on the Accentuation of the three so-called Poetical Books of the Old Testament—Psalms, Proverbs, and Job.
By W. WICKES, D.D. With an Appendix containing the Treatise, assigned to R. Jehuda Ben-Bil'am, on the same subject, in the original Arabic. Demy 8vo., paper cover, price 5s.

P. Ovidii Nasonis Ibis.
Ex novis Codicibvs edidit, Scholia vetera Commentarivm cvm prolegomenis Appendice Indice addidit R. ELLIS, Collegii Trinitatis apud Oxonienses Socivs. Demy 8vo., cloth, price 10s. 6d.

Euripides: Helena.
Edited, with Introduction, Notes, and Critical Appendix, for Upper and Middle Forms, by C. S. JERRAM, M.A., late Scholar of Trinity College, Oxford. Extra fcap. 8vo., cloth, price 3s.

Sophocles. The Plays and Fragments.
With English Notes and Introductions, by LEWIS CAMPBELL, M.A., Professor of Greek, St. Andrews, formerly Fellow of Queen's College, Oxford. 2 vols., price 32s.

Published for the University by **HENRY FROWDE**, 7 Paternoster Row, London.

ALSO TO BE HAD AT THE

CLARENDON PRESS DEPOSITORY, 116 High Street, Oxford.

Anecdota Oxoniensia

TEXTS, DOCUMENTS, AND EXTRACTS

CHIEFLY FROM

MANUSCRIPTS IN THE BODLEIAN

AND OTHER

OXFORD LIBRARIES

CLASSICAL SERIES. VOL. I—PART III

ARISTOTLE'S PHYSICS, BOOK VII

COLLATED BY

RICHARD SHUTE, M.A.

Oxford
AT THE CLARENDON PRESS
1882

[*All rights reserved*]

𝔏𝔬𝔫𝔡𝔬𝔫

HENRY FROWDE

OXFORD UNIVERSITY PRESS WAREHOUSE

7 PATERNOSTER ROW

ARISTOTLE'S PHYSICS

BOOK VII

A TRANSCRIPT OF THE PARIS MS. 1859

COLLATED WITH THE PARIS MSS. 1861 AND 2033

AND

A MANUSCRIPT IN THE BODLEIAN LIBRARY

WITH

AN INTRODUCTORY ACCOUNT OF THESE MANUSCRIPTS

BY

RICHARD SHUTE, M.A.

SENIOR STUDENT AND TUTOR OF CHRIST CHURCH

Oxford

AT THE CLARENDON PRESS

1882

[*All rights reserved*]

in these MSS., though he himself can only have collated them (if at all) for chapters 2 and 3; since he is, as we have seen, at the time of the publication of the Berlin Edition, ignorant of the very existence of a distinct first text for chapter 1 and the earlier part of chapter 2. Moreover, as we shall find, he has certainly not collated chapters 4 and 5 in any of these MSS.[1]

Since the date of this discovery of Spengel's all subsequent editions, including the smaller text of Bekker, have given the first text of the earlier part of the book as it appears in Spengel's paper. No one apparently has collated the three Paris MSS., and no one has discussed the question as to whether the fourth and fifth chapters of the book, as given in the Berlin text, belong to the first or the second text; though Simplicius, the latest but, for this book, the only trustworthy Greek commentator on the Aristotelian Physics, states distinctly that the two texts run throughout the book, and further, that in all cases the first is of greater authority than the second.

Prantl, the latest editor of the *Physics*, does indeed refer repeatedly to 'codd.' in his apparatus criticus in the first part of the book: but, as he never vouchsafes to tell us which of the three MSS. this plural reference points to; as, further, these codices are not always in agreement on the readings so referred to; and as more than once no one of them has the text as he gives it, we are forced to the conclusion that his 'codd.' means nothing more than the thrice-reprinted text of Spengel, with which, as far as I can discover, his text, allowing for the emendations which he makes himself or adopts from other scholars, is exactly in accordance. It is of course possible that he may have either himself looked up one or two marked passages in these MSS., or have entrusted this task to some scholar resident in Paris; but of this there is no direct evidence, while there is the strongest proof that he can never have read the latter chapters of the book in any of these three MSS.

I am concerned to prove that these MSS. give throughout the

---

[1] In his smaller edition of the Physics (Berlin, 1843) Bekker gives the first version of the first part of the book with a reference to Spengel's article, relegating the second version to small type throughout the first three chapters; but as there is no apparatus criticus to that edition no fresh information is given.

book the first text as known to Simplicius, or at least one much more nearly resembling it than is to be found in any of Bekker's MSS.

Of the three Paris MSS. by far the most important is that numbered 1859. It is a fourteenth-century MS., very carefully and accurately written. It has very few mistakes, though naturally a certain number of omissions, generally by reason of an ὁμοιοτέλευτον. These omissions are however, with a single exception, corrected in the margin by what seems to be the same hand, at all events by a hand of the same century. This MS. differs from the other two Paris MSS. (and from an Oxford MS. to which I shall refer later) much more widely than these three differ from each other. This MS. is also by far the nearest of the four to Morel's text, differing from it only nine times in the portion covered by Morel's quotation; two or three of these points of difference are definitely mistakes in Morel's text; one is due to his insertion of a marginale; and the remaining differences, though not to be accounted for on these grounds, are not so wide or important as to justify us in discarding the conclusion, otherwise very probable, that Morel used this MS. in that portion of his edition.

Next in importance comes the MS. numbered Paris 2033, which, as is twice stated in different parts of the MS., was copied in Crete, after the fall of Constantinople, by Michael Apostoles. The handwriting is beautiful, but the MS. seems to have been copied from a much worse original than MS. 1859, and in two or three cases inserts sentences or parts of sentences from the second text.

Paris 1861 comes very close to 2033, and generally, but not invariably, follows it in its errors and insertions from the second text. It is a sixteenth-century MS., and on the whole does not seem to be a direct copy of 2033, but rather to be derived from a common archetype, probably nearly coeval with, but certainly inferior to, Paris 1859.

Lastly, there is in the Bodleian Library at Oxford a MS. (Misc. ccxxxviii), most carelessly copied and several times corrected from MSS. of the second text, which none the less in its general tenor follows the text of the three Paris MSS., approximating most nearly to Paris 2033, though in some striking readings it agrees with Paris 1859 against the readings of the other two MSS.

The general relations of these MSS. may be estimated by the following table:—

Denoting Paris 1859	by A	A stands alone against BCD	55 times.
„ Paris 1861	„ B	B „ „ ACD	17 „
„ Paris 2033	„ C	C „ „ ABD	3 „
„ Bodleian Misc. ccxxxviii.	„ D	D „ „ ABC	44 „
		AB stand against . CD	3 „
		AD „ „ . BC	8 „

Lastly, there are two cases of triple readings A..D..BC, and A..C..BD.

Though the number of times when D stands alone as against the other three MSS. is not far short of that in which A stands alone, yet the importance of the variants in the cases where D is unique is far inferior to that of those where A is unique. The majority of unique readings in D are simple errors, and do not militate against the general law that B C D constitute one sub-group, and that A is the solitary representative of another.

As to these MSS. as a whole. It is universally admitted that they are the only MSS. which give us the genuine first text for the first chapter and the earlier part of the second. With regard, then, to this portion of the book, there is little to note, since here our MSS. have the field to themselves; and, though they differ in certain points from Morel's text, these differences are individually of slight importance.

Little also need be said of the third chapter, though for a somewhat different reason. Here our MSS. also indisputably give the first text; but here they do not stand alone. A considerable number of other MSS. give the correct text for either a large part or the whole of this chapter, and for the latter part of the second chapter. Each separate MS. and each family of MSS. has of course its peculiar errors, and therefore a text may be constituted from the comparison of them all which is superior in accuracy to any of them taken singly, and even to any single group. The Berlin text of this third chapter stands in this position. It differs not greatly from our MSS., but is probably superior in accuracy to them and to any other single group.

It is with regard to the fourth and fifth chapters that the question of the authority of these MSS. assumes the greatest importance.

ARISTOTLE'S PHYSICS. BOOK VII.   159

Here, as we have seen, the Berlin and all subsequent editions give only a single text, though we have Simplicius' authority for the existence of a double text throughout. I believe that the text given in all these editions is a mixture of the two known to Simplicius, probably more closely approaching the first than the second, while our four MSS. either give the true first text throughout or at least with very slight intermixture of the second.

This I hold to be distinctly proveable of the fourth chapter, while with regard to the fifth the matter is less certain, since in that chapter Simplicius quotes less frequently than usual the *ipsissima verba* of Aristotle; but even there the balance of evidence is definitely, though slightly, in favour of our four MSS.

I shall therefore in this introduction limit myself to citing passages from these two latter chapters, as to which only there is any doubt of the superiority of our MSS.; and shall attempt to establish that, in cases of divergence between these MSS. and the Berlin text, the former are always, or almost always, nearer the first text of Aristotle as it was known to Simplicius.

Taking the more striking cases of divergence in order, we find first in p. 248 a, ll. 21–22 of the Berlin edition, ὥσπερ εἰ κάταντες, τὸ δ' ἄναντες. Here our MSS. have ὥσπερ ἂν εἰ τὸ μὲν κάταντες τὸ δ' ἄναντες. Simplicius in his commentary, folio 251 b, has ὡς ἂν εἰ τὸ μὲν ἐπὶ κατάντους ἐκινεῖτο τὸ δ' ἐπὶ ἀνάντους.

In the Berlin edition, 248 b, l. 1, we have the word διῆλθε. All our four MSS. and Simplicius give διελήλυθε. In lines 5–7 of the same page, the Berlin text has ἀλλ' ὅσα μὴ ὁμώνυμα πάντα συμβλητά: our four MSS. and Bekker's MS. H give ἀλλ' ὅσα μὴ συνώνυμα ἄπαντα ἀσύμβλητα. On this passage the words of Simplicius are ἰστέον δὲ ὅτι ἡ γραφὴ τοῦ ῥητοῦ τούτου διάφορος φέρεται. ὅπου μὲν 'ἀλλ' ὅσα μὴ ὁμώνυμα ἄπαντα συμβλητά,' ὡς καὶ ὁ 'Αλέξανδρος ἔγραψεν' ὅπου δὲ ' ἀλλ' ὅσα μὴ συνώνυμα ἄπαντα ἀσύμβλητα.' τινὲς δὲ τὴν ἐν τῷ ἑτέρῳ ἑβδόμῳ βιβλίῳ γραφὴν ἐνταῦθα μετατεθείκασιν ἔχουσαν οὕτως· ' ἀλλ' ἆρά γε ὅσα μὴ ὁμώνυμα ἄπαντα συμβλητά.'

Here the easier reading is undoubtedly that of Alexander, which is substantially the same as that of the second text; but, for that very reason, we should prefer the second reading given by Simplicius as

ARISTOTLE'S PHYSICS. BOOK VII.

equally belonging to MSS. of the first text, which also appears in our four MSS.

If one reading be found only in MSS. of the first text, while the other is, with slight variation, common to one family of MSS. of the first text and to all those of the second, we have some ground at least for assuming that the reading common to the first and second text is a correction from the latter into the former; while the reading which occurs only in MSS. of the first text is likely to be the original reading of that text. From this passage, however, and from another to which we shall call attention later, we have some reason for doubting whether the distinction between the first and second texts of this book was so sharply drawn in the days of Alexander as it was at the time of the commentary of Simplicius.

A still more important passage occurs in lines 17–19 of the same page. Here we have—

Berlin text.	Our four MSS.
ἀλλ' ἐνίων καὶ οἱ λόγοι ὁμώνυμοι οἷον εἰ λέγοι τις ὅτι τὸ πολὺ τὸ τοσοῦτον καὶ ἔτι ἄλλο τὸ τοσοῦτον, καὶ τὸ ἴσον ὁμώνυμον, καὶ τὸ ἐν δέ, εἰ ἔτυχεν, εὐθὺς ὁμώνυμον.	ἀλλ' ἐνίων καὶ οἱ λόγοι ὁμώνυμοι, οἷον εἰ λέγοι τις ὅτι¹ πολὺ τὸ τοσοῦτον καὶ ἔτι, καὶ τὸ διπλάσιον τόσον, ἀλλὰ τὸ τοσοῦτον καὶ τὸ ἴσον ὁμώνυμον, καὶ τὸ ἐν δέ, εἰ εὐθὺς ἔτυχεν, ὁμώνυμον.

The words of Simplicius are, ὁ γὰρ λόγος τοῦ πολλοῦ ὁ λέγων ὅτι πολύ ἐστι τὸ τοσοῦτον καὶ ἔτι, ὁμώνυμος καὶ αὐτός ἐστιν. ἄλλο γὰρ τῷ εἴδει τὸ ἐν ὕδατι τοσοῦτον καὶ ἔτι, καὶ ἄλλο τὸ ἐν ἀέρι, ... καὶ ὁ τοῦ διπλασίου δὲ λόγος ὁ λέγων δύο πρὸς ἓν ὁμώνυμός ἐστι. καὶ γὰρ τὸ ἐν αὐτὸ ὁμώνυμόν ἐστιν. (Fol. 252 b.)

Two things here are sufficiently clear. First, that both versions of the text are corrupt; secondly, that Simplicius has got the reading of our four MSS. and not that of Bekker's text. What the true reading may be, it is difficult to conjecture. It may possibly have been something of this kind: Οἷον εἰ λέγοι τις ὅτι πολὺ τὸ τοσοῦτον καὶ ἔτι ὅτι διπλάσιον τόσου. ἀλλὰ τὸ τοσοῦτον καὶ τὸ διπλάσιον καὶ τὸ ἴσον ὁμώνυμα, καὶ τὸ ἐν δὲ εὐθύς, εἰ ἔτυχεν, ὁμώνυμον. I am inclined to omit the article before διπλάσιον, and thus make τὸ τοσοῦτον the subject of both asser-

---
[1] Paris 1859 omits ὅτι and τὸ before τοσοῦτον (bis).

ARISTOTLE'S PHYSICS. BOOK VII.

tions (πολύ ἐστι τὸ τοσοῦτον—τὸ τοσοῦτον διπλάσιον τόσου ἐστί). It seems to me that this omission makes the line of argument clearer and more intelligible. If the article before διπλάσιον is (as I think) a mere copyist's error for ὅτι, then the inserted καί would be a very natural emendation of a subsequent editor.

The MSS. followed by the Berlin text seem to me to represent a later and post-Simplician attempt to remedy the evil by omitting words which, in their corrupted form, were devoid of sense.

In the twenty-fourth line of this page

The Berlin text has	Our MSS. and Simplicius write
καὶ κατὰ μέγεθος ὡσαύτως.	καὶ κατὰ τὸ μέγεθος ὡσαύτως.

In the fifteenth line of the page 249 a

The Berlin text has	Our MSS. and Bekker's F give
ὁ μὲν γὰρ χρόνος ἀεὶ ἄτομος τῷ εἴδει, ἢ ἅμα κἀκεῖνα εἴδει διαφέρει.	ὁ μὲν γὰρ χρόνος ὁ αὐτὸς ἀεὶ ἄτομος τῷ εἴδει. ἢ ἅμα κἀκεῖνα εἴδει διαφέρει.

In this case the best reading known to Simplicius, and perhaps to Alexander, differs widely from either of these readings. There is no trace of the reading of the Berlin text; but Simplicius tells us that one of the readings acknowledged by Alexander is that which we now find in our MSS. and in Bekker's F (Simplicius, fol. 253 b). Simplicius himself says that this reading really belongs to the second text; but if so, it must have been inserted into some MSS. of the first text before the time of Alexander, and Alexander himself was apparently unaware of its doubtful origin. But is this not rather a proof of the supposition which we before referred to, that the distinction between the two texts is not so precise in the time of Alexander as in that of Simplicius?

A few words later (l. 17) there occurs a passage where our MSS. are certainly incorrect, but where their error gives us a most valuable hint towards the restoration of the correct text. In this place the words are

In the Berlin text.	In our MSS.
ἔτι δ' ἐὰν ᾖ, οἷον εἰ πόδες, βάδισις, εἰ δὲ πτέρυγες, πτῆσις, ἢ οὔ, ἀλλὰ τοῖς σχήμασιν ἡ φορὰ ἄλλη.	ὅτε δ' ἐν ᾧ οὐ ἀλλὰ τοῖς σχήμασιν ἡ φορὰ ἄλλη.

ARISTOTLE'S PHYSICS. BOOK VII.

The true reading here is ἔτι δ' ἂν δι' οὗ, οἷον εἰ πόδες, βάδισις, εἰ δὲ πτέρυγες πτῆσις, ἢ οὔ, ἀλλὰ τοῖς σχήμασιν ἡ φορὰ ἄλλη, which is given in Cod. K (Bekker), and is supported by the authority of Simplicius, fol. 254 a. It seems likely that the homoioteleuton (οὗ, οὐ) caused the omission of the words οὗ, οἷον εἰ πόδες, βάδισις, εἰ δὲ πτέρυγες πτῆσις, ἢ in the archetype of our family of MSS., and that the words ἔτι δ' ἂν δι', now meaningless, were then altered into ἔτι δ' ἐν ᾧ, in some attempt to correct the text (the truncated δι' would naturally be taken for a mistaken repetition of the δ' immediately preceding). The ὅτι for ἔτι is obviously a mere later copyist's slip. The MSS. followed by Bekker probably give a case of the insertion of the words omitted from some correct MS. into one which had the imperfect reading of our MSS., in which insertion, as often happens, the insertor did not notice that a correction, as well as an insertion, was necessary in order to bring his text into conformity with the more correct MS.

In lines 30–31 of the same page

The Berlin text gives	Our MSS.	Simplicius, fol. 254 (2nd) a.
ἔστι τὸν μὲν ταχὺ τὸν δὲ βραδέως λαθῆναι.	ἔστι[1] δὲ τὸν μὲν ταχέως τὸν δὲ βραδέως λαθῆναι.	ἔστι γὰρ τὸν μὲν ταχέως λαθῆναι τὸν δὲ βραδέως.

In page 249 b, l. 4.

Berlin text.	Our MSS.	Simplicius, fol. 254 (2nd) a.
ἀλλ' ἔστω ἰσοταχὲς τὸ ἐν ἴσῳ χρόνῳ τὸ αὐτὸ μεταβάλλον.	ἀλλ' ἔστω τὸ[2] τὸ αὐτὸ μεταβάλλειν ἐν ἴσῳ χρόνῳ ἰσοταχές.	ἔστω, φησὶν, ἰσοταχὲς εἶναι ἐπὶ ἀλλοιώσεως τὸ τὸ αὐτὸ μεταβάλλειν ἐν τῷ ἴσῳ χρόνῳ.

l. 14.

Berlin text.	MS. Paris 1859.
ἀλλὰ δὴ πότερον εἰς τὸ πάθος δεῖ βλέψαι, ἐὰν ᾖ ταὐτὸν ἢ ὅμοιον, εἰ ἰσοταχεῖς αἱ ἀλλοιώσεις, ἢ εἰς τὸ ἀλλοιούμενον, οἷον εἰ τοῦ μὲν τοσονδὶ λελεύκανται τοῦ δὲ τοσονδί; ἢ εἰς ἄμφω, καὶ ἡ αὐτὴ μὲν ἡ ἄλλη τῷ πάθει εἰ τὸ αὐτό.	ἀλλὰ δὴ πότερον εἰς τὸ πάθος δεῖ βλέψαι, ἐὰν ᾖ τὸ αὐτὸ ἢ ὅμοιον, εἰ ἰσοταχεῖς αἱ ἀλλοιώσεις, ἢ εἰς τὸ ἀλλοιούμενον, οἷον εἰ τοῦ μὲν τοσονδὶ λελεύκανται, τοῦ δὲ τοσονδί; ἢ εἰς ἄμφω καὶ εἰ αὐτὴ μὲν ἡ ἄλλη τῷ πάθει εἰ τὸ αὐτό.

[1] ἔχει Paris 1861 and Paris 2033 by a clerical error.
[2] τὸ om. Paris 1861 and Paris 2033.

The right reading of the last line but one of this passage is to be arrived at by combining that of the Berlin text with that of MS. Paris 1859. For this right reading is καὶ εἰ ἡ αὐτὴ μὲν ἢ ἄλλη τῷ πάθει κ.τ.λ. This reading is actually to be found in another MS. in the Bodleian Library. (Cod. Baroc. 79.)

In lines 21–22 the Berlin text, following MS. E, reads θάττων δὴ εἰ ἐν ἀνίσῳ. All other MSS., with one exception, agree with our four in reading θάττων δ', εἰ ἐν ἴσῳ ἕτερον, which reading is in agreement with the words of Simplicius, who writes θάττων δὲ γένεσις ὅταν ἐν τῷ αὐτῷ ἴσῳ χρόνῳ μὴ τὸ αὐτὸ ᾖ τὸ γεγονὸς ἀλλ' ἕτερον, fol. 264 (2nd) b. [The pages here are wrongly numbered in the Aldine edition of Simplicius.]

So far for the fourth chapter, as to which, I think, our instances show sufficiently that the text of these four MSS. represents an older and more consistent family than that of the Berlin edition. With regard to the fifth chapter, the case, as I before said, is more doubtful. The differences between the text of this chapter and that of the Berlin edition are much more frequent than those of the preceding chapters, but they are rarely of much importance; and it is usually quite impossible to cite the authority of Simplicius on one side or the other, since, as we have noticed, in this chapter he but rarely quotes the words of Aristotle, while the unimportance of the differences between the two texts makes it almost impossible to infer from his commentary which of two variants he had before him. Often, moreover, in this chapter we find that he is following a reading clearly different from any known to us.

As to the difference between the two texts generally, we may say, that whereas our four MSS. usually give us both the letter acting as symbol for some quantity and the name of that order of things of which it is a quantity—τοῦ Β βάρους .. τοῦ Δ χρόνου, etc.— the MSS. followed by the Berlin text omit either the one or the other—ἡ αὐτὴ δύναμις τὸ αὐτὸ ἐν τῳδὶ τῷ χρόνῳ τοσηνδὶ κινεῖ, p. 250 c, ll. 4–5, and conversely, τὸ Ε τὸ Ζ κινεῖ ἐν τῷ Δ τὴν Γ, l. 10. But in these latter MSS. there is an explanatory sentence, οἷον τῆς Α δυνάμεως ἔστω ἡμίσεια ἡ τὸ Ε καὶ τοῦ Β τὸ Ϛ ἥμισυ, ll. 7–8. This sentence is not wanted in our MSS., and does not appear there. At first

164   ARISTOTLE'S PHYSICS. BOOK VII.

sight the explanatory words inserted in our MSS. look like glosses which have crept into the text, but the fact of the absence of this sentence in these MSS. shows us the two versions as two different methods of arriving at the same result. I doubt much whether the one method can be proved to be more Aristotelian than the other.

There are only two passages in this chapter where the words of Simplicius help us at all to a judgment between the two texts.

The first occurs in ll. 9–12 of p. 250 of the Berlin text.

Berlin text.	Our four MSS.	Simplicius, fol. 256(3rd)b.
καὶ εἰ τὸ Ε τὸ Ζ κινεῖ ἐν τῷ Δ τὴν Γ, οὐκ ἀνάγκη ἐν τῷ ἴσῳ χρόνῳ τὸ ἐφ' οὗ Ε τὸ διπλάσιον τοῦ Ζ κινεῖν τὴν ἡμίσειαν τῆς Γ.	καὶ εἰ τὸ Ε τὸ Ζ κινεῖ ἐν τῷ Δ χρόνῳ τὴν Γ τὸ μῆκος, οὐκ ἀνάγκη ἐν ἴσῳ χρόνῳ[1] τὸ ἐφ' οὗ τὸ Ε[2] τὸ διπλάσιον τοῦ Ζ βάρους κινεῖν τὴν ἡμίσειαν τῆς Γ.	καὶ εἰ τὸ Ε τὸ Ζ κινεῖ ἐν τῷ Δ χρόνῳ τὴν Γ, οὐκ ἀνάγκη ἐν τῷ ἴσῳ χρόνῳ τὸ ἐφ' οὗ τὸ Ε διπλάσιον τοῦ Ζ βάρους κινεῖν τὴν ἡμίσειαν τῆς Γ.

The Aldine text of Simplicius gives the last few words in the form τὴν ἡμίσει αὐτῆς Γ, which is obviously merely a misprint. It is to be noticed that the reading here given from Simplicius is not the one which he follows in his commentary, which was apparently quite different from either of our two texts; but he himself prefers the reading I have quoted. The evidence, then, of this passage is, as far as it goes, in favour of our MSS., but I do not think much weight can be attached to it, since in a case of this kind variations of text would be almost necessary from the very beginning, it being purely an indifferent matter whether the sentence should be written in the one form or the other. Nor do I lay much stress on the fact that in several places throughout the chapter the commentary of Simplicius comes much nearer to our MSS. than to the Berlin text, for it might be argued that the glosses of Simplicius himself, or of some other commentator, had crept into the text.

The remaining passage, however, is of more importance. It is that in which Aristotle examines the paralogism of Zeno as to the falling medimnus of corn.

The two versions here are

[1] Bodleian MS. omits χρόνῳ.   [2] Z; Paris 1859 by clerical error B; so also Bodleian.

ARISTOTLE'S PHYSICS. BOOK VII.

Berlin text.	Our four MSS.
Διὰ τοῦτο ὁ Ζήνωνος λόγος οὐκ ἀληθής, ὡς ψοφεῖ τῆς κέγχρου ὁτιοῦν μέρος. οὐδὲν γὰρ κωλύει μὴ κινεῖν τὸν ἀέρα ἐν μηδενὶ χρόνῳ τοῦτον ὃν ἐκίνησεν ἐμπεσὼν ὁ ὅλος μέδιμνος.	Καὶ διὰ τοῦτο Ζήνωνος λόγος οὐκ ἀληθὴς ὡς ψοφεῖ τῆς κέγχρου ὁτιοῦν μέρος. οὐδὲν γὰρ κωλύει μὴ κινεῖν τὸν ἀέρα ἐν μηδενὶ χρόνῳ τοῦτον ὃν ἐκίνησε πεσὼν ὁ ὅλος μέδιμνος.

In this passage it seems to me that the reading ἐμπεσών cannot possibly be defended; for Aristotle is not speaking of that upon or into which the medimnus falls, but of the air through which it falls. It is not even clear whether the noise of which he speaks is that of the fall upon the earth, or merely the entirely different and equally real noise of the fall through the air, but in either case he is thinking merely of that air which is the instrument of both sounds alike. Simplicius here reads καταπεσών, which differs from the reading of our four MSS. only in being a little more precise; but Simplicius is here quoting the words of Zeno himself; and it seems probable that Aristotle, who is not quoting Zeno, but arguing against him, may have preferred to put the argument in the wider rather than in the narrower form.

The result, then, of our inquiry is, that whereas it is universally admitted by scholars that these MSS. alone give the true first text unbroken for the first three chapters of this book, the evidence of Simplicius is strongly in favour of the belief that the same thing is true of the fourth chapter; while as to the fifth chapter, we should, were the evidence between the two texts exactly balanced, be naturally and rightly inclined to prefer the claims of the four MSS. which give us the correct text throughout the rest of the book. But as a matter of fact, even as to this chapter, the balance of evidence is definitely, though but slightly, in favour of our four MSS. Hence, I think, we may safely conclude we have before us in these MSS. a nearly correct representation of the first text of the seventh book as it was known to Simplicius.

But it is not only with regard to the seventh book that the question of the comparative authority of these MSS. is of importance. Throughout the whole of the Physics these MSS., and especially Paris 1859, give a number of variants which usually accord better with the words of Themistius, Simplicius, and Johannes Philoponus, than those of any MS. quoted by Bekker, though they often nearly approach the readings of the Aldine Editio Princeps. The resemblance to Simplicius is throughout closest, but it is not one which can give rise to the supposition that these MSS. spring from an archetype which was corrected from Simplicius himself, as this resemblance is usually one rather of meaning than of phrase. Of this resemblance I will give only one example.

In the first book, p. 188 a, ll. 19-25, Aristotle is concerned to prove that almost all philosophers have in some sense or other assumed opposition as a necessary factor in the evolution of the universe. The words with which the chapter (v.) begins in the Berlin text are as follows:—

Πάντες δὴ τἀναντία ἀρχὰς ποιοῦσιν οἵ τε λέγοντες ὅτι ἓν τὸ πᾶν καὶ μὴ κινούμενον (καὶ γὰρ Παρμενίδης θερμὸν καὶ ψυχρὸν ἀρχὰς ποιεῖ, ταῦτα δὲ προσαγορεύει πῦρ καὶ γῆν) καὶ οἱ μανὸν καὶ πυκνόν, καὶ Δημόκριτος τὸ στερεὸν καὶ κενόν, ὧν τὸ μὲν ὡς ὂν τὸ δ' ὡς μὴ ὂν εἶναί φησιν· ἔτι θέσει, σχήματι, τάξει. ταῦτα δὲ γένη ἐναντίων· θέσεως ἄνω κάτω, πρόσθεν ὄπισθεν, σχήματος γωνία εὐθὺ περιφερές.

In the apparatus criticus it is noted that the MSS. F and I read γεγωνιωμένον for γωνία. But it is perfectly clear that according to either reading the text is defective. For we obviously need a contrary to γεγωνιωμένον or γωνία. Bekker, with too much reliance on the authority of E, has not troubled himself about the absurdity of the passage, in which, forsooth, Aristotle, having taken in hand to prove that the three prime differences of Demokritus are reducible to pairs of opposites, gives us under the head of σχῆμα one pair of opposites and a detached term. But in truth in the MS. E itself the error is yet greater, for not only is there no opposite to γωνία, but ὄπισθεν, the needful opposite to πρόσθεν, is also omitted; a fact which Bekker does not notice in his apparatus criticus. If then we follow E we shall have only two pair of opposites where we need four. If we do not, we may look further abroad for the correction of the passage, and we find what we need in our Paris MS. 1859, where the last two lines run thus:— ταῦτα δὲ γένη ἐναντίων· θέσεως, ἄνω κάτω, πρόσθεν ὄπισθεν, σχήματος, γεγωνιωμένον ἀγώνιον, εὐθὺ περιφερές.

This reading, which is obviously required by the sense of the passage, is supported by the commentary of Simplicius, fol. 39 a, l. 14, and by one other MS., that which has been transferred from the Cathedral Library at Paris to the National Library.

I have thought it, therefore, worth while to transcribe the whole of the Seventh Book from the MS. Paris 1859. I have corrected no errors, nor even re-inserted the omissions, although these latter are, as I have said, almost always inserted in the margin, apparently by the original scribe himself. I have placed all these inserted omissions in the apparatus criticus, together with the variants from the other three MSS. which follow generally the same text.

I shall be more than satisfied with the result if I shall be judged to have done somewhat to shake the immoderate empire of the Paris MS. 1853, Bekker's E. To the authority of this MS. all recent German editors have enslaved the text of the Aristotelian physical works. Valuable and beautiful as that MS. is, I believe that the excessive worship paid to it is an obstacle, and not an aid, to the further emendation of the text of Aristotle.

A = Parisiensis 1859; B = Parisiensis 1861; C = Parisiensis 2033;
D = Bod. Misc. ccxxxviii.

Ἅπαν τὸ κινούμενον ὑπό τινος ἀνάγκη κινεῖσθαι· εἰ μὲν γὰρ ἐν ἑαυτῷ μὴ ἔχει τὴν ἀρχὴν τῆς κινήσεως, φανερὸν ὅτι ὑφ' ἑτέρου κινεῖται· ἄλλο γὰρ ἔσται τὸ κινοῦν· εἰ δ' ἐν αὑτῷ, ἔστω¹ τὸ εἰλημμένον ἐφ' οὗ τὸ ΑΒ ὃ κινεῖται καθ' αὑτό, ἀλλὰ μὴ τούτου τι κινεῖσθαι. πρῶτον μὲν οὖν τὸ ὑπολαμβάνειν τὸ ΑΒ ὑφ' ἑαυτοῦ κινεῖσθαι διὰ τὸ ὅλον τε κινεῖσθαι καὶ ὑπ' οὐδενὸς τῶν ἔξωθεν ὅμοιόν ἐστιν ὥσπερ εἰ² τοῦ ΚΛ κινοῦντος τὸ ΛΜ καὶ αὐτοῦ κινουμένου, εἴ ²μὴ φάσκοι τις τὸ ΛΜ κινεῖσθαι ὑπό τινος³ διὰ τὸ μὴ φανερὸν εἶναι πότερον τὸ κινοῦν καὶ πότερον τὸ κινούμενον· εἶτα τὸ μὴ ὑπό τινος κινούμενον οὐκ ἀνάγκη παύσασθαι κινούμενον τῷ ἄλλο ἠρεμεῖν, 242 a. ἀλλ' εἴ τι ἠρεμεῖ τῷ ἄλλο πεπαῦσθαι κινούμενον, ἀνάγκη ὑπό τινος αὐτὸ κινεῖσθαι. τούτου γὰρ εἰλημμένου πᾶν τὸ κινούμενον κινήσεται ὑπό τινος. ἐπεὶ γὰρ εἴληπται τὸ κινούμενον ἐφ' ᾧ τὸ ΑΒ, ἀνάγκη διαιρετὸν αὐτὸ εἶναι· πᾶν γὰρ τὸ κινούμενον διαιρετόν. διῃρήσθω δὴ κατὰ τὸ Γ. τοῦ δὴ ΓΒ μὴ κινουμένου οὐ κινηθήσεται τὸ ΑΒ· εἰ γὰρ κινήσεται, δῆλον ὅτι τὸ ΑΓ κινοῖτ' ἂν τοῦ ΓΒ⁴ ἠρεμοῦντος, ὥστε οὐ καθ' αὑτὸ κινηθήσεται καὶ πρῶτον, ἀλλ' ὑπέκειτο καθ' αὑτὸ κινεῖσθαι καὶ πρῶτον. ἀνάγκη ἄρα τοῦ ΓΒ μὴ κινουμένου ἠρεμεῖν τὸ ΑΒ. ὃ δὲ ἠρεμεῖ μὴ κινουμένου τινός, ὡμολόγηται⁵ ὑπό τινος κινεῖσθαι, ὥστε πᾶν ἀνάγκη τὸ κινούμενον ὑπό τινος κινεῖσθαι· ἀεὶ γὰρ ἔσται τὸ κινούμενον διαιρετόν, τοῦ δὲ μέρους μὴ κινουμένου ἀνάγκη καὶ τὸ ὅλον ἠρεμεῖν. ἐπεὶ δὲ πᾶν τὸ κινούμενον ἀνάγκη κινεῖσθαι ὑπό τινος, ἐάν γέ ⁶τι κινῆται⁶ τὴν ἐν τόπῳ κίνησιν ὑπ' ἄλλου κινουμένου, καὶ πάλιν τὸ κινοῦν ὑπ' ἄλλου κινουμένου κινῆται⁷ κἀκεῖνο ὑφ' ἑτέρου καὶ ἀεὶ οὕτως,

¹ ἔσται Β.   ² ἡ BCD.   ³ μὴ ὑπολαμβάνει τις τὸ ΛΜ κινεῖσθαι διὰ τὸ μὴ συνορᾶν πότερον ὑπὸ ποτέρου κεκίνηται [κινεῖται D], πότερον τὸ ΔΕ ὑπὸ τοῦ ΕΖ ἢ τὸ ΕΖ ὑπὸ τοῦ ΕΔ. ἔτι τὸ ὑφ' ἑαυτοῦ κινούμενον οὐδέποτε παύσεται κινούμενον τῷ ἕτερόν τι στῆναι κινούμενον· εἰ τι παύεται κινούμενον τῷ ἕτερόν τι στῆναι κινούμενον τοῦθ' ὑφ' ἑτέρου κινεῖσθαι· τούτου γὰρ φανεροῦ γιγνομένου ἀνάγκη πᾶν τὸ κινούμενον κινεῖσθαι ὑπό τινος C et D e textu secundo; neque aliter B nisi quod post secundum στῆναι κινούμενον reiterat ἀνάγκη τοίνυν.   ⁴ ΑΒ Β.   ⁵ ὡμολόγητο BCD.   ⁶ κινεῖσθαι D.   ⁷ κινεῖται BC, κινεῖσθαι cor. κινεῖται D.

(15)

ἀνάγκη εἶναί τι τὸ πρῶτον κινοῦν, καὶ μὴ βαδίζειν εἰς ἄπειρον[1]. μὴ γὰρ[2] ἔστω ἀλλὰ γενέσθω ἄπειρον· κινείσθω δὲ τὸ μὲν Α ὑπὸ τοῦ Β, τὸ δὲ Β ὑπὸ τοῦ Γ, τὸ δὲ Γ[3] ὑπὸ τοῦ Δ, καὶ ἀεὶ τὸ ἐχόμενον ὑπὸ τοῦ ἐχομένου, ἐπεὶ οὖν ὑπόκειται τὸ κινοῦν κινούμενον κινεῖν ἀνάγκη ἅμα γίνεσθαι τὴν τοῦ κινουμένου καὶ τὴν τοῦ κινοῦντος κίνησιν· ἅμα γὰρ κινεῖ[4] τὸ κινοῦν καὶ κινεῖται τὸ κινούμενον· φανερὸν ὅτι[5] ἅμα ἔσται τοῦ Α καὶ τοῦ Β καὶ τοῦ Γ καὶ ἑκάστου τῶν κινούντων καὶ κινουμένων ἡ κίνησις. εἰλήφθω οὖν ἡ ἑκάστου κίνησις καὶ ἔστω τοῦ μὲν Α ἐφ' ἧς Ε, τοῦ δὲ Β ἐφ' ἧς Ζ, τῶν ΓΔ ἐφ' ὧν ΗΘ. εἰ γὰρ ἀεὶ κινεῖται ἕκαστον ὑφ' ἑκάστου, ὅμως ἔσται λαβεῖν μίαν ἑκάστου κίνησιν τῷ ἀριθμῷ· πᾶσα γὰρ κίνησις ἔκ τινος εἴς τι, καὶ οὐκ ἄπειρος τοῖς ἐσχάτοις· λέγω δὴ ἀριθμῷ μίαν κίνησιν τὴν ἐκ τοῦ αὐτοῦ εἰς τὸ αὐτὸ τῷ ἀριθμῷ ἐν τῷ αὐτῷ χρόνῳ τῷ ἀριθμῷ γιγνομένην. ἔστι γὰρ κίνησις καὶ γένει καὶ εἴδει καὶ ἀριθμῷ ἡ αὐτή, γένει μὲν ἡ τῆς αὐτῆς κατηγορίας, οἷον οὐσίας ἢ ποιότητος, εἴδει δὲ [6]ἐκ τοῦ αὐτοῦ τῷ εἴδει[6], οἷον ἐκ 242b. λευκοῦ εἰς [7]μέλαν ἐξ[7] ἀγαθοῦ εἰς κακὸν ἀδιάφορον τῷ εἴδει· ἀριθμῷ δὲ ἡ ἐξ ἑνὸς τῷ ἀριθμῷ ἐν τῷ αὐτῷ χρόνῳ οἷον ἐκ τοῦδε τοῦ λευκοῦ εἰς τόδε τὸ μέλαν, ἢ ἐκ τοῦδε τοῦ τόπου εἰς τόνδε ἐν τῷδε τῷ χρόνῳ· εἰ γὰρ ἐν ἄλλῳ, οὐκέτι ἔσται ἀριθμῷ μία κίνησις, ἀλλ' εἴδει. εἴρηται δὲ περὶ τούτων[8] ἐν τοῖς πρότερον. εἰλήφθω δὲ καὶ ὁ χρόνος ἐν ᾧ κεκίνηται τὴν αὑτοῦ κίνησιν τὸ Α, καὶ ἔστω ἐφ' ᾧ Κ· πεπερασμένης δ' οὔσης τῆς τοῦ Α κινήσεως καὶ ὁ χρόνος ἔσται πεπερασμένος[9]. ἐπεὶ δ' ἄπειρα[10] τὰ κινοῦντα καὶ τὰ κινούμενα, καὶ ἡ κίνησις ἡ ΕΖΗΘ ἡ ἐξ ἁπασῶν ἄπειρος ἔσται. ἐνδέχεται μὲν γὰρ ἴσην εἶναι τὴν τοῦ Α καὶ τοῦ Β καὶ τὴν τῶν ἄλλων,[11] ἐνδέχεται δὲ μείζους τὰς τῶν ἄλλων[11] ὥστε εἴ[12] ἀεί τε μείζους, ἀμφοτέρως ἄπειρος ἡ ὅλη. λαμβάνομεν γὰρ τὸ ἐνδεχόμενον. ἐπεὶ δ' ἅμα κινεῖται καὶ τὸ Α καὶ τῶν ἄλλων ἕκαστον, ἡ ὅλη κίνησις ἐν τῷ αὐτῷ χρόνῳ ἔσται καὶ ἡ τοῦ Α· ἡ δὲ τοῦ Α ἐν πεπερασμένῳ[13]· τοῦτο δ' ἀδύνατον. οὕτω μὲν οὖν δόξειεν ἂν δεδεῖχθαι τὸ ἐξ ἀρχῆς, οὐ μὴν ἀποδείκνυται διὰ τὸ μηδὲν δείκνυσθαι ἀδύνατον· ἐνδέχεται γὰρ ἐν πεπερασμένῳ χρόνῳ ἄπειρον εἶναι κίνησιν, μὴ ἑνὸς ἀλλὰ πολλῶν. ὅπερ συμβαίνει καὶ ἐπὶ τούτων· ἕκαστον γὰρ κινεῖται τὴν ἑαυτοῦ κίνησιν, ἅμα δὲ πολλὰ κινεῖσθαι οὐκ ἀδύνατον. [14]ἀλλ' εἰ[14] τὸ κινοῦν

[1] ἄπειρα BCD. [2] δὲ BCD. [3] Δ BC. [4] om. B. [5] om. BCD. [6] εἰς τὸ αὐτὸ τῷ εἴδει inserit D. [7] μέλαν ἢ ἐξ BCD. [8] τούτου D. [9] hic D inserit e textu secundo verba καὶ οὐκ ἄπειρος εἴη. ἀλλ' ἐν τῷ αὐτῷ χρόνῳ ἐκινεῖτο τὸ Α καὶ τὸ Κ (cor. Β) καὶ τῶν ἄλλων ἕκαστον nihil tamen prioris omittit. [10] ἄρα D. [11] om. BD, C habet ἐνδέχεται δὲ μείζους sed erasum. [12] εἰς BCD. [13] πεπερασμένῳ, ὥστε εἴη ἂν ἄπειρος ἐν [τῷ Β] πεπερασμένῳ BCD necnon A in margine. [14] ἀλλὰ D.

πρῶτον κατὰ τόπον καὶ σωματικὴν κίνησιν ἀνάγκη ἢ ἅπτεσθαι ἢ συνεχὲς εἶναι τῷ κινουμένῳ, καθάπερ ὁρῶμεν ἐπὶ πάντων, ἀνάγκη τὰ κινούμενα καὶ τὰ κινοῦντα συνεχῆ εἶναι ἢ ἅπτεσθαι ἀλλήλων, ὥστ' εἶναί τι ἐξ ἁπάντων ἕν. τοῦτο δὲ εἴτε πεπερασμένου εἴτε ἄπειρον οὐδὲν διαφέρει πρὸς τὰ νῦν· πάντως² γὰρ ἡ κίνησις ἔσται ἄπειρος ἀπείρων ὄντων, εἴπερ ἐνδέχεται καὶ³ ἴσας εἶναι καὶ μείζους ἀλλήλων· ὃ γὰρ ἐνδέχεται, ληψόμεθα ὡς ὑπάρχον. εἰ οὖν τὸ μὲν ἐκ τῶν ΑΒΓΔ ἄπειρόν τι ἐστίν, κινεῖται δὲ τὴν ΕΖΗΘ κίνησιν ἐν τῷ χρόνῳ τῷ Κ οὗτος δὲ πεπέρανται, συμβαίνει ἐν πεπερασμένῳ χρόνῳ ἄπειρον διιέναι ἢ τὸ πεπερασμένον ἢ τὸ ἄπειρον. ἀμφοτέρως δὲ ἀδύνατον· ὥστε ἀνάγκη ἵστασθαι καὶ εἶναί τι πρῶτον κινοῦν καὶ⁴ κινούμενον. οὐδὲν γὰρ διαφέρει τὸ συμβαίνειν ἐξ ὑποθέσεως τὸ ἀδύνατον· ἡ γὰρ ὑπόθεσις εἴληπ- 243 a. ται ἐνδεχομένη, τοῦ δ' ἐνδεχομένου τεθέντος οὐδὲν προσήκει γίγνεσθαι διὰ τοῦτο ἀδύνατον.

2. Τὸ δὲ πρῶτον⁵ κινοῦν, μὴ ὡς τὸ οὗ ἕνεκεν, ἀλλ' ὅθεν ἡ ἀρχὴ τῆς κινήσεως ἅμα τῷ κινουμένῳ ἐστί· λέγω δὲ τὸ ἅμα, ὅτι οὐδέν ἐστιν αὐτῶν μεταξύ· τοῦτο γὰρ κοινὸν ἐπὶ παντὸς κινουμένου καὶ κινοῦντός ἐστιν. ἐπεὶ δὲ τρεῖς αἱ κινήσεις, ἥ τε κατὰ τόπον καὶ ἡ κατὰ τὸ ποιὸν καὶ ἡ κατὰ τὸ ποσόν, ἀνάγκη καὶ⁶ τὰ κινοῦντα τρία⁷ εἶναι, τό τε ἀλλοιοῦν,⁷ καὶ τὸ αὖξον ἢ φθῖνον. πρῶτον οὖν εἴπωμεν περὶ τῆς φορᾶς· πρώτη γὰρ αὕτη τῶν κινήσεων. ἅπαν δὴ τὸ φερόμενον ἢ ὑφ' ἑαυτοῦ κινεῖται ἢ ὑπ' ἄλλου. ὅσα μὲν οὖν αὐτὰ ὑφ' αὑτῶν κινεῖται, φανερὸν ἐν τούτοις ὅτι ἅμα τὸ κινούμενον καὶ τὸ κινοῦν ἐστίν· ἐνυπάρχει γὰρ αὐτοῖς τὸ πρῶτον⁸ κινοῦν, ὥστ' οὐδέν ἐστιν ἀναμεταξύ. ὅσα δ' ὑπ' ἄλλου κινεῖται, τετραχῶς ἀνάγκη γίγνεσθαι· τέτταρα τῆς⁹ εἴδη τῆς ὑπ' ἄλλου φορᾶς, ἕλξις ὦσις¹⁰ ὄχησις δίνησις. ἅπασαι γὰρ αἱ κατὰ τόπον κινήσεις ἀνάγονται εἰς ταύτας· ἡ μὲν γὰρ ἔπωσις ὦσίς τίς ἐστιν, ὅταν τὸ ἀπ' αὑτοῦ κινοῦν ἐπακόλουθον¹¹ ὠθῇ, ἡ δ' ἄπωσις, ὅταν μὴ ἐπακολουθῇ κινήσαν, ἡ δὴ ῥῖψις ὅταν σφοδροτέραν ποιήσῃ τὴν ἀπ' αὑτοῦ κίνησιν τῆς κατὰ φύσιν 243 b. φορᾶς, καὶ μέχρι τοσούτου φέρεται ἕως ἂν κρατῇ ἡ κίνησις. πάλιν ἡ δίωσις καὶ σύνωσις ἄπωσις καὶ ἕλξις εἰσίν· ἡ μὲν γὰρ δίωσις ἄπωσις, ἢ γὰρ ἀπ' αὑτοῦ ἢ ἀπ' ἄλλου ἐστὶν ἡ ἄπωσις, ἡ δὲ σύνωσις ἕλξις, καὶ γὰρ πρὸς αὑτὸ καὶ πρὸς ἄλλο ἡ ἕλξις. ὥστε καὶ ὅσα τούτων εἴδη, οἷον σπάθησις καὶ κέρκισις· ἡ μὲν γὰρ σύνωσις, ἡ δὲ δίωσις. ὁμοίως δὲ καὶ αἱ¹² ἄλλαι συγκρίσεις καὶ διακρίσεις· ἅπασαι γὰρ ἔσονται διώσεις ἢ συνώσεις, πλὴν ὅσαι ἐν

γενέσει καὶ φθορᾷ εἰσίν. ἅμα δὲ φανερὸν ὅτι [1] οὐδ' ἔστιν [1] ἄλλο τι γένος κινήσεως ἢ σύγκρισις καὶ διάκρισις· ἅπασαι γὰρ διανέμονται εἴς τινας τῶν εἰρημένων. ἔτι δ' ἡ μὲν εἰσπνοὴ ἕλξις, ἡ δὲ ἐκπνοὴ ὦσις. ὁμοίως δὲ καὶ ἡ πτύσις, καὶ ὅσαι ἄλλαι διὰ τοῦ σώματος ἢ ἐκκριτικαὶ ἢ ληπτικαὶ κινήσεις· αἱ μὲν γὰρ ἕλξεις εἰσίν, αἱ δ' ἀπώσεις. δεῖ δὲ καὶ τὰς ἄλλας τὰς κατὰ τόπον ἀνάγειν· ἅπασαι γὰρ πίπτουσιν εἰς τέσσαρας ταύτας. τούτων δὲ πάλιν ἡ [2] ὄχησις [2] καὶ ἡ δίνησις εἰς ἕλξιν καὶ ὦσιν. ἡ μὲν γὰρ [4] ὄχησις [2] κατὰ τούτων τινὰ τῶν τριῶν τρόπων ἐστίν· τὸ μὲν γὰρ ὀχούμενον κινεῖται κατὰ συμβεβηκός, ὅτι ἐν κινουμένῳ ἐστὶν ἢ ἐπὶ κινουμένου τινός, τὸ δ' ὀχοῦν [5] ὀχεῖ ἢ ἑλκόμενον ἢ ὠθούμενον ἢ δινούμενον, ὥστε κοινή ἐστιν ἁπασῶν τῶν τριῶν ἡ ὄχησις. ἡ δὲ δίνησις σύγκειται ἐξ ἕλξεώς τε καὶ ὤσεως· ἀνάγκη γὰρ τὸ δινοῦν τὸ μὲν ἕλκειν τὸ δ' ὠθεῖν· τὸ μὲν γὰρ ἀφ' αὑτοῦ τὸ δὲ πρὸς αὑτὸν [6] ἄγει. ὥστ' εἰ τὸ ὠθοῦν καὶ τὸ ἕλκον ἅμα τῷ ὠθουμένῳ καὶ τῷ ἑλκομένῳ, φανερὸν ὅτι τοῦ κατὰ τόπον κινουμένου καὶ κινοῦντος οὐδέν ἐστι μεταξύ. ἀλλὰ μὴν τοῦτο δῆλον καὶ ἐκ τῶν ὁρισμῶν· ὦσις μὲν γάρ ἐστιν ἡ ἀφ' αὑτοῦ ἢ ἀπ' ἄλλου πρὸς ἄλλο κίνησις, ἕλξις δὲ ἡ ἀπ' ἄλλου πρὸς αὑτὸ ἢ πρὸς ἄλλο, ὅταν θᾶττον ἡ κίνησις ᾖ τοῦ ἕλκοντος [7] τῆς χωριζούσης [7] ἀπ' ἀλλήλων τὰ συνεχῆ. οὕτω γὰρ συνεφέλκεται θάτερον. τάχα δὲ δόξειεν ἂν εἶναί τις ἕλξις καὶ ἄλλως· τὸ γὰρ ξύλον ἕλκει οὐχ οὕτως. τὸ δ' οὐθὲν διαφέρει κινουμένου τοῦ ἕλκοντος ἢ μένοντος ἕλκειν. ὁτὲ μὲν γὰρ ἕλκει οὗ ἔστιν, ὁτὲ δὲ οὗ ἦν. ἀδύνατον δὲ ἢ [8] ἀφ' αὑτοῦ πρὸς ἄλλο ἢ ἀπ' ἄλλου πρὸς αὑτὸ κινεῖν μὴ ἁπτόμενον, ὥστε φανερὸν ὅτι τοῦ κατὰ τόπον κινουμένου καὶ κινοῦντος οὐδέν ἐστι μεταξύ. ἀλλὰ μὴν οὐδὲ τοῦ ἀλλοιουμένου καὶ τοῦ ἀλλοιοῦντος. τοῦτο δὲ δῆλον ἐξ ἐπαγωγῆς· ἐν ἅπασι γὰρ συμβαίνει ἅμα εἶναι τὸ ἔσχατον ἀλλοιοῦν καὶ τὸ ἀλλοιούμενον ὑπὸ τῶν εἰρημένων. ταῦτα γάρ ἐστι πάθη τῆς ὑποκειμένης ποιότητος· ἢ γὰρ θερμαινόμενον ἢ γλυκαινόμενον ἢ πυκνούμενον ἢ ξηραινόμενον ἢ λευκαινόμενον ἀλλοιοῦσθαί φαμεν, ὁμοίως τε τὸ ἄψυχον καὶ τὸ ἔμψυχον λέγοντες, καὶ πάλιν τῶν ἐμψύχων τά τε μὴ αἰσθητικὰ τῶν μερῶν καὶ αὐτὰς τὰς αἰσθήσεις. ἀλλοιοῦνται γάρ πως καὶ αἱ αἰσθήσεις· ἡ γὰρ αἴσθησις ἡ κατ' ἐνέργειαν κίνησίς ἐστι διὰ τοῦ σώματος, πασχούσης τι τῆς αἰσθήσεως, καθ' ὅσα μὲν οὖν τὸ ἄψυχον ἀλλοιοῦται, καὶ τὸ ἔμψυχον, καθ' ὅσα δὲ τὸ ἔμψυχον οὐ κατὰ ταῦτα πάντα τὸ ἄψυχον· οὐ γὰρ ἀλλοιοῦται κατὰ τὰς αἰσθήσεις, καὶ τὸ μὲν λανθάνει, τὸ δ' οὐ λανθάνει πάσχον.

[1] οὐδέν ἐστιν D.   [2] ὄχησις BC.   [3] om. D.   [4] ὄχησις BC.   [5] ὠθοῦν BCD.
[6] αὑτόν CD.   [7] ἡ χωρίζουσα BCD.   [8] ἡ B.

οὐδὲν δὲ κωλύει καὶ τὸ ἔμψυχον λανθάνειν ὅταν μὴ κατὰ τὰς αἰσθήσεις 245 a. γίγνηται ἡ ἀλλοίωσις. εἴπερ οὖν ἀλλοιοῦται τὸ ἀλλοιούμενον ὑπὸ τῶν αἰσθητῶν, ἐν ἅπασί γε τούτοις φανερὸν ὅτι ἅμα ἐστὶ τὸ ἔσχατον ἀλλοιοῦν καὶ τὸ πρῶτον ἀλλοιούμενον· τῷ μὲν γὰρ συνεχὴς ὁ ἀήρ, τῷ δ᾽ ἀέρι τὸ σῶμα. πάλιν δὲ τὸ μὲν χρῶμα τῷ φωτί, τὸ δὲ φῶς τῇ ὄψει. τὸν αὐτὸν δὲ τρόπον καὶ ἡ ἀκοὴ καὶ ἡ ὄσφρησις· πρῶτον γὰρ κινοῦν πρὸς τὸ κινούμενον ὁ ἀήρ. καὶ ἐπὶ τῆς γεύσεως ὁμοίως· ἅμα γὰρ τῇ γεύσει ὁ χυμὸς ὡσαύτως δὲ καὶ ἐπὶ τῶν ἀψύχων καὶ ἀναισθήτων· ὥστ᾽ οὐδὲν ἔσται μεταξὺ τοῦ ἀλλοιουμένου καὶ τοῦ ἀλλοιοῦντος [1]. οὐδὲ μὴν τοῦ αὐξανομένου τε καὶ αὔξοντος· αὔξάνει γὰρ τὸ πρῶτον αὖξον προσγινόμενον, ὥστε ἓν γίγνεσθαι τὸ ὅλον. καὶ πάλιν φθίνει τὸ φθίνον ἀπογινομένου τινὸς τῶν τοῦ φθίνοντος. ἀνάγκη οὖν συνεχὲς εἶναι καὶ τὸ αὖξον καὶ τὸ φθίνον, τῶν δὲ συνεχῶν οὐδὲν μεταξύ. φανερὸν οὖν [2] ὅτι τοῦ κινουμένου καὶ τοῦ κινοῦντος πρώτου καὶ ἐσχάτου 245 b. πρὸς τὸ κινούμενον οὐδέν ἐστιν ἀνὰ μέσον.

3. Ὅτι δὲ τὸ ἀλλοιούμενον ἅπαν ἀλλοιοῦται ὑπὸ τῶν αἰσθητῶν [3] καὶ ἐν μόνοις ὑπάρχει τούτοις ἀλλοίωσις ὅσα καθ᾽ αὑτὰ λέγεται πάσχειν ὑπὸ τῶν αἰσθητῶν [3], ἐκ τῶνδε θεωρητέον. τῶν γὰρ ἄλλων μάλιστ᾽ ἄν τις ὑπολάβοι ἔν τε τοῖς σχήμασι καὶ ἐν [4] ταῖς μορφαῖς καὶ ἐν ταῖς ἕξεσι καὶ [5] ταῖς τούτων λήψεσι καὶ ἀποβολαῖς ἀλλοίωσιν ὑπάρχειν· ἐν οὐδετέροις δ᾽ ἔστιν. τὸ μὲν γὰρ σχηματιζόμενον ὅταν ἐπιτελεσθῇ, οὐ λέγομεν ἐκεῖνο ἐξ οὗ ἐστίν, οἷον τὸν ἀνδριάντα χαλκὸν ἢ τὴν πυραμίδα κηρὸν ἢ τὴν κλίνην ξύλον, ἀλλὰ παρωνυμιάζοντες τὸν μὲν χαλκοῦν τὸν δὲ κήρινον, τὸ δὲ ξύλινον τὸ δὲ πεπονθὸς καὶ ἠλλοιωμένον προσαγορεύομεν· ξηρὸν γὰρ καὶ ὑγρὸν καὶ σκληρὸν καὶ θερμὸν τὸν χαλκὸν λέγομεν καὶ τὸν κηρόν. καὶ οὐ μόνον οὕτως, ἀλλὰ καὶ [5] τὸ ὑγρὸν καὶ τὸ θερμὸν χαλκὸν λέγομεν, ὁμωνύμως τῷ πάθει προσαγορεύοντες τὴν ὕλην. ὥστ᾽ εἰ κατὰ μὲν τὸ σχῆμα καὶ τὴν μορφὴν οὐ λέγεται 246 a. τὸ γεγονὸς ἐν ᾧ ἐστὶ τὸ σχῆμα, κατὰ δὲ τὰ πάθη καὶ τὰς ἀλλοιώσεις λέγεται, φανερὸν ὅτι οὐκ ἂν εἶεν αἱ γενέσεις αὗται ἀλλοιώσεις. ἔτι δὲ καὶ εἰπεῖν οὕτως ἄτοπον ἂν δόξειεν, ἢ ἀλλοιοῦσθαι τὸν ἄνθρωπον ἢ τὴν οἰκίαν ἢ ἄλλο ὁτιοῦν τῶν γεγενημένων· ἀλλὰ γίνεσθαι μὲν ἴσως ἕκαστον ἀναγκαῖον ἀλλοιουμένου τινός, οἷον τῆς ὕλης πυκνουμένης ἢ μανουμένης ἢ θερμαινομένης ἢ ψυχομένης, οὐ μέντοι τὰ γινόμενά γε ἀλλοιοῦται, οὐδ᾽ ἡ γένεσις αὐτῶν ἀλλοίωσίς [7] ἐστιν. ἀλλὰ μὴν οὐδ᾽ αἱ ἕξεις οὔθ᾽ αἱ τοῦ σώματος οὔθ᾽ αἱ τῆς ψυχῆς ἀλλοιώσεις [7], αἱ μὲν γὰρ ἀρεταὶ αἱ δὲ κακίαι τῶν ἕξεων· οὐκ ἔστι δὲ

[1] B inserit οὐδὲ μὴν τοῦ αὐξανομένου καὶ ἀλλοιοῦντος. [2] δὲ D. [3] om. BCD.
[4] om. D. [5] ἐν Β. [6] om. D. [7] om. BCD.

οὔτε ἡ ἀρετὴ οὔτε ἡ κακία ἀλλοίωσις, ἀλλ' ἡ μὲν ἀρετὴ τελείωσίς τίς ἐστιν¹. ὅταν γὰρ² λάβῃ τὴν ἑαυτοῦ ἀρετήν, τότε λέγεται τέλειον ἕκαστον· τότε γὰρ ἐστι³ μάλιστα τὸ κατὰ φύσιν, ὥσπερ κύκλος τέλειος, ὅταν μάλιστα γένηται κύκλος βέλτιστος, ἡ δὲ κακία φθορὰ τούτου καὶ ἔκστασις. ὥσπερ οὖν οὔτε τὸ τῆς οἰκίας τελείωμα λέγομεν ἀλλοίωσιν· ἄτοπον γὰρ εἰ ὁ θριγκὸς καὶ ὁ κέραμος ἀλλοίωσις, ⁴ἢ εἰ θριγκουμένη⁴ καὶ κεραμουμένη ἀλλοιοῦται ἀλλὰ μὴ 246b. τελειοῦται ἡ οἰκία· ⁵τὸν αὐτὸν τρόπον⁵ καὶ ἐπὶ τῶν ἀρετῶν καὶ τῶν κακιῶν καὶ τῶν ἐχόντων ἢ λαμβανόντων· αἱ μὲν γὰρ τελειώσεις, αἱ δὲ ἐκστάσεις εἰσίν, ὥστ'-οὐκ ἀλλοιώσεις. ἔτι δὲ καὶ φαμεν ἁπάσας εἶναι τὰς ἀρετὰς ἐν τῷ πρός τι πῶς ἔχειν. τὰς μὲν γὰρ τοῦ σώματος, οἷον ὑγίειαν καὶ εὐεξίαν, ἐν κράσει καὶ συμμετρίᾳ θερμῶν καὶ ψυχρῶν τίθεμεν, ἢ ⁶αὐτῶν πρὸς αὑτὰ⁶ τῶν ἐντὸς ἢ πρὸς τὸ περιέχον· ὁμοίως δὲ καὶ τὸ κάλλος καὶ τὴν ἰσχὺν καὶ τὰς ἄλλας ἀρετὰς καὶ κακίας. ἑκάστη γάρ ἐστι τῷ πρός τι πῶς ἔχειν, καὶ περὶ τὰ οἰκεῖα πάθη εὖ ἢ κακῶς διατίθησι τὸ ἔχον· οἰκεῖα δ' ὑφ' ὧν γίγνεσθαι καὶ φθείρεσθαι πέφυκεν. ἐπεὶ οὖν τὰ πρός τι οὔτε αὐτά ἐστιν ἀλλοιώσεις, οὔτε αὐτῶν ἐστιν ἀλλοίωσις οὐδὲ γένεσις, οὔθ' ὅλως οὐδὲ μεταβολὴ οὐδεμία, φανερὸν ὅτι οὔθ' αἱ ἕξεις οὔθ' αἱ τῶν ἕξεων ἀποβολαὶ καὶ λήψεις ἀλλοιώσεις εἰσίν, ἀλλὰ γίνεσθαι μὲν ἴσως αὐτὰς καὶ φθείρεσθαι ἀλλοιουμένων τινῶν ἀνάγκη, καθάπερ καὶ τὸ εἶδος καὶ τὴν μορφήν, οἷον θερμῶν καὶ ψυχρῶν ἢ ξηρῶν καὶ ὑγρῶν, ἢ ἐν οἷς τυγχάνουσιν οὖσαι πρώτοις. περὶ ταῦτα γὰρ ἑκάστη λέγεται κακία καὶ ἀρετή, ὑφ' ὧν ἀλλοιοῦσθαι πέφυκε τὸ ἔχον· ἡ μὲν γὰρ ἀρετὴ ποιεῖ ἀπαθὲς ἢ ὡς δεῖ παθητικόν, ἡ δὲ κακία παθητικὸν 247a. μὲν ἐναντίως καὶ ἀπαθές. ὁμοίως δὲ καὶ ἐπὶ τῶν τῆς ψυχῆς ἕξεων· ⁷ἅπασαι γὰρ⁷ καὶ αὗται τῷ πρός τι πῶς ἔχειν, καὶ αἱ μὲν ἀρεταὶ τελειώσεις, αἱ δὲ κακίαι ἐκστάσεις, ἔτι δὲ ἡ μὲν ἀρετὴ εὖ διατίθησι πρὸς τὰ οἰκεῖα πάθη, ἡ δὲ κακία κακῶς. ὥστ' οὐδ' αὗται ἔσονται ἀλλοιώσεις· οὐδὲ δὴ αἱ⁸ ἀποβολαὶ καὶ αἱ λήψεις αὐτῶν. γίνεσθαι δ' αὐτὰς ἀναγκαῖον ἀλλοιουμένου τοῦ αἰσθητικοῦ μέρους. ἀλλοιωθήσεται δ' ὑπὸ τῶν αἰσθητῶν· ἅπασα γὰρ ἡ⁹ ἠθικὴ ἀρετὴ περὶ ἡδονὰς καὶ λύπας τὰς σωματικάς, αὗται δὲ ἢ ἐν τῷ πράττειν ἢ ἐν τῷ μεμνῆσθαι ἢ ἐν τῷ ἐλπίζειν. αἱ μὲν οὖν ἐν τῇ πράξει κατὰ τὴν αἴσθησίν εἰσιν, ὥσθ' ὑπ' αἰσθητοῦ τινὸς κινεῖσθαι, αἱ δ' ἐν τῇ μνήμῃ καὶ τῇ ἐλπίδι ἀπὸ ταύτης εἰσίν, ἢ γὰρ οἷα ἔπαθον μεμνημένοι ἥδονται, ἢ ἐλπίζοντες οἷα μέλλουσιν. ὥστ' ἀνάγκη πᾶσαν τὴν τοιαύτην ἡδονὴν ὑπὸ τῶν αἰσθητῶν

¹ om. D.   ² om. BC.   ³ om. D.   ⁴ ἢ εἰ ἡ θριγκουμένη C.   ⁵ τὸν αὐτὸν δὴ τρόπον D.   ⁶ αὐτὰ πρὸς αὐτὰ BCD.   ⁷ ἅπασαι μὲν γὰρ D.   ⁸ καὶ BCD, sed D cor. καὶ αἱ   ⁹ om. D.

γίγνεσθαι. ἐπεὶ δ' ἡδονῆς καὶ λύπης ἐγγιγνομένης καὶ ἡ κακία καὶ ἡ ἀρετὴ ἐγγίγνεται, περὶ ταύτας γάρ εἰσίν, αἱ δ' ἡδοναὶ καὶ αἱ λῦπαι ἀλλοιώσεις τοῦ αἰσθητικοῦ, φανερὸν ὅτι ἀλλοιουμένου τινὸς ἀνάγκη καὶ ταύτας ἀποβάλλειν καὶ λαμβάνειν. ὥσθ'[1] ἡ μὲν γένεσις αὐτῶν μετ' ἀλλοιώσεως, αὕτη δ' οὐκ ἔστιν ἀλλοίωσις. ἀλλὰ μὴν [2] οὐδ' αἱ [3] τοῦ νοητοῦ μέρους ἕξεις ἀλ- 247b. λοιώσεις, οὐδ' ἔστιν αὐτῶν γένεσις. πολὺ γὰρ μάλιστα τὸ ἐπιστῆμον ἐν τῷ πρός τί πως ἔχειν λέγομεν. ἔτι δὲ καὶ φανερὸν ὅτι οὐκ ἔστιν αὐτῶν γένεσις. τὸ γὰρ κατὰ δύναμιν ἐπιστῆμον οὐδὲν αὐτὸ κινηθὲν ἀλλὰ τῷ ἄλλο ὑπάρξαι γίγνεται ἐπιστῆμον. ὅταν γὰρ γένηται τὸ κατὰ μέρος, ἐπίσταταί πως τῇ καθόλου τὸ ἐν μέρει. πάλιν δὲ τῆς χρήσεως καὶ τῆς ἐνεργείας οὐκ ἔστι γένεσις, εἰ μή τις καὶ τῆς ἀναβλέψεως καὶ τῆς ἀφῆς οἴεται γένεσιν εἶναι, καὶ τὸ ἐνεργεῖν ὅμοιον τούτοις. ἡ δ' ἐξ ἀρχῆς λῆψις τῆς ἐπιστήμης γένεσις οὐκ ἔστιν οὐδ' ἀλλοίωσις· τῷ[3] γὰρ ἠρεμῆσαι καὶ στῆναι τὴν διανοίαν ἐπίστασθαι καὶ φρονεῖν λεγόμεθα, εἰς δὲ τὸ ἠρεμεῖν οὐκ ἔστι γένεσις· ὅλως γὰρ οὐδεμιᾶς μεταβολῆς, καθάπερ εἴρηται πρότερον. ἔτι δ' ὥσπερ ὅταν ἐκ τοῦ μεθύειν ἢ καθεύδειν ἢ νοσεῖν εἰς τἀναντία μεταστῇ τις, οὐ φαμὲν ἐπιστήμονα γεγονέναι πάλιν, καίτοι ἀδύνατος[4] ἦν[5] τῇ ἐπιστήμῃ χρῆσθαι πρότερον, οὕτως[6] οὐδ' ὅταν ἐξ ἀρχῆς λαμβάνῃ τὴν ἕξιν· τῷ γὰρ καθίστασθαι τὴν ψυχὴν ἐκ τῆς φυσικῆς[7] ἀρετῆς φρόνιμόν τι γίνεται[8] καὶ ἐπιστῆμον. διὸ καὶ τὰ παιδία οὔτε μανθάνειν δύνανται οὔτε κατὰ τὰς αἰσθήσεις ὁμοίως κρίνειν τοῖς πρεσ- 248 a. βυτέροις· πολλὴ γὰρ ἡ ταραχὴ καὶ ἡ κίνησις. καθίσταται δὲ καὶ ἠρεμίζει πρὸς ἔνια δ' ὑπ' ἄλλων, ἐν ἀμφοτέροις δὲ ἀλλοιουμένων τινῶν τῶν ἐν σώματι καθάπερ ἐπὶ τῆς χρήσεως καὶ τῆς ἐνεργείας, ὅταν νήφων γένηται καὶ ἐγερθῇ. φανερὸν οὖν ἐκ τῶν εἰρημένων ὅτι τὸ ἀλλοιοῦσθαι καὶ ἡ ἀλλοίωσις ἔν τε τοῖς αἰσθητοῖς γίγνεται καὶ ἡ ἐν τῷ αἰσθητικῷ μορίῳ τῆς ψυχῆς, ἐν ἄλλῳ δ' οὐδενὶ πλὴν κατὰ συμβεβηκός.

4. Ἀπορήσειε δ' ἄν τις πότερόν ἐστι κίνησις πᾶσα πάσῃ συμβλητὴ ἢ οὔ. εἰ δή ἐστι πᾶσα συμβλητὴ καὶ ὁμοταχὲς[9] τὸ ἐν ἴσῳ χρόνῳ ἴσον κινούμενον, ἔσται περιφερής τις εὐθείᾳ ἴση, καὶ μείζων δὴ[10] καὶ ἐλάττων. ἔτι ἀλλοίωσις καὶ φορά τις ἴση, ὅταν ἐν ἴσῳ χρόνῳ τὸ μὲν ἀλλοιωθῇ τὸ δ' ἐνεχθῇ, ἔσται ἴσον [11] πάθος μήκει [11] ὥστ' οὐκ ἔστιν ἀλλοίωσις φορᾷ ἴση οὐδ' ἐλάττων. ὥστ' οὐ πᾶσα συμβλητή. ἐπὶ δὲ τοῦ κύκλου καὶ τῆς εὐθείας πῶς συμβήσεται; ἄτοπον

[1] ἔτι BCD.   [2] οὐδὲ τοῦ BCD.   [3] τὸ BC.   [4] ἀδύνατον B.   [5] ἢ D.
[6] ὅταν BCD.   [7] ἡδονῆς BC.   [8] γένηται B.   [9] ὁμοταχὲς BC.   [10] δὴ BCD.
[11] post haec verba BCD inserunt ἀλλ' ἀδύνατον· ἀλλ' ἄρα ὅταν ἐν ἴσῳ χρόνῳ ἴσον κινηθῇ τότε ἰσοταχές· ἴσον δὲ οὐκ ἔστι πάθος μήκει, necnon A in margine, sed omittit χρόνῳ.

γὰρ εἰ μὴ ἔστι[1] κύκλῳ ὁμοίως τοῦτο[2] κινεῖσθαι καὶ τοῦτο[2] ἐπὶ τῆς εὐθείας, ἀλλ' εὐθὺς ἀνάγκη ἢ θᾶττον ἢ βραδύτερον, ὥσπερ ἂν εἰ τὸ μὲν κάταντες, τὸ δ' ἄναντες. ἔτι δὲ[2] διαφέρει οὐδὲν τῷ λόγῳ εἴ τις φησὶν ἀνάγκην εἶναι θᾶττον εὐθὺς ἢ βραδύτερον κινεῖσθαι. ἔσται[4] γὰρ μείζων καὶ ἐλάττων ἡ περιφερὴς τῆς εὐθείας, ὥστε καὶ ἴση. εἰ γὰρ ἐν τῷ Α χρόνῳ τὸ μὲν τὴν Β διελήλυθε τὸ δὲ 248 b. τὴν Γ, μείζων ἂν εἴη ἡ Β τῆς Γ. οὕτω γὰρ[5] τὸ θᾶττον ἐλέγετο· οὐκοῦν καί, εἰ ἐν ἐλάττονι ἴσον, θᾶττον· ὥστ' ἔσται τι μέρος τοῦ Α ἐν ᾧ τὸ] Β τοῦ κύκλου τὸ ἴσον δίεισι, καὶ[6] τὸ Γ ἐν ὅλῳ τῷ Α τὴν Γ. ἀλλὰ μὴν εἰ ἔστι συμβλητά, συμβαίνει τὸ ἄρτι ῥηθέν, ἴσην εἶναι εὐθεῖαν κύκλῳ. ἀλλ' οὐ συμβλητά, οὐδ' ἄρα αἱ κινήσεις. ἀλλ' ὅσα μὴ συνώνυμα ἅπαντα ἀσύμβλητα· οἷον διὰ τί οὐ συμβλητόν, πότερον ὀξύτερον τὸ γράφιον ἢ ὁ οἶνος ἢ ὁ νήτη; [7]ὅτι γὰρ ὁμώνυμα οὐ συμβλητά· ἀλλ' ἡ νήτη τῇ[7] παρανήτῃ συμβλητή, ὅτι ταὐτὸ σημαίνει τὸ ὀξὺ ἐπ' ἀμφοῖν. [8]ἆρ' οὖν[8] οὐ ταὐτὸ τὸ ταχὺ ἐνταῦθα κἀκεῖ; πολὺ δ' ἔτι ἧττον ἐν ἀλλοιώσει καὶ φορᾷ. ἢ πρῶτον μὲν τοῦτο οὐκ ἀληθὲς ὡς εἰ μὴ ὁμώνυμα συμβλητά. τὸ γὰρ πολὺ ταὐτὸ σημαίνει ἐν ὕδατι καὶ ἀέρι, καὶ οὐ συμβλητά, εἰ δὲ μή, τό γε διπλάσιον τὸ αὐτό, δύο γὰρ πρὸς ἓν καὶ οὐ συμβλητά. ἢ καὶ ἐπὶ τούτων ὁ αὐτὸς λόγος· καὶ γὰρ τὸ πολὺ ὁμώνυμον. ἀλλ' ἐνίων καὶ οἱ λόγοι ὁμώνυμοι, οἷον [9]εἰ λέγοι τις[9] πολὺ[10] τοσοῦτον καὶ ἔτι καὶ[11] τὸ διπλάσιον τόσου· ἀλλὰ [12]τοσοῦτον καὶ τὸ ἴσον ὁμώνυμον, καὶ τὸ ἓν δὲ[13] εἰ[14] εὐθὺς ἔτυχεν, ὁμώνυμον. εἰ δὲ τοῦτο, καὶ τὰ δύο, ἐπεὶ διὰ τί τὰ μὲν συμβλητὰ τὰ δ' οὔ, εἴπερ ἦν μία φύσις; ἢ ὅτι ἐν ἄλλῳ πρώτῳ δεκτικῷ· ὁ μὲν οὖν ἵππος καὶ [15]ὁ κύων συμβλητά[15], πότερον λευκότερον· ἐν ᾧ γὰρ πρώτῳ ταὐτό[16], ἡ ἐπιφάνεια· καὶ κατὰ τὸ μέγεθος ὡσαύτως. ὕδωρ δὲ καὶ φωνὴ οὔ· ἐν ἄλλῳ γάρ. ἢ δῆλον 249 a. ὅτι[17] ἔσται οὕτω γε πάντα ἓν ποιεῖν, ἄλλῳ δὲ ἕκαστον φάσκειν εἶναι, καὶ ἔσται ταὐτὸν ἴσον καὶ γλυκὺ καὶ [18]λευκὸν ἐν[18] ἄλλῳ. ἔτι δεκτικὸν οὐ τὸ τυχὸν [19]οὗ δεκτικόν ἐστιν[19] ἀλλ' ἑνὸς τὸ πρῶτον. ἀλλ' ἆρα οὐ μόνον δεῖ τὰ συμβλητὰ μὴ ὁμώνυμα εἶναι ἀλλὰ καὶ μὴ ἔχειν διαφορὰν μήτε ὃ μήτε ἐν ᾧ; λέγω δὲ οἷον χρῶμα[20].... τισται μᾶλλον μὴ κατά τι χρῶμα[21], ἀλλὰ κατὰ τὸ λευκόν. οὕτω

[1] om. BCD.   [2] τουτὶ D.   [3] οὐδὲ BC.   [4] ἔσω BCD.   [5] γὰρ καὶ D.
[6] om. B.   [7] om. B.   [8] οὐκοῦν D.   [9] εἰ λέγοι τις ὅτι CD et A in margine, B omittit τις.
[10] καλὸ τὸ BCD.   [11] om. BCD.   [12] ἀλλὰ τὸ BCD.   [13] om. B.   [14] om. D.
[15] post haec verba B et C inserunt ἢ καὶ ἐπὶ τούτων ὁ αὐτὸς λόγος, καὶ γὰρ τὸ πολὺ τὸ τοσοῦτον καὶ ἔτι καὶ τὸ διπλάσιον τόσου· ἀλλὰ τὸ τοσοῦτον καὶ τὸ ἴσον ὁμώνυμον. εἰ δὲ τοῦτο καὶ τὰ δύο ἐπεὶ διὰ τί τὰ μὲν συμβλητὰ τὰ δ' οὐ εἴπερ ἦν μία φύσις; ἢ ὅτι ἐν ἄλλῳ πρώτῳ δεκτικῷ; ὁ μὲν οὖν ἵππος καὶ ὁ κύων συμβλητά.   [16] ταὐτόν BCD ut saepe alias.
[17] ὅτι οὐκ D.   [18] λευκὸν ἀλλ' ἐν D.   [19] om. D.   [20] BCD inserunt ἔχει διαίρεσιν· τοιγαροῦν οὐ συμβλητὸν κατὰ τοῦτο, οἷον πότερον κεχρωμάτισται, necnon A in margine.   [21] Post haec D inserit ἀλλ' ᾗ χρῶμα.

καὶ περὶ κίνησιν ὁμοταχὲς τὸ ἐν ἴσῳ χρόνῳ κινηθὲν ἴσον τοσονδὶ τοῦ μήκους· εἰ δὴ τοῦ μήκους ἐν τῳδὶ τὸ μὲν ἠλλοιώθη τὸ δ' ἠνέχθη, ἴση ἄρα αὕτη ἡ ἀλλοίωσις καὶ ὁμοταχὴς τῇ φορᾷ; ἀλλ' ἄτοπον. αἴτιον δ' ὅτι ἡ κίνησις ἔχει εἴδη, ὥστ' εἰ τὰ ἐν ἴσῳ χρόνῳ ἐνεχθέντα ἴσον μῆκος ἰσοταχῇ ἔσται, ἴση ἄρα ἡ εὐθεῖα καὶ ἡ περιφερής. πότερον οὖν αἴτιον, ὅτι ἔστιν ἡ φορὰ γένος, ἢ ὅτι ἡ γραμμὴ γένος; ὁ μὲν[1] χρόνος αὐτὸς ἀεὶ ἄτομος τῷ εἴδει. ἡ ἅμα κἀκεῖνα εἴδει διαφέρει· καὶ γὰρ ἡ φορὰ εἴδη ἔχει ἂν ἐκεῖνο[2] ἔχῃ εἴδη ἐφ' οὗ κινεῖται. ὅτε δ' ἐν ᾧ οὐ ἀλλὰ τοῖς σχήμασιν ἡ φορὰ ἄλλη, ὥστε τὰ ἐν ἴσῳ ταὐτὸ μέγεθος κινούμενα[3]· τὸ αὐτὸ δὲ τὸ ἀδιάφορον[4] εἴδει. ὥστε τοῦτο σκεπτέον, τίς διαφορὰ κινήσεως. καὶ σημαίνει[5] ὁ λόγος οὗτος ὅτι τὸ γένος οὐχ ἕν τι, ἀλλὰ παρὰ τοῦτο λανθάνει πολλά, εἰσὶ δὲ τῶν ὁμωνυμιῶν αἱ μὲν πολὺ ἀπέχουσαι [6]αἱ δὲ ἔχουσαί τινα ὁμοιότητα[7], αἱ δ' ἐγγὺς ἢ γένει ἢ ἀναλογίᾳ, διὸ οὐ δοκοῦσιν ὁμωνυμίαι εἶναι οὖσαι. πότε οὖν ἕτερον τὸ εἶδος, ἆρά γε ἂν ταὐτὸ ᾖ [7]ἐν ἄλλῳ ἢ ἂν[7] ἄλλο ὂν ἐν ἄλλῳ καὶ τίς ὅρος; ἢ τῷ κρινοῦμεν ὅτι ταὐτὸν τὸ λευκὸν καὶ τὸ γλυκὺ ἢ ἄλλο; ὅτι ἐν ἄλλῳ φαίνεται ἕτερον, ἢ ὅλως οὐ ταὐτό; περὶ δὲ δὴ ἀλλοιώσεως πῶς ἰσοταχὴς [8]ἑτέρα ἑτέρᾳ[8]; [9]εἰ δή ἐστι[9] τὸ ὑγιάζεσθαι ἀλλοιοῦσθαι, ἔστι δὲ τὸν μὲν ταχέως τὸν δὲ βραδέως ἰαθῆναι καὶ ἅμα τινάς[10], ὥστ' ἔσται ἀλλοίωσις ἰσοταχής· ἐν ἴσῳ γὰρ χρόνῳ ἠλλοιώθη. ἀλλὰ τί ἠλλοιώθη; τὸ γὰρ 249b ἴσον οὐκέτι ἐστὶν ἐνταῦθα λεγόμενον, ἀλλ' ὡς ἐν τῷ ποσῷ ἰσότης, ἐνταῦθα ὁμοιότης. ἀλλ' ἔστω τὸ[11] τὸ αὐτὸ μεταβάλλειν ἐν ἴσῳ χρόνῳ ἰσοταχές. πότερον οὖν ἐν ᾧ τὸ πάθος ἢ τὸ πάθος δεῖ συμβάλλειν, ἐνταῦθα μὲν δὴ ὅτι ἡ ὑγίεια ἡ αὐτή ἐστι λαβεῖν ὅτι οὔτε μᾶλλον οὔτε ἧττον ἀλλ' ὁμοίως ὑπάρχει. ἐὰν δὲ τὸ πάθος[12] ᾖ οἷον ἀλλοιοῦται τὸ λευκαινόμενον καὶ τὸ ὑγιαζόμενον, τούτοις οὐδὲν τὸ αὐτὸ οὐδ' ἴσον οὐδ' ὅμοιον, ἢ ἤδη[13] ταῦτα εἴδη ποιεῖ ἀλλοιώσεως[14] καὶ πόσα φοράς. εἰ μὲν οὖν τὰ κινούμενα εἴδει διαφέρει, ὧν εἰσὶν αἱ κινήσεις καθ' αὐτά[15] καὶ μὴ κατὰ[15] συμβεβηκός, καὶ αἱ κινήσεις εἴδει διοίσουσιν· εἰ δὲ γένει, γένει, εἰ δ' ἀριθμῷ, ἀριθμῷ. ἀλλὰ δὴ πότερον εἰς τὸ πάθος δεῖ βλέψαι, ἐὰν ᾖ τὸ αὐτὸ ἢ ὅμοιον, εἰ[16] ἰσοταχεῖς αἱ ἀλλοιώσεις, ἢ εἰς τὸ ἀλλοιούμενον, οἷον εἰ τοῦ μὲν τοσονδὶ λελεύκανται τοῦ δὲ τοσονδί, ἢ εἰς ἄμφω καὶ εἰ αὐτὴ μὲν ἢ ἄλλη τῷ πάθει, εἰ τὸ αὐτό, ἴση δ' ἢ[17] ἄνισος εἰ ἐκεῖνο ἄνισον. [18]καὶ ἐπὶ[18] γενέσεως δὲ[19] φθορᾶς τὸ αὐτὸ σκεπτέον. πῶς ἰσοταχὴς ἡ γένεσις; εἰ ἐν ἴσῳ

[1] μὲν γὰρ BCD. [2] ἐκεῖνος D. [3] κινούμενα ἰσοταχῆ D. [4] ἀδιάφορον τῷ D.
[5] σημαίνει γε D. [6] om. BCD. [7] om. BCD. [8] ἑτέρᾳ ἑτέρας BCD. [9] εἰ
δὴ ἔχει B. [10] om. BCD. [11] om. BC. [12] πάθος δεῖ BCD et A in margine.
[13] εἴδη BCD. [14] BCD ins. καὶ οὐκ ἔστι μία, ὥσπερ οὐδ' ἡ φορά, ὥστε λεκτέον πόσα εἴδη ἀλλοιώσεως inserunt et A in margine. [15] om. B. [16] BCD. [17] om. BC. [18] περὶ BC.
[19] καὶ inserunt BCD.

(23)

χρόνῳ τὸ αὐτὸ καὶ ἄτομον, οἷον ἄνθρωπος ἀλλὰ μὴ ζῷον· θάττων δὲ[1] εἰ ἐν ἴσῳ ἕτερον· οὐ γὰρ ἔχομέν τινα δύο, ἐν οἷς ἡ ἑτερότης ὡς[2] ἡ ἀνομοιότης. καὶ[3] ἔστιν ἀριθμὸς ἡ οὐσία, πλεῖον[4] καὶ ἐλάττων ἀριθμὸς ὁμοειδής, ἀλλ' ἀνώνυμον τὸ κοινὸν καὶ τὸ ἑκάτερον[5] ὥσπερ τὸ πλεῖον[6] πάθος ἢ τὸ ὑπερέχον μᾶλλον, τὸ δὲ ποσὸν μεῖζον.

5. Ἐπεὶ δὲ τὸ κινοῦν κινεῖ ἀεί τι καὶ ἔν τινι καὶ μέχρι του. [7]λέγω δὲ τὸ μὲν ἔν τινι, ὅτι ἐν χρόνῳ, τὸ δὲ μέχρι του[7] ὅτι ποσόν τι μῆκος· ἀεὶ γὰρ ἅμα κινεῖ καὶ κεκίνηκεν ὥστε ποσόν τι ἔσται ὃ ἐκινήθη καὶ ἐν ποσῷ. εἰ δὴ[8] τὸ μὲν 250 a. Α τὸ κινοῦν, τὸ δὲ Β τὸ κινούμενον, ὅσον δὲ κεκίνηται μῆκος τὸ Γ, ἐν ὅσῳ δὲ ὁ χρόνος ἐφ' οὗ τὸ Δ· ἐν δὴ τῷ ἴσῳ χρόνῳ ἡ ἴση δύναμις, ἡ ἐφ' οὗ Α, τὸ μὲν[9] ἥμισυ τοῦ Β βάρους τὸ Ζ διπλασίαν[10] τῆς Γ τοῦ μήκους κινήσει. τὴν δὲ[11] τοῦ Γ ἡ αὐτὴ ἐν τῷ ἡμίσει τοῦ Δ χρόνου τῷ Η. οὕτω γὰρ ἀνάλογον ἔσται, εἰ ἡ αὐτὴ δύναμις ἡ Α τὸ αὐτὸ τὸ Β ἐν τῷδε τῷ χρόνῳ τῷ Δ τοσήνδε κινεῖ τὴν Γ καὶ τὴν ἡμίσειαν τῆς Γ ἐν τῷ ἡμίσει τοῦ Δ χρόνου[12]. καὶ ἡ ἡμίσεια ἰσχὺς τῆς Α τὸ ἥμισυ κινήσει τοῦ Β βάρους τὸ Ζ ἥμισυ[13]. ὁμοίως δὴ ἕξουσι καὶ ἀνάλογον ἡ ἰσχὺς πρὸς τὸ βάρος ὡς ἡ Α πρὸς τὸ Β, ἡ Ε πρὸς τὸ Ζ, ὥστε ἴσον ἐν ἴσῳ χρόνῳ κινήσουσι. καὶ εἰ τὸ Ε τὸ Ζ κινεῖ ἐν τῷ Δ χρόνῳ[14] τὴν Γ τὸ μῆκος, οὐκ ἀνάγκη ἐν ἴσῳ χρόνῳ, τὸ ἐφ' οὗ τὸ Β[15] τὸ διπλάσιον τοῦ Ζ βάρους κινεῖν τὴν ἡμίσειαν τῆς Γ. Εἰ δὴ[16] τὸ Α δύναμις [17]τὴν τὸ Β κινήσει[17] ἐν τῷ Δ χρόνῳ ὅσην τὸ Γ, τὸ ἥμισυ τοῦ Α ἐφ' ᾧ Ε τὴν τὸ Β οὐ κινήσει ἐν τῷ χρόνῳ ἐφ' οὗ Δ, οὐδ' ἔν τινι τοῦ Δ τῆς Γ, ἀνάλογον περὶ[18] τὴν ὅλην Γ ὡς τὸ Α πρὸς τὸ Ε. ὅλως γὰρ εἰ ἔτυχεν οὐ κινήσει οὐδέν· οὐ[19] γάρ, εἰ[20] ὅλη ἰσχὺς τοσήνδε ἐκίνησεν, ἡ ἡμίσεια[21] κινήσει οὔτε ποσὴν οὔτ' ἐν ὁποσῳοῦν· εἷς γὰρ ἂν κινοίη τὸ πλοῖον εἴπερ ἡ τῶν νεολκῶν τέμνεται[22] ἰσχὺς εἰς[23] τὸν ἀριθμὸν καὶ τὸ μῆκος ὃ πάντες ἐκίνησαν. καὶ διὰ τοῦτο[24] Ζήνωνος λόγος οὐκ ἀληθὴς ὡς ψοφεῖ τῆς κέγχρου ὁτιοῦν μέρος. οὐδὲν γὰρ κωλύει μὴ κινεῖν τὸν ἀέρα ἐν μηδενὶ χρόνῳ τοῦτον ὃν ἐκίνησε πεσὼν ὁ ὅλος μέδιμνος· [25]οὐδὲ δὴ[25] τοσοῦτον μόριον, ὅσον ἂν κινήσειε τοῦ ὅλου εἰ εἴη καθ' αὑτό, τοῦτο οὐ κινεῖ. οὐδὲ γὰρ οὐδέν ἐστιν ἀλλ' ἢ δυνάμει ἐν τῷ ὅλῳ. εἰ δὲ τὰ δύο καὶ ἑκάτερον τῶνδε ἑκάτερον κινεῖ τοσόνδε ἐν τοσῷδε[26], καὶ συντιθέμεναι αἱ δυνάμεις τὸ σύνθετον ἐκ τῶν μερῶν[27] τὸ ἴσον κινήσουσι μῆκος καὶ ἐν ἴσῳ χρόνῳ· ἀνάλογον γάρ. ἆρ' οὖν οὕτω καὶ ἐπ' ἀλλοιώσεως καὶ ἐπ' αὐξή-

[1] δὴ καὶ BCD.   [2] καὶ D.   [3] καὶ εἰ BCD.   [4] ὁ πλείων D.   [5] ἕτερον BD.
[6] om. D.   [7] om. BC.   [8] δὲ D.   [9] μὲν οὖν BCD.   [10] διπλασίον D.   [11] δὲ ἡμίσειαν BCD.   [12] χρόνῳ C.   [13] om. BCD.   [14] om. D.   [15] Ε BC.   [16] δὴ ἡ BCD.
[17] τὴν Β κινήσει BC, τὴν Β κίνησιν D.   [18] πρὸς CD.   [19] εἰ D.   [20] ἡ BCD.   [21] ἡμίσεια οὗ D.   [22] τέμνεται D.   [23] εἴς τε BCD.   [24] τοῦτο ὁ BCD.   [25] οὐδὲ δεῖ δὴ D.
[26] τῷδε D.   [27] βαρῶν BCD.

σεως; τί μὲν γὰρ τὸ αὖξον, τί δὲ τὸ αὐξανόμενον, ἐν ποσῷ δὲ χρόνῳ καὶ ποσὸν τὸ μὲν αὔξει τὸ δ' αὐξάνεται. καὶ τὸ ἀλλοιοῦν καὶ ἀλλοιούμενον ὡσαύτως τί καὶ ποσὸν κατὰ τὸ μᾶλλον καὶ τὸ ἧττον ἠλλοίωται καὶ ἐν ποσῷ χρόνῳ, ἐν διπλασίῳ διπλάσιον καὶ τὸ διπλάσιον ἐν διπλασίῳ, καὶ τὸ ἥμισυ ἐν ἡμίσει χρόνῳ ἢ ἐν ἡμίσει ἥμισυ· ἢ ἐν ἴσῳ διπλάσιον. εἰ δὲ τὸ ἀλλοιοῦν ἢ τὸ[1] αὖξον τοσόνδε ἐν τοσῷδε ἢ αὔξει ἢ ἀλλοιοῖ, οὐκ ἀνάγκη καὶ τὸ ἥμισυ ἐν ἡμίσει καὶ ἐν ἡμίσει τὸ ἥμισυ, ἀλλ' οὐδὲν εἰ ἔτυχεν ἀλλοιώσει ἢ αὐξήσει ὥσπερ καὶ ἐπὶ τοῦ βάρους.

[1] om. C.

Anecdota Oxoniensia.

Already Published.

The English Manuscripts of the Nicomachean Ethics,
Described in relation to Bekker's Manuscripts and other Sources. By J. A. STEWART, M.A., Classical Lecturer, Christ Church. Small 4to. 3s. 6d.

Nonius Marcellus,
de Compendiosa Doctrina, Harleian MS. 2719. Collated by J. H. ONIONS, M.A., Senior Student of Christ Church. Small 4to. 3s. 6d.

Commentary on Ezra and Nehemiah.
By Rabbi Saadiah. Edited by H. J. MATHEWS, M.A., Exeter College, Oxford. Small 4to. 3s. 6d.

Buddhist Texts from Japan.
Edited by F. MAX MÜLLER. Small 4to. 3s. 6d.

Sinonoma Bartholomei.
A Medico-Botanical Glossary from a Fourteenth-Century MS. in the Library of Pembroke College, Oxford. Edited by J. L. G. MOWAT, M.A., Fellow of Pembroke College. Small 4to. 3s. 6d.

In the Press.

The Psaltar na Rann,
By Ængus Cele De, or, the Culdee. Edited, from a MS. in the Bodleian Library, by WHITLEY STOKES, LL.D.

A Fifteenth-Century Medico-Botanical Glossary.
Edited, from a MS. in the Bodleian Library, by J. L. G. MOWAT, M.A.

Also, uniform with the above.

Passio et Miracula Beati Olaui.
Edited from a Twelfth-Century MS. in the Library of Corpus Christi College, Oxford, with an Introduction and Notes, by FREDERICK METCALFE, M.A. Small 4to., stiff covers, 6s.

Gascoigne's Theological Dictionary: 'Liber Veritatum.'
Selected Passages, from the MS. in the Library of Lincoln College, Oxford, illustrating the Condition of Church and State, 1403-1458. With an Introduction by JAMES E. THOROLD ROGERS, M.P. Small 4to., cloth, 10s. 6d.

CLARENDON PRESS, OXFORD.

RECENT PUBLICATIONS.

A Practical Introduction to Greek Accentuation.
By HENRY W. CHANDLER, M.A., Waynflete Professor of Moral and Metaphysical Philosophy, Fellow of Pembroke College, Oxford. Second Edition, revised. Demy 8vo., cloth, price 10s. 6d.

A Manual of Greek Historical Inscriptions.
By E. L. HICKS, M.A., formerly Fellow and Tutor of Corpus Christi College, Oxford. Demy 8vo., cloth, price 10s. 6d.

A Treatise on the Accentuation of the three so-called Poetical Books of the Old Testament—Psalms, Proverbs, and Job.
By W. WICKES, D.D. With an Appendix containing the Treatise, assigned to R. Jehuda Ben-Bil'am, on the same subject, in the original Arabic. Demy 8vo., paper cover, price 5s.

P. Ovidii Nasonis Ibis.
Ex novis Codicibvs edidit, Scholia vetera Commentarivm cvm prolegomenis Appendice Indice addidit R. ELLIS, Collegii Trinitatis apud Oxonienses Socivs. Demy 8vo., cloth, price 10s. 6d.

A Grammar of the Homeric Dialect.
By D. B. MONRO, M.A., Fellow of Oriel College. Demy 8vo., cloth, price 10s. 6d.

Sophocles. The Plays and Fragments.
With English Notes and Introductions, by LEWIS CAMPBELL, M.A., Professor of Greek, St. Andrews, formerly Fellow of Queen's College, Oxford. 2 vols., price 32s.

Published for the University by HENRY FROWDE, 7 Paternoster Row, London.

ALSO TO BE HAD AT THE

CLARENDON PRESS DEPOSITORY, 116 High Street, Oxford.

Anecdota Oxoniensia

TEXTS, DOCUMENTS, AND EXTRACTS

CHIEFLY FROM

MANUSCRIPTS IN THE BODLEIAN

AND OTHER

OXFORD LIBRARIES

CLASSICAL SERIES. VOL. I—PART IV

BENTLEY'S PLAUTINE EMENDATIONS

BY

E. A. SONNENSCHEIN, M.A.

Oxford
AT THE CLARENDON PRESS
1883

[*All rights reserved*]

London

HENRY FROWDE

OXFORD UNIVERSITY PRESS WAREHOUSE

7 PATERNOSTER ROW

BENTLEY'S
PLAUTINE EMENDATIONS

FROM

HIS COPY OF GRONOVIUS

BY

E. A. SONNENSCHEIN, M.A.

UNIVERSITY COLLEGE, OXFORD
PROFESSOR OF CLASSICS IN THE MASON COLLEGE, BIRMINGHAM

Oxford
AT THE CLARENDON PRESS
1883

[*All rights reserved*]

London

HENRY FROWDE

OXFORD UNIVERSITY PRESS WAREHOUSE

7 PATERNOSTER ROW

BENTLEY'S PLAUTINE EMENDATIONS

FROM HIS COPY OF GRONOVIUS.

BENTLEY'S notes and emendations on the text of Plautus contained in this volume are extracted from the margin of a copy of the Vulgate (Gronovius, Lugd. Batav. et Roterod., 1669), now in the Bodleian Library (Auct. S. infra I. 27). On the title page are the initials R. B., with letters indicating the place of the volume in a library; and the initials recur p. 1162. The fly leaf contains some additional notes, written, like the marginal correction, in Bentley's unmistakeable hand. Besides these, the volume contains the hand of at least two other persons: (1) a certain Sheldon Mervyn (or Mervin), whose name appears on the fly leaf and *Dedicatio* p. 1, and who seems to have been the first possessor; (2) Gilbert Wakefield, the editor of Lucretius, whose name and arms appear on a printed plate attached to the cover, and whose hand is found in a few marginal notes, some in ink and some in pencil, scattered through the volume. One passage (Curc. II 1. 21), in which Wakefield's reading 'Lien crepat' (also published in his Silva Critica, Cambridge, 1789-95, V p. 100) is struck out in pencil, suggests the possibility that some of the pencil marks are by a fourth hand.

The history of the volume after the time of Bentley appears to have been as follows: (1) At Bentley's death (1742) it became the property of his nephew, Richard Bentley, who inherited all his uncle's classical books containing MS. notes (see Monk, Life of Bentley, p. 660). (2) It was probably purchased by Wakefield at the sale of the younger Bentley's books at Leicester in the year 1786: at any rate a copy of this very edition, described further as containing MS. notes, appears in the Sale Catalogue (no. 114), and there seems little reason to doubt that this is the volume in question. Wakefield himself, referring to Bentley's reading in Amphitruo, III 2. 54, remarks (Silva Critica, III p. 69), '*sic bene restitutum reliquit summus Bentleius in exemplari ejus, quod forte fortuna ad meas manus devenerit.* AL. Ah! propitius sit potius. JUP. CONFIDO fore.' Here the phrase 'forte fortuna' would apply well enough to purchase at a sale[1]. (3) It was purchased by Richard Heber at the Wakefield Sale in 1802 for the sum of two shillings and six-pence (*vide* no. 987 in the priced catalogue of the sale). (4) It passed into the possession of the Bodleian Library, possibly by gift of Heber or by purchase at the Heber Sale (1834–36).

It is generally believed that Bentley's library was, unlike those of so many other scholars, successfully kept together; and no doubt a valuable portion of his books passed *en masse* through the hands of Richard Cumberland, who received them as a present from the younger Bentley, into the British Museum. But this was not the fate of all: several books with MS. notes by Bentley became the property of Anthony Askew, M.D., who doubtless bought them at the sale of part of Bentley's library which took place immediately after his death. These books were again thrown into the market at the Askew Sale (1785); and though some of them have found their way into public libraries[2], others may possibly still be buried in private collections.

The emendations of Bentley amount in all to 1094, and fall into three classes: (1) Those conjectures which coincide neither with the thoughts of other editors nor with recently-discovered MSS., and which are therefore new to the world. (2) Those conjectures which have since been independently made by modern editors or found in recently-discovered MSS. (3) Those readings which he borrowed, or may have borrowed, from previous editors or commentators, and simply 'entered' as approved by himself. These three classes are distinguished by different kinds of type[3]. In the last two classes the name of the scholar

---

[1] In another place Wakefield evidently misread Bentley's hand; see Silva Critica, IV p. 233, where he gives as Bentley's reading on Amphitruo Prologue 46:
Sed moris nunquam illinc fuit patri meo.
Bentley's correction in the margin stands 'moris illi n. f.' (not illinc'). A similar inaccuracy of Wakefield's is found in Silva Critica, V p. 107.

[2] E.g. an Aeschylus (1580), a Menander and Philemon (1709), a Terentianus Maurus (1684), and an interleaved copy of the 'Emendationes ad Tusculanas,' with many additional notes and corrections in Bentley's hand, all of which are in the Cambridge University Library; one at least of the volumes in the British Museum (Nicandri Theriaca, 1557) has likewise reached its present destination through the Askew Sale.

[3] See Explanations of Signs, p. 194.

whom Bentley has anticipated, or to whom the reading may be due, is added in brackets. The following table exhibits the numerical relations of the three classes in the various plays[1]:—

	I	II	III	TOTAL
Amphitruo	9	9	40	58
Asinaria	11	8	23	42
Aulularia	12	8	22	42
Captivi	5	9	11	25
Curculio	10	11	20	41
Casina	3	43	22	68
Cistellaria	0	2	1	3
Epidicus	16	21	22	59
Bacchides	12	13	38	63
Mostellaria	15	32	54	101
Menaechmi	9	19	34	62
Miles Gloriosus	26	30	57	113
Mercator	11	20	37	68
Pseudolus	13	16	32	61
Poenulus	14	48	31	93
Persa	1	5	15	21
Rudens	19	23	53	95
Stichus	3	2	11	16
Trinummus	5	17	15	37
Truculentus	1	15	10	26
	195	351	548	1094

It will be seen that half of the total number belong to class III; 546 corrections are by the hand of Bentley himself, and of these, 195 are new. Whether the 351 readings of class II can be claimed for Bentley, or whether the honour of them belongs to the various modern scholars who first published them, may be left to the decision of future editors of Plautus.

The readings contained in the present volume, taken together with

---

[1] The reader must be cautioned not to expect anything more than approximate accuracy in a table of this kind. The causes of possible error are numerous.

those of the copies of Pareus and Camerarius in the British Museum[1] and those contained in the notes on Bentley's editions of Horace (A. D. 1711) and Terence (A. D. 1726), represent Bentley's work upon the text of Plautus, so far as known at the present day. The emendations of the copies of Pareus and Camerarius amount to about 1140 in number; those of the editions of Horace and Terence to about 360. We have here, therefore, a considerable body of critical matter—not indeed so extensive as it appears at first sight, since the same reading frequently occurs in two, and occasionally in three, of the sources, but still important enough to claim examination and to justify the attempt to discover the relation of the various sources to one another, and their comparative value. It will be the object of this Introduction to determine: I. The relation of the Bodleian MS. notes to the British Museum MS. notes. II. The relation of the copies with MS. notes to the Plautine emendations in the notes to Horace and Terence. III. The approximate date of the emendations in MS. Under this head it will be necessary to examine, (1) the internal evidence, (2) the evidence of the handwriting.

I. The problem presented by the recensions in the three copies with MS. notes is a curious one. The Pareus has about the same number of emendations as the Gronovius[2]; but, while a considerable number are common to the two[3], each has many valuable readings of its own, which are not found in the other. Neither recension is, therefore, independent of the other: on the contrary, Bentley appears to have used both copies during the period of his Plautus studies, and to have entered his emendations sometimes in the one, sometimes in the other, according to his convenience[4]. At the same time the considerable amount of common matter makes it probable that at some time or times Bentley transferred bodily from one copy to the other, rejecting only what on more mature thought he disapproved. Such transference, however, appears to have taken place in particular plays rather than from the one

[1] Press Marks 682. b. 10 and 682. c. 11. A collation of these readings has been published in an Appendix to the *Captivi* of Plautus, by E. A. Sonnenschein, 1880.
[2] In the following enquiry the copy of Camerarius is left out of account, as containing very few emendations, and being altogether of far less importance than the other two.
[3] I. e. those marked with an asterisk in the present volume; see Explanations of Signs, p. 195.
[4] I am informed by the Rev. Professor J. Wordsworth, of Oxford, that there is a similar relation between the several copies of the New Testament with MS. notes by Bentley.

volume, as a whole, to the other; and it must certainly have been previous to the stage of criticism which the volumes, as we have them, represent. In no single play can the one recension be entirely accounted for from the other. Thus in the *Bacchides*, while the Gronovius is on the whole decidedly superior[1], the Pareus and the Camerarius contain one emendation ('Inimiciorem' for 'Inmitiorem,' III 4. 1) in which Bentley ingeniously anticipates the reading of the Ambrosian palimpsest, and which is probably superior to the reading of Gronovius, which he does not correct.

In the *Captivi*, on the other hand, the Pareus is far more complete; yet the Gronovius has 'larviae' on III 4. 66, while in the Pareus Bentley leaves 'larvae' uncorrected: the metre requires a trisyllabic word[2]. In the *Epidicus* the Gronovius seems decidedly superior up to the end of Act II: but after that point the Gronovius almost ceases, whereas the Pareus has as many emendations in the last as in the first act, the whole number of readings of the Pareus being, however, in the *Epidicus*, only 22. In the *Mostellaria* the Gronovius has several emendations in Acts IV, V (lines 947-1155 in Ritschl's edition), while the Pareana cease altogether after Act III (i. e. of the edition of Gronovius, Ritschl line 966). In the first three acts there are many passages in which the Gronovius seems superior, e. g. I 1. 72, I 2. 11, I 2. 35, I 3. 75, II 1. 42, II 2. 95; but many in which it is inferior, e. g. I 3. 29, I 3. 53, I 3. 80, II 1. 66, II 1. 75, III 2. 127 (Par. IV 1. 41). In several plays it is very difficult to decide which copy has the advantage. Isolated instances are remarked upon in the foot-notes: the reader may be specially referred to those on *Casina* III 5. 1, *Curculio* II 3. 67, *Miles Gloriosus* II 4. 10, 11.

[1] Cf. especially IV 9. 145, where the conjecture 'uti' (for 'veluti') agrees with the note on Horace, Epistles II 1. 67, and is not found in the Pareus. Again in II 3. 86 the reading of Pylades ('Quantillum' for 'Quantulum') which is adopted, agrees with the note on Terence. Haut. IV 2. 1 but is not in the Pareus. Other passages in which the Gronovius is superior are III 4. 4, IV 6. 24, IV 7. 1.

This word 'larvia,' which Bentley seems to have devised as a Plautine equivalent of 'larva' (which modern editors usually write 'larüa'), is characteristic of the Gronovius; it is found in Amph. II 2. 145, Aul. IV 4. 15, Capt. III 4. 66, Cas. III 4. 2, Men. V 4. 2, Merc. V 4. 20, 22. That it is a form deliberately approved by Bentley appears from the fact that it is adopted in the note on Horace, Epistles I 2. 34. It is found once in the Pareus (Aul. IV 4. 15). In the Gronovius the correction is always made in the same way (by writing the letters *via* in the margin), in exactly the same hand and with the same dark and glossy ink.

It is clear therefore that for a study of Bentley's work on Plautus, both the copies with MS. notes are essential. The same may be said of the emendations in the notes upon Terence and Horace, which form the subject of the next heading.

II. The relation of the copies with MS. notes to the emendations in the notes on Terence and Horace is also an interesting one. To what extent are the latter coincident with the former, to what extent inconsistent[1]?

[1] The question has been already treated, in regard to the emendations in the copy of Pareus ('Pareana'), by Dr. H. Schenkl in an article in the *Zeitschrift für die oesterreichischen Gymnasien* (*Zweiunddreissigster Jahrgang*, 1881). His position is that the inconsistencies between the notes on Terence and the 'Schediasma' on the one hand, and the 'Pareana' on the other, are so grave and numerous as to compel the inference that the latter represent an earlier stage of criticism.

His line of argument is presented under two heads: (*a*) That while Bentley is inexorable against all hiatus in his edition of Terence, the Pareana show a certain tolerance towards hiatus; (*b*) That the divergences between the quotations and emendations of Plautus in the notes on Terence and Horace and the Pareana make it impossible to explain the former from the latter. With regard to (*a*) Dr. Schenkl's argument proceeds on the assumption that what is true of the verse of Terence is true of that of Plautus. This was not Bentley's view: and any conclusions founded upon the assumption that it was, are wholly invalid. The following quotation from Bentley himself (ad Eun. III 1. 18) disposes of the argument of Dr. Schenkl. Speaking of the hiatus ('*hiare*') he says, '*Quod etsi Plautus sibi indulgeat in caesura, nunquam id facit Terentius*;' and in the notes on Terence we actually find him quoting Plautus with hiatus in caesura, e. g. Trin. Prol. 18 (on Phormio Prol. 26 and Haut. Prol. 1);

Huic nomen Graece est Thesauro fabulae

and again in Capt. V 2. 24 (on Andr. I 5. 54).

Thus the readings of the Pareana in *Pseud.* I 1. 24

Interpretari | alium posse neminem

in Stich. II 1. 81 (Ritschl 235)

Ecastor auctionem | haud magni preti

in Merc. II 2. 12

Tantum est. DE. *Lysimache salus.* | LY. *Euge Demipho*

and in Pseud. III 2, 67

Ut nostra properes amoliri | omnia

and similar cases, are entirely consistent with the principles and practice of Bentley in the year 1726.

To what extent Bentley would, in 1726, have allowed Plautus '*hiare*' in other cases than in caesura, it is difficult to say. The Pareana give no clear sound on this point. Thus his correction in Stich. II 1. 63

Consensi: paene sum fame | emortuus

seems to allow the hiatus; whereas in Mil. I 1. 49

Edepol memoria'st optuma. AR. *Offae me monent*

his correction is based upon a disinclination to allow hiatus in the same place.

Under the heading (*b*) Dr. Schenkl quotes several cases in which the notes on Terence present valuable emendations of which the Pareana give no hint, e. g. those on Eun. II 3. 65, both of which are accepted by Ritschl (Bacch. IV 4. 27, Mil. V 36). In two other passages the notes

In order to determine this point with accuracy, the present writer has extracted and examined all the Plautine emendations in the notes on Terence and such of those in the notes on Horace as could be discovered from the index or from references in editions of Plautus. The results may be summed up as follows :—Of about 346 quotations from Plautus in the notes on Terence, 250[1] simply follow the text of the Vulgate edition or of Pareus, occasionally with insignificant changes, 15 contain slips or misprints, 6 contain conjectural readings by other editors or commentators before Bentley. This leaves 75 cases in which there are genuine conjectures of Bentley's own. Of these 75 emendations, 37 are fully accounted for by one or other of the copies with MS. notes[2], 2 are partly accounted for by the Pareus, and 36 remain to represent the advance of Plautine criticism in the edition of Terence as compared with the copies with MS. notes.

From these statistics it is evident that Bentley did not, in the year 1726, regard his MS. emendations of Plautus as antiquated: on the contrary, he appears to have used them throughout in preparing his notes on Terence. When he had occasion to quote Plautus, he regularly quoted the passage as emended in one or more of his copies with MS. notes; where these did not contain any emendation, he either quoted one of the standard texts of his time—Pareus or Gronovius[3]—or else emended the

---

on Terence complete a partial emendation of the copy of Pareus (Cist. II 1. 26, on Andr. IV 3. 13 and Hec. V. 4. 30; and Mil. II 1. 8 on Phorm. Prol. 26).

But here too Dr. Schenkl's results must be received with caution. He has exaggerated the case by admitting as instances of divergence numerous cases in which approval of a line as given by Pareus is inferred *ex silentio*. He has treated mere slips or misprints of the edition of Terence as serious conjectures (see notes on Andr. I 1. 92, Eun. III 5. 22, V 4. 14, Adelph. II 4. 1). He has laid no stress on the other side of the question—the extent of the agreement between the Pareana and the notes on Terence: nor has he stated the extent of absolute inconsistency, i.e. the extent to which Bentley in his Terence *rejects* emendations of the Pareus in favour of a different conjecture.

[1] It should be noted that all these are, with one exception, passages in which *no correction is registered* in the copies with MS. notes. The one exception is Merc. II 1. 4 (on Haut. II 1. 13).

[2] 14 are in the Pareus alone, 8 in the Gronovius alone, 1 in the Camerarius alone, 13 in both the Pareus and the Gronovius, 1 in both the Gronovius and the Camerarius.

[3] That he quoted mainly from Pareus is shown by the numbers of the lines. Thus Stich. II 1. 18 (on Haut. IV 7. 8) can be found only by a reference to Pareus; in the Vulgate it is I 3 8. Similarly Most. V 3. 26 (on Andr. I 1. 13) is V 2. 26 in the Vulgate; Most. III 3. 13 (on Eun. II 2. 36) is III 2. 108. The same holds in a dozen other cases. In writing his notes on Cas. III 5. 36 (on Eun. IV 6. 5), and Epid. II 2. 117 (on Haut. III 3. 48), it looks precisely as if he were

passage himself on the spot. In a very few passages, it is true, he rejected one of his previous emendations, or modified it, in favour of a new thought [1]. In at least two others the notes on Terence appear to exhibit a less advanced stage of criticism than the Gronovius; see Rud. I 1. 6, Trin. II 2. 78 (cf. on Haut. III 1. 72 and Adelph. V 8. 23).

III. The question of date is connected with that just discussed, and has already been treated, in regard to the copy of Pareus, by Dr. H. Schenkl in the article alluded to above. Dr. Schenkl's argument is twofold. (1) He maintains that Bentley must have completed a critical recension both of Terence, as represented in the edition of 1726, and of Plautus, so early as the year 1709, when he 'announced his intention of bringing out an edition not only of Plautus but also of Terence [2].' (2) He maintains that the 'Pareana' represent an altogether earlier stage of criticism than the notes on Terence and the Schediasma. His conclusion is that the Pareana were written considerably before the year 1709, and are therefore a comparatively immature work. At the same time he makes handsome acknowledgment of the 'considerable number of the most plausible and acute emendations—in many cases the result of unwearied and protracted labour—which will take their due place in all future editions of Plautus.'

The second position of Dr. Schenkl has been already sufficiently answered. The MS. notes in the Pareus—and, it may be added, those in the Gronovius—do not represent an immature stage of criticism. The metrical principles of the Pareus are the metrical principles of the notes on Terence and the Schediasma: and, while it is quite true that the notes on Terence contain 36 emendations not in the copies with MS. notes, this number seems altogether insufficient as a basis upon which to establish the hypothesis of a later and improved recension [3].

---

transferring his own remarks in his copy of Pareus into his notes on Terence; in the former passage the Pareana have 'leg. expeto (MS. expeto),' and in the notes on Terence, reading expeto, he remarks, 'Sic MS. Regius bonae notae.'

[1] Such passages are Merc. II 1. 4 (cf. the Pareus with note on Haut. II 1. 13), and Aul. II 8. 23, Men. III 3. 34, Trin. II 2. 78, Rud. I 1. 6, Asin. II 4. 86, Bacch. II 2. 14 (cf. the Gronovius with notes on Terence, quoted at the foot of the page).

[2] In the *Emendationes ad Tusculanas*, appended to the edition of Davies, of the year 1709.

[3] If Bentley had had such a complete recension before him, we should not so often find him quoting lines which will not scan, e. g. Poen. I 2. 185 (on Ad. IV 2. 52).

Nor is Dr. Schenkl's evidence on his first position any sounder. He relies, firstly, upon the 'promise' of the year 1709; secondly, on the statement that we do not hear of any subsequent study of Latin comedy, on the part of Bentley, till the year 1726, when the edition of Terence was hastily put together and published. It may be replied: (*a*) That a promise of this kind would in any case be unsafe ground for inferring that the materials for fulfilling it were ready to hand. But further, the reader who turns to the original passage in which the supposed 'promise' is contained (ad Tusc. III 12), will be somewhat surprised at the terms in which it is expressed. After emending a passage from the *Amphitruo* (II 1, 1-23), Bentley continues, '*Non enim nunc locus est, ut ista latius prosequar: sed si erit unquam ut Plautum Terentiumque lima nostra expolitos in lucem edam, et haec et alia infinita fusius tenuiusque deducta conspicies.*' In the edition of Horace (1711) we find him using similar language (ad Serm. II 5. 79), '*Sed haec pluribus, si a majoribus negotiis otium erit, ad ipsum Terentium.*' This pious aspiration, that he might some day produce an edition of Plautus—which is not mentioned in the second passage quoted—as well as of Terence, began its marvellous career as a promise so early as Monk's Life of Bentley, where we are told that 'he held out expectations of publishing some time or other both Plautus and Terence;' in Maehly, 'he promised a Plautus and Terence' (Richard Bentley, eine Biographie: Belege, p. 150); in Dr. Schenkl's article 'he had manifestly completed the critical recension of both authors!'

(*b*) It is a mistake to say that we hear of no study in the field of Latin comedy between 1709 and 1726. In the year 1713 Bentley was occupied on his edition of Terence: and many a point of metre must have been discussed with Hare during the years that preceded their rival editions

---

Neque mihi jam video propter tete victitandum sorbilo.
In other passages we find him approving readings which are manifestly imperfect. Thus on Eun. V 4. 14 he quotes Mil. II 2. 84 thus:
Dicam *hanc* Athenis advenisse cum amatore aliquo suo;
upon which Ritschl exclaims 'imprudens puto.' Similarly in Trin. II 1. 20 (on Eun. V 8. 57), he reads
Quod ebibit, quod comest, quod facit sumpti;
and in Most. III 1. 15 (Hec. IV 4. 12),
.... Verum ut res sese habet.
Neither of these lines will scan, and on both Ritschl remarks, '*quod mirere patienter tuli: sa Bentleium.*'

of Terence. Besides, our information about Bentley's private reading is very meagre; and any inference based upon the silence of his biographer is quite valueless.

While therefore the Plautine emendations in the *Emendationes ad Tusculanas* make it quite clear that Bentley had read both his Terence and his Plautus, and read them critically, before the year 1709, there is no evidence that a complete recension of the text of Terence was finished in that year; and the completed recension of Plautus is a myth.

This evidence, therefore, for a date considerably anterior to 1709 falls to the ground. But it is difficult, nay, impossible, to set up any definite date in its stead, from the fact that the emendations were obviously not all written at the same period. This would in any case be probable from internal evidence; it is proved conclusively by an examination of the handwriting. Bentley's hand presents a wide range of variation, but three stages are distinctly discernible, not counting his boyish hand [1]: (1) The hand of his early manhood: the writing of which is sloped, and shows more tendency to looping than in his later hand; specimens may be seen in several of his books with MS. notes in the British Museum [2], in the fly leaf of the Manilius in the library of Trinity College, Cambridge (B. 17. 29), and in the letter to De Veil preserved in the Trinity College collection [3] of Bentley's correspondence (Wordsworth, vol. i. p. 254). (2) The hand of his middle age. It is more upright than the other, and not as a rule looped; it keeps its letters more separate from one another, and shows a remarkable tendency to running the ends of words off small. This is the hand most characteristic of Bentley, and is seen in the large majority of his books in the British Museum, and in several documents in Trinity College library,—the *Ephemeris* of the year 1701 [4], the postscripts to the letters to Kuster (1708)—the letter to J. Clericus of 1710—and the margin of the Manilius and Terence (B. 17.

[1] E. g. the hand of the verses on the Papist conspiracy, written at College (Trinity College Collection, p. 2).
[2] E g. the Stephanus (687. h. 5), the Aphthonius (683. b. 2).
[3] The letter is there marked 'copy,' but I believe it to be original.
[4] A fly leaf, under the date July 26, 1701, contains the following entry: 'Saturday. Mr. Hutchinson, Mr. Porter, Mr. Green and Mr. Leighton played at Bowls in ye College Bowlinggreen [sic] all chapell time, in ye Evening service: seen out of my window by me (who was then lame and could not be at Chapel) & Will. Jaist.' This is amusing when compared with Monk, vol. II, p. 341.

33). The *terminus a quo* for this hand appears to be about the year 1700, when Bentley was 38 years of age, and the *terminus ad quem* about the year 1725, when he was 63. A letter of the year 1693, preserved in the British Museum (Additional MSS. 6911), exhibits a hand midway between the 'characteristic' and the earlier hand: the *terminus ad quem*, therefore, of the latter would seem to be about the year 1690. (3) His old age hand, which is large and rather shaky, and which exhibits other signs of breaking up: it regularly employs the 'Greek *ε*.' Specimens may be seen in the letter to Sir H. Sloane of the year 1728, now in the British Museum (Sloane MSS. 4037), in the MS. notes on Markland's *Epistola Critica*, published 1723 (Brit. Mus. 681. c. 25), and those on Burmann's Ovid, published 1727 (Brit. Mus. 681. d. 6); and also in occasional passages in others of his books with MS. notes (e. g. in the Terence, Brit. Mus. 687. f. 16, p. 345). This hand can be traced back to the year 1728[1].

Applying these results to the copies of Plautus with MS. notes, we find that they are for the most part written in the 'characteristic' or middle hand, but that occasional specimens of the earlier, and frequent specimens of the later, hand present themselves. Thus on the flyleaf of the Gronovius (see p. 224) the writing down to the middle of the page ('p. 772. 35'... 'Festus') is in the early hand, while the rest ('Prologo Casinae'... 'R. B.') is in the characteristic hand. The late hand is found occasionally in the Pareus, and still more frequently in the Gronovius (e. g. Amph. I 1. 264, 2. 28, Asin. III 3. 71, Aul. III 5. 33, Most. I 3. 13[2], Rud. I 2. 77, II 6. 1, III 2. 37, 49, Trin. II 4. 44, V 2. 31).

From a consideration, therefore, of the handwriting two inferences seem to follow: (1) the notes on Plautus were written at widely different times; a few date from Bentley's early manhood, the majority from the first two decades of the eighteenth century, and a few more from the

[1] It is worth notice that in the large majority of the volumes with *Adversaria*, the notes are in a hand or hands dating from after the year 1700. These volumes represent a large amount of critical work on the most various authors, and are important evidence that Bentley's activity as a scholar did not cease after his appointment to the Mastership of Trinity, as is sometimes said.

[2] It is curious that in the Mostellaria the handwriting changes from Act IV on (Ritschl 947); and it is just at this point that the notes become more numerous than those of the Pareus (see above p. 185). These notes then appear to be more recent additions.

period of his old age: (2) as Bentley used the two copies of Plautus till so late in his life, it is improbable that he possessed any other copy representing a more complete recension of the text by his own hand. Otherwise he would have entered his emendations in that copy rather than the Gronovius. At the same time it is not evident why he did not at once enter in one of the above copies the emendations now extant only in the Terence. Perhaps he considered them sufficiently recorded in the latter work; and we know that he was working under pressure.

An estimate of the absolute value of the emendations contained in this volume is not here attempted. But whatever the verdict of scholars may be on this point, certain general results may perhaps be anticipated. That Plautine criticism is under immense obligations to Bentley is indisputable; but a more careful examination of the actual work left on record by him will perhaps lead to the conclusion that the debt is rather indirect than direct, rather to the principles of comic metre and prosody laid down in the Terence than to emendations of particular passages, and that the supreme position of Bentley as a critic of Plautus can be explained only by this indirect obligation [1]. There is no evidence that Bentley ever gave to Plautus the thorough study, in detail, which he gave to Terence, Horace, and Manilius; nor does he seem to have collated any MS. except that of the King's Library (*J*), which contains only the first eight plays (cf. notes on Pseud. III 2. 55, IV 6. 36) [2].

On the other hand, if the positive gain at the present day from the volumes with MS. notes appears small, it must be remembered that many of their best emendations were published a century and a half ago in the Terence, and about one-third have either been made independently by modern scholars, working on Bentley's lines and drawing the inferences from his principles, or discovered in the Ambrosian MS. In an

[1] Cf. the panegyric of Ritschl in his dedication of the Trinummus to Hermann, '*ad emendandum Plautum post magnum Bentleium duci unico.*' The question of the obligations of Bentley to Guyet is a curious one: see the note of Wagner in his Aulularia, p. xiv (1st edition). An examination of Guyet's emendations, as published by M. de Marolles in his edition of Plautus (Lutetiae, 1658), certainly shows that Bentley borrowed many emendations from the French scholar whom he frequently attacked; among them must be included the celebrated *virgeum* for *virgarum* in Mil. II 6. 22, which is put down to Bentley by Ritschl, and the *festra* of Rud. I 1. 6 (cf. note on Haut. III 1. 72). On the other hand Bentley's general independence in conjecture is unmistakeable, and Guyet's inferiority in metrical insight comes out very clearly in the Cantica.

[2] For *B*, he relied on Pareus, whose notes he did not always study with sufficient care.

FROM HIS COPY OF GRONOVIUS.   193

estimate of Bentley's work on Plautus, these must be taken into account; they often furnish remarkable evidence of his insight and sagacity, and bear the best possible testimony—the testimony of verification—to the general soundness of the principles on which Plautine criticism rests. The evidence of this *consensus* is indeed so important and reassuring, that critics may be almost reconciled to the late publication of the *Bentleiana*; though it must not be forgotten that, had Bentley's work been made public property fifty years ago, Plautine criticism might on several important points have been saved a considerable *détour*[1].

In conclusion the editor would express his sincere thanks to the Curators of the Bodleian Library, for permission to publish the Bentleiana contained in this volume, and to others who gave him valuable help or advice in the progress of his work—the Ven. Archdeacon Palmer, the Rev. Prof. J. Wordsworth and F. Madan, Esq., of Oxford, Prof. R. C. Jebb, of Glasgow, Rev. R. Sinker of Cambridge, E. M. Thompson, Esq., and A. W. K. Miller, Esq., of the British Museum, and Arthur Beanlands, Esq., of Durham.

[1] See Bücheler in the *Deutsche Literaturzeitung* (Oct. 2, 1880), who comments upon Bentley's recognition of anapaestic verse in Plautus (on Pseud. IV 1. 33) and the remarkable restoration of the form *iurigare*.

EXPLANATION OF SIGNS, ETC.

To the left of the square bracket stands the word or phrase of the Vulgate text which Bentley corrects ; to the right, his correction. These corrections are printed in three different kinds of type : those which he borrowed or may have borrowed from previous editions (Class I) stand in ordinary Roman type, and are followed by the name of the scholar from whom he borrowed : those which have been since made independently by modern scholars or found in recently discovered MSS. (Class II) are printed in *italics*, and followed by the name of the scholar or MS. in question : those which are new at the present day are printed in **Clarendon** type. A few corrections stand in Roman type, and are not followed by any name in brackets ; these are by Bentley himself, but fall under none of the above categories, having been published by him either in the edition of Terence or that of Horace ; a reference to the place is given in a footnote (e. g. on Men. V 4. 2, Most. I 3. 19). Comments and notes by Bentley, i. e. such as are not corrections of the text, are also given in Roman type (cf. Most. I 2. 1, 39, Bacch. IV 9. 4, Men. II 3. 74).

Where Bentley strikes out a word in the text, the fact is indicated by ' del.' on the right of the bracket, whether Bentley himself employs this word or not. The type of the word ' del.' varies according as the emendation belongs to the first, second, or third class. On the other hand ' leg.' (i.e. lege, legendum) is only added where Bentley himself employs the word in the margin.

An upright stroke at the right of the square bracket (|, /, |) indicates the close of a line ; it is the sign which Bentley himself employs (cf. Cas. II 8. 34, III 5 ; Mil. II 4. 11). A horizontal stroke in the same place (—,)⁻ indicates that a word is to be joined on to the following line (cf. Bacch. IV 1. 11, Curc. V 3. 10). A † in the same place represents Bentley's tick with which he marked a line which he suspected, but could not correct (cf. Curc. II 3. 44, etc.) : sometimes particular words are underlined to indicate suspicion, with or without a tick in the margin ; this sign is represented by a similar line beneath the word or a part of the word to the left of the bracket (cf. Asin. I 1. 46, 50). A caret (∧, ∧) indicates the omission of a word (cf. Most. I 3. 65). A minus sign after the name of a scholar indicates that his reading differs only in some trifling point from that of Bentley (e. g. Mil. IV 8. 3).

A single asterisk after a correction indicates that the same correction is made in the copy of Pareus; two asterisks, that it is made in the copy of Camerarius; three asterisks, that it is made in both these copies, i.e. that it occurs in all three copies with MS. notes. Indications are also given, in foot notes, of all the passages in which the Pareus or the Camerarius collide with the Gronovius: and all the passages in the notes on Terence, which contain identical or varying corrections of the same passages, are referred to.

In determining the classes to which the various emendations are to be assigned, the chief modern editions of the whole or part of Plautus have been collated, and also the editions of Pareus and M. de Marolles (1658). For other editors before Bentley and for MSS. the critical apparatus of Ritschl and his followers have been the main helps. But, while accuracy has been aimed at, it is quite possible that the assignment of 'class' may sometimes be in error; some emendations put down as new (Class I), may possibly be extant in a modern periodical, and some which are assigned to a modern scholar (Class II) may be really due to an editor before Bentley. In such a matter absolute completeness is neither attainable nor necessary.

LIST OF ABBREVIATIONS.

A = Codex Ambrosianus (Ambrosian palimpsest)
Acid. = Acidalius
Ald. = Aldus
Ang. = Angelius
B = Codex Vetus
Ba = first hand of B
Bb = second hand of B
Bentl. = Bentley
Bentl.(C.) = Bentley in his copy of Camerarius
Bentl.(G.) = Bentley in his copy of Gronovius
Bentl.(P.) = Bentley in his copy of Pareus
Bo. = Bothe

Bos. = Bosius
Bossc. = Bosscha
Br. = Brix
C = Codex Decurtatus
Cam. = Camerarius
D = Codex Ursinianus
del. = dele
Diom. = Diomedes
Dou. = Dousa
E = Codex Ambrosianus (thirteenth century)
Fl. = Fleckeisen
Fr. = Francken
Gep. = Geppert
Gron. = Gronovius
Grut. = Gruter

Gul. = Gulielmius
Guy. = Guyet
Gz. = Goetz
Herm. = Hermann
J = Codex Britannicus
Lachm. = Lachmann
Lamb. = Lambinus
leg. = lege (legendum)
Li. = Lindemann
Ling. = Lingius
Lips. = Lipsius
Loe. = Loewe
Lor. = Lorenz
Meurs. = Meursius
Mül. = C. F. W. Müller
Mur. = Muretus
Non. = Nonius
om. = omitted

P. = Pareus
Pall. = Codices Palatini (quoted in the notes of Pareus)
Pi. = Pius
Pist. = Pistoris
Pyl. = Pylades
Quich. = Quicherat
Rl. = Ritschl
Rz. = Reiz
Sca. = Scaliger
Sci. = Scioppius
Scriv. = Scriverius
Speng. = Spengel
Uss. = Ussing
Wag. = Wagner
Wei. = Weise
Z = Editio Princeps

BENTLEY'S PLAUTINE EMENDATIONS.

AMPHITRUO.

Prol. 19 Mercurii] Mercurio (Guyet)
32 affero] fero (Acidalius)
46 mos nunquam illic fuit] **moris illi n. f.**[1]
71 Sive] *Seu* (Fleckeisen)
82 Ut] del. (Fruterius)
95 Nunc] Nunc vos (Lambinus, Pareus)

I.

1. 14 (Fl. 168)] Sotad.[2] [i. e. versus Sotadicus]
18 (172)] Sotad.
19 (173)] Bacch.
28 (183) hominem] **del.** [sic]
    mi] *mihi* (Bothe)
29 (184) ea] **del.**
49 (204) delegit] délegit
66 (221) legiones] del. (Guy.)
67 (222) Item] *del.* (Ussing)
72 (227) canunt contra] contra canunt[2] (Guy.)
136 (292) homo?] homo, (Pareus)
203 (359) familiae]*familiai*[2] (Bo.)
211 (367) audaciae] audaciai[2] (Camerarius)
221 (377) Eloquere]Loquere[2](Aldus)
264 (420) cistula] *cistellula* (Bo.)
270 (426) tabernaculo] tabernaclo (*D*)
272 (428) tabernaculo] tabernaclo (Guy.)

1. 302 (458) meam,] **mea**[2]
2. 1 (463) hodie] del. (Quidam ap. Acid.)
13 (475) concordiam conjugis] conjugis concordiam (Pylades)
28 (490) suspicio] consuetio[2] (Scioppius)

II.

1. 13 (563) hodie] / [2] [2]
15 (565) ludificari] **ludos facere**
16 (566) nunquam]umquam(*J*—,P.)
19 (569) te] / [2] [2]
48 (595) Neque] **Atque**
   mirum] **nihilo mirum**
57 (604) satin'] **satine**
82 (629) jam imperavi] *imperavi jam* (Bo.)
2. 29 (661) sese] se (Pyl.)
   ajebat] aibat (Guy.)
60 (692) factum est] **del.**
71 (703) velis] vis (MSS.)
73 (705) resolvas] rem solvas (Pistoris)
   —te solvas (Sci.)
76 (708) rogare] del. (Cam.)
103 (735) id] del. (Ald.)
105 (737) abivisti] abiisti (Pyl.)
113 (745) tu] del. (Guy.)

[1] Withdrawn; cf. Silva Critica IV. p. 233, and Introd. p. 181 (note 1).
[2] I. e. agreeing with 'quae.'

BENTLEY'S PLAUTINE EMENDATIONS

2. 145 (777) larvarum] **larviarum**[a]
149 (781) est profecto] profecto est (Guy.)
153 (785) Amphitruonem] *alium A.*[1] (Uss.)
164 (796) Praecurristi] Praecucurristi (P.)
175 (807) ajebas] aibas (Guy.)
182 (814) haec] hic
  facta'st] factu'st } (Pyl.)
189 (821) impudicitiae] impudicitiaī (Gruter)
non potes capere] capere non potes (Z, P.)

III.

1. 15 (875) Frustrationem] *Frustrationes* (Müller)

1. 15 (875) maxumam] *maxumas* (Müll.)
2. 22 (903) verecunda] iracunda[a] (Lamb.)
   potin' es] potin[a] (Cam.)
24 (905) arbitrare] arbitrere (P.)
27 (908) neque] neque ego (P.)
49 (930)]†
54 (935) confide] confido (MSS.)
4. 17 (1000) cispellam] aspellam[2] (*J*)

IV.

3. 14 (1048) aedibus] aedis (Cam.)
15 (1049) sive uxorem... sive adulterum] seu ux.... seu ad.[3] (Guy.)
18 (1052) aedibus] aedis (Cam.)

ASINARIA.

Prol. 3 Gregique] **Gregi**
4 jam nunc] *nunc jam* (Lingius)

I.

1. 36 (Goetz and Loewe 50)] v. 69
46 (61) praenoscimus
50 (65) obsequelam[4]
62 (77) obsecutum illius] *ejus obsecutum* (Bo., Wei.)
69, 70 (51, 52)] del. (v. 36)[5]
85 (98) id] istuc (Guy.—)
92 (105) forte] **fortasse**

3. 31 (183) pedissequae] pedisequae[a] (Pylades)
56 (208) ajebas] *aibas* (Bo.)

II.

2. 9 (275) hercle] **hercule**[6]
12 (278) huic occasioni] *occasioni huic*[7] (Fl.)
20 (286) frausus] *frausu*[i] (Quich.)
siet] sit (Cam.)
60 (326) derogita] rogita[a] (Cam.)
81 (348) novisse] nosse[a] (Guy.)
105 (372) caveto] **cave tu**[a,8]

[1] Bentl. originally thought of 'alium peperisti,' as his caret before 'peperisti' shows.
[2] Also on Haut. II 3. 20.
[3] Bentl. in his copy of Camerarius reads 'Si' for 'Sive' (at the beginning of the line).
[4] In his copy of Pareus Bentl. suggests 'obsequentiam.'
[5] I. e. Bentl. transposes these verses to their proper place after 36; so Acidalius and Gz.
[6] Bentl. originally thought of 'hercle tu.'   [7] Bentl. (P.) reads 'ai huic sese occasionit.'
[8] Here the emendation in the copy of Pareus and that given above supplement one another.
[9] Cf. Capt. II 3. 71.

(18)

3. 6 (386) conservas] / *
    7 (387) aedibus] del.* (Gulielmius, Acidalius)
    9 (389) extemplo] exemplo (*J*, P.)
    24 (404) hic] *del.*
    25 (405) incedit] cedit* (Scaliger)
    26 (406) Si] **ME. Si**
4. 22 (428) dedi] *dedo* (Gz.)
    86 (493) me tamen] tamen me¹ (P.)

III.

1. 6 (508) matris] **matri***
    27 (530) periculum] periclum (Pyl.)
    magnum] del.* (Pyl.)
2. 14 (560) nunc] del. (Guy.)
    23 (569) sies] **sis**
3. 9 (599) Negotiosus²
    53 (643) Le.] del. (Z)
    haec] hic (Pyl.)

3. 65 (655) populi] popli (*J*, P.)
    66 (656) imperator
    71 (661)]†
    herum] **humerum**³
    127 (717) olim] del. (*J*, Pyl.)
    131 (721) perpetuum] **perpetem**⁴

IV.

1. 40 (785) est] sit (Z)
    44 (789) habere illam] illam habere (Acid.)
2. 7 (816) tu haec] haec tu⁵ (Guy.)

V.

2. 45 (895) illam] illanc (Cam.)
    46 (898) Art.] Ph. (Acid.)
    es] **oris**⁶
    57 (907) nequeo] queo (*J*, P.)
    71 (921) odio] **suo odio***
    GREX 6 (947) sic] del.⁷ (Pyl., P.)

AULULARIA.

I.

2. 7 (Gz. 85) nunc] del. (Cam.)

II.

1. 46 (168) eburata] **ebur**
2. 20 (197) onerat] *ornat** (Bosius, Francken)
    54 (231) quasi nunquam] **quam si non**
    73 (251) -que sum] **sumque**
4. 4 (283) Co.] del.⁷

4. 6 (285) St.] An. (Z)
    16 (295) filiae] filiaï (Sca.)
    23 (302) sibi] del. (P.)
    27 (306) te] **te Congrio**
    aequom est] **est aequom**
    36 (315) esse parcum] *parce* (Wag.)
5. 14 (340) si quod] **si quo**⁸
8. 2 (372) bene] bene me* (Sca., Guy.)
    filiae] filiaï* (Sca.)
    23 (243) intro huc propere] deL*
    26 (396) Cui] *Si cui* (Uss.)

---

¹ Cf. on Andr. I 1. 92, where he reads 'fortasse.' ² By Bentl.?
³ This is not in Bentl.'s bold, characteristic hand, but cf. Aul. II 2. 54, III 5. 33, etc.
⁴ Cf. Amph. I 1. 125, II 2. 100, Truc. II 2. 23.
⁵ Bentl. (P.) omits 'tu.' ⁶ Withdrawn.
⁷ Here Bentl. (P.) shows a distinct advance. ⁸ Cam. read 'si qui.'
⁹ Cf. Bentl. on Haut. I 1. 20, where he proposes 'Ni intro huc propero currere.'

III.

2. 16 (430) crudum an coctum] cootum an crudum
5. 27 (501) pedissequos] pedissequos* (Pyl.)
   33 (507) pulchrum] *paulum* (Brix)
   45 (519) arcularii] |
6. 2 (538) audivisti] audivistin'* omnia] | (P.)
   3 (539) E] del.* (P., Gul.)
   4 (540) filiae] filiaï (Sca.)
   28 (564) totus est] totust (Guy.)

IV.

2. 8 (615) aurum] del.
4. 1 (628) Foras] I foras (Lamb.)

4. 3 (630) Ego] del.
   7 (634) rogitas] rotas [i.e. rogas* (Cam.)]
   9 (636) quidagam?] ecquidagam?
   15 (642) Larvae] Larviae*
   16 (643) Facisne]Faci'ne [*i.e. Facin*] mihi] del. (Reiz, Wei.)
   19 (646) vellem] velles
   22 (649) rursum] *rursus* (Rz., Bo.)
   25 (652) St. non] Eu. non (P.)
5. 1 (661) Emortuus] Emortuum (P.)
   3 (663) jam] *jam iterum* (Müller)
6. 13 (679) Indeque] *Inde* (Bo.)
8. 5 (705) illuc] illo (Cam.)
   7 (707) Indeque] Inde (Cam.)
10. 67 (797) filiae] filiaï (Guy.)

CAPTIVI.

I.

1. 6 (Fl. 74) non?] non est?¹ (P.)
   33 (101) suum] del.
2. 36 (139) egone] *ego* (Bo.)
   60 (163) est] *del.* (Bosscha)
   76 (179) Hx.] *del.* (Li.)
   77 (180)] p. 210 [*i.e.* III 1. 37.]

II.

2. 76 (326) luculentos] lutulentos (P.)
   107 (355) collaria] *collari* (Li.)
3. 71 (431) caveto] *cave tu*² * (Bo., Bosscha)

III.

1. 3 (463) cupit] cupiat*
   9 (468) Itaque] Ita* (Guy.)
   19 (479) inquam] del.* (Guy.)

4. 19 (552) Tr. ain'] Ar. ain' (P.)
   66 (598) larvae] larviae
   114 (647) et] del.* (Guy.)
5. 27 (685) Meum] *Me meum* (Fl.)
5. 67 (725) Nisi] *del.** [*transferred to end of previous line.*]

IV.

1. 13 (780) hunc] ob hunc (P.)
2. 21 (801) extemplo] del. (*J*)
   52 (832) vel] del. (Guy.)
   76 (856) te] *tute* (Li.)
   85 (865) huncce] hunc (*BJ*)

V.

3. 7 (984) indistis] indidistis (P.)
4. 4 (1001) omni'] *del.** (Li.)
   CATERVA (1032) liberet] haberet patrem suum] suum patrem

¹ Bentl. (P.) inserts 'scortum' after 'invocatum.' ² Cf. Asin. II 2. 105.
² Here Bentl. (P.) is in advance, reading 'Cotidiano'; so also on Haut. IV 5. 7.

CURCULIO.

I.

1. 27 sinit] sirit* (Muretus, Cam.)
   39 eveniat] **evenit***
   43 Id] **Id ita**
   45 exedat] excidat (Lamb.)
   67 Curiam] Cariam (P.)
   84 afferri] *ferri* (Fl.)
   93 Viden'] *Vide* (Bo.)
3. 1 (Gz. 158) forum] forium* (Pyl.)
   49 (205) utimur] utemur* (Pius)
   54 (210 me] del. (P.)

II.

3. 1 (280) atque] *del.* (Fl.)
   5 (284))]†
   11 (290) conferunt] *conserunt* (Fl.)
   13 (292) bibentes] libentes (Acid., *E*)
   15 (294) offendero,]—¹
   16 (295) Ex
       exciam] excutiam* (Cam.)
   28 (307) dextram] dexteram (*J*)
   32 (311) Viden'] Vide* (Pyl.)
   37 (316) vis] *del.* (Bo.)
   39 (318) Os]† [*Bentl.* marks Ös]
   43 (322) opus est] opu'st (P.)
   44 (323))]†
   55 (334)]†
   58 (337)]†
   60 (339) dextram] *dexteram*

3. 62 (341) Lyconem trapezitam] *trap. Lyc.* (Wei.)—267 [i. e. III 36]
   66 (345)]†
   67 (346) meo] **del.²**
   68 (347) daret operam] **operam daret**
   69 (348)]†
   72 (351)]†
   77 (356) opposuit] opposivit² (Cam., P.)
   88 (367) panem] pane (Nonius, P.)
   90 (369)]†
       tabellas] tabulas (*Z*)

III.

   4 (374)]†
   31 (401) non] *haud** (Bo.)

IV.

2. 22 (508) suadendo] **sua dando**
   26 (512) Cu.] Cᴀ. (*B*)
   33 (519) opus est] **del.**
3. 13 (545) tu mihi tabulas] **tabulas mihi**⁴
   14 (546) mihi luscos] **luscos mihi**⁵
   15 (547) ullu'st] *ullus est* (*F*)
   17 (549)]†*
4. 11 (567)]†
   22 (578)]†

---

¹ Cf. V 3. 10, 11 and note.
² Here, and in the next line, Bentl. (P.) represents a more advanced stage. By deleting 'meo,' instead of transferring it to the next line, Bentl. made the problem of line 69 insoluble: hence his †. Bentl. (P.), following Grut. and Guy., gives the key to the true solution of all three lines.
³ Cf Bacch. II 3. 72, Most. II 1. 35, Truc. Arg. 4; and note on Eun. V 3. 3.
⁴ Bentl. (P.) reads 'tu mihi,' deleting 'tabulas.'
⁵ The figures (2 1), by which Bentl indicates the change, are, contrary to his wont, placed under the words, instead of over them: the 2 stands above the 'u,' the 1 above the 'm,' of 'quidem.'
⁶ Here Bentl (P.) supplies the wanting emendation, by deleting 'tui.'

V.

2. 3 (601)]†
    7 (605) parentesne] parentes nè
    (*BJ*)
    prohibeas?] prohibeas
    23 (621) te] del. (*Z*)
    37 (636) PL.] PL. *hem* (FL)

2. 47 (647) spectacula] spectacla (P.)
   48 (648) nescio quis] *nescio qui* (Bo.)
   51 (651) Meministin'] **Meministi**
3. 2 (680) expertus sum] **expertu'**
   sum
   10 (688) tibi?]—
   11 (682) Aut¹

CASINA.

I.

1. 18 nisi] *si*'* (Bo.)
   30 facem.] facem;
   41 Jejunium] Jejunum * (Guy.)

II.

2. 22 ingratis] *ingratiis*¹* (Bo., Geppert)
3. 16 amo] /* (Bo., Gep.)
   17 enecas] /* (Bo., Gep.)
   18 tibi] /* (Bo., Gep.)
   es] | * (P.)
   59 Miser] Mi (P.—)
5. 10 uxorene] *uxoren'* (Bo., Gep.)
   27 emortuus] mortuus (Acid.)
   30 habeat] habet * (Cam.)
   42 Tace parum] St! tace parumper
   (Cam., P.)
6. 41 , amabo] ambo *² (Guy.)
   45 cupit] cupis (P.)
8. 10 magistia] mastigia (P.)
   34 viros] | (P.)
   57 Emitto] Emito (P.)
   lolligiunculas] lolligunculas (Pall.
   3, 4; see notes of P.)

8. 58 triticeas] triticeias (P.)
   71 noxa] noxia * (Cam.)

III.

1. 1 Alcesime] /* (Bo., Gep.)
   15 doctus] doctus et (Lamb.)
3. 22 est officium] *officium'st* (*A*)
4. 2 ludificatus est larva] **ludificatu'st**
   larvia⁴
   14 ea] del.
   18 hodie.] hodie (P.)
5. 1 occidi] /³ (Gep.)
   2 tremunt] / (Gep.)
   3 perfugii] / (Gep.)
   4 modis] / (Gep.)
   5 audaciam] / (Gep.)
   6 obsecro] / (Gep.)
   22 audi] / (Bo., Gep.)
   23 nos] / (Bo., Gep.)
   24 Coepit] / (Bo., Gep.)
   disciplinam] / (Bo., Gep.)
   25 linguae] / (Bo., Gep.)
   34 repente] /* (Bo., Gep.)

¹ Bentl. intends to transfer 'Aut' to the preceding line.
² Bentl. (P.) closes the line at 'postulat,' and thus is in advance of this correction.
³ Bentl. (P.) II 6. 34.
⁴ Cf. Amph. II 2. 145, Aul. IV 4. 15, Capt. III 4. 66, Men. V 4. 2, Merc. V. 4. 20, 22; P. Bo.
and Wei. here read 'ludificatu'st lariia.'
* This division of lines, which is not in Bentl. (P.), anticipates *A* (see Gep.).

5. 35 credo]/* (Bo., Gep.)
    hodie]/* (Bo., Gep.)
 36 audi]/*[1] (Bo., Gep.)
 37 Dejuravit] Dejeravit /[2] (Bo., Gep.)
 45 amator]/* (Bo., Gep.)
 46 facete]/* (Bo., Gep.)
 47 dixi]/* (Bo., Gep.)
    protulerunt] | * (P.)
 48 Pardalisca]/* (Bo., Gep.)
 49 te]/* (Bo., Gep.)
 50 mœrorem]/* (Bo., Gep.)
 51 gladium]/* (Bo., Gep.)
    te]/* (Bo., Gep.)
 52 hodie]/* (Bo., Gep.)
    vivunt] | * (P.)
 53 opinor]/* (Bo., Gep.)
 54 ademit]/* (Bo., Gep.)

5. 55 orat]/* (Bo., Gep.)
 56 iri]/[3] (Bo., Gep.)

IV.

1. 10 laute exornatusque] lauteque exornatus (Guy.)
2. 14 , sis ergo] sis ergo, (P.)
   18 socerus] *socius*[4] (Gep.)
3. 10 hymen]/* (Bo., Gep.)
 11 licet]/* (Bo., Gep.)
 12 copia]/* (Bo., Gep.)
    indomabilis] | * (P.)
 13 nimis tenax] lego, **nimi' sternax**,* Virgil.
 14 uspiam]/* (Bo., Gep.)
 15 foras]/* (Bo., Gep.)

CISTELLARIA.

I.

1. 72 Gustu] *Gustui** (Bo.)

II.

1. 28 periculum] periclum (P.)
 30 reliquom] *reliqūom*[5] (Bo.)

EPIDICUS.

I.

1. 4 (Gz. 5) Certe] Recte (Sca., *A*)
   salve] **Epidice salve**
 9 (11) Ep.] Ep. **Laevae ?**
 27 (29) quid rogas?] **quid tu rogas?**
 29 (34) dicis tu] **dicis id tu** [6]
 82 (90) amat] *amavit* (Wei.)
2. 8 (111) es] *del.* (Bo., Wei.)
 21 (124) item] fidem*** (Lamb.)

2. 27 (130) mandasti] *mandavisti** (Bo.)
 38 (141) est] del.
 40 (143) Dic] Ep. Dic (P.)
    a quo] *quo a* (Mül.)
 43 (146) periculo] periclo (P.)
 46 (149) periculum] periclum (P.)
 48 (151) de] del.* (Non., Acid., *A*)
 59 (162) dormitandum] *dormitandi* (*A*, Gz.)

---

[1] Also on Eun. IV 6. 5.
[2] Here Bentl. (P.) marks the end of a line, but does not alter the 'Dejuravit' of P.
[3] Cf. on Andr. II 3. 28, where he reads 'sese' for 'se': and note on Eun. V 5. 26.
[4] 'Cod. Rover. solus,' see Gep.   [5] Cf. on Andr. I 1. 127.   [6] *J* has 'dicis /// tu.

II.

2. 7 (191) amorem] amore (Cam.)
   apud nescio quam] **nescio apud quam**
8 (192) Ap.] Ep. (P.)
   hercle] **hercule**
10 (194) conjice] **conjice et—**
11 (195) Itaque] **-que**[1]
19 (203) ambo advenire] advenire ambo (Guy.)
20 (204) sine] *sine ut* (Rz.)
21 (205) Recipiam] Pr. *Recipe* (Br.)
41 (225) Utin'] **Utn'**
   eat] *fuerit* (*A*)
43 (227) potesse] **potes-**
44 (228) Illis] **-se illis**[1]
50 (234) Cani] Cani' (P.—, *B*)
   ademptum'st] adeptu'st (P., *A*)
54 (238) me] *del.* (*A*, Br.)
55 (239) exaudiebam] exaudibam (*B*, Bo.)
60 (244) Liberare quam volt] **Quam volt L**
61 (245) Illi. ibi] **Illa ibi filium**] / (Bo.)
62 (246) audio] / (Bo., Gz.)
   (247) actum] *actum'st* (*A*, Br.)
66 (251) sunt tabellae] tabellae sunt (Guy.)
68 (253)]†
69 (254)†

2. 74 (259) ubi est] ubi id est (P.)
   79 (264) reperitote] **repperito**[2]
   83 (268) corrumpit] **corrupit**
   87 (272) venerit] venit (P.)
   88 (273) hic] hunc (*B*)
   94 (279) nisi] *nisi si* (Bo., Wei.)
   98 (283) sapis] /[*]
      et placet.]—
   99 (284) acturus] **acturus es**
   104 (286) Filii] *Fili*[*]
   111 (296) minas] minis (Gron.)
   119 (304) abeas] abitas (P., *B*)
   120 (305) i, numera,] i numero, (Sca.)
3. 8 (313) Quam] *Quà* (Bo.)
   aliqua] aliquam (*B*)

III.

1. 1 (320) exenteror] / Versus Cretici et Paeonici
   2 (321) eveniant] /
   3 (322) sit] /
4. 26 (462) nisi] *nisi si* (Bo.)
   88 (525)[*] [*]] **scilicet**[4]

IV.

2. 26 (596) ratus] /[*]
   quibus]—
   31 (601) habeto] habe (Guy.)

V.

1. 55 (662) accurrentur] accurrentur (*B*, P.—)

---

[1] Cf. II 2. 43 and 44.
[2] Bentl. (P.) has 'reperi tute.'
[3] Cf. II 2. 10 and 11.
[4] P. has 'scilicet esse,' and so Wei.

FROM HIS COPY OF GRONOVIUS.   205

BACCHIDES.

I.

1. 25 (Rl. 59) aut] haut (P., etc.)

II.

1. 2 (171) Ephesum] **Epheson***
2. 11 (188) Pl. vivit] vivit. Pl. (P.) nempe] num* (Sca.)
   14 (191) recte] del.[1]**
   33 (211) Bacchis] del.**(Bo.)
3. 21 (255) Dei] Divi (Bo.)
   70 (304) extemplo] extempulo* (Bo.)
   72 (306) apud] ad (Hermann) deposuimus] deposivimus* (Acid.)
   73 (307) Dianae] in Dianae (P.)
   74 (308) Theotimus est] Theotimu'st* (Guy.)
   Megalobuli] Megalobuzi (Meursius, Pi., P.)
   78 (312) in ipsa] ipsa in (P.) conditum] **concreditum*** (iv. 9. 141)
   86 (320) Quantulum] Quantillum[2] (Pyl.)
   98 (332) auro habeat soccis] soccis habeat auro (Pyl., P.)
   120 (354) Ephesum] **Epheson***

III.

1. 12 (379) tui] te tui (P.)
   14 (381) Tua] **Tu tua**[3]

3. 24 (428) pugillatu] pugilatu** (Lamb.)
   36 (440) attingas] attigas (Dousa)
   41 (445) attingas] attigas* (Non.)
   58 (462) annis majus est] est annis majus (Bo.)
   85 (489) illam] illam jam (P.)
   95 (498) atque] del.[4] (Wei.)
4. 4 (503) meo] del. (A)
   24 (om.) malim] mavelim (Cam.)
6. 6 (535) et tollam] contollam (Cam., P.)
   15 (544) videatur] invideatur (P.)
   19 (548) Atque] **del.**
   29 (558) ego] **equidem**
   36 (565) Occiperes] **Ocoeptares**
   41 (570) parum] parvam[5]* (Sca.)

IV.

1. 11 (583) Ecquis exit]—[6] (Bo., Rl.)
4. 36 (687) dedisti] dedidisti (Acid., P.)
   58 (709) intendebam] intendam (P.)
   100 (752) periculo] periclo (Bo.)
6. 13 (783) criminatus est] criminatu'st (P.)
   18 (788) ut] del. (D F Z)
   24 (794) exeo] **exibo**
   27 (797) agitatur] agitur*** (Guy.)
7. 1 (799) Constringe] **Constringito**
   5 (803) gnato meo] meo gnato (Herm.)

[1] Also on Haut. II 3. 3; but there Bentl. also deletes 'ille.'
[2] Also on Haut. IV 2. 1.   [3] Rl. reads 'Tua tu.'
[4] Bentl. (P.) accepts the conj. of Cam. 'amicosque' for 'amicos atque.' To delete the 'atque' seems a later thought.
[5] Also on Eun. I 2. 117.
[6] I.e. Bentl. joins these words on to the first line of the next scene, as Bo. and Rl.

(25)   E   [I. 4.]

7. 13 (811) detuli] tetuli ** (*Ba*)
18 (816) diligunt :] diligunt, (P.)
22 (820) Terrae] *Terraï* (Bo.)
ambulat]inambulat(Pyl., P.)
35 (833) Pauxillum]   Pauxillulum
(Pyl.)
8. 52 (893) Opis] Opi'
9. 4 (928) subegerunt] subegĕrunt
13 (937) Sinon] Sino (Angelius)
41 (965) periculo] periclo (*C D*)[1]
42 (966) Postea] Post (Acid.)
94 (1017) Prius] Ni.⁸ Prius (*B*)

9. 118 (1041) tu] del. (Guy.)
145 (1068) inepta] incepta (P.)
veluti] uti*
146 (1069) incederem]   cederem ⁵ ⁶
(Sca.)

V.

2. 9 (1127) tonsitari] /
10 (1128) certo est] /
16 (1134) lactem] lao*
20 (1139) absunt] | (*B*)
23 (1142) Hae] *Haec*⁴ (Bo.)

MOSTELLARIA.

I.

1. 33 (Rl. 34) huid] quid (P.)
40 (41) tu] del. (P.)
42 (44) superior] superior quam herus (P.)
52 (55) carnificum]   carnificinum
(Sca., Cam.)
54 (57) si huc reveniat] simitu ut
huo revenerit
63 (66) rus abi] abi rus⁵ (P.)
70 (73) Venire] *Venit*⁕ (Bugge)
id] illud (P.)
72 (75) erres] *del.* (Lorenz)
78 (82) mensium] mensum (Lamb.)
2. 1 (85)] Bacchiaci
11 (94) credatis] creduatis
12 (95) ita esse] *esse ita* (Herm.)

2. 13 (96) scio]—⁸ (Herm.)
14 (96) nunc] /
15 (97) audietis] /
17 (100) esse hanc rem]*rem esse*⁷(Bo.)
23 (105) indiligensque]   indiligens
(Pyl.)—Cretici
35 (116) faciunt] *sarciunt* (Palmer)
39 (120)] Bacchiaci
3. 2 (158) quem] quom (*B*)
9 (165) hae] haec (Cam., P.)
13 (169) amatores]*amantes*⁴(Lachm.)
16 (172) decet] deceat* (Cam.)
19 (175) gratis] gratijs⁸⁕
mihi] mi'*
21 (178)vituperari]*vituperarier*⁕(Bo.)
23 (180) aut] et*
30 (187) stultam] stultam,

¹ These MSS. however have 'e periclo.'
² So also on Hor. Epist. II 1. 67 ; Guy. reads 'uti nunc.'
³ Bentl. (P.) also corrects ' Piraeeum' to ' Piraeum.'
⁴ I. e. to be joined on to the next verse.
⁷ C omits ' hanc.'   Bentl. (P.) follows Gron. in striking out the insertion of P. ' autem' after
'Simul ;' here he makes a further change in the line.
⁸ Withdrawn.   ⁹ Also on Adelph. IV 7. 26.

³ Blotted.
⁶ Blotted.

(26)

FROM HIS COPY OF GRONOVIUS. 207

3. 37 (194) plane] /*
41 (198) credas,] *credas* ⎫
42 (199) mea dicta] *mea dicta*, ⎬ *(Bo.)
  nosce : rem] *nosce* ⎭
  rem :
  vides] vide (Sci.)
47 (205) me] del. (Guy.; Ritschl, alternative correction[1])
48 (204) suo] fo. *suo aere* (Rl.) vel (*suo*) *sumtu*[2]
61 (218) nunc] nunc me (P.)
65 (222) me]   p. 171[3]
    ʌ
66 (223) nisi] ni (Z, P.)
73 (230) egere] aut egere (P.)
75 (232) Quom] Quom me (Gruter) referri] *referre benemerenti*[4] (Rl.)
81 (238) hisce] *his decem*[5] (Bo.)
85 (244) collocassem]   locassem[5] (Guy.) — I 3. 144
87 (242) patronum] patronam (Guy.)
88 (245) nihil] nihili[5] (P.)
92 (249) sim] *siem* (Bo.)
96 (253) tibi peculi] *peculi tibi* (Bo.)
107 (264) ullam aliam] aliam ullam[5] (MSS.)
121 (278) oleant] olent[5] id unum] unum id (Guy.)
123 (280) est] esse (Gellius) maxumaque] maxuma (Gellius)

3. 136 (294) hinc tu] tu hinc (MSS.)
138 (296) Libet] *del.* (Rl.)
151 (309) opus est] opu'st (P.)

II.

1. 33 (380) ubi] jam ubi
35 (382) autem hic] hic autem (Guy.)
  deposuit] deposivit (P.)
42 (389) ego] del.
  faciam] terrefaciam—pavefaciam (Gul.)
46 (393) est] *del.* (Wei.)
49 (396) animo ut] *ut animo*[6] (Bo.)
52 (399) tu jam] jam tu[5] (Guy.)
59 (406) meque] me (Pyl., P.)
2. 2 (432) me] med (Guy.)
   4 (434) imposuisse] imposuisse[7] (P.)
  ilico'st] 'st ilico[7] (Guy., Scriverius)
22 (452) qui] *del.* (Bo.)
23 (453) pedibus] *del.*[8] (Bo.)
33 (463) isto] istoc (P.)
37 (468) attingite] leg. attigatis (Diomedes)
44 (475) quid est?] del.[5] (Cam.)
47 (478) sceleste] *sceleris*[9] (Spengel)
53 (484) ausculta] ausculta tu.
70 (501) necavit] necuit
71 (502) ibidem] *del.* (Rl.)
73 (504) haec sunt] hæce (Guy.—)
90 (523) atque] del.[5] (Guy.)

---

[1] Bentl. (P.) reads 'Solam ei me soli.'   [2] In Bentl. (P.) the latter suggestion only.
[3] I.e. Aul. IV 10. 46. Bentl. has deleted the word in the margin, which he first thought of inserting after 'Dii,' and then after 'me'; and it is now illegible.
'Benemerenti' is from Cam.   [5] See Bentl. (P.)
[6] Bentl. (P.) reads 'ut animo sis' for 'animo ut sis': correct Appendix to Captivi, p. 151.
[7] Bentl. (P.) reads 'Scies in undam inposuisse, haut causa ilico'st.'
[8] Bentl. (P.) deletes 'ambas' instead of 'pedibus.'   [9] Bentl. (P.) reads 'scelesti.'

(27)   E 2

2. 94 (527) fugies] fuge* (Z)
95 (528) invocabis] *invoca** (Rl.)
te] *ted*¹ (Fl.)

III.

1. 19–22 (553, 557–9) are bracketed by Bentl. (Acid.)
25 (552) Dixtin] *Dixtine* (Bo.)
30 (557) eo] **eo me**
88 (616) compellat] compellat meum (Cam.)
91 (618) Objici] / (Rl.)
128 (657) Mulum] Nullum (MSS.)
2. 120 (807) incommodum est] *est incommodum* (Bo.)
127 (814; P. IV 1. 41) humano ingenio] humani ingeni²(P.)
128 (815; P. IV 1. 42) perspectas] perspecta* (B)
147 (832; P. IV 1. 61) ludificatur] *ludificat** (Bo.)
156 (842; P. III 3. 20) Latius] **Satius**

2. 165 (852; P. III 3. 29) aqua] **agna**
3. 15 (918; P. IV 3. 15) didimus] dedimus (P.)

IV.

2. 32 (947; P. IV 4. 9) nimium] **nimirum**
35 (950; P. IV 4. 12) aedibus] in aedibus (Pyl., Cam., A)
42 (958; P. IV 4. 19) in] del. (P.)
43 (959; P. IV 4. 20) in] del. (P.)
72 (988; P. IV 4. 49) intus] intus est (Z, A)

V

1. 29 (1077; P. V 2. 72) advenit] *adveneril* (Bugge)
65 (1114; P. V 2. 107) sarmen] sarmenta (Pyl., P.)
2 (P.3). 20 (1141) faciunt] del. (Guy.)
28 (1149) Tr.] Th. (P.)
33 (1155) adiit] **adit**

MENAECHMI.

Prol. 37]†
62 quam] quum (Acid.)
75 enim] del.*

I.

1. 6 (Rl. 82) accidit] leg. accedit* (Z)
9 (85)]†²
2. 2 (111) esse] *del.* (Herm.)
5 (114) foras] del. (P.)
revocas;] **me**

2. 6 (115) Rogitas] / (Rl.)—p. 724, 4 [i. e. Merc. I. 2. 108]
9 (118) loqui est] est loqui⁴ (Z)
10 (119) te] *del.*⁴ (Herm.)
20 (129) congratulantes] gratulantes (Pyl.)
3. 34 (217) Deum] deorum (P.)

II.

2. 6 (278) amabunt] ament⁵ (Cam.)

---

¹ Bentl. (P.) corrects 'invocabis' but not 'te.'
² Bentl. (P.) reads 'teque' for 'atque te,' and is thus in advance of Bentl. (G.)
³ Bentl. (P.) supplies 'aut' after 'compediti.'
⁴ Bentl. (P.) reads 'necessum' for 'necesse.'   ⁵ Cf. on Andr. IV 1. 12.
⁶ Bentl. (P.) reads 'quisquis es' for 'scis quis ego sum.'

FROM HIS COPY OF GRONOVIUS. 209

2. 9 (282) insanus est] insanust (P.)
10 (283) Dixtin'] Dixin' (P.)
27 (301) habeo] *ego habeo*[1] (*A*)
35 (309) equidem] *quidem** (Bo.)
45 (320) est ? non] an (Guy.)
58 (333)]†
3. 20 (371) voluit me] me voluit (P.)
atque] neque (P.)
38 (389) Egone] *Egon*' (Bo.)
63 (416) Peristi] Periisti (Guy.)
74 (428) eadem] eâdem
79 (433) es] del. (Acid.)
82 (437) solis] leg. solem * (Lamb.)
83 (438)]†
86 (441) perî] *perii* (Bo.)
88 (443) qui] quin'

III.

2. 6 (471) hercle] *hercule** (Bo.)
nisi] ni (P.)
7 (472)]†
30 (495) homini] homini hic (Cam., P.)
32 (497) Postea] Post* (*B*)
34 (499) nomen non] *non nomen** (Bo.)
43 (508) atque] *atque eam* (Rl.)
3. 27 (551) equidem] *quidem* *(Bo.)
31 (555) manum] *manum ut* (Bo.)
32 (556) Ut si] *Si*'[2] (Bo.)
34 (558) sciat] resciat[3]

IV.

1. 1 (559)]†
2. 33 (598) optumum] opimum * (Rittershusius)
82 (645) tibi] mihi[4] ('Quidam' apud Lamb.)
83 (646) ut] uti (Cam., P.)
88 (651) Menaechmus est] Menaechmust (Guy.)
91 (654) nos defessi] defessi* (Lipsius)
100 (663) ME.] *del.** (Bo.)
Ego] *Eo** (Bo.)
domum ?] *domum* (Bo.)
105 (668) sese] se*[5] (Pyl.)

V.

2. 1 (753) usus] usu'
5 (757) corpus] oorpu'
6 (758) merx mala est tergo] mala merx ergo'st[6] (P.)
7 (759) affert] fert (*Ba*)
8 (760) autumem] †
sermo sit] sermo'st (P.)
9 (761) dura] curae (*Bb*)
10 (762)]†
11 (762) expetit] expetit ut ad sese] *ad se ut* (Rl)
12 (763) id] *del.* (Bo.)
sit] |
53 (804) degerit] gerit

---

[1] Bentl. (P.) reads 'hercule' for 'hercle.'
[2] Bentl. (P.) reads 'sequitur' and 'censeat' for 'sequantur' and 'censeant.'
[3] Cf. on Haut. II 3. 104, where Bentl. reads 'jam sciat.'
[4] Bentl. (P.) simply underlines 'tibi.'
[5] Bentl. (P.) offers three suggestions, the last two of which were evidently made on the same occasion, as the handwriting and ink are identical.
[6] Probably Bentl. meant to read, as P. reads, 'ut aetas mala'st.'

2. 115 (868) minare] minaris (Guy.)
4. 1 (889) esset] esse¹* (Pi.)
   2 (890) larvatus] larviatus*
5. 6 (904) mea sit] mea'st *(Cam.)
   7 (905) educatus est] educatust (P.)
   18 (917)]†

5. 18 (917) insanire] **furere**
   22 (921) percipit] **percipit eum**
   45 (948) itan'] itane (*Bb*, Acid.)
   54 (957) nunc] del. (Guy.)
   62 (965) usque ad noctem:] *usque*:
       ad noctem (Bo.)

MILES GLORIOSUS.

I.

1. 24]†

II.

1. 22 (Rl. 100) amabat] *amat** (Bo.)
   26 (104) ut] del.* (Acid.)
   33 (111) amabat] *amat* (Bo.)
   39 (117)]†²
2. 1 (156) defregeritis] defregeritis
   2 (157) Videritis] Videritis
   5 (160) videritis] videritis⁴
   15 (170) fuerit] foret* (Cam., *A*)
   18 (174) vostrorum]vostrum* (Guy., *A*)
   20 (176) conservos est] conservos*
       (*Z, A*)
   80 (235) circumtentus est] circumtentust (P.)
   96 (251) abiit] *abit*⁵ (*A*)

2. 107 (262) familiarem] familiarium
       (P., *A*)
   115 (270) me] meae* (Guy., *A*)
   116 (271) atque] *del.** (Bo.)
3. 3 (274) alium]*malam rem**⁶ (*A*)
   9 (280) hic] *del.** (Bo.—)
   11 (282) te] del.*⁷ (Cam.)
   23 (294) fraudom] fraudem (P.)
   50 (321) Sc.] del. (*B*)
   51 (322) Pa. Quid jam? Sc. quia luscitiosus. Pa. vae verbero! edepol tu quidem] So. Quid jam? Pa. quia lusciosus. So. vae⁸ verbero! Pa. edepol tu quidem.
4. 9 (362) polita] pol ita (P.)
   10 (363) perpropere]—⁹
   11 (364) iste]¶¹⁰

¹ Also on Hor. Epist. I 2. 34.   ² Also on Hor. Epist. I 2. 34; but not in Bentl. (P.)
³ Bentl (P.) accepts the correction of Lips. 'id quod di volunt.'
⁴ Cf. on Eun. V 8. 34, where Bentl. reads 'Quemquem' and 'hic.'   ⁵ Bentl. (P.) reads 'iit.'
⁶ Also on Phorm. III 3. 11. Bentl. originally thought of 'alienum' (as Bo.), but afterwards substituted 'malam rem.'
⁷ Bentl. (P.) also reads 'sci' for 'scis.'   ⁸ Bentl. (P.) deletes 'vae,' as Guy. and Bo.
⁹ Cf. Curc. V 3. 10, 11; Mil. IV 6. 45, 46. Bentl. (P.) reads 'praepropere' for 'perpropere.'
¹⁰ This correction rests upon the misprint of the Vulgate ('quod' instead of 'quando,' which is the reading of all the MSS.). This is an instance of careless work on Bentl.'s part: when he

(30)

FROM HIS COPY OF GRONOVIUS.   211

4. 37 (390) esse] del.*¹ (Pyl., Sci.)
   40 (393) in vigilantes] in vigilan-
           tem ²
   51 (405) prius] *del.*³ (*A, Rl.*)
           mihi] del.¹
   55 (409) absumtus es] absumtus ⁴
           (Guy.)
5. 12 (422) tecum?] tecum⁵ (P.)
   17 (427) tu] del.* (Pyl.)
   58 (468) parierietem] parietem (P.)
6. 12 (492) magno malo] *malo magno*⁶
           (*A*)
   22 (502) virgarum] leg. virgeum * ⁸
           (Guy.)
   31 (511) tibi] mihi ** (Lamb.)
           datur]de te datur * ⁶(Lamb.)
   35 (515) tecum] *te*⁵ (Li.)
   50 p. 658 (   )]⁷ del. (P.)
   56 (536) Licet] del.
   67 (548) hospitae ajo] hospital *
   71 (552) Aqua aquae] Aquae aqua⁸
   82 (565) egone] ergo

III.
1. 5 (om.) is bracketed by Bentl.⁹ (*A*)
   9 (601) cate]† leg. *aut cautela* *
           (Rl.)
   20 (614) Immo] del.
   26 (620) te¹⁰
           ex] *del.* (Wei.)
           summis
   36 (630) pernix sum] *sum pernix*
           (Bo.)
           pedes] *pede* (Bo.)
   37 (631) albus capillus] albu' ca-
           pillus
   41 (635) periculum] periclum (Guy.)
   45 (641) aliquantulum] aliquantum
           (P.)
           meo] del.* (Guy.)
   55 (656) equidem] *quidem*¹¹ (Bo.)
           eductum] *educatum* (Bo.)
   66 (658) res] del.¹²
   67 (661) fateare,] *fateare*

made this suggestion he could not have had Pareus before him, still less his own excellent correction in his copy of Pareus ('probri' for 'propudii') in which he anticipates the reading of *A*.   ¹ Bentl. (P.) reads 'esse' for 'est,' as Cam.

² Bentl. (P.) reads 'vigilanti,' as Brix; *A* has INUIGILANTI according to Rl., UIGILANTI according to Gep.

³ Bentl. (P.) reads 'mihi ob oculos,' which was probably the reading of *A*.

⁴ Bentl. (P.) corrects P. by the help of Vulg.

⁵ Also on Adelph. IV 2. 52.   ⁶ Bentl. (P.) reads 'prius tecum postulare.'

⁷ Repeated by a printer's error on the next page.

⁸ *A* has AQUAAEQ; Bentl. (P.) reads, 'Aqua aqual' (and so Rl.).

⁹ This at the foot of the page.

¹⁰ Bentl.'s signs, as they stand, seem to point to his having read 'Ea te expetere: opibus summis te mei honoris gratia,' though he does not expressly say that 'te' is to follow 'summis.' After deleting 'ex', he saw no way of avoiding hiatus (either after 'mei' or 'expetere') and so left his correction incomplete. Bentl. (P.) simply deletes 'ex'.

¹¹ Bentl. (P.) reads 'eum quidem' for 'equidem' (leaving 'eductum' unchanged).

¹² Bentl. (P.) reads 'Lepidiorem ad omnis res, nec magis qui amico amicus sit,' as Bergk, Br. and Uss.

BENTLEY'S PLAUTINE EMENDATIONS

1. 70 (664) Opus] Opusne (P.)
   75 (669) PL.] PA. (P.)
   76 (670) PE.] PL. (P.)
   82 (676) apud me] del.¹
   84 (678) autem] del. (Lamb.)
       uti volo] utere²
   89 (683)]†³
   99 (692) Praecantatrici] Praecentrici⁴
   108 (701) te in] del.*⁵
   116 (710) habeo] *habebo**⁶ (Bo., *A*)
   120 (714) ego haec] egomet (Acid., P., *A*)
   122 (716) tu] del. (P.)
   133 (727) Sicuti] *Sicut* (*A*, *Rl.*)
   138 (733)]†
   147 (742) Qui] Quin (P.)
   150 (745) introduxi] induxi (Grut.)
   157 (752) Nam] *del.** (Rl.)
   159 (754) hoc] hoc hospes (Cam., P.)
   170 (765) agitur] agitur nunc (Pyl., P.)
   179 (774) perpurgatis] purgatis *
       (Guy.)
       operam] operas*

1. 181 (776) istunc] istuc⁷ (*Z*, P.)
   196 (791) Utique] que⁸
   202 (797) faveae suae ancillae] famulae⁹ suae
2. 3 (815) manipulares]maniplares(P.)
3. 1 (874) mea] del.¹⁰
   10 (883)]†
   13 (886) habuere] habere (MSS., Pyl.)
   20 (893) inscientes] scientes (Beroaldus)
   21 (894, 895) nulla meretrix] *mulier merx* (Br.—)
   27 (901) architectus est] architectust (P.)
   45 (919) architectique]   *architectonesque* (Rz.)
   61 (935) accibo] acciebo (P.—)

   IV.
1. 9 (955) quis] qui*
       nostro hic auceps] auceps
       nostro hic (P.)
   23 (970) incipit] *cupit**¹¹ (Bo.)

¹ Bentl. (P.) reads 'et mea unde' for 'ut transeuntem' (retaining 'apud me').
² Here Bentl. (P.) simply underlines 'uti,' indicating the presence of an error, but not correcting it.
³ Here Bentl. (P.) suggests a correction (liberum med), whereas Bentl. (G.) merely indicates the presence of an error.
⁴ Bentl. (P.) follows Sca. in reading ' Praecantrici.'
⁵ Also on Andr. IV 1. 57. Bentl. (P.) also gives 'te in eum rursus,' as Guy.
⁶ Bentl. (P.) also corrects 'quom' of Pareus to 'qui mi,' as Cam. Vulg. has 'quin.'
⁷ Bentl. (P.) reads ' Nec fuisse aeque' for ' Fuisse adaeque' of Vulg.
⁸ It is not clear what Bentl. meant by striking out the first two syllables ('Uti'). He probably intended to substitute the reading of the MSS. 'Itaque' for the 'Utique' of Cam.; but then found that the line would not scan without some further change.
⁹ Bentl. (P.) reads ' famulo.'
¹⁰ Bentl. (P.) reads ' unà ' for ' mea ' (and so *B C D*, Rl.)
¹¹ The strict interpretation of Bentl.'s signs is that he read ' incupit' for 'incipit,' as he only underlines two syllables of the latter word ('in<u>cupit</u>'). But this was probably not his intention.

FROM HIS COPY OF GRONOVIUS.   213

1. 24 (971) uti] ut (P.)
   34 (981) instruxisti] instruxti (Cam., P.)
   35 (982)]†
   36 (983) istanc] istam (P.)
2. 4 (994) nam] del. (Guy.)
   7 (997) corporis est] corporist (P.)
   10 (1000)]†
   18 (1009) pedissequus] pedisequus (Z)
   19 (1010) eveniat] veniat
   26 (1017) domum] donum (P.)
4. 15 (1151) periculum] periclum (A, Rl.)
   18 (1154)]†
   26 (1162) Volo] del.
   53 (1190) ut properet]*properet*(Wei.)
   56 (1193) protinus] *protinam*[3] (Bo.)
6. 6 (1221) ut volui] del.[4] (Guy.; Rz. in Fl. Epistula Critica, p. xxvii; Lorenz)
   18 (1233) fastidiosus est] fastidiosust (P.)

6. 29 (1244) exspectet] te exspectet (Cam., P.)
   30 (1245)]† [2]
   37 (1252) clementi] *clementi id*[3] (Mül.)
   43 (1258) Nescio,] *Nescio*[4]
   45 (1260) astare] *stare—*[5] (Bo.)
   46 (1260, 1261) Nequeo] / (Bo.) defit]†
7. 19 (1302) pretiosum] pretium[6]
8. 2 (1312) viden'] vide[7]
   3 (1313) audistin'] audin'[8](Guy.—)
   6 (1316) salutem] salutem me (P.)
   9 (1319) omnia] del. (Gul., Lamb.)
   22 (1332) atque] *del.* (Bo., Rl.)
   23 (1333)]†
   41 (1351) agite, ite] ite, agite
   48 (1358)]†
   51 (1361) me] ne (P.)
   60 (1370) praeter me esse] esse praeter me
9. 15 (1392) Mulieres] Omnes[9]

MERCATOR.

I.
1 (Prol.). 4 (Rl. 13) facere amatores] *amatores facere* (Rl.)
   6 (15) credo] credo ab humanas] humanis[6] (B)

1. 17 (4)]†
   47 (50) injustitiam lenonum] *lenonum injustitiam* (Rl.)
   64 (64) esse] esse se[**] (Cam.)
   66 (66) tum] del.[10]

---
[1] Bentl. (P.) deletes 'otiose.'
[2] Here Bentl. (P.) and Bentl. (G.) are at the same stage. Bentl. (P.) underlines the troublesome syllables '-movere istam.'   [3] Bentl. (P.) reads 'clementi mi.'
[4] Bentl. (P.) strikes out 'hu! ha!' of P.
[5] Cf. Carc. V 3. 10, 11; Mil. II 4. 10, 11.
[6] Here Bentl. (P.) simply indicates the presence of an error.
[7] Guyet read 'Quem omnes.'   [8] Bentl. (P.) suspects 'Humanas.'
[9] Also on Andr. I 1. 27.   [10] Bentl. (P.) suspects 'positum' of P.

(33)   F   [I. 4.]

BENTLEY'S PLAUTINE EMENDATIONS

1. 69 (69) se] sese (PyL, P.)
   80 (81) esse me] *me esse*[1] (Rl., Wei.)
   84 (85) allaudat] collaudat[3]
   91 (92) iisce] MSS. isset[5] [i.e. *BCD*]
2. 4 (124) enicato] *enicat*[*] (Rl.)
   5 (114) plenissume[4]
   9 (118) jurgandum est[6]
   10 (119) illud] del. (P.)
   11 (120) Cura est] *Curae est*, (Rl.)
   16 (137) Cн.] del.
   17 (126) Ac] *del.*[4] (Rl., Wei.)
   19 (128)]†[7]
   39 (150) esse sequentem] sequentem esse[8] (Sca.)
   47 (159) Quid] *Quid id*[*] (Bo.)
   57 (167) nullus est] nullust (P.)
   63 (175) te] del. (P.)
   69 (181)] 1 (P.)
   70 (185)] 5[9] (P.)
   71 (182)]† 2 (P.)
   72 (183) I] *In*'[*][10] (Bo.)
   nugare] *nugaris*[*] (Bo.)

2. 73 (184)] 4 (P.)
   74 (186)] 6 (P.)
   76 (188) confabulatus est] confabulatust (P.)
   78 (190) abstrudebas] **aliquo abstrudebas**[11]
   79 (191) nos nostris] *nostris nos*[*] (Bo., Lachm.)
   80 (192) &] del.[*] (Cam.)
   88 (201) Occurri] Occucurri (Cam., P.)
   98 (211)] Typographus omisit sex versus.[12]
   107 (220) ilico] **te ilioo**[13]
   109 (222) quin] del. (P.)

II.

1. 2 (226) somniis] somnis (P.)
   9 (233) custodiam eam] custodelam[*] (Grut.)
   15 (239) uxoris dotem ambadedisse] **ambadedisse dotem uxoris**[14]

[1] Rl. assigns this correction to P.; but it is not in his first, second, or third edition.
[2] Withdrawn.
[3] Bentl. (P.) underlines 'eljsce' of P.
[4] Bentl. (P.) suspects the line.
[5] Bentl. (P.) reads 'jurigandum'st.'
[6] Bentl. (P.) corrects 'balneae' (of P.) to 'balineae' (Vulg.).
[7] Bentl. (P.) deletes 'scire me' of P.
[8] Bentl. (P.) reads 'esse obsequentem,' as Cam.
[9] Bentl. (P.) reads 'rogo' for 'interrogo.'
[10] Pareus has printed a 3 at the head of this line; Bentl. in copying seems accidentally to have omitted it.
[11] Bentl. (P.) reads 'eam abstrudebas,' as Lachm., and Rl.
[12] At the foot of the page. These 'six verses' are found in Pareus and other editions.
[13] This correction makes the verse, as it stands in the Vulg., unmetrical; for 'Posteaquam' (which is an emendation of Cam.), Bentl. perhaps intended to read 'Postquam' (as *Z*) or otherwise to correct 'Postea,' the reading of the MSS. Bentl. (P.) marks the line as suspicious.
[14] This seems to be Bentl.'s intention. He probably first thought of 'dotem uxoris amb.' (as Herm., Bo.), and then on reflection put a figure 1 over 'ambadedisse,' and a second stroke by the side of the 1 over 'dotem,' to indicate that the latter word should stand after 'amb.' The appearance of the whole is thus, 'uxoris dotem ambadedisse.'

FROM HIS COPY OF GRONOVIUS. 215

1. 20 (244) uxorom] uxorem[1] (P.)
   24 (248) visus est] visust* (Z, A)
2. 13 (284) salve. ô] salveto (Cam., P.)
   55 (327) valeto] vale* (Guy.)
   58 (330) hominem] del.
3. 1 (335) nullus est] *nullust** (Rz.)
   3 (337) Santin'] Satin'[1] (P.)
   8 (342) meum] *me meum** (Wei.)
   12 (346) consilii] *consili*
   20 (355) igitur] / (Rl.)
   21 (356) sic amare] | (P., Rl.)
   23 (358) inveni] / (Rl.)
   24 (359) amoeni] | (P., Rl.)
   27 (362) Nec] | Nec[2] (P., Rl.)
   28 (362) adsit.] / (Rl.)
   29 (363) est] | (P., Rl.)
   44 (381) docto] dicto[1] (P.)
   63 (397) facit] faciat[1] (P.)
   85 (422) Ligitare] Litigare[1] (P.)
4. 19 (487) at erit id] erit | * (Guy.)
   20 (488) Achillem] **Id Achillem**

III.
1. 13 (511) illim] *illi** (Bo.)
   advecta huc] huc advecta (P.)
4. 12 (842)] 756[3] [*i.e.* V 2. 1]
   29 (614) nullus est] nullust (P.)
   43 (628) meâ] *del.* (Bo.)
   58 (643) dedit mihi] mihi dedit (P.)

IV.
3. 1 (700) ne] nec (P.)
5. 7 (822) alumne] alumne mi (Pyl., P.)

V.
1. 5 (834) familiae] *familias** (Bo.)
2. 1 (842)] 741 [*i.e.* III 4. 12]
   5 (846) Civitatem] leg. **œvitatem**[4]
   6 (847) decem] *del.* (Bo.)
   38 (880) sinistram] sinisteram (P.)
4. 4 (965) ce te] cette (Cam., P.)
   19 (980)]†
   Ly.] Ev. (P.)
   20 (981) larva] **larvia**
   22 (987) larva] **larvia**

PSEUDOLUS.

I.
1. 35 (Rl. 37) quantus es] quantum'st[5] (Sca., Passerat, A)
   63 (65) Jocus] **Jocu**[6]
   81 (83) adjutas] *adjuvas*† (F, Bo.)

1. 84 (86) reddam] reddibo*[4]
   88 (90) persequi tenebras] tenebras persequi[4] (P.)
   122 (124) in] **del.**[7]
   124 (126) populo] poplo (P.)
3. 55 (289) monstres?]monstres. (Guy.)

---

[1] Correction of misprint, cf. Mil. II 3. 23.
[2] The stroke is put before the first word in the line.
[3] Bentl. does not say in which place he would delete the line (or two lines).
[4] Rl. reads 'voluptatem,' but remarks: 'Nisi tamen aliud subest: quamquam nec *salutem* nec *quietem* nec *aequitatem* nec *hilaritatem* placet.'
[5] In the text Bentl. has changed 'quantus es' into 'quantu's;' in the margin he has written 'tum'st.' Bentl. (P.) reads 'quantum'st.'
[6] Also on Hor. Serm. II 2. 99.   [7] Bentl. (P.) deletes 'utrum.'

216   BENTLEY'S PLAUTINE EMENDATIONS

3. 60 (294) Omnes] *Omnes homines*[1]
(Bo.)
roges] | * (*B*)
mutuum—(*B*)
85 (319) fugitivam canem] *canem fugitivam* (Bo.)
91 (325) habeo] jam habeo (P., Rl.)
117 (351) hominum] homo hominum ** (Guy.—)
128 (362) haec ista] **ista haec**
136 (370) alium] aliud (*Z*, *F*)
4. 17 (410) huc,] huc (P.)
5. 1 (415) <u>amatoribus</u>] leg. **ganeonibus**
Sic Terent. Ganeo, damnosus.[3]
64 (479) hoc] *del.* (Rl.)[3]
93 (508) hercle] *hercule* (Bo.)

II.

1. 6 (581) malorum] majorum (Dou., P.)
2. 61 (656) ahenea] *ahena* * (*A*, Bo.)
3. 6 (672) omnes sunt] *omnes* (*A*, RL)
4. 19 (709) an] **anne**
24 (714) Charine] o **Charine**
58 (748) scitus est] scitust (P.)
76 (766) ipsum] *del.* (Bo.)

III.

2. 6 (795) hunc] **del.**[6]
27 (816) laserpicii] laserpici (*B*, *C*, *D*, *F*[4], Rl.)
44 (833) Eae ipsae sese] *Eae ipsae se*[5] (Wei.)
49 (838) tuis] tuis istis (Pyl., P., *A*)
53 (844) in] del. (Gul., P., *A*)
55 (843) demissis] **del.**[4]
63 (852) milvinis] miltinis (MSS.)
67 (856) Uti] Ut* (MSS.)
90 (880) illos] *del.* (Fl.)[7]
92 (882) suavitate] leg. suavi suavitate* (Grut., *A*)
95 (885) dabit] dabis (P.)
99 (889) nimium jam] **nimi' jam**[8]
107 (897) petivit] **expetivit**[9]

IV.

2. 20 (976) illa] illa mea (Cam., P.)
33 (990) tibi me recte] *tibi recte me* (Bo.)
37 (994) mihi] del. (Guy.)
3. 9 (1024) mecum] meum (P.)
5. 3 (1054) Mihi] del.* (MSS.)
4 (1055) Et] *del.* (Bo.)
5 (1056) scio.] *scio*
6. 4 (1066) Simo] *del.*[10] (Bo.)

[1] Bentl. (P.) does not insert 'homines,' though he closes the line at 'roges.'
[2] At the foot of the page.
[3] Bentl. however does not alter the order of the words 'te rogo.'
[4] I. e. these MSS. have the termination '-ci.'
[5] Bentl. (P.) reads 'Ipsae se,' as Guy. and Rl.
[6] Bentl. (P.) deletes 'BA. Quid est? Co.' Both corrections are based upon the reading of Cam. ('Quia enim' for 'Quia'); cf. note on IV 6. 36.
[7] Rl. reads 'illo,' but adds 'nisi delendum est potius.'
[8] Bentl. (P.) deletes 'jam.'
[9] Bentl. (P.) reads 'petiit' for 'petit' (P.), thus leaving hiatus in caesura (and so Wei.).
[10] Bentl. (P.) reads 'Simo. SI. quid jam? BA. quid jam? nihil est' *etc.*

6. 21 (1083) ajebat] aibat * (Guy.)
26 (1088) nec] neque|¹
27 (1089) Meministine]   Potest.
   Meministin'
36 (1098) quidem] del.²
38 (1100) molarum] molas (P.)
7. 4 (1105) esse] del. (Guy.)
38 (om.) heus, adolescens] *adolescens* (Wei.)

7. 44 (1143) curio] corio
71 (1167) ludo] ludos (Lamb., P.)
81 (1177) solitus es] solitus (P., Rl.)
82 (1178) solitus es] solitus (P.)
92 (1189) fœmina] femina (P.)
124 (1222) nisi] ni³
8. 7 (1244) Dolum] *Dolonem* (Ei 'quos ridet Beckerus Qu. p. 64' [Rl.])

POENULUS.

Prol. 47 ignarures] *gnarures** (Bo.)
  71 abiit] **abit**⁴
  95 in] del.
 118 reliquom] *reliqüom* (Bo.)

I.

1. 35 (Gep. 161) damno et] del. (Guy.)
2. 61 (268) En] *del.** (Wei.)
   62 (269) nebulae cyatho] **vel obolo aerato**
  130 (336) tu] del. (Guy.)
  197 (402) Respexit] **Respexisti**
3. 13 (415) promisisti] promisti* (D, Guy.)
  36 (437) Illinc] Illic (P.)

II.

 3 (443) illum] ullum (P.)
47 (486) auscultas] **aut ausoultas**

III.

1. 6 (500) Sciebam] Scibam (Guy.)
   39 (533) dictum] **dicta**
   64 (558) agendum. propera] **agendum propere***
   74 (568) incedit] *cedit* (Bo.)
3. 8 (613) tibi,] *tibi, et* (Wei.)
    9 (om.) Et] *del.* (Wei.)
       leviter] leniter (P.)⁵
   10 (614) scio.] *scio*
   22 (626) id] del.⁴*
   25 (629) tui] del.
   26 (630) leviter] leniter* (MSS.)
   32 (636) iratus est] iratust (P.)
   36 (640) est] at⁷
   79 (683) huc] del.* (Guy., A)
4. 8 (709) reliqua] *reliqüa* (Bo.)

---

¹ Bentl. (P.) deletes 'ab me,' retaining 'nec potest' at the end of the line, as Rz. and Rl.
² Here Bentl. bases his correction upon the correction of Cam. ('Quin jam quidem illam'), instead of upon the reading of the MSS. ('Qui illam quidem jam'); cf. note on III 2, 65. Bentl. (P.) marks the reading of Cam. (in P.) as suspicious, but does not correct it.
³ Bentl. (P.) reads 'moriri' for 'emoriri.'   ⁴ Bentl. (P.) deletes 'ad.'
⁵ Bentl. (P.) deletes the whole line, as Gep.   ⁶ Also on Eun. I 2. 69.
⁷ The stroke through the 'e' is faint and smudged. Bentl. seems to have thought of deleting the word and then to have changed his mind.

218 BENTLEY'S PLAUTINE EMENDATIONS

4. 20 (721) censetis] **censes**[1]
   21 (722) venerit] venit* (Guy.)
5. 28 (764) allegaverunt] *allegarunt* *
   (Bo.)
6. 2 (788) mehercle] hercle * (Wei.)

IV.

2. 30 (842) facis] del.*
   33 (845) tu] **tu tuum**
   44 (856) memorandum] memora
      dum (P.)—900, 7 [*i.e.* V
      2. 103]
   62 (874) perdeam
   68 (880) habeto] **habe**
   78 (890) ajebat] aibat (Guy.)

V.

2. 61 (1010) volui] volt (P., *A*)
   63 (1012) si] *sis* (Bo.)
   65 (1014) uti] ut (*A*, Bo.)
   92 (1040) mihi hospitalis tessera]
      hospitalis tessera mihi
   157 (1105) novit] noverit (P.)
3. 35 (1147) leviter] leniter* (MSS.)
   52 (1142) haec] hae (P.)
4. 46 (1205) benefeceris] benefecerit *
      (Acid.)
   69 (1228) multo] multos (P.)
   75 (1234) faciatis] *facitis* * (Herm.)
   77 (1236) vox] vos (P.)
   79 (1238) timeo,]/*[2]
      (1239) quid]— *

POENULO SUPPOSITA.

1 (1356) meo] / *
2 (1357) mulieres] / *
   (1358) filias] | (P.)
3 (1359) meas] / *
4 (1360) domo] /
   (1361) perditus.] | (P.)
5 (1362) cognosceret] /
6 (1363) mihi!] /
   (1364) minae,] /
7 (1365) Lyce:] /
   (om.) perditus.] | *
8 (1366) novellicus,] / *
      Utrum is est novelle no-
      vellicus,] Utrumvis est,
      vel leno, vel lycus*(P.)—
      913, 21 [i.e. V 5. 53]

9 (1368) noveris:] / *
10 (1369) credidi:] / *
   (1370) magis] /
11 (1371) obsecro,] / *
12 (1373) addecet,] / *
13 (1375) liberas,] / *
   (1376) manu.] | (P.)
14 (1377) tuum] / *
15 (1378) dabo,] /
16 (1380) consulam.] / *
17 (1381) est.] /
   (1382) negotium?] | (P.)
18 (1383) abducêre.] / *
19 (1384) foris:] / *
20 (1385) simul.] / *
21 (1386) cogito] / *

---

[1] Bentl. (P.) reads 'AD. censeo. AG. Hominem' for 'censetis? Hominem.'
[2] Bentl. (P.) reads 'hercule, mi Patrue' for 'hercle: Patrue.'   [3] At the foot of the page.

FROM HIS COPY OF GRONOVIUS. 219

22 (1388) sient.]/*
23 (1389) obsecro.]/*
24 (1390) improbo.]/*
25 (1391) scio;}/*
   (1392) mecum] | (P.)
26 (1393) carcerem.]/*
27 (1394) volo,]/*
28 (1395) sententiam,]/*

29 (1397)] | Ita (P.)
31 (1399) tibicinam:]/*
32 (1400) sient.]/*
33 (1401) tuum.]/*
34 (1402) sequor.]/*
35 (1403) Carthaginem?]/*
36 (1404) Ilico.]/*
37 (1406)] | HA. Faciam (P.)

PERSA.

II.

2. 28 (210) mali] male (B)
  29 (211) arbitratus est] arbitratust (P.)
  34 (216) dic tu:] *dic tu. P. Dic tu* (Wei.)
  48 (230) fœde] del.
  57 (239) quid est?] *P. edictum est mihi.* (Rl.—[1])
  58 (240) PÆ.] *del.* (Rl.—[2])
4. 14 (285) gratis] *gratiis*[3] (A)
  24 (295) ipsum] del. (Guy.)

III.

1. 18 (346) melius est] meliust (P.)
  25 (353) ego] del. (Guy.)

1. 41 (369) melius est] meliust (P.)
3. 16 (421) lucro] lurco (Non., Z, P.)
  29 (434) augentarii] argentarii (P.)

IV.

1. 1 (449) an] *ac* (Bo.)
3. 65 (534) complures] compluries (P.—)
4. 23 (572) ferreo] ferro (P.)
  113 (665) periculo] periclo (P.) datur] dabitur[3]
8. 4 (734) fateor] fateor, (P.) habere] habeo (B)

V.

2. DORDALUS] DORDALUS, TOXILUS (F, Z, P.)

[1] In Rl. this speech ('Edictum est .... prius') is assigned to Sophoclidisca.
[2] Also on Adelph. IV 7. 26.
[3] Also on Haut. IV 7.8, where Bentl. reads 'haec sexaginta' for 'sexaginta haec.'

RUDENS.

Prol. 24 perduunt] perdunt (P.)
27 scelestus est] scelestust*(Guy.)

I.

1. 2 (Fl. 84) vobis] nobis (P.)
   6 (88) fenestrasque] festrasque[1]
   (Guy.)
2. 21 (109) nos] del.* (Guy.)
   23 (111) mox] *del.** (Rz.)
   53 (141) melius est] meliust (P.)
   56 (144) periculum] periclum (P.)
   58 (146) Amore] Amori (Sci.)—92
   [i. e. I 2. 92]
   77 (166) potuit] *potuit rectius* (Rz.)
5. 2 (259) precantum me] me precantum (*B*)
   10 (268) caeruleas] caerulas* (Guy.)
   24 (282) inopesque] inopesque,
   (Guy.)

II.

1. 5 (294) Hisce] Hice[2]
   hae] haec[3]*
   7 (296) exercitu] **exercitio**
2. 2 (307) ajebat] *aibat** (Rz.)
   13 (319) mali] *del.** (Rz.)
3. 68 (399) se sic] sic se[3] (Guy.)
4. 17 (433) Veneris] *del.** (Rz.)
   19 (436) periculo] periclo (Guy.)
5. 19 (476) vinculis] vinclis (*B*)
6. 1 (485) HOMO] *homo esse*[4] (Wei.)
   3 (487) quid] **quidquam**

6. 25 (509)]†
   anteposita est] **posita**
   65 (549) hanc unam] unam hanc
   (Guy.)
7. 19 (577) pluvit] *pluit* (Rz.)

III.

1. 9 (601) Videbatur] Videtur* (Guy.)
   21 (613) fano]— [5] (Rz.)
   22 (614) Clamoris] **clamor**
2. 5 (619) innocentium] innocentum*
   (*B*)
   11 (625)]†
   custodiam] *custodelam**(Rz.)
   12 (626) perveniat] **pervenit** *
   25 (639) exoptavi] optavi* (Guy.)
   28 (642) innocentes] innocentes intus (P.)
   29 (643) jus] **jusque** *
   32 (646) audeat violare] **violare
   auderet** [6]
   35 (649) * * *] liberas (P.)
   37 (651) parricidii] *parricidi* (Rz.)
   perjurii] *perjuri* (Fl.)
   plenus] plenissumus (P.)
   42 (656) fecit hercle] hercle fecit
   (Guy.)
   49 (663) ecce] *eccas** (Rz.)
4. 10 (715) Nive] Neu (*B*, P.—)
   27 (732) murteta juncis] *juncis murteta* (Bo.)
   38 (743) Mea!] *del.* (Wei.)
   56 (761) Veneris] Veneri* (Guy.—)

[1] On Haut. III 1. 72 Bentl. reads 'fenestrasque,' remarking that the word 'fenestra,' both in Plautus and Terence, is pronounced as a dissyllable, and approving the spelling 'festra,' quoted by Festus.
[2] Also on Eun. II 2. 38; and so Bo.
[3] Bentl. (P.) reads 'sic sese.'
[4] Bentl. (P.) reads 'sese esse.'
[5] I. e. Bentl. makes one line of 21 and 22.
[6] Bentl. (P.) reads 'audeat violare.'

FROM HIS COPY OF GRONOVIUS. 221

5. 4 (783) quidem] **equidem**
16 (795) istas] del.* (Guy.)
19 (798) affer] **affer e domo**¹
25 (805) advenit] **venit**
47 (827) equidem] *quidem*² (Rz.)
6. 23 (861) Quin] Quin'³* (Guy.—)
27 (865) quid] numquid⁷*

IV.

1. 14 (905) vaniloquentia] loquentia⁴*
2. 11 (916) praeposui] praeposivi (P.)
13 (918) sententiam]   servitutem*
(Cam., Rz.)
32 (937) pransurus est] pransurust (P.)
3. 54 (993) audivisti] audisti* (Guy.)
69 (1008) exurgeri] exugeri* (Guy.)
70 (1009) exurgebo] exugebo*(Guy.)
101 (1040) tetulerit] tulerit* (Guy.)
105 (1044) est ignotus, notus:] *ignotu'st, notu'st*:⁵ (Rz.)
4. 19 (1063) Utin'] *Utin'* (Bo.)
27 (1071) potius est] potiust (P.)
28 (1072) dat] **das**
29 (1073) Quoad] Quod (*B*)
31 (1075) hic noster] **noster hic**⁶
36 (1080) tu] del.
39 (1083) usus est] **'st usus**⁶
80 (1124) milvum] *miluum* (Bo.)
82 (1126) parte] del.⁶ (Guy.)

4. 91 (1135) ostenderis] **ostendas**⁷
98 (1142) quidquid] quid* (Cam.)
113 (1157) est] *sit* (Rz.)
118 (1162) ite] i* (Guy.)
6. 1 (1205) melius est] meliust (P.)
6 (1210) tamen] del. (Guy.)
8 (1212) rogato] *roga* (Wei.)
20 (1224) opus est] opust⁸ (P.)
7. 3 (1229) danunt] dant⁹ (*B*)
6 (1232) melius illi] *illi melius*⁰
(Rz.)

V.

1. 1 (1281) mortalium] *mortalis*⁰ (Rz.)
2. 13 (1300) robigine] **robigine verum**¹⁰
15 (1302)]†
27 (1314) denaria Philippea] mnae Philippiae ¹¹ *—(P.—)
seorus] sorsus (P.)
49 (1336) dejura] *dejera*⁰ (Rz.)
68 (1355) arbitratus est] arbitratust (Guy.)
3. 4 (1360) ó] *del.* (Rz.)
28 (1384) Promisisti] **Promisti**
29 (1385) Promisisti] **Promisti**
33 (1389) ergo] **ego**
47 (1403) taceto] tace (Guy.)
52 (1408) facias] facis (P.)
53 (1409) Liberta] Libera (P.)

¹ Rz. proposed 'affer huc domo.'
² Also on Andr. I 1. 13; and so Rz.
³ Bentl. (P.) reads 'si non' for 'non.'
⁷ Bentl. (P.) reads 'ostendas.'
⁸ Also on Haut. II 3. 104.

⁸ Cf. Men. II 3. 86; Stich. III 2. 45.
⁴ Also on Haut. I 1. 20; and so Rz.
⁶ Bentl. orig. thought of 'usust,' as Guy. and Bo.
⁹ Also on Phorm. I 3. 14.
¹⁰ Bentl. (P.) puts a caret after 'robigine.'

¹¹ Bentl. writes the plural terminations (-ae -ae) under the marginal note of Gron. 'mna Philippia.'

(41)   G   [I. 4.]

STICHUS.

I.

2. 19 (Rl. 77) indaudiverim] inaudiverim (Cam., *A*)
60 (117) id] del.
89 (146) placet] places (Gul., *A*)
3. 9 (163) pauxillulam] pauxillam (Guy.)
11 (165) oboriuntur] *oriuntur* (Wei.)
13 (167) hoc] **hoc verbum**
21 (175) puero] del. (Acid.)
28 (182) esum] del. (Gul.)
60 (213) quot] **quae**
89 (243) multum [1]

II.

2. 64 (389) Ridiculosissumos] Ridiculissumos* (Acid.)

III.

2. 45 (501) Quae ne et]Quaen'(Acid.—P.—)

IV.

1. 30 (536) eccilla] *eccillam* (Bo.)

V.

3. 8 (681) obsonatus est] obsonatust (P.)
5. 19 (760) cantationem] cantionem (Non., Saracenus)
7. 1 (769) possiet] possit (Guy.)
4 (772) omnes] nunc omnes (P.)

TRINUMMUS.

I.

1. 9 (Rl. and Ed. 31) succreverunt]succrerunt (Acid., P.)
2. 8 (46) ego] *ego te* (*A*, Herm.)
14 (52) bene valere] *valere** (*A*, Bo.)
45 (82) aliena] alieno (P.)
92 (129) Dedistine] *Dedisti* (Rz., Bo., Fritzsch)
occideret?] *occideret*. (Bo.)
172 (209) facta] *del* [2]* (*A*)

II.

1. 1 (223) vorso,]/*
2 (224) indipiscor:]/*

concoquo] *coquo* (*A*)
defetigo.]/
3 (226) est.]/*
4 (227) est,]/*
(228) expetessam,]/
5 (229) firmiorem:]/*
6 (230) siet:]/*
16 (243)]/ilico
17 (243) liquitur.]/
(244) audes,]/
2. 39 (321) non] del.* (Gron., *A*)
69 (350) **IMMUNIFICO**] immuni* (Grut., *A*)

---
[1] Bentl. probably intended to delete the word, as Bo.
[2] Also in the Schediasma.

2. 78 (359) Charmidae]   Charmidaï¹
         (Sca., Grut.)
4. 30 (431) te] del.³ (Guy., *A*)
  44 (445) hau !] haud³ (MSS.)
  45 (446) malas.] **malas** ?⁴
  50 (451) novisse] **nosse**
  158 (559) quidem] del.
  186 (586) ô pater !] ô **pater pater**

III.

2. 65 (691) dedisse]dedidisse (Cam.)

IV.

2. 162 (1004) tinniit] *tinnit*⁵ (Herm.)
3.   5 (1012) abieris] aberis⁵ (Cam.)
    25 (1032) NIHIL] nihili⁵ (Sca.)

V.

2. 31 (1155) CH.] CH. **Lysiteles,**
   50 (1174) foras] del. (Guy.)
   52 (1176) subito] del. (Guy.)
   53 (1177) satin'] satine⁵ (Grut.)
   64 (1188) licet] del. (Guy.)

TRUCULENTUS.

Arg. 3 Utique] leg. Utque (P.)
    4 supposuit]   supposivit (Sca.,
      Lamb.)

I.

1. 51 (Schoell 70) quidem]   *equidem*
                            (Br.)
   60 (om.) is bracketed by Bentl.
                         (Lamb., P.)

II.

2. 8 (263) Imprudens]   Impudens⁵
      (Lamb., *A*) **mihi**   RB

2. 46 (301) perdidere] perdiderunt (*C,
                           D, Z*)
4. 5 (356) Dinarche] *mi Dinarche* (Bo.)
   67 (421) ego tota] del. (Guy.)
   90 (444) perferre] perferri (P.)
5. 8 (459)] | Lucri (P.)⁵
           exsecuta :] / ⁵
   9 (460) supposivi.] / ⁵
     (461) oportet] *te oportet* (Spengel)
           aggrediri,] / ⁵
   10 (462) exsequare.] / ⁵
   11 (463) incedo :] / ⁵
   28 (481) veniret] veniat⁵ (Guy.)

---

¹ On Adelph. V 8. 23 and Haut. V 5. 21. Bentl. adopts the reading of Mur. and Acid. 'Charmidae hujus.'
² Also on Hec. I 1. 7.
³ Also on Eun. V 8. 36 ('haut'). Bentl. (P.) corrects the 'Haud' of P. to 'Haut.'
⁴ This note of interrogation is like that after 'Laevae,' Epid. I 1. 9. On Eun. V 8. 36 the line is quoted without a note of interrogation.
⁵ Cf. Bentl. on Amph. II 1. 57.

7. 1 (551) damnigeruli,] / * (Speng.)
   3 (553) expoliat.] / *
   4 (554) me,] / *
  40 (599) gemens.] | P.
  41 (600) suspirium.] / *
  42 (601) femur.] / *
     (602) verberat?] /¹*

III.
2. 14 (682) commoveo,] leg. commeo,
         (Cam., P.—)

IV.
2. 2 (712)] / ama
     exinani.] /

¹ Also on Eun. III 1. 38.

NOTES OF BENTLEY FROM THE FLY-LEAF
OF HIS COPY OF GRONOVIUS.

P. 772. 35. leg. At te dii deæque quantum'st : : servassint quidem.
P. 775. v. 88. Certum est mihi ante tenebras tenebras persequi.
P. 437. Eadē plane de Pellione Hieronymus Grofiotius Epistola ad Jacobū
      Lectiū an : Dom : 1583 apud Goldastū nū. 83. Is quidē erat
      amicus summus Gulielmii.
P. 144. Meursius de Luxu Roman : legib.
      Ædepol mortalem perseparcū prædicas.
     i. e. perparcū : ut persefacul pro perfacul. Festus.
     — Prologo Casinæ.
     Latine Plautus cum latranti nomine.
     Camerarius ad *Marcum* Plauti prænomen refert, ob literam caninam *R*.
     Sed hoc absurdum. Petitus ad *Casinam* quasi *Canissam* : stulte :
     Salmasius ad eandem, quod omnes mulieres sint oblatatrices [sic, i. e.
     oblatratrices] et clamosæ. Et hoc frustra. Tu refer ad Plautum ; quod
     verbum etiam canis genus significat. Festus. Plauti appellantur canes,
     quorum aures languidæ sunt ac flaccidæ ut latius videantur patere.
     Idem alibi in *Ploti*. M. Accius poeta, quia Umber Sarsinas erat, a
     pedum planitie initio Plotus, postea Plautus cœptus est dici. Sed
     auctor Prologi, qui non est ipse Plautus, priorem Etymologiam secutus
     est. *R. B.*

APPENDIX.

The following letter of Bentley is taken from Appendix III to a tract, entitled 'An exact and circumstantial History of the Battle of Floddon [sic],' with notes by Robert Lambe,' London, 1774, a copy of which is in the Bodleian Library. The editor speaks (Notes, p. 79) of the 'very curious letter in Appendix No. III, printed from a manuscript[1],' and adds, 'Having no date or superscription, I do not certainly know to whom it was addressed.'

Indications are, however, not wanting as to both recipient and date. The internal evidence seems to show with regard to the recipient (1) that he was living, at the time, near to Dr. Mountague, probably at, or in the neighbourhood of Durham[2]; (2) that he had a son at Cambridge. With regard to the date, we have (1) the reference to Wetstein, who is probably the 'able foreigner,' and his visit to Paris in the year 1716, for the purpose of collating MSS. for Bentley; and (2) the general subject of the letter. It would appear therefore to fall some time after, probably soon after, the year 1716.

All these indications agree perfectly with the supposition that the recipient was the Rev. Thomas Rud, Librarian of the Dean and Chapter of Durham, and formerly master of Durham Grammar School; a gentleman with whom Bentley is known to have corresponded on the subject of the proposed edition of the New Testament. A certain Thomas Rudd [sic] of Trinity College, took his B.A. degree at Cambridge in the year 1717, and an earlier Thomas Rudd, also of Trinity, graduated in the year 1687. The former is probably the son alluded to in Bentley's letter; the latter may have been the father. The difference in the spelling of the name is probably not a matter of any consequence.

[1] The letter is given as printed by Lambe: several passages suggest a doubt as to the accuracy of the transcription.
[2] Dr. Mountague died in London.

APPENDIX.

LETTER OF BENTLEY [TO REV. T. RUD, D.D.?]

REV. SIR,

I received your very obliging letter. It would make my long tedious work much more easy and light to me, if all the persons, whose courtesy I am forced to make address to, were as frank and forward as yourself. You will be sensible, that the effect of this labour of mine depends upon authority, not reason and criticism. I could sit still in my study, and with little trouble make Greek and Latin agree, and tally together, with plausible, if not certain, nay, even with certain emendations. How many such, when I collated my first manuscript, have I written in the bottom of the page, as conjectures of the true Latin reading? These, in the progress of more and older manuscripts, I have since found to have been plain, and from the first hand, in the old Saxon exemplars. You know the difference of these two propositions. I guess, I argue, I persuade, that it was once so written, though all the copies go against it; and I show you, that it is yet actually so, in an old manuscript of King Athelstan's, St. Cedas, St. Cuthbert's of the age of 1200 years. The one pleases, and convinces ingenuous men, and well-willers to the Scriptures, and the other stops the mouths even of Pagans and Freethinkers. This consideration makes me resolve to spare no labour, nor any charge, to have all the books that our own country, and even foreign countries, can afford to me. I have advanced fifty pounds to an able foreigner, to go to Paris, and to collate some manuscripts of equal, or greater antiquity than our own. For I have never yet used one old book, if it were but of twenty scattered sheets, that I did not get something particular by it. It is odd and pleasant to see how the readings lie scattered through the copies. There shall be three true readings against the present Pope's text, within the compass of three verses, and these shall be fetched out of three several manuscripts; what hits in one failing in the other two. Therefore I am encouraged by success; all that I meet with help somewhat. Give me then number enough, and I am sure all will exactly tally. And for this reason, I must intreat you to send me down those other manuscripts, that contain the Acts and the Epistles, though they do not reach to the age desired; I mean those, which you take to be the best of them, and which are in square, rather than in oblong volumes, *cæteris paribus*. It is but a small addition of carrier's charge, and I am glad to pay it, both hither, and back again. I think, that I told you before, that I am comparatively poor in the Acts and the Epistles, which makes me send for help out of France. I have but two copies that reach 800 years, and these do not always come up to that which I seek for. But what is odd, junior books supply that sometimes, which the ancient ones fail in.

Coloss. ii. 4. *Hoc autem dico ut nemo nos decipiat en pithanologia in sublimitate sermonum.* For so the Popes, so the former editions, so both my old manuscripts read. And yet it is plain, that nobody could so translate it. *Sublimitas sermonum* is *upsilogia*, or *meteorologia*, never *pithanologia*. I soon guessed it to be an error of the Scribes, for *subtilitate*

APPENDIX.

sermonum. For thus the old Glossaries at Paris, printed by Stephens, from a copy of a thousand years of age, *subtilitate pithanologia*; and in Gloss. Graecolat. *peithanologia*, *subtilitas verborum*.

But after this, I found in four manuscripts, of the King's Library, not one of which is above 600 years old, *subtilitate verborum*, from the very first hand. This I also impute to some useful criticks in the Western countries, about 700 years ago, who then collated the present manuscripts of the Bible with the oldest copies then extant, and rectified the innovations: These emendations they published, under the title of *Correctorium Bibliæ*, none of which have been yet printed, but quoted occasionally by Zegerus and Lucas. I shall get transcripts of them from abroad. If you meet with any such in your library, they make but few sheets, I pray that you would communicate them to me. This I say is the reason why a true reading shall be in a manuscript of 600, that is now wanting in those, of now of a thousand years of age. Because these correctors, of 700 years ago, had still older books, and the following transcribers, if learned, adjusted their copies, according to their directions. Of your two old books I shall give, as of all the rest, which are a thousand years old, a specimen of the writing in a copper-plate, that posterity may see, what good authorities I follow. I wish that you would look, what comments of Bede, or of the other tractators, Austin, Ambrose, &c. you have, of a competent age; for I shall give you the trouble to examine particular places therein, when I begin to build; for, at the present, I am but digging my stones out of the quarries.

I am glad, that your son put it into my power to oblige you; and I shall more rejoice, if he gives me a farther occasion to show, that I am,

Sir,
Your obliged, humble servant,
RICHARD BENTLEY.

My service and thanks to Mr. Dean.*

---

* [Note by Lambe: 'Dr. Montague [sic], Dean of Durham'.]

Anecdota Oxoniensia

TEXTS, DOCUMENTS, AND EXTRACTS

CHIEFLY FROM

MANUSCRIPTS IN THE BODLEIAN

AND OTHER

OXFORD LIBRARIES

CLASSICAL SERIES. VOL. I—PART V

HARLEIAN MS. 2610, *OVID'S METAMORPHOSES I, II, III.* 1–622
XXIV LATIN EPIGRAMS FROM BODLEIAN OR OTHER MSS.
*LATIN GLOSSES ON APOLLINARIS SIDONIUS
FROM MS. DIGBY* 172

COLLATED AND EDITED BY

ROBINSON ELLIS, M.A., LL.D.

Oxford
AT THE CLARENDON PRESS
1885

London
HENRY FROWDE

Oxford University Press Warehouse
Amen Corner, E.C.

COLLATIO COD. HARLEIANI 2610
OVIDII METAMORPHOSEON I, II, III. 1-622

EPIGRAMMATA LATINA XXIV
EX CODICIBVS BODLEIANIS ET SANGALLENSIBVS

GLOSSAE IN APOLLINAREM SIDONIVM
EX CODICE DIGBEIANO 172

EDIDIT

ROBINSON ELLIS, M.A., LL.D.
SOCIVS COLLEGII TRINITATIS APVD OXONIENSES

Oxford
AT THE CLARENDON PRESS
1885

[All rights reserved]

London
HENRY FROWDE

Oxford University Press Warehouse
Amen Corner, E.C.

PRAEFATIO.

I.

Codex Harleianus 2610 (A) Ouidii Metamorphoseon continet cum libris I II tertium ad finem usque uersus 622. Scriptus est, ut opinatur E. M. Thompson, cui submissa est cura codicum qui in Museo Britannico seruantur, exeunte fere saeculo X, in Germania; certe in I. 298 super *uineta* exaratum est, eadem manu ut uidetur, *winstete*, super *agitataque robora* I. 303 *getribenen bŏma*. Codex ut inter antiquissimos sic inter optimos Metamorphoseon existimandus est (1) si orthographiam spectes (2) si lectiones. Dixi de his fusius in Diario Cantabrigiensi XII. 62 sqq.; hic pauca tantum strictim commemorabo.

1. In compositis ubi *con* praecedit uel *in*, singularem scriba exhibuit constantiam. Nam fere semper permansit intactum utrumque, *inposuit* (ter) *inposuere inritamenta inrupit inmaduisse inmedicabile inmittite immensa inmenso inrorauere inpiger inpatiens inperfecta inperfectus inpultos inpulit inpulsu inpedientibus inpedit inminet inmania inlustre inperat* (bis) *inplerat inpleuere inplent inmunis inmixta inperfectus inreprehensa inprudens inrita*. Excipiuntur haec *immensa* I. 38, *imminet* I. 52, 146, *impia* I. 200, *irritus* I. 273, *impluit* I. 573, *irrita* III. 336, *immotus* III. 418, *impubes* III. 422. Nonnumquam cum *in* scriptum fuisset, alia littera superposita est, ut *ińridet* I. 221. Rariora cum *con* composita, pleraque tamen sine mutatione *conpraensus conplectitur conlocat conpagibus conpagine conplexibus conplexus*, nisi quod *complet* est in III. 312; *conubia* I. 480 sic exhibetur, ut a peritioribus scriptum constat fuisse.

Aliter se res habet in eis quae *ad* compositum habent. Habet quidem A *adspirate admouerat adfectas adsidua adflatu adstitit adsensit adrides adsonat admiratur adsbicere;* sed et *assiduis asiduo affectasse assensibus åffert affatur afflat annuit assere apparuit accliuo asbice asbexit:* quorum similia sunt *summouet* I. 664, *summisit* III. 23, 502; semel *subplice* pro *supplice* II. 396.

Non raro accusatiuus pluralis in -*is* occurrit, *seminicis* I. 228, *mollis* I. 685, *penatis* I. 773, *uomentis* II. 119, *patentis* II. 179, *feruentis* II. 229, *tris* II. 738, *leuis* III. 43; quibus fortasse addenda sunt *uocís* III. 369, *moles* III. 376; semel pro nominatiuo *instabilis* II. 164; *igneis* pro accusatiuo II. 271.

PRAEFATIO.

Si pro *est* bis inueni I. 89 *saĕst* pro *sata est*, II. 86 *regeres* quod ex *regerest* uitiatum est. Hoc ideo notandum duco quod immutato iam usu saeculi Ciceroniani multo frequentius *est* scriptum fuisse quam *st* credibile est a poetis qui Augusti exeuntem principatum contigerunt.

In uocabulis ubi fluctuat usus scribendi inter praemissam *h* et omissam, scriba A plerumque eam rationem secutus est quae ex optimis codicibus potior fuisse colligitur, *harundine* I. 471, *harundinibus* I. 684; I. 707 *ªarundine h* habet superscriptam: itaque quinquies *harena*, bis *arena* legitur; semel *ªarenosi* I. 702. Minore constantia scriba modo *umor, umerus*, modo *humor, humerus* exarauit; ter enim *umor umidus umenti*, bis *humor*, semel *humoribus*, semel *humida*, semel *ªumida* repperi: ut a prima manu quater *u*, quater *hu* scriptum uideatur. Qua ratione usus *umerus* ter, quater *humerus* numeraui; *umeros ªumeros ªumeri*, at uero *humeros humeros humero humuri* (III. 109).

Notabile etiam illud quod semper in A aut *ecquis* aut *hecquis* siue *ªecquis*, numquam *etquis* apparet: pro *hei* autem I. 523 A habet *ei*, quae potior orthographia est.

Constat antiquiores semper *-uos -uom* pro *-uus -uum* posuisse; id Ouidiani moris fuisse testantur haec uestigia in A, *uerŏm* I. 223, *uacuos* II. 165, *suŏs* II. 186, *riŭos* II. 456, *flauăs* III. 617.

Graecam *o* nominatiui saepius exhibet A, *Parnasos Tauros Cephisos Peneos Caicas* (h. e. *Caicos*) *Ismenos Aglauros Agrihodos Harpalos Naxos Tenedos Claras* (h. e. *Claros*.)

2. Venio ad locos ubi A aut noua aut meliora praebet plerisque codicum. Ex his praecipua duco *circuit* I. 730 quod solus A habet: ceteri enim *terruit*, uitiose: I. 327 *Innocuos ambo, cultores numinis ambo* A m. pr., *ambos* his ceteri; II. 183 *Iam genus agnoscit piget* h. e. *agnosci*, ceteri *Iam cognosse genus piget;* II. 589 *tetro facta uolucris Crimine* ubi ceteri *diro;* II. 691 *tenuit*, quod unice uerum habeo, ceteri *timuit* inepte; III. 421 *Et dignas Baccho, dignas et Apolline crines*, ceteri *dignos;* I. 718 *praereptam sanguine repĕm*, ceteri *rupem*, quod post *praereptam* nimium quantum languet; quamquam incertum est *sepemne* Ouidius, an *sedem* scripserit: II. 476 *aduersam prensis a fronte capillis Strauit humi pronam* A recte pro *auersam* quod habent ceteri; II. 462 *Aspicit infantem totoque salutifer orbi Cresce puer dixit*, multi *totique*. Vt Ouidius, sic ante Ouidium Propertius *Septem urbs alta iugis, toto quae praesidet orbi.*

Sunt et alia, quae lecturis relinquo. Neque tamen infitior nonnumquam uitium traxisse alioqui perbonum codicem: quae commemorare futtile est, satis enim patebunt. Illud uere dicturus uideor, post Marcianum codicem non extare digniorem qui intente consideretur hoc nostro A.

Non alienum consilio meo existimaui lectiones adicere codicis perantiqui (fortasse saec. VIII, sic enim habitus est ab Hermanno Hagen quamquam nono adsignatur a Merkelio Praef. ad Met. p. 8), Bernensis 363, quem aestate anni 1883 Bernae inspexi. Hic codex fragmenta Metamorphoseon continet haec I. 1-199, 304-309, 773-778; II. 1-22; III. 1-56. Excusserat haec ante me Hagenus, miseratque ad Riesium, qui ea edidit in apparatu critico editionis suae.

II.

Secuntur Epigrammata XXIV, maximam partem inedita, nisi quod XX *Res male tuta puer, nec te committe quibusdam* iam ex Haureauano libro de Hildeberti carminibus innotuit, XXIV *Fonte lauat genitor quem crimine polluit uxor* in Riesii Anthol. Lat. 688, Baehrensii P. L. M. III. p. 171 editum est. Quae utraque denuo publicaui, alterum quia meliore codice usus sum Haureauano, alterum quod in codice Sangallensi 250 titulus extat, unde difficillimi carminis expeditur significatio. Cetera ex codicibus traxi Bodleianis, praeter unum XXIII quod in Sangallensi 397 legitur, necdum, quod sciam, lucem expertum est: certe non inueni apud Canisium neque in Duemmleri Sylloge Poet. Lat. aeui Carolini, quamquam quod ibi edidit Duemmlerus *Arboris est altrix quondam uagina medullae* non solum re congruit, sed uerba multa habet communia, uideturque ex eo conflatum.

Quo tempore scripta sint haec epigrammata, non satis exploratum est: neque ideo medio aeuo, quod dicitur, adsignanda sunt quia ex codicibus proueniunt multa huiusmodi continentibus. Nam Rawl. B. N. 109 unde I-XII traxi, saec. XII exeunte uel XIII ineunte exaratus, habet is quidem non pauca quae uel eius aeui sunt uel non diu ante composita, cuius rei testes sunt uersus in medio concinentes cum fine (*Leoninos* uocant), quorum exemplum pulcherrimum et paene exquisita arte elaboratum extat codicis p. 17. Idem codex multa habet Hildeberti, Cenomanensis Episcopi, quaedam quae Marbodo inputantur, uelut f. 29[b] *Plurima cum soleant sacros euertere mores* (cf. Leyseri Syllog. p. 370); non pauca quae aut uerbis (uelut *marca*) aut nominibus personisque aut etiam rebus seriorem aetatem prae se ferant. Inmiscentur tamen his alia et potiora et, me iudice, antiquiora; uelut illa *Virginis insano Iulianus captus amore* (912 Anthologiae Riesianae), *Iupiter astra, fretum Neptunus, Tartara Pluto* (793 R.), *Ad cenam Varus me nuper forte uocauit* (796 R.), *Graecinum uirgo, puerum Graecinus amabat* (797 R.); monosticha quattuor (34, 37, 65, 78) ex illis quae Baehrensius edidit P. L. M. III. 236-240; quae si quis recentiora

PRAEFATIO.

statuere conetur, uelim iustis argumentis id conuincat. Est enim res subtilissimi iudicii, neque a quoquam nisi post maximas inquisitiones pro explorata habenda. Nam quod nonnulli dictitant, carmina si in codice aliquo iuncta reperiantur, eiusdem fere saeculi esse, id nec uerum esse et a uero abhorrere permultis exemplis cognoui. Vnum afferam: in Cod. Laud. 86 f. 116ᵃ tria extant epigrammata quae se sic excipiunt.

De Cherulo* (Schneidewin Mart. Suppositiciorum XI).

Cherule, tu cenas apud omnes, nullus apud te;
Alterius siccas pocula, nemo tua.
Multa foris poscis, paucis contentus apud te:
Largus in alterius, parcus in aede tua.
Iam uel redde uicem uel desine uelle uocari.
Dedecus est semper sumere, nilque dare.

De Neuolo.

Iuras dasque fidem tibi te nullam sociasse.
Neuole, digna fide credimus absque fide.
De nulla nunquam, de nulla, Neuole, iuras.
Quod mihi tu iuras, hoc ego iuro tibi.
Si nullam tangis, nec uis aliquam tetigisse,
Ergo pudicus eris, Neuole? non sequitur.

2. digne *Digb.* 65 *f.* 69ᵃ.   3. De nullo *L.* De nulla *D.* de nullo Neuole iures *D.*
5. Neuole nec tangis ne uis *D.*

De eodem (Mart. I. 97).

Cum clamant omnes loqueris tunc, Neuole, tantum,
Et te patronum causidicumque putas.
Hac ratione potest nemo non esse disertus,
Ecce tacent omnes; Neuole, die aliquid.

Videlicet coniuncta sunt cum Martialis uero epigrammate duo quae ab alio profecta sunt. Horum scriptor latet: Riesio (A. L. II. p. xxx) uidetur medio aeuo uixisse qui prius *de Cherulo* scripsit. Eius iudicio quamquam multum tribuo, non extra dubitationem res est. Nam si ita se res habet, miror duos uersus illos (3, 4) *Multa foris poscis paucis contentus apud te Largus in alterius, parcus in aede tua* etiam in Rawl. 109 f. 68ᵇ seorsim scriptos extare. Qui si digni uidebantur qui saec. XII uel XIII a loco suo reuulsi pro disticho excerperentur, uel si is qui saec. XII uel XIII pro distichó eos habuit de libro

---

* Hoc epigramma amicus Gruteri, Paulus Melissus, Francus, in epistula testatur uocibus harmonicis a Gasparo Othmaro, musico suauissimo, concinnatum saepe se inter sodales puerum cecinisse (Schneid. Mart. Epig. p. 635).

PRAEFATIO.

uetustiore sumpsit iam excerptos, retro sensim ad ea tempora extrudimur quae intra fines medii aeui non sunt. Epigramma ipsum si spectes, nihil inest quod ad saec. X aptius quam ad priora referatur. Illud *apud te* (1, 3) Martialis imitatorem sapit, sed hunc cuiusuis saeculi : quod *nemŏ* correptum est, quod *tuā* claudit pentametrum, quod *uelle* cum infinitiuo post *desine* positum est, quod iterum (6) clauditur pentameter breui syllaba qualis est *nilque dare*, haec mihi uidentur eius esse temporis, quo supererat adhuc sensus Latinae locutionis, quaesitioris prosodiae ; quod *aede* pro *aedibus* usurpatum est, caue hoc uitium ducas latine balbutientium ; est enim *aede* hic oeco siue conclaui, ut apud Plautum in Casina III. 5. 31 et Curtium VIII. 6. Potest igitur epigramma non infra Theodosium esse. Longe aliter iudico de sequente *Iuras dasque fidem* : quamuis enim incerti temporis sit, antiquum uix potest esse, quod ex uno illo *non sequitur* satis arbitror demonstratum.

Ex carminibus quae hic edidi primorem locum tenent XIII et XVI. Prius extat in cod. Digb. 172, qui inter complura neque eodem scripta tempore, intertextum habet uersibus quibusdam *de poenitentia, de decem plagis, de triplici Herode* etc., elogium Chrysopolitae cuiusdam, quem amasium Byzantini imperatoris fuisse conicio. Antiquum certe uidetur : cum rarissima sit apud scriptores medii aeui caesura post quartum trochaeum qualis est *conpenso nouissima* (3), ut nihil dicam de ipsa correptione litterae huius *o* ubi praesentem notat indicatiui. Quid quod ad uersum *Quem procul a patria principis egit amor* proxime accedit quod de se dicit Helpis uxor Boetii *Quam procul a patria coniugis egit amor ?* At carmen XVI *de illis qui contra naturam agunt* nulli credo legentium gratum non erit, siue ob ingenium scriptoris, siue ob castitatem sermonis et eurhythmian. Sane multi sunt in hoc uitio insectando qui post saec. X uixerunt, eruntque qui et hos uersus et XVII et XX huic potissimum aetati adsignandos arbitrentur. Neque infitior productas syllabas breues ante uocalem *coitūs et, furōr ubi, amōr et* a seueriore prosodia abhorrere ; sed frequentissimus hic error in carminibus nisi exactiorum recurrit post 300 A.D. A Christiano conscriptum XVI ex argumento arguitur ; sed quo potissimum tempore, uix ausim definire, cum hactenus nulli uideatur innotuisse. Ex reliquis eminet ingeniosum illud *Tela Cupido tene, quoniam non ille sed illa* (II), quod de puero licet interpretari quem amator sic deperibat tamquam uera puella esset. Solum hoc ex his παιγματίοις ad speciem accedit epigrammaton Graecae Anthologiae. Neque ideo tamen asseuerantius antiquioribus tribuerim, cum certius κριτήριον uetustatis absit. Sed quoquo tempore scriptum est, uitium iam traxerat cum Rawl. 109 exarabatur : nam coniectura tantum uersum 3 restitui.

Sed de his alii iudicabunt : nec quidquam nobis ultra dicendum superest,

PRAEFATIO.

nisi ut codicum Digb. 65, 172, Laud. Lat. 86 paulo exactius speciem aetatemque describam.

Digb. 65 codex est saec. XII exeuntis, scriptus pulcherrime una manu, binis columnis. Insunt uersus uarii, plerique medium aeuum prae se ferentes, saepe Leoninum concentum: quibus antiquiora nonnulla innectuntur. Nam f. 57ª habet carmen notissimum *Dulcis amica ueni*, f. 58 *Versus Serlonis cognomento Paridisi de monachis*, f. 59ª *De illis qui contra naturam agunt* tum *Potus Milo sapis*, f. 59ᵇ *Cum mea me mater grauida portaret in aluo* siue de Hermaphrodito, tum *Natura facienta uirum grauis incidit error*, mox f. 61ª *Fama est fictilibus cenasse Agathoclea regem* Ausonianum, *In noctem prandes, in lucem turgide cenas* quod Hildeberto Riesius inputat (A. L. II. p. xxxi), post Haureauum ego politius quam pro huius genere dicendi reor, tum *Diogenes declamabat mundum periturum* recentioris monetae, tum Godefridi Wintonensis *Nos faenum, leporem canis, alba ciconia uermem* (Wright Satirical Poems of the Twelfth Century I. p. 135), f. 61ᵇ uersus Traiano adscriptos *Vt belli sonuere tubae* denique *Thrax puer astricto glacie dum ludit in Hebro* (A. L. 709 R.).

Digb. 172 ex diuersissimis consarcinatus est. Scriptura inest saeculorum XII XIII XIV XV; epigrammata duo quae p. 20 edidi manus saec. XIV exarauit. At Glossae Sidonianae, quae est nostrae opellae pars tertia, saec. XII assignantur a Macraio et Westwoodio.

Laud. Lat. 86 manus ostendit saeculorum XII XI XIII. Foliis 94-133 insunt epigrammata uaria, partim antiqua, partim recentioris saeculi, et haec quidem non ante saec. XIII exarata. Cf. Catal. codicum Laudianorum quem Oxonii edidit H. O. Coxe anno 1858.

III.

De Glossis in Sidonii Epistulas pauca tantum dicenda sunt. Ita enim de eis censeo; breuiora quaedam quibus uocabula Sidonii explicarentur non ita multo post ipsius Sidonii saeculum conscripta fuisse; his mox alia adficta et insuper his alia ac plerumque uitiosiora in illud corpus coaluisse quod in Cod. Digb. 172 extat et a me primum in lucem pertractum est. Nam sunt in his Glossis non pauca bonae frugis nec spernendi pretii: quorum sufficit exempla duo apponere. Nam ad IV. 1 Glossator haec tradit *Exoccupatu .i. magna occupatione. Quoniam exoccupatus est una dictio et ex ibi positum significat intensionem occupationis. Ex quandoque augmentatiue ponitur, quandoque priuatiue, ut exaucloratus auctoritate priuatus. Augmentatiue ut hic exoccupatus.* Verum hoc nec a quoquam hactenus notatum. Testor lexicographos, apud quos frustra *exoccupatus* requiritur. Iterum ad VII. 2 haec scripta sunt *Hoc caelum ut hoc celte celtis instrumentum est quo caelatur .i. sculpitur*. Itaque ex grammatico aliquo innotuerat glossatori neutrale *celte tis:* cuius rei adhuc testis desideratur.

Scriptores in his glossis laudantur non solum notiores uelut Terentius Cicero Vergilius Horatius Ouidius Lucanus Persius Iuuenalis Statius Claudianus Hieronymus Isidorus sed etiam obscuriores, Petronius Macrobius Symmachus alii qui me fugerunt. Sed ante omnia Iustinianei iuris elucet cognitio: ut non immerito suspiceris ex eis qui has glossas concinnarunt legis peritum fuisse. Est et illud in his notabile, quod qui ultimus eas tractauit, uerba inmiscuit modo Anglica, modo Gallica, qualia saec. XII uel XIII usurpabant. Placebunt haec, ut spero, doctioribus nostri saeculi Skeatio Earlio Sweetio: nec sane exiguum momentum fuerunt cur commentarium ederem, ut utilia plerumque, sic et futtilia aliquando amplexum. Nam est ubi longissime a uero glossator aberrauit: quae plerumque omisi. Nec raro a loco suo glossae migrarunt: quas reuocaui. Sed non eget excusationis is qui scriptori inter praestantissimos non sui tantum sed omnium temporum—utor iudicio Eduardi Freeman—etiam tantillum nouae lucis uidebitur offudisse. Ecquandone extabit Sidonii interpres dignus ipsius saeculo, dignus nostro?

ERRATA ET ADDENDA.

Met. II. 520   quantú A *non* quant.
III. 187   adstitit A *non* astitit.
Epigr. XIII. 4 *Pro* gaudia *conicio* praemia.
Gloss. Sidon. p. 56. l. 17   cornibus *non* comibus.

INCIPIT P. N. O. METAMORPHO SIS A METAMORPHOSEON I. Lib. p. ouidii Bern.

1-199 *Extant in* Bern.
2 dii ceptis, A; concoeptis, Bern.; di mutastis et illas, A, Bern.
3 Aspirate, A; Adspirate, Bern.
7 digestaque, A¹; indigestaque, A².
8 *om.* Bern.; eodem, A.
10 prebebat, A.
       aere
12 arce, A (arce *incertum*).
13 brachia, Bern., A.
14 amphitrite, Bern.; amphitrites, A.
15 Vtque erat tellus, Bern.; Vtqᵃ erat et t., A, *sed* ᵃ *incerta*; pontus et ether, A.
16 inna bilis, A; *spatio relicto duarum litterarum*.
18 quod, Bern.; corpora in unum, A.
19 pungnabant, A; humen., A, Bern.
21 litem † limitem, Bern.
22 abstulit, A.
23 ethere, A; aere, Bern.
25 concordia, Bern.; legauit,
       † ligauit
   A; locauit, Bern.
29 hic, Bern.
30 sua, A, Bern.; humor, A, Bern.
31 Vltima, A, Bern.; possi-
       i
   det, A.
33, 34 *inuerso ordine*, Bern.
33 redegit, A; coegit, Bern.

35 orbes, Bern.
36 Tum, A, Bern.; diffundit, Bern.; diffudit, A.
37 litora, A², Bern.; litera, A¹.
38 immensa, A; Imensa, Bern.
       nc   v
39 cigxit declidia, A.
41 partimque recepta, A; campoque recepto, Bern.
42 litora, A, Bern.
43 ualles subsidere campos, Bern.
45 Atque duae dextra caelum, A.
50 inter utramque, A; in utrumque, Bern.
52 Imminet, A, Bern.
53 Pondere aquae leuior, A, Bern.; igne, A.
56 fluminibus, A; fulgora, Bern.; uentes, A.
59 regat, A; rotat, Bern.
60 Cum lanent, A.
61 nabateaque, Bern., A.
63 Vespere, A¹; lit²ora, A.
64 zephiro, A, Bern.; Scithiam septemque triones, A, Bern.
66 assiduis, A, Bern.
67 imposuit, Bern.; inposuit, A.
69 Atque ea, Bern.; dissepserat, Bern.; diªcerpserat, A.
70 Queque diu pressa massa latuere sub illa, A; Cum quae pressa diu fuerant caligine caeca, Bern.

71 efferuescere, A, Bern.
72 animalibus, Bern.
74 habita/te, A.
75 cepit, A.
76 capᵃcius, A.
77 Deerat, A, Bern.; cetera, A, Bern.
81 retinebant, Bern.
82 sat usia peto, Bern.; pluuialibus, Bern.
83 moderantum, A.
84 cetera, A.
85 Os hominis ubi me, Bern.; uidere, A, Bern.
       a
89 satest, A.
91-93 *om.* A, Bern.
94 uiserat, Bern.; uisceret, A.
98 carnua, Bern.
99 erat, A.
101 immunis, Bern.; inmunis, A¹.
102 Saucea, *pr.* A.
        c
103 gogente, Bern.
        e
104 fotus, A.
105 herentia, A¹; herentia A²; poma, Bern.
107 aeternum, A; euris, Bern.
108 Mulgebant, Bern.; zephyri, Bern.; zephiri, A.
114 sub/it, A.
115 preciosior, A.
116 Iupiter, A; Iuppiter, Bern.
117 inaequalis, Bern.; autumnus, Bern.; autumnos, A.

[I. 5.]

118 quatuor, A; .IIII., Bern. ͦͬ
120 astricta, Bern.; adstricta, A.
121 domos, Bern.; domus, A¹; domos, A².
125 aenea, A, Bern.
126 promtior, A.
127 celerata, A¹; ²celerata, A².
128 inrupit, A; irrupit, Bern.; peroris, Bern.
129 fugitque, Bern.
130 dolisque, Bern.
131 Insidiaeque tuis, Bern.
132 dabu̇nt, A; neque, A, Bern.
133 prius *pro* diu, Bern.
134 exsultauere, Bern.
135 aurę, A.
139 stigisque, A; stygiis, Bern.; admouerat, A, Bern.
140 irritamenta, Bern.; inritamenta, A.
142 Prodiderat, A, Bern.; prodiit, Bern.
144 raptu, A; ʰospes ab ʰospite, A.
146 Imminet, A, Bern.; exicio, A; coṅgis, A.
147 terribilis, Bern.
149 cede, A; madentis, Bern.
150 astrea, A; astra ea, Bern.
151 aeter, A.
152 Affectasse, A, Bern.; gigantas, A, Bern.
153 mon̊tes, Bern.
154 olympum, Bern.; olimpum, A.
155 subiecto pelion ossę, A; subiectae pelion ossae, Bern.
156 *om.* A.

158 Inmaduisse, A; Immaduisse, Bern.
159 ferę *pro* suae, A; monumenta, A; monimenta, Bern.
160 fatiem, A.
162 sciri ////, A.
165 Feda licaonie, A; ͥlicaoniae, Bern.
166 Ingentes, A, Bern.; animo̧, A.
167 onciliumque, A; conciliumque, Bern.
173 hac fronte, A; hac parte, Bern.
175 audatia, A.
177 marmorⁱᵒ, A.
180 Cesariem, A.
181 ora, *om.* Bern.
182 ulla, A.
183 fuit, Bern.; quã, A; parabat, A, Bern. ᶜᵘᵐ
184 angipedum, Bern; brachia, Bern.; brahia, A; caelo, A. ᵘ
189 sub terras, A, Bern.; stigo, A.
190 temptanda, A; tentata, Bern.; corpus, A, Bern.
191 Inse, Bern.
192 nimphae, A.
193 satirique, A. ᵃᵘᵖᵉʳⁱ
196 pueri, Bern.
197 ui uos, Bern.
198 erit aⁿte, Bern.; Lycaon, A, Bern.
199 Contremuere, A; Non fremuere, Bern.; ausu, Bern.
200 impia, A; saeuit, A.

201 Cesareo, A; extinguere, A.
202 tantę subito, A.
203 perorruit, A.
205 ioui, *om. in textu, add. in marg.* A.
206 *om.* A.
208 Iuppiter, A.
209 penas, A; dimittite, A.
211 aures, A.
212 Olympo, A.
214 nox ę, A.
216 Menela, A.
217 E cum Cilleno, A; licei, A.
218 Arcados hic sedes et inospita, A; tyranni, A. ͬ
221 Cęperat inridet, A; Lycaon, A.
 .i. sed ᵛ
223 dubitabile //// uerom, A.
225 Comprimere haec. *Hic uersus transuerso margine dextro scriptus est in* A.
226 eo est, A; *ante* missi *rasura est in* A; molossa, A.
228 seminicis, A.
229 igne, A.
230 inposuit, A.
231 In dominum, A.
232 ipse, A; nactusque, A.
233 ab ipso, A.
238 Canicies, A.
239 occuli, A; imago est, A.
241 erinis, A.
244 probant, A.
245 Adiciunt, A; assensibus, A.
247 orbi, A.
248 qui sit, A.
250 cetera, A.

LIBER I. 3

252 Rex superum trepidare
    uetat sobolemque, A.
254 ęter, A.
256 adfore, A; b.e. affore *ex* adfore.
258 proloṡ obsessa, A.
259 ciclope, A.
260 Pęna, A.
261 demittere, A.
262 aeoliis, A.
263 ñimbes, A.
264 nothum, A; nothus, A.
269 Fit fragor et densi, A; nymbi, A.
271 Nuntia, A; affert, A.
272 coloni, A.
273 irritus, A.
274 suo est, A.
275 Ceruleus, A.
276 omnes, A; tyranni, A.
280 inmittite, A.
282 aequora, A.
285 exspaciata, A; *super quod eadem m. scripsit* sper-cipennonte.
289 Indecta, A¹; alcior, A.
292 erat deerant quoque litora, A.
293 cimba, A.
295 supra, A.
297 anchora, A.
298 tegunt, A; uineta, A.
299 quo, A.
300 deformes, A; phocę, A.
301 lucos urbesque, A.
302 in altis, A.
303 Incursant agitataque,
        anestoLent * getribenenboma

304–309 *extant in Bern.*
304, 5 *sic habet* A; Nat (*marg.* nabat) lupus inter oues nec uires fulminis apro, *omissis quae interposita sunt. Bern. sic* Nat iupus inter oues nec ui res fulminis apro Vnda uehit tigris fuluos trahit unda leonis.
305 apro, A.
306 Curura ues, Bern.; nec, runt A; prosunt, A.
307 Quesitisque, A; sistere possit, A; sistere posset, Bern.
308 dicidit, A.
309 tumolos inmensa, A; Imensa, Bern.; licentia, A.
312 domant inop/es ieiunia uictus, A.
313 actaeis phocas, A.
316 stetit arduus, A.
317 parnasos, A; superatque cacumine nubes, A.
318 caetera texerat aequor, A.
319 rete, A¹; adhehit, A.
320 Oreadas *ex* Orecidas, A; adorant, A.
321 tetin, A *ex rasura*.
324 Iuppiter, A.
325 milibus, A.
326 *in transuerso sinistro margine scriptum habet* A; milibus, A.

327 †ambo, A; ambo, A; *serior manus addidit.*
329 ethera, A¹.
331 sapraque, A.
332 Extantem, A; humeros, A; h *serius add.*
333 Ceruleum, A.
334 conchęque, A.
335 bucina, A.
337 Bucina, A.
338 Litora, A; latentia, A.
340 infata receptus, A.
343 litus, A.
347 fronte, A.
349 silencia, A.
350 phirrā affatur, A.
351 O soror et coniunx, A.
354 quoscumque, A; ocasus, A.
355 cętera, A.
356 aduc, A.
360 dolores, A.
361 quandoque, A.
362 *sinistro margine paginae scriptum habet* A.
363 possim, A.
368 axilium, A.
369 cephesidos, A.
370 Et *pro* ut, A; sed *pro* sic, A.
371 inrorauere, A.
372 fastigia, A.
379 Dicite qua, A.
382 cinctasque, A.
384 Obstipuere, A.
387 Ledere, A.
388 caecisque, A.
389 verba deae sortis, A.
390 Hinc promethides placidamque promettbida, A.

* *Credo* anestozent.   † *Credo sic scripsisse Ouidium.*

391 Mulcet et aut fallax ait
  est sollertia nobis (est
  ᵃ *post rasuram*), A.
397 nocebat, A.
398 Discedunt, A.
399 iusso, A.
401 duritiam, A.
403 mittior, A.
405 coepto, A.
407 umida, A¹; ᵇumida, A²;
  ᵇ *pallidiore atramento.*
408 E, A.
410 mittatur, A.
411 spacio, A.
416 Cętera, A.
   ᵛ
417 fetus humor ab igne, A.
418 humidaeque, A.
421 coepere, A.
425 glebis, A.
426 Inueniunt et in his quaedam inperfecta suisque,
  A; *omissis uerbis* modo
  coepta sub ipsum Nas-
  cendi spatium.
427 *om. suo loco* A; *habet in
  summa pagina adiectum.*
428 humeris, A; sepe, A.
   ᵛ
429 rodis, A.
430 umor, A¹; ᵇhumor, A².
432 umidus, A¹; ᵇumidus, A².
435 estu, A.
437 Reddidit, A.
   ᵇ
438 python, A.
439 incognite, A.
442 clammis, A; fugatibus, A.
443 exhastaque, A.
445 posset, A.
447 Pythea, A; perdomitę,
  A¹; *nunc erasa est*ᵇ.
448 Hic, A; pedibusque, A.

449 esculeae, A.
452 quam non, A.
455 uicta, A.
457 humeros, A.
460 *Post* Strauimus *rasura
  est in* A, *ut quid ibi
  fuerit in incerto sit : sed
  in marg. add. est* in-
  numeris. phitona, A.
   † inuitare
462 Indignare, A.
467 Inpiger, A; pharnasi, A.
468 Atque, A; promisit, A.
470, 1 *post* 472 *habet* A.
470 Quod fecit auratum est,
  A.
471 elisum est, A; *sed el post
  erasas quae fuerant litteras*; harundine, A.
   ⁿ
472 inimpha, A.
473 Lesit, A.
474 alter nomen, A.
475 Siluarum latebris, A.
476 * Exuuię/ris, A.
477 om. A.
479 Inpaciens, A; nemora,
  A.
480 himen, A; conubia, A.
483 uelud, A; taedas, A.
484 Pulcra, A; suffundit, A.
485 herens, A.
490 Phębus, A.
491 .illum, *om.* A.
492 adolentur, A.
493 quas forte, A.
498 comerentur, A.
501 Brahiaque, A.
502 Si qua latent, A.
503 leuis, A.
505 Nympha, A *et* 504; pe-
  neia, A; ostis, A.
506 aquilam *ex* aquilem, A.

509 nocent, A; sum, A.
    ipse
511 moderatius insequor ostis
  A.
516 Et claras tenedos pate-
  reaque, A.
517 Iuppiter, A; quid, A.
518 nerbis, A.
519 Certa tamen, A.
    amplo
520 inuacuo, A.
521 opiferque, A.
522 herbarum subiecta, A.
523 Ei mihi, A.
526 inperfecta, A.
528 festes, A.
529 inpulsos, A.
530 Aucta uia forma est, A.
531 plandicias, A; monebat,
  A.
535 inhesuro, A.
537 conpraensus, A.
538 reliquit, A.
542 Imminet, A; sparsum,
   ſ
  A; aflat, A.
544-546 *sic scripti sunt in* A,
  Victa labore fugae tel-
  lus ait bisce uel istam
  Quae fecit ut iedar
  mutando perde figuram
  Fer pater inquit opem
  si flumina numen ha-
  betis.
550 brachia, A, *sed post rasuram.*
551 felox, A.
552 obit, A²; abit, A¹.
555 Complexusque, A.
560 laetis, A.
561 uisent longas, A.
564 iuuenile, A.
567 Annuit, A; atque, A.

* *Fuitne* exuuieis?

LIBER I. 5

568 aemonię, A; cludit, A,
569 tempę, A; peneus, A.
570 soluitur, A.
573 Impluit, A.
579 sparcheus et inrequietus enipheus, A.
580 Eridenusque, A¹; amfrisus et aetas, A.
585 luget et amissam, A.
588 i^uppitur, A¹.
591 Altorum nemorum sed demonstrauerat umbras, A.
597 fugebat, A.
598 lircea, A.
599 inducta alta, A.
601 despexit in agros, A.
604 nec umenti sensit, A.
605 atque, A¹, *ni fallor*; vtque, A².
610 persenserat, A.
615 Iuppiter et terra genitam mentitus, A.
.i. indicare
617 addicere, A.
622 Pelice, A.
623 ferto, A.
627 C&era, A.
cum
628 quoq., A; at/io, A.
634 limasaque, A¹.
635 braⁿhia, A.
636 brachia, A.
637 Conataque, A.
641 seseque exterrita fugit, A.
642 Naides, A.
647 lacrimas sed si, A.
649 Litera, A.
650 Corporis indiuum, A.
652 niuae, A.
654 reperta es, A.

656 alta, A.
ⁱ
659 secundę, A.
660 uir et de grege, A.
662 pręclausaque, A.
664 summouet, A.
666 ipse procul, A.
667 Occubat, A¹; occupat,
v
A²; speculator, A.
668 p^horonidos, A.
670 Peleiaṭ, A.
672 tegimenque cappillis, A.
m
674 tegimenque repouit, A.
tantum
675 natūmodo, A.
677 adductis, A.
678 noua, A; arte, A.
679 poteras, A; consedere, A.
o
680 agit neque enim pecuri, A.
681 captamque, A.
684 harundinibus, A.
685 mollis, A.
687 querit, A.
690 Interra ędriadv, v super rasuram, A.
691 nymphae syringa, A.
692 satiros, A.
693 umbrosa silua feraxque, A.
694 ortiguam, A.
698 om. A.
699 capud, A.
702 ʰarenosi, A.
703 inpedientibus, A.
705 Pan quoque conprensā sibi iam syringa putareṭ, A.
707 ʰarundine, A.
710 consilium, A.

711 conpagine cęrae, A.
713 cillenius, A.
v
719 Deicit, A; repem, A.
720 quodque inter tot lumina lumen, A.
721 Extinctum est, A.
722 Excipit hunc, A.
723 inplet, A.
725 erinī, A.
v
726 Pelicis, A; stimolos qi, A.
*727 circuit orbem, A.
728 inmenso, A.
733 queri finemque, A.
734 conplexus, A.
737 stigias, A.
738 linita dęest, A.
739 Fit quod, A; et, A¹; e, A²; sęę, A.
741 ʰumerique, A.
742 om. A.
u
743 bone, A.
744 Officiu que, A.
745 timuitque, A; tim *post rasuram*.
746 retemptat, A.
747 linigera, A; creberrima, A.
v
748 Nunc epaphis, A; desimine, A.
751 pheton, A.
752 credentem, A.
755 pheton, A.
756 climine n, A; conuitia, A.
757 genitrix ait illae, A.
758 hec opprobria, A.
negari
759 referri, A.
761 assere, A.

* *Ex hoc uno elucet praestantia codicis.* Ceteri omnes terruit.

OVIDII METAMORPHOSEON

762 iplicuit, A; brachia, A.
s. est   i
765 Ambiguum, A; demine,
   i
   A (clemine *potius*).

767 Brachia, A.
770 Nocte, A.
   v
771 si ficta neget, A.   fero
773-779 *extant in* Bern.

773 labor est patrios, Bern.;
   v
   longos, A; penatis, A.
776 loetus, A.
777 & hera, A.

INCIP. lib. II **Bern.** *Inter I et II spatium est duorum uersuum in* **A.**

1-22 *Extant in* Bern.
1 colū nis, A.
2 pyropo, Bern., A.
3 tegebat, A, Bern.
4 lumiņae, Bern.
5 Materiam, A, Bern.; mulcifer, A.
6 et accelerat, Bern. *pro* caelarat; celarat, A.
7 inminet, A; iffinet, Bern.
9 Protheaque, A; ballenarumque, A, Bern.
10 Aegona, Bern.; inmania, A; iffiania, Bern.
11 uidetur, Bern.
12 uiridi, Bern.
14 Ñ, Bern.; sororem, Bern.
16 nymfas, Bern.; cetera, Bern., A.
17 imposita est, Bern.; inposita est, A; celi, A.
18 se a *pro* sex, Bern.
   † adclini
19 Quos, Bern.; adcylii, Bern.; acclino, A, *sup. lineam*; limite, Bern.
20 dubitati, A, ti *post rasuram*.
21 sua fert, Bern.; uertit, A.
22 neque enim, A; propiora uidebat, Bern.
24 claro, A², o *ex rasura*; smaragdo, A², o *ex rasura*.

25 At, A.
26 spatuis, A.
29 autūnis, A¹; al. uuae, marg. A.
   p
30 hiems, A.
32 aspicit, A.
         a
34 pheton, A; inficienda, A.
35 inmensi, A.
         a
36 sidųs, A; *post* nominis *scriba* A *scripserat* usum, *quo eraso addidit* huius.
37 climine, A.
38 Pingnora, A; generis, A, *man. recent.*
39 ʰunc, A; horrorem, A, *quod cum erasum esset iterum in margine scriptum est.*
41 iusit, A¹, altera s *post addita.*
43 clymine, A.
49 Penituit, A.
50 inlustre, A.
51 facta tibi est, A.
52 negare, A.
53 non es, A.
54 pheton, A.
         a
55 conneniunt, A.
57 contingere possit, A.
58 adfectas, A.
59 Nec, A.

60 om. A.
61 dextera, A.
62 agit, A; et qd, A.
       s
63 nix, A.
64 Eniᵘtur, A.
66 Sit, A; trepidet, A.
            que corrum
68 Tunc quoque subiectis, A.
69 Ne ferat in ƥceps t& hys, A.
70 adsidua, A.
71 celeri quo lumine, A¹; celeri quoque lumine, A².
       o
72 * Hitur, A.
73 Impetus, A; eueor, A.
74 Fingebat hos currus, A, *et in marg.* Deicit hoc curru. poteris nec, A.
75 † nec te citus auferet, A.
81 Ņɟec nonivs //// arcus, A.
82 brachio, A¹.
83 brachio, A¹.
84 quadripedes, A¹.
   ? reges
86 regeres, A; ubi acres, A.
       v
88 fenesti, A; sum, A.
89 res quesinⁱt, A.
90 credes, A¹; credas, A².
91 timendo, d *ex* t, A.
92 aspice, A.
93 occulos in pectora posses (*ex* posset), A.
94 deprehendere, A *sic.*

* *Fuitne* Itur?   † *Hinc legerim* ne te citus auferet axis, *ut* ne *particula affirmatiua sit.*

LIBER II.

95 quidquid, A ; diues *om.* A.
96 Deque, A.
98 poenam, A.
99 pheton, A.
100 blandi signare, A¹.
105 Ergo quā licuit cunctatus, A, *om.* genitor.
106 uoleania, A.
109 chri solithi, A ; positaeque, A ; gemme, A.
111 pheton, A.
114 cogit at cogens, A.
115 Lucifer e celi, A.
116 Quem pater ut, A.
117 uelud, A¹ ; uelut, A².
118 inperat, A.
119 uomentis, A.
121 Quadripedes, A.
124 Inposuitque comes, A.
125 sollitito, A.
126 saluē, A ; saltem, *marg.*
    A ; parāre, A.
128 uolentes, A.
129 derectos, A ; quique, A.
131 Zanarumque, A.
135 p̄ me, A.
136 celestia, A.
139 ducit adarcam, A.
140 Inter utrumque, A ; cetera, A.
142 esperio, A ; litore, A.
143 Humida, A.
144 etfulget, A.
147 *om.* A.
149 Que tutus spectes, A.
150 iuuenali, A.
151 manibusque leues, A.
153 pyrois eous et aethon, A.
154 Quartusque phlegon solis equi, A.

155 Flammifferos inplent, A.
156 tetᵇis, A.
157 Repulit, A ; inmensi, A ; mundi, A.
159 leuatis, A.
160 ortus istem, A.
163 labent, A ; pontere, A.
164 instabilis, A.
165 sic onera ad sua eta uacuos, A.
168 Quadriiuge, A.
169 paueńt, A.
170 Nec sic qua sit, A; iperet, A.
172 temptarunt equore tingui, A.
174 formidabiles, A.
175 sūsit, A.
176 bootē, A.
178 despexit ab ęthera, A.
179 pheton, A ; patentis, A. ; obortę, A.
183 * Iam genus agnoscit, A ; rogantem, A¹ ; rogando, A².
185 borea quo uecta, A² ; qui uicta, A¹ ; remansit, A.
186 *bis scriptus est in* A ; *semel in imo margine folii* 16ᵃ
    sic Frena suos rector quę diis uotisque reliquit, *iterum summo fol.*
    16ᵇ *sic* Frena suus rector quam dis uotisque reliquit.
188 moetitur, A.
190 ocasus, A.
192 *post 194 scriptus est in* A; aequorum, A.

193 Sparsaque, A ; maracula, A.
194 simulacra, A.
195 geminos, A, -nos *post rasuram.*
196 utrūque, A.
197 spacium, A.
198 madiā, A.
201 summo, A ; licentia, A ; tergo, A.
202 Exspaciantur, A.
203 inpetus, A.
204 Ac sine legerunt, A ; fixit, A.
205 p̄ uia, A.
206 perde cliua, A.
208 Inferiorque, A¹; Inferivsque, A².
209 Admiratur, A.
210 Corriptiur, A.
211 Fixaque, A ; sucis, A.
214 menibus, A.
215 totas, A ; gentes, A.
217 taurosque, A ; molus, A.
218 Et modo si caprius creberrima, A.
219 eeagrius hęmus, A.
220 ethne, A.
221 Parnasosque, A ; erix et oynthus et othrys, A.
222 rodope, A ; nimasque, A.
223 Dindimaque et mycalem promtus ptusque. cum
225 dum, A.
226 appennius, A.
227 pheton, A.
228 Aspicit, A.

* *Et hic ueram manum Ouidii deprendas scripto* agnosci.

229 Feruentisque, A; uelud, A; profunda *erasum in* A, *et post id spatium uolantes.*
230 trahaet, A; sensit, A.
233 calligine, A.
235 om. A.
236 populus, A.
237 libiae, A; humoribus, A.
238 cum nymphę, A.
239 booetia cirnon ? dircen, A.
240 Arethusa· drimoné ephyre phirennidas, A.
242 manem, A; ᵐᵃⁿ ⁿᵗ *incerta littera quam in spatio omisi.* medus
tanaṣis, A; undas, A.
243 Peneosque, A; teuthranteusque caicas, A, *ni fallor.*
244 Et tǽ//, A¹; Cessit et, A²; ismenos cum phocaico, A.
245 Arsurosque, A; Xanthus flauusque Lycormas.
246 recurutis, A; maeandrus, A.
247 Nigdoniusque melas et atenarius, A.
249 Thermodoonque, A; gangisque, A; phasis et hister, A.
250 Alpheos *ex* Alpheus, A; sperchiedes, A¹; sperchiedos, A².
251 ᵃffluit, A.
253 ᵃcystro, A.
255 capud, A.

256 uacant, A.
257 eborum, A; strimone, A.
258 aniṁ/s, A, *sed* m *in* ne *mutata;* renum rodanumque, A.
259 thibris, A.
261 Ignis *pro* Lumen, A; siccae quoque campus arenae, A.
264 Extabant, A; eˣ, A.
266 delfines, A.
270 aquis, A; brachia, A.
271 Exerere, A; igneis, A.
274 uisera, A.
275 sustulit omnipotens (oṁps), A.
278 sacraque, A.
281 perere, A.
283 tostos en asbice crines, A.
284 Inque oculis tantum tantum super ora fauillae, A.
287 ferro, A.
288 peccori, A.
289 tura, A.
291 sortę, A.
292 et hab& here, A.
293 ne fratris, A.
294 celj, A; utrumque, A.
295 utrumque, A; si uitia ueṣṭit, A; axis, A.
296 *om.* A.
297 humeris, A.
299 etripe, A.
300 super est, A.
301 Dixerat hoc, A; neque enim, A; uapore, A.
303 Retulit, A.
308 uibrataque fulmina, A.

310 dimitteret, A.
313 seuis, A.
318 lacere, A; cursus, A² *ex* currus.
319 pheton, A.
320 Vuluitur, A; longoque *per nubila* poli tractu, A, *sed* poli *alia manus uidetur addidisse.*
325 hesberiae, A.
326 Siṗgnant, A. *ex*
328 etcidit, A.
329 obductus, A¹.
332 ustus, A² *post rasuram et marg.* A.
335 taḍ tū, A; percensuit al. transcenderat, A.
337 Reperit, A; ripa, A.
341 cesis, A.
342 phǽonta, A; querelas, A.
343 Nonte, A; adsternunturque, A.
344 inpleraṅt, A.
347 terrae procumberae, A.
348 Diriguisse, A.
349 iampetie, A.
352 brachia, A.
353 conplectitur, A.
354 utrum, A; ʰumerosque, A.
355 Ambiet extabant, A.
356 trahit inpetus, A.
358 euellere, A.
360 Sanguinęe, A; uulnere, A.
364 Vnde, A.
366 gestanda, A.
367 steneleia cygnus, A.
368 uinctus, A.
369 proprior, A.
371 querelis, A.

LIBER II.

372 inples ut, A. [uit]
374 Dissimulantque, A.
376 Pinna, A.
377 cyngnus, A.
378 Tradit, A; iniusti, A. [e]
379 Stagna, A.
381 Squalibus, *marg.* Squalidus, A.
384 adicit, A.
385 inquid, A. [t]
386 inrequieta, A.
389 diei, A.
393 Nomeruisse, A; rexerat, A.
396 Subplice, A.
399 seuit, A.
400 Seuit, A; inputat, A.'
401 ingentis, A.
403 firmas ubique, A.
405 inpensior, A.
408 letasque, A.
409 Dum redit & idque, A; Nonacrines, A. [t, a]
410 Haesid, A.·
411 molire, A.
412 positas, A; ubi fibula, A. [cui]
413 neglegitos, A. [c]
415 mencalon, A.
416 longe est, A.
417 sol læus, A.
418 cetīderat, A.
419 huic humero, A. [ut]
422 &, A.
424 Sunt o sunt iniuria tantum, A.
425 cultumque, A.

428 silue, A. [talue]
429 Apdiat, A. [u]
430 preteris se, A.
431 ea uirgine, A (a *conuersa in* x). [ex, e]
432 parentem, A. [a]
433 Inpedit, A.
434 posset, A.
436 quem, A.
437 Qusue, A.
439 Vnde, A.
441 coro, A; dictina, A. [h]
442 Menalon, A; cede, A.
443 Aspitit, A.
446 nymeruq', A¹; numorūmq', A²; haram, A. [e]
447 Eu, A¹; H ευ, A²; uultū, A.
448 nec ut, A.
456 atritas, A; riuos, A. [v]
459 limphys, A.
460 Parrasis, A. [h]
464 ne, A.
465 saecedere cetu, A.
467 idonia, A¹; idonia, *serior manus*. [e]
469 fuerit de pellice, A.
470 Cvi, A; obuertens, A.
473 No//ta, A; testatur, A; esse, A.
474 Haud inpune, A; namque, A.
475 inportuna, A.
476 aduersam, A.
479 unges, A.
480 Officiuque, A.

* *Videtur esse* quantu hausta.

484 gutere, A.
485 manet *pro* tamen, A.
486 Asiduoque, A.
489 Ah, A.
491 Ah, A.
492 uenantjum, A.
496 lycaonię, A¹; lycaonia, A².
497 ter, *om.* A; ferena talibus actis, A.
498 saltos, A.
499 erimandidos ampit, A.
501 Et agnoscenti, A.
503 accedere fugit, A.
504 Uolnifico, A.
505 Arguit, A.
506 et pariter raptos, A.
507 Inposuit, A; uiciniaque, A.
508 pelex, A.
509 tethin, A.
511 uiam & sricitantibus, A.
514 Mentior, A.
515 uulnera, A.
516 ille ubi, A.
517 preuissimus, A.
518 Est uero quisquam Iunonem ledere, A.
520 *quant asta potentia nostra est, A. [v]
522 inpono, A.
524 argolicā, A.
526 Conlocat, A; talamo, A; lycana sumit, A. [h]
527 Aduos, A; lęse, A; contepmptus, A.
530 aequorae pelex, A.
531 Dii, A; adn., A.
533 Iam, A.
534 Quantū, A.
538 seruaturus, A.

[I. 5.]

539 cyneno, A.
541 contrarias, A¹; contra-
   rius, A².
542 larissęa coronea, A.
543 haec meǎnia, A.
547 garula ramis, A.
548 cicitetur, A.
549 Auditaeque, A; carpit,
   A.
553 erichtonium, A; crea-
   tum, A.
554 Clausaerat, A.
555 nates, A¹; natis, A².
556 ne reserata, A; reserata
   super rasuram.
559 Pandrasas, A.
560 Aglauros, A; deducit, A.
561 adporrectumque, A.
565 Admonuisse peñaş potest,
   A; piricula, A.
566 rogabis, A ex rasura.
567 Me petit ipsa licet licet,
   A.
569 phocarca, A; telure, A.
571 nec me contempne, A.
572 uentis, A.
573 summa, A; arenis, A.
575 absumpsit, A.
577 nequiquam, A; harena,
   A.
580 brachia cęlo, A.
581 Brachia cep., A; horres-
   cere, A.
582 Reiecerę, A; ʰumeris,
   A.
583 egerat, A.
585 Sed neque, A; nec pectora, A.
586 nec ut, A.
588 Eueor, A.

589 si, om. A; *tetro facta
   uuolucris, A.
590 Myctimenon, A.
   i. nobile
592 parium, A.
599 coronea, A.
600 auditor, A.¹
603 adsueta capit, A.
606 Iacta, A.
607 punce, A.
608 E dixi, A.
609 in ūna, A.
   &
610 ut, A.
612 Poenit, A.
615 erǎit, A; manuque, A.
617 Conlapsamque, A; facta,
   A.
   ne
621 gemitusque, A.
624 Lactantis, A.
625 Discussit, A.
627 iniustaque iusta, A.
   d
628 laba, A; eostem, A.
629 utroque, A.
630 cyronis, A.
633 Semiuir, A.
635 humeros, A.
636 caricto, A.
638 ocyrphe, A.
639 fugit, A.
640 uaticinos, A.
642 Aspicit, A; totoque, A;
   orbi, A.
646 prohibebᵉre, A.
647 Exque deo corpus fies
   exangue, A.
649 nunc iam mortalis, A.
651 tum cum curaberae, A.
652 serpentis, A; sautia, A.
653 et *pro* ex, A; numine,
   A.

656 lambuntur oborte, A.
657 inquid mea fata, A.
658 inquid mea, A.
660 futurā, A.
663 Inpetus est in equa, A.
664 extrema biformis, A; biformis *super rasuram*.
665 extremę querele, A.
666 fuerunt, A.
   něc
667 Mox ǎuidem uerba, A.
668 eque, A.
669 hinitus, A; brachia, A;
   ǐ
   herbas, A.
   ǐ
670 digito, A.
674 abire, A.
675 deder͠, A.
676 tuu, A; philirius, A;
   hęros, A.
678 ne si, A.
679 elimas seniaque, A.
681 baculo siluestre sinistre,
   A.
682 canis, A.
684 pylios me morantur, A.
685 atlandide matre, A.
688 uicina hunc rura cane-
   bant, A.
691 Hunc †tenuit balanda-
   que, A.
692 hosbes, A.
693 Nec, A.
694 repentatur, A.
695 Edidit, A; reddit hosbes,
   A.
700 Ira, A.
701 suo pariter, A; foemina,
   A.
704 et meme perfide, A.
709 Munychiosque, A.

* Plerique MSS. diro.   † Et hoc unice uerum existimo.   Nihil est timuit quod plerasque edd. inuasit.

LIBER II.

710 arbustaq., A.
712 palĭdis arce, A.
714 aspicit, A.
715 * eunde, A.
716 uidis, A ; miluius, A.
718 gyrum, A.
719 auis, A.
720 acteas auis, A ; ap//ces, A.
723 quanto quam, A.
725 poṉpae, A.
726 Obstupuit, A ; pennis, A.
729 abuit, A ; ignis, A.
730 diuersa relicto, A.
731 fuducia, A.
734 Conlocat, A ; totum apareat, A.
735 somnus, A.
738 Tris, A ; pandra, A.
739 aglauros, A.
741 scicitarier, A.
744 iuppiter, A.
747 est, om. A.
748 Aspicit, A ; istem, A.
749 aglauros, A ; secraeta, A.
751 &cedere, A.
753 susbiria, A.
755 om. A.
756 creatum, A.
757 styrpem, A ; federa, A.
758 Ingratamque deo fore ingratamque minerue, A.
759 aurum, A.
761 ualibus, A.
765 belli, A.
766 neque enim succere, A.

767 etrema, A.
768 uidit intus etedentem, A.
770 uisăque, A.
771 pigra, A ; reliquit, A.
773 om. A.
774 uultuque deę ad susbiria duxit, A.
775 matices, A.
776 recta bis A.
777 liuent, A ; lurent MS. Digb. 65. p. 774.
777 sufusa, A.
779 uigilatibus, A.
781 homineṣ, A.
782 illum, A.
783 adfata est, A.
785 aglauros, A.
786 inpressa, A ; repulit, A.
787 obliqo, A.
788 successuramque, A.
789 baculussique, A ; quod, A.
792 papauera, A.
793 Adflatuque, A.
795 Ingentes, A.
797 nata, A.
799 amantis, A ; inplet, A.
800 Insbiratque, A ; perosa, A.
801 plumone, A.
802 spatium causae, A ; erret, A.
803 Germanamque, A.
805 magno, A ; irritata, A.
806 oculto, A.
807 Axia, A.
808 solet, A.

* an eundo ?

809 lit̃.
810 subponitur, A.
811 om. A.
814 limine, A.
815 Exclusara, A ; plandimenta, A.
817 Hinc me ego non, A ; moritura, A.
820 conati, A.
823 post 826 A ; pungues, A.
825 inmedicabile, A.
827 hiemps, A ; pectorę, A.
828 clusit, A.
829 canata, A.
831 etsangue, A.
834 Cępit, A ; at^{h}lanciades, A ; dictas, om. A.
840 Suscipit indignę, A.
841 montano ex montane, A ; pascit, A.
843 certe, A.
844 Litora hic et 843 A.
847 Magestas, A.
854 &stant, A.
855 si, A.
862 sberata, A.
863 uix ha uix cetera, A.
864 At, A ; exultat, A.
865 N nunc, A ; harenis, A.
867 plaudende, A.
868 Inped., A.
869 consederet auri, A.
870 siccoque ad litorae, A.
871 primo, A ; in imis, A^1 ; in undis, A^2.
874 cornu, A.
875 imposita est, A.

III.

1-56 extant in Bern.
1 in magine, A.
2 dicteaque, Bern.
4 Inperat, A.
6 depreendere, Bern.
8 phebeique oracula suplex, A.
10 *phebõs, A ; occuret, A.
11 inmunis, A ; immunis, Bern.
12 duę, A.
13 boetiaque, A ; que *om.* Bern.
14 discesserat, A ; descenderet, Bern.
18 Autoremque, Bern.
19 cephesi, A, Bern.
20 speciosam, A.
21 mugittibus inpulit, A ; impulit, Bern.
22 respiciens *pro* sequentes, A *iterum*; sequentis, Bern.
23 sũmisit, A, Bern.
24 Kadmus, Bern. ; ait, A ; peregrinaque, A.
25 et †inignotos, A.
28 uiolatũ, A ; secure, Bern.
29 aculmine denso, A.
30 conpagibus, A.
31 fecundis, A.
32, 33 *bis scripti sunt in* Bern.
32 pignis, A.
33 uenenis, Bern. *bis.*
34 *om.* Bern., Trisque micant, A.
35 profeciti, Bern.
36 gradu *om.* Bern.; dea usaque, Bern.

37 capud, A.
39 unde, A; *sed manca linea qua* n *incipit*; relinquit, A ; reliquit, Bern.
40 atonitas, A.
41 squamosus, A.
42 immensos, A ; inmensos, Bern.
43 leuis, A ; leueş se rectus, Bern.
45 spectejs, A ; seperat, A.
46 si uelli, Bern.
47 siue timor ipse, Bern.
48 c̃plexibus, A, Bern.
49 adflatu, A ; afflatu, Bern. ; funesti, Bern. ; tabae, A.
52 tegimendi repta leonis, A; tegimen derepta leoni, Bern.
53 splendentia, A *pro* splendenti lancea ; telo, Bern.
55 leto data corpora, A; laetataque, Bern.
56 spatiosa corporis, A.
57 *om.* A.
58 fidissima corpora, A.
61 inpulsu, A.
62-86 *om.* A.
89 cedebat, A. do
90 guture, A.
92 obstiti, A.
95 consederat, A.
96 congnoscere promptu, A.
99 tolorem, A.

100 delapsa, A.
101 su^bpendere, A.
104 Parcet et upresso, A.
105 Semmina, A.
107 apparuit, A.
108 nudantia cona, A.
109 humuri, A ; brachia, A.
110 Existunt, A.
111 aⁿlea, A.
112 surgerere, A.
113 Cetera, A.
114 himoque, A.
115 oste, A.
116 Nec, A.
120 Hunc, A.
121 exbirat, A.
124 sortiata, A.
125 Sanguineam tepido tangebant, A.
127 munitu tridonidis, A.
128 pecitque, A.
129 sido nidus hosbes, A.
130 iussus phoebeis, A.
131 stabant thaebe, A.
132 Ex illo, A.
133 Continge^rant, A ; ad *pro* adde, A.
134 natas natosque, A ; nepotes, A.
136 hominem *om.* est, A.
137 subpremaque, A.
138 secundus, A.
140 ^herili, A.
142 & nim, A.
145 et aequo mediastas, A.
147 hiantius, A.
150 l festa *pro* inuecta, A.

* *Supposita* e *neglegentius scripta, altera superius addita est.*   † *Error ortus est ex* ingnotos.

LIBER III.   13

152 idem, A; uap̧orebus, A.
154 fatiunt, A ; intermituntque, A.
155 crupressu, A.
156 garsaphᶦae, A ; succinte, A.
157 extremum, A ; mortale, A.
158 Aṇ̃te, A.
159 punice, A.
160 toſes, A.
161 addextrum, A.
162 patulos incinctus hiatus, A.
163 ueneta, A.
165 post quam, A.
168 Vincula, A.
170 quam uiserat, A.
171, 172 *inuerso ordine scripti sunt in* A.
171 nimphę fialeque ranisque, A.
172 specas, A; phialę, A.
173 lymphis, A.
176 fate, A.
178 nudae uiso, A.
180 Inpleuere, A.
185 uestae, A.
186 quaquam, A.
187 obliqumque tamen *astitit.
188 uelle, A ; abuisse, A.
191 Addit haec claudis, A.
195 cacuminē taures, A.
196 brachia, A.
197 uęḷlat, A.
198 autonoeius, A.

202 fugit, A ; lacrima/ *incerta littera quam per/ notaui.*
204 regulia, A.
205 inpedit, A.
206 uideri, A; melamphus, A.
207 Isnouatesque saxa, A ; dederunt, A.
208 Gnosius Isno(*ex* a)uates, A ; melāphus, A.
210 Pamphagus et dorceus et oribasus, A.
211 lelape, A.
212 plerelas, A.
213 Hilaeusque, A.
215 Fęminis, A¹ ; Fęmenis, A²; harpya, A.
216 sitionius, A.
217 canasche stictaeque.
220 ciprio, A; licysce, A.
221 ab illo, A.
222 Harpolos et meianeus, A.
223 lyconide, A.
224 agrihodos, A ; hiiator, A.
226 aditusque, A.
227 secuntur, A.
229 libaebat, A.
230 Actheon, A.
231 rosonat, A.
232 me lanchates, A.
233 orestrophus, A.
234 exierat, A; compendia, A.
235 Precipitata, A.
239 querelis, A.
240 gnibus, A.
241 brachia, A.
242 latratibus, A.
243 acteona, A.
246 oblata, A.
247 uidere, A.

249 Unde que, A.
251, 2 *extant in* A.
256 coniux, A.
257 dade, A, *nisi fallor.*
258 pellice, A.
261 semeles, A; ĥuria, A.
262 iuria, A.
266 soror *om.* A.
267 est et iuria, A.
269 uni, A.
272 mersas *pro* mersa suo, A; in undas, A.
275 posuit ad temporae, A¹.
280 Ad nomen euere, A. multi
281 tuḷịt, A.
282 inere, A.
283 pignos, A.
285 Ionone, A.
286 ēplexus, A.
291 timor es deus ille deorum, A.
293 semel equalem, A.
296 exierat iam uox, A.
299 c̶o̶n̶s̶c̶e̶n̶d̶i̶t̶ consendit, A (*sic*).
300 inmixitaque fulgora, A.
303 de iecerat igne typhoea, A.
305 ciclopum, A.
308 agenorē, A.
309 etherios.
310 Inperfectus, A.
312 complet, A.
314 datum *om.* A; nes/eides, A.
317 bachi, A.
319 grauis, A.
320 malos uestra prophecto est, A.
323 Quaereret ////// uenus, A *relicto spatio.*

---

* *Legendum uidetur* abstitit.

327 aut tūnos, A.
329 actoris, A.
331 genitiuaque, A.
332 Arbitu̥r, A; sumptus *om.*
   A; ioco(o *ex* a)fa, A.
336 irrita, A.
337 adempit, A, *nisi fallor.*
338 honores, A.
340 Inreprehensa, A.
341 Prima fidei uocisque datę temptamina, A.
343 Inplicuit, A; cęphisos, A.
345 nimpha iam tum, A.
350 letique, A.
351 cephesius, A.
352 nuper, A.
356 Aspicit, A; recia, A.
357 nimphę, A.
358 prior, A; resonabiles, A.
360 Caͬrula, A; abebat, A.
362 Iuno quia cum, A.
363 Sub Ioue, A.
365 fugeret, A; post quam hoc, A.
366 delv(v *ex* o)sa, A¹.
367 preuissimus, A.
369 uocis, A.
371 ingaluic̄, A.
373 circumlitat aedis, A.
374 Admota, A; uiuatia sulphura flāmę, A.
376 moles, A.
377 sint illa paratae, A.
378 remitat, A.
379 seductis, A.
380 ʰecquis, A; resbonderat, A.

381 atque, A; demiͥsit, A.
384 quod, A.
386 Huṇ, A.
387 Responsora, A; retulit, A.
389 iniceret sberat obrachia, A.
390 c̄plexibus aufert, A.
392 Retulit, A; nichil, A.
393 frontibus, A.
395 que *om.* A.
396 Et tam̄ uigiles curpus misaerabile, A.
397 et a corpore sucus, A.
398 Corpore somnus abit, A.
401 figura, A.
403 cęptus, A.
404 dispectus, A.
406 adsensit, A; rhamnusia, A.
407 in limis, A.
409 Contigerat aliud sue pectus, A.
411 humor, A.
415 ceruit, A.
417 quod undę, A.
418 Atstupet, A; immotus, A.
421 *dignas, A; dignas, A.
422 Impubesque, A.
425 inprudens, A.
427 Inrita, A.
428 uisus, A.
430 quod uidetur in illo, A.
432 fugatia, A.
434 imaginis umbre, A.
440 leuatos, A.
442 Nec quis, A.
443 opportuna, A.
444 Haec quem, A.

449 męnia, A.
451 liquidis quociens, A; liymphis, A.
452 tociens, A.
456 quaem, A.
459 adrides, A.
460 singna, A.
462 aures, A; nostris, A.
464 meueoque, A.
465 roge; *ceteris omissis quae secuntur.*
469 admit, A.
470 ęuū, A.
475 lacrimas.
476 cum *om.* A.
478 Disse̥re, A.
479 Asbicere, A.
480 summo reduxit ab ore, A.
482 tenuem percusa rubore, A.
483 quapͥ, A; candidida, A.
486 asbexit, A; undas, A¹; unda, A².
488 matui *ceteris omissis quae secuntur,* A.
489 atenuatus, A.
490 et tecto, A.
492 uires sed quae, A.
493 amaueret, A.
499 solitam—undam *om.* A.
500 Haec, A.
502 sūmisit in erba, A.
503 mors, A.
504 infrena, A.
506 Naides, A; inposuere caͦpillis, A.
507 adsonat, A.
511 archaides, A.
512 Atulerat, A; anguris, A.

* *Et hoc notandum.* Crinis *genere feminino inuenitur in Plaut. Most. I.* 3. 69 *et Attae epigrammate ap. Non.* 201.

LIBER III.

513 aechiodes, A; et *pro* ex, A.
517 lhuius, A.
518 nec bachi̊a, A.
519 quam iam haud procul, A.
524 Eueniat, A.
525 Meque et ab his, A; uȧidiˡs, A.
526 echine, A.
528 ullulatibus, A.
530 ḍad sacra, A.
532 Attollit, A.
533 uiḍeaˡnt et adunaque, A.
534 magice, A.
535 strictus, A.
537 Obscenique, A; timphana, A.
539 posuisti, A.
540 *om.* A.
543 sistis, A.
545 profrondibusillelucuque, A.
547 moles, A,
548 patrum, A.
550 sonare, A.
554 ussus, A.
555 Sed medius murra crinis, A.

556 Purpurẹaque, A.
557 attutū, A.
559 čtempnere, A.
561 aduenit hebis, A.
564 huc cetera, A.
565 frustaque, A.
566 Acryor, A; inritaturque, A.
567 moderaminȧeque, A; nocebȧunt, A.
568 torrentē, A¹; torrenti, A²; qua obstabat nil, A.
569 decurre, A.
571 obice, A.
576 quondam, A.
577 Aspicit hunc pentheus oculis, A; tremendus, A.
578 quenqȧuam, A; uix et, A.
579 peraiture, A.
581 moresque, A.
582 acetes, A.
583 pelle, A.
584 duris colerentur rura iuuencis, A.
585 Lanigeros greges, A.
587 salamo, A.
590 nichil, A.

591 Preterea quas num, A; apellẹȧre, A.
592 scopulos, A; iȧsteᵈm, A.
595 Taygentēque hydasque, A.
596 pupibus altos, A.
597 cbiẹ, A.
598 Applicor, A; adduco litora, A.
599 immittit arenae, A¹.
601 et / urgo, A; recentis, A.
602 Admoneo, A; ducit, A.
603 promitit, A.
604 Prospitio, A.
605 sotiorum primus ofeltes, A.
607 Virgineā, A.
612 est *om.* A.
615 Dirtiᵘs, A; cᶜonsendere sūmat, A.
616 Otior antemnas, A.
617 libis, A; flauaᵒs, A; et prorẹ, A.
618 alcimodoᵉn, A; quere quiemque, A.
621 sacri uiȯlare, A.
622 Perpetior, A.

EPIGRAMMATA CODICVM BODLEIANORVM.

EPIGRAMMATA CODICIS BODLEIANI RAWL. B. N. 109.

I.

p. 32.
Dūm colo militiam, dum uates desero musas,
    In ceruice graui uulnere laedor ego.
Musa mouet caput et 'merito sic accidit' inquid
    'Prospera non poteras, aspera disce pati.'

II.

p. 44.
Tela, Cupido, tene, quoniam non ille sed illa
    Sustinet esse meus uel mea, tela tene.
Tela tene. quid amo quod amat non *reapse*? Sed huius
    Quod fugit, huius ero? non ero. Tela tene.
Tela tene, quia non teneo quod amo tenuisse.   5
    An dixi, quod amo? non amo. Tela tene.
Tela tene, uel tange parem. ne feceris, imo
    Dico tibi, sine, uel tange, Cupido, parem.

III.

p. 67.
Viuere non possum sine te neque uiuere tecum,
    Illud namque metus impedit, illud amor.
O utinam sine te uel tecum uiuere possem,
    Sed mallem tecum uiuere quam sine te.

IV.

p. 68.
Lingua non oculo, Nestor lasciue, loquaris.
    Odi blanda senis uerba supercilii.
Frons numerat menses, frontis cute scribitur aetas,
    Praetenditque suos arida ruga dies.

I. 1. celo miliciam.   2. ledor.   II. 3. quod amat non absit.   III. *Ouid. Am.* iii. 11. 39 Sic ego nec sine te nec tecum uiuere possum. *Mart.* xii. 47. 2 Nec tecum possum uiuere nec sine te.

EPIGRAMMATA

     Nestor, in annosa legimus tua tempora carta:
        Frons uetat haec in se mollia uerba legi.
     Inueterate puer, non consonat actio fronti,
        Et frons a uerbis dissidet ipsa tuis.
     Inberbis ueteres lasciuia dedecet annos,
        Nutus lasciui nuntius est animi.
     Nondum, blande senex, tecum tua uerba senescunt,
        Nec faciunt mores tempora longa suos.
     Vt mores fugias, non te, non effugis annos;
        Hoc age quod iuuenis, non agis hoc iuuenis.
     Vae tibi, cuius opus non corrigit ipsa senectus.
        Vae tibi, qui pectus non sinis esse senex.
     Cum tibi barba seni iam marceat in sene mento,
        Barbatam mentem non sinis esse tuam.
     O lasciue senex, monstrum est lasciua senectus,
        Et cum quo mores insenuere mali.

V.

     Quamuis canities te, Naeuole, Nestora monstret,
        Mens lasciua   conprobat esse uirum.
     Naeuole, cum fragili uix uiuas corpore Nestor,
        Iupiter extincto Nestore uiuis adhuc.
     Nestoris atque Iouis concordia, Naeuole, nulla est.
        Nulla senectuti luxuriaeque fides.
     Naeuole, tam diuersa duo, tam dissociata
        In te conueniunt, luxuriose senex.
     Naeuole, lasciuis tenero lasciuior haedo,
        Et frustra Veneri posse placere studes.
     Fastidit Venerem Venus exsaturata clientem.
     Ergo luxuriae, Naeuole, pone modum.

VI.

     Potus, Milo, sapis, non potus desipis idem.
        Si bibis ut sapias, desipis ut sapias.

IV. 7. frontis.   9. In uerbis.   10. nuncius.   11. Nundum.   15, 16. Ve.
20. *fortasse* cum qua.   V. 1. canicies.   2. laciua *excidit* tamen.   3. uiuat.   8. luxuriosa.   9. edo.   10. *an* cupis?   VI. *Extat etiam in Digbeiano* 65, p. 59ᵃ Ad disputatorem bene potum.

Nec tibi si sicco facundia uixerit ore,
   Nec nisi pota nimis Musa diserta tua est.
Qui sapis ex Bacc*h*o, qui non sapis aure sed ore,
   Hoc unum sapio quod nihil ipse sapis.

VII.

p. 72.

Esto superba minus dum te prece uexo, Superba,
   Et melior fieri nomine disce tuo.
Omnia quae uincis post omnia te quoque uince.
   Immemor esse tui nominis esto memor.

VIII.

ib.

Thraso, tuis si facta forent tua consona dictis,
   Non foret ut quis te largior esset homo.
Pollicitis multos ditat tua prodiga lingua,
   Sed uix aut numquam dicta sequetur opus.
Vtile consilium est, ne quid promiseris ulli,
   Sed sine pollicitis da dare si qua uoles.

p. 92.

Insperata magis sunt munera grata frequenter,
   Et nil promittens debitor esse fugit.
Nam qui promittunt non dant, sed debita soluunt;
   Nec data, quae non est ius retinere, uoco.
Non retinere licet quia reddere cogit honestas,
   Virtutumque simul mater honesta fides.

IX.

p. 95.

Si tibi grana placent, spicas attunde flagellis,
   Si nuclei dulces sunt tibi, frange nucem.
Si laetis rebus uis participare, labora.
   Nam parit ingratus munera grata labor.

---

3. facundia D *habet* Nec tibi si sicco facundia suggerit ore.   5. bacco.   6. nichil.
VIII. 1. Thraso *uitio serioris aeui*.   4. sequentur *Post* 12 *secuntur in codice spuria haec*
Tullius esse fidem describit in officiorum Libro cum fuerint singula dicta prius. Ergo fide salua
mixta Tulli (*cod.* tullii) ratione, Quae dare promittis non retinere licet.   IX. 2. nŭclei *cf.*
Mart. xi. 86. 3.

X.

Corrupere duo Flauiam, parit illa gemellos,
   Et cum nesciret quis pater esset, ait,
Vni si dentur, cum sit pater unus eorum,
   Forsitan alter erit, decipiamque duos.
Ne pater amit/at, ne nutriat aemulus ambos,
   Vnum cuique dabo, decipiamque minus.

XI.

Maxima uenandi causa est tibi, nulla legendi.
   Brutus es et brutis, Quintiliane, uacas.

XII.

Non re sed uerbis est Sextus amicus amici,
   Si sit opus, poscit, ferre recusat opem.

EPIGRAMMA COD. DIGBEIANI 172.

XIII.

Versu(s) monimenti.

Hic ego qui iaceo ganymedes Chrysopolita,
   Quem procul a patria principis egit amor,
Gaudia perpetuis conpenso breuissima poenis.
   Talia consequitur †gaudia talis amor.
Quid species, quid lingua mihi, quid profuit aetas?
   Da lacrimas tumulo, qui legis ista, meo.

Paginae 97, 98 *praeter epigrammata quae edidi habent haec Anthologiae Riesianae* Virginis insano Iulianus captus amore (912 R.). Iupiter astra, fretum Neptunus, Tartara Pluto, Regna paterna tenent, tres tria quisque suum (793 R.), Ad cenam Varus me nuper forte uocauit (796 R.) Graecinum uirgo, puerum Graecinus amabat (797 R.). X. 1. Flāuiam *uide ad* VIII. 1 Corrūpere. 5. amitat emulus XIII. *Videtur epitaphium esse amasii cuiusdam ex principibus Byzantinis. Nam Chrysopolis suburbium Byzantii notissimum. Crediderim puerum Chrysopolitanum cum forma nimis placuisset principi inuidiam conflasse et ob hanc rem fortasse episcoporum monitu in exilium actum fuisse. Miror tamen huiusmodi elogium Latine scriptum extare, si uere puer Graecus fuit.* 1. ganimedes crisipolita.   2. *Simile est quod de se dicit* Helpis *uxor Boetii ap.* Burm. Anth. i. p. 321 Quam procul a patria coniugis egit amor. *Post hoc epigramma sequitur in cod. distichon de decem plagis, deinde sex uersus sic inscripti* Versus cuiusdam metriste. Fraus tua non tua laus, facinus non gloria forme Minuere te fecit sic tibi materiam. Fax tua non tua pax feritas non gratia lingue Scribere te docuit sic tibi grammaticam. Lis tua non tua uis amor non musica muse Iungere te iussit sic tibi rethoricam; *quibus alius aliquis subnexuit* Isti sex uersus proprii sunt heu(? n)riolato Cum sit peruersus, sic dic ita (*f.* dicito) de michiloto.

EPIGRAMMATA COD. DIGBEIANI 65.

XIV.

fol. 12^b. QUOMODO ARISTOTELES FECIT ALEXANDRUM RECEDERE AB ATHENIS.

Magnus Alexander bellum mandarat Athenis.
  Infestus populo totius urbis erat.
Ibat Aristoteles caute temptare tyrannum,
  Si prece uir tantus flectere posset eum.
Quem procul intuitus, sceptrum capitisque coronam   5
  Testans, 'non faciam si qua rogabis' ait,
Mutat Aristoteles causam subtiliter, urbem
  Obsideat, frangat moenia Marte, petit.
Poenituit iurasse ducem, bellumque roganti
  Dat pacem, lusus calliditate uiri.   10

XV.

fol. 57^a. DE FORMA ROMAE.

Vt doceat cunctis se solam nobiliorem
  Vrbibus, effigiem Roma leonis habet.
Miror tam gracilem de tanto corpore uocem,
  Miror posse regi tam magnum lumine solo.

XVI.

ol. 59^a. DE ILLIS QVI CONTRA NATVRAM AGVNT.

Heredes Sodomae uestros aduertite uultus,
  Infames usus diraque facta canam.
Principio rerum mater natura creatis
  Indixit legem, iussa sequente modo.
Fecerat illa uirum; mulier cum facta fuisset,   5
  'O modo facta uirum femina,' dixit, 'habe.'
Lege data tali uir duxit, femina nupsit.
  Et uarii sexus gratia iuncta fuit.

XIV. 1. mandaret.   2. tocius.   3. Aristotiles tirannum.   7. Aristotiles.   9. Penituit.
XV. 3. *Ante* Miror *q adscriptum*.   XVI. *Cum his uersibus comparandi sunt uersus Sodoma inscripti apud Cyprianum, Tom. III. Part iii. p.* 289, *ed. Hartel, et quos Leoninos appellant* Quam prauus mos est pueros praeferre puellis Cum sit naturae ueneris modus iste rebellis *in Cod. Laud.* 86. p. 94.   7. dūxit.

EPIGRAMMATA

  Laetus erat coitus et qui coiere beati,
10   Et celebres ritus disposuere sibi.
  Arrisit natura fauens successibus horum.
   'Haec quoque uenturis foedera' dixit 'erunt.'
  Impia posteritas successit et omnia uertens
   In uitium posuit libera colla sibi.
15   Impia libertas turpes processit in usus,
   Viuat ut arbitrio quilibet ecce suo.
  Heu mala res, mala progenies, mala secta furoris.
   Quam male respondent ultima principiis.
  Vlteriusne loquar? loquar an scelerata silebo?
20   Eloquar, at uobis inuidiosus ero.
  Cum puer intonsus rapitur, cum femina tristis
   Accusat turpi condicione mares,
  Quam scelerata uenus, quam perniciosa uoluptas.
   Haec est quae secum contrahit omne nefas.
25   Naturae legem seruant animalia muta,
   Subsequitur tauro femina iuncta suo.
  Non equs urit equm, non hircus iungitur hirco,
   Diuersi generis collige iuncta duo.
  Ergo quis iste furor? ubi sunt exempla parentum?
30   Et leges et amor et pudor et licitum?

XVI[b].

 A. Fontibus addis aquas et siluas frondibus auges,
   Et nullo quae sunt arida rore rigas.
 B. Non eget aequor aquis, non frondibus indiget Ida,
   Ida tamen frondes accipit, aequor aquas.

XVII.

  Natura faciente uirum grauis incidit error.
   Erroris uitio femina uirque fuit.

11. Arriset. 12. federa. 24. contrait. 26 sqq. *Ouid. Met.* ix. 731 Nec uaccam uaccae nec equas amor urit equarum. Vrit oues aries, sequitur sua femina ceruum. Sic et aues coeunt interque animalia cuncta Femina femineo correpta cupidine nulla est. 27. equum *Post* 30 *sequitur sine interuallo tetrastichon* XVI[b]. Fontibus—aquas, *sed praemisso d quod plerumque additur ubi noua res inducta est. Sed manifestum est uersus* Fontibus—rigas, *ab eo dici qui mulierum causam contra pedicones agit, hos respondere disticho* Non eget—aquas. *Sequitur in cod. hexastichon* Potus Milo sapis, *tum* De hermafrodito Cum mea me mater (786 R.), *tum* XVII Natura faciente uirum, etc.

CODICVM BODLEIANORVM. 23

Simplice materia simplex faciebat et unum,
  Dumque unum faceret, fecit utrumque simul.
Semiuir hic nullo poterit custode teneri,   5
  In cuius uenerem sensus uterque uenit.

XVIII.
DE QVADAM VIDVA.

Luce tuum defles mutata ueste maritum,
  Et deplorato coniuge nocte bibis.
Quid mirum? maestos desiccat lacrima uultus,
  At Bacchi reficit cor tibi triste liquor.
Semper luce fleas et ames conuiuia nocte;   5
  Famosum nostro tempore nomen habes.

XIX.

fol. 60ᵇ.
Lapsus in aeternum fatali lege soporem,
  Officii linquis taedia longa tui.
Ante tibi requiem nox inportuna negabat:
  Nunc dormire simul nocte dieque potes.

XX.

fol. 70ᵃ.
Res male tuta puer nec te committe quibusdam.
  Multa domus multos fertur habere Ioues.
Non tamen expectes Ganymedis crimine caelum,
  Hac modo militia nullus ad astra uenit.
Laud. Lat. 86.
f. 111.
Consecrat aetherias solis Iunonibus arces   5
  Lex melior, manes masculus uxor habet.
Cum doleat culpam suspecti Iuno mariti,
  Mercedem culpae non dolet esse polum.

XXI.

Digb. fol. 70ᵃ.
Aurum Parthorum Crassus sitiebat, et aurum
  Ore bibens sociis proelia morte facit.

XVIII. 3. *mire pro* desiccantur lacrimae maestis uultibus.   XX. *Hoc epigr. nuper edidit Hauréau in libro quem de Hildeberti carminibus conscripsit,* p. 187. *Cuiuscumque est aeui, dignum reor quod accuratius edam; integrum in Laud. Lat.* 86 *inueni, Digb.* 65 *uu.* 1-4 *solos habet.* 1. comit*e, Digb.,* non te *L.* 3. Nolo quod affectes *L.* ganimedis *DL.* 5. iunioribus *cod. Haur.*

EPIGRAMMA COD. LAVD. LAT. 86.

XXII.

fol. 114ᵃ.

Haec duo carta salus, mihi nobis, missa fuerunt,
 Sic commune datum, sic speciale fuit.
Missa mihi socioque salus, res una duobus.
 Nos facit esse tuos res licet una duos.
5 Ambo salutati fuimus, resalutat uterque,
 Sic quod utrique dabas nunc ab utroque capis.
Scripta mihi solus misisti, solus habeto,
 Solus ego soli scripta remitto tibi.
Sic ego, sic socius, ego carmen, uterque salutem,
10 Ecce reportamus, debita quisque sua.

EPIGRAMMATA CODD. SANGALLENSIVM.

XXIII.

397. fol. 42ᵇ.

Quae fueram quondam tenerae uagina medullae,
 Altrix nunc rigidi roboris esse notor.
Ossea nunc patulum producunt germina ramum:
 Siluescit membris dammula pulchra suis.

XXIV.

250. p. 70.
184. p. 245.
347. p. 147.

VERSVS DE QVODAM PATRE QVI BENE NVTRIVIT
FILIVM MATRE EIVS MORTVA ET EVNDEM INTERFECIT
QVIA NOVERCAM SVAM ID EST PATRIS VXOREM POLLVIT.

Fonte lauat genitor quem crimine polluit uxor,
 Et puerum refouet qui iuuenem perimat.

XXII. 3. *Ennod. Epist.* ii. 1. 10 *Hartel* Tu tamen inter ista quasi specialis mali pressus nece concluderis, nesciens temperandum quod per multorum dispersum corda commune est. vi. 35 Hoc munus speciale conputo.   XXIII. *Explicatur altero epigrammate cod. Sang.* 869 (*Dümmler* ii. *p.* 382) DE OSSE DAMMULAE PER QUOD ARBUSCULA CREUIT AD IMPERATOREM HLUDOUICUM Arboris est altrix quondam uagina medullae. Tibia germen habet, nempe bonum omen erit. Quod cortex humore caret, quod durior ipso est Robore miramur, talis in osse uigor. Nil Caesar tibi magne uacat, uenabere dammas, Ossibus ex quarum silua orietur. Age. *Et hoc quidem ex nostro uidetur desumptum.*   XXIV. *Ediderunt Riesius A. L.* 688, *Baehrensius P. L. M.* iii. *p.* 171 *sed ut disticha distraherent. Ex titulo nostri codicis apparet unum esse epigramma.*   1. Fonte *sc. baptismatis.* polluet *Riesius.* uxor *nouerca pueri.*

CODICVM SANGALLENSIVM.

Ante suum gremium portat portatus alumnum,
 Vnum gestat equus, sed duo terga premunt.
Mergitur Hippolytus, mori*t*urus amore nouercae.
 Quem quia fata iuuant, flumina nulla nocent.
In causa Hippolyti uersa est natura parentum,
 Saeua nouerca fouet, quem pater ipse necat.

3. Portat ante portatus alumnum suum gremium *cod.* 250. portatus *in equo puer iam uir factus portat in gremio infantem quem ex se nouerca peperit ut ambo simul mergantur.* 5. Hippolytus *hic est amator nouercae.* ippolitus *cod.* 250. mersurus *codd.* 250, 397. mersu *cod.* 184. moriturus *Riesius. An est* mersurus *intransitiuum?* 6. *h. e.* quamuis mersu *flumine non perit.* 7. causam *cod.* 250. 8. quia *pro* quem 250. *Debuerat nouerca saeuir in priuignum, pater indulgere filio.*

GLOSSAE IN SIDONIVM.

MS. Digb. 172
f. 143.
I. I.

Gaii Sollii Apollinaris Sydonii epistolarum liber primus incipit. Sydonius
Constantio suo salutem.

SIDONIVS iste gratia et rogatu Constantii uiri illustrissimi et magnae scientiae hunc librum in quo ad eum proemiat ex quibusdam transscriptis quarundam epistolarum quas uariis personis et de diuersis causis et negotiis in diuersis temporibus transmisit Con- 5 stantio scribit. Continentur itaque in hoc libro .ix. distinctiones librorum quorum .vii.
Constantio principaliter scribit. Duos uero ultimos secundario. Nam .viii. scribit
Petronio et .ix. Firmino, in quibus ad eum proemiat. illi tum duo .vii. libris Constantii annectuntur, ut ex illis .ix. libris unum fiat uolumen Constantio transmissum. In prima igitur epistola hoc modo tractat, ostendens se auctoritati Constantii fauere debere. 10 Secundo loco ostendens quos uelit imitari in quantumcumque potest et quos non possit imitari et quare non possit ostendit. Tertio loco demonstrans se erga Constantium hunc librum componere, licet multorum detrahentium *super* incepto opere timeat inuidiam, etiam *si* securus sit ab eorum detractione *super* libro panegyrico quem uersibus et metris compositum de laude principum con*scribit*. 15

Major .i. magne. *causa* quoniam de diuersis negotiis scriptae sunt. *persona* quoniam ad diuersas personas scriptae sunt. Quas iubet Constantius supra quamlibet epistolam nominare. *tempus* quoniam in diuersis temporibus. *retractatis* .i. relectis. *exemplaribus* .i. transscriptis. *enucleatis* .i. correctis. Quoniam transscripta multoriens falsa sunt uitio scriptorum. *rotunditatem* in uerbis perfectis. *praesumptuosis*. Quoniam illi magnae 20 scientiae fuerant. *nam de Marco Tullio*. Hic ostendit se non posse imitari Tullium quem Iulius Titianus qui de secta erat Frontonis, maximae scientiae homo, uoluit (eum) imitari et non potuit, in quodam libro uidelicet quem scribit de laude illustrium feminarum. Et quia non potuit Iulius iste Tullium imitari, ideo consocii sui et consectanei .i. de eadem secta siue sententia Frontonis uocauerunt eum simiam oratorum. *propter* 25 *quod* sic uerte literam. *propter quod ceteri quique Frontonianorum* .i. qui erant de secta Frontonis *aemulati* inuidi .i. indignantes *cur* .i. quia *et cet*. Et ideo uocauerunt eum *simiam oratorum*. *ueternosum* uetus et graue, *immane* .i. magnum. *temporum suorum* .i. in tempore suo. *meritorumque praerogatiuam* .i. meritis suis prae aliorum meritis, exigentibus omnibus, praeferebantur. *examinationi* .i. iudicio. *recensendas* .i. legendas. 30 *perquam* .i. ualde. *haesitabundos* .i. dubios. *deinceps* quoniam maximam laudem et famam

10. fauere se debere.   13. supra.   14. si om. supra.   panegerico.   15. componit.
18. relictis.   30. praeferebatur.   legendas *an* relegendas?   31. hesitabundos.

GLOSSAE IN SIDONIVM.

prius s. in pan*egi*rico consecutus est, nunc deinceps dubium est an tantam famam consequi possit ex hoc libro epistolarum. *genuinum* .i. naturalem. *molarem* molares dentes sunt illi interiores quibus teritur cibus. et notat hic per hanc dictionem *fixerit* morem inuidorum qui cum detrahunt aliis dentes molares simul conterunt. *actutum* .i. cito.

      Sydonius Agricolae suo salutem et suam benedictionem.   5
      Saepenumero .i. multoriens. *popularis fama* apud populum. *In quantum* quia oportet epistolam breuem esse. *laudans in te* .s. animi nobilitatem quia talis principis cupis scire mores et habitus. *minus familiariter* .i. maxime extraneis qui non sunt de familia eius. *dote* .i. munere. *ut laudibus* sic lege literam *ut inuidia ne* .i. etiam *regni* .i. in regno maiorum non *defraudet* aliquid et non possit aliquid minuere et detrahere *laudibus* 10 eorum. *exacto* .i. magno et perfecto. *ceruix* .i. collum eius breue non est nec contractum ut caput adhaerens sit humeris, et est ceruix illud ubi conueniunt occipud et collum. *orbes* .i. ocellos. et nota quod hic non describitur uir femineae pulcritudinis sed uir uiribus plenus et cingulo militiae aptissimus et uir robustus. *cilia* oculorum. *flectantur* digitis trahantur. *tegulae* legulae aurium sunt tenues et molles carniculae 15 quae sub auribus pendent. *flagellis* .i. cirris quae recte dicuntur 'loc.' *incuruus* .i. subcuruus .i. non nimis longus. *non obesi* .i. nimis crassi. *succulenti* .i. pleni succo .i. aliquantulum de natura crassi. *recedente aluo* quia circa uentrem gracilis erat et circa pectus spissus. *tuberosum* .i. grossum et durum. *musculis* musculos appellat carnem illam quae utrimque protuberat. *internodia* .i. genua. *mascula* .i. uirilia et grossa. 20 *poplitum* poplites dicuntur 'hamme.' *crura* nota differentiam inter crus et femur. Quoniam femur a genibus est supra, crus uero a genibus est infra. *suris* suras appellat illud grossum carnis quod protuberat in tibiis. *antelucanos* .i. matutinos. *quamquam sit sermo secretus* hoc est interpositio et hoc silentio dicit. *secretus* nobis duobus .s. Sidonio et Agricolae. *pro consuetudine potius quam ratione* hoc dicit propter haeresim arria-25 nam quam Got*hi* celebrabant. Et iste Theodoricus Christianus erat. *sellam* .i. sedem. *armiger* .i. miles. Timebat enim sibi quoniam tirannus erat. *pellitorum* a pellibus ferinis quibus induebantur ut T*h*eodoricum si opus esset defenderent. *pro foribus* .i. extra fores. *exclusa* hoc tractum est a ueteri testamento. In tabernaculo enim erant duo loca diuisa a se per uelum quoddam ductum ex transuerso tabern*acu*li s. sancta sanctorum et 30 sancta. In sanctis sanctorum erat altare t*h*ymiamatis et arca foederis et propiliatorium.
      i. accedere
Ad quem locum non licebat Aaron ascendere nisi semel in anno in die propitiationis. In sanctis autem quae et dicebantur cancella erat altare holocaustorum ubi cotidie sacrificabant. Ista autem pars tabernaculi in qua stabant soli leuitae dicebatur cancellum propter uelum ductum ex transuerso tabernaculi. Nam cancellare est lineam 35 ex transuerso ducere. Vnde cancellarius qui male scripta huiusmodi linia dampnat et inde dicitur cancellatis manibus .i. in modum crucis impositis. Isti igitur pelliti non

    1. panagerico.   2. *genuinum* i. naturalem] *sc. qui cum homine nascitur* (*Schol. Pers. I.* 115).   3. figerit.   6. multociens.   14. apt'ssim' *h. e.* aptus *uel* aptissimus.   25. Sidonio et Agricolae *om.* quam FG.] *Cod. Sidonii Laud.* 104 *habet* potius quam pro ratione.   goti. 28. teodoricum.   30. taberna.   31. timiamatis. propiciatorium.   34. pars tab. ex transuerso tab.   36. lima.

GLOSSAE IN SIDONIVM. 29

erant intra uela sed extra in cancellis .i. non erant in illa domo in qua erat rex
sed in proxima propter eorum murmur. *tractabitur* .i. dignum dilatione. *expedietur* .i.
dignum ut statim tractetur. *solio* .i. sede. *stabulis* ut uideat equos. *neruo* s. arcus.
loro .i. freni. *thecatum* .i. in theca i. in repositione i. in forello. *spicula* .i. sagittam.
implet .i. chordam ponit in illorum conatis capitibus. *admonet* .i. quaerit. *si ab* quasi 5
dicat, Quoniam forte contigit sed raro quod ipse uidens feram aliquam alonge fallitur
.s. ignorans an sit ceruus an cerua et huiusmodi. sed *ictus* eius *destinantis* .i. trahentis
numquam *fallitur* .i frustratur. *profestis* .i. procul a festis. *priuato* priuatum con-
uiuium est non regis sed inferiorum. *cedentibus* .i. plicantibus prae nimio honere argenti.
suspiriosus prae labore et pondere sciforum. *toreumatum* toreuma est lectus tornatilis et 10
tamen hic ponitur pro uestibus quae super lectum sternuntur. *peripetasmatum* .i. corti-
narum a peri quod est circum quia circum domum uel lectum ducuntur. Et sunt uela
a circumducendo dicta eo quod per funes circumducantur per ambitum domus. peri enim
circum petasma uelum. *conchiliata* .i. rubricata. Quoniam in concha latet piscis qui
dicitur murex ex cuius sanguine fit rubra uestis. *bissinum* recte dicitur 'cheinsil,' et 15
est uestis tenuissima et albissima. *paterae* i. scifi. *babundantiam Gallicanam.* Quoniam
Galli parce comedunt et non ultra modum. *Italam* ubi cito comedunt uel cito
seruientes eunt fercula portantes. *publicam* .i. multos seruientes. *priuatam.* Quoniam
quidam seruiebant de coquina et alii de penu non intermiscue. *de luxu sabbatario*
quoniam in sabbatis illi tenebant et celebrabant maxima festa ut nunc Iudaei. *secundas* 20
.i. 'des'
fastidit .i. taediat .i. indignatur. *facere secundas* .i. habere. *tesseras* deceptorias, et etiam
indignatur *timere* secundas aduersarii. *sine colludio* colludium dicitur a con .i. simul
et ludo. *bilis* .i. ira. *recrudescit* .i. iterum fit cruda uel crudelis relicto ludo. *pulsantes*
ostium s. ut possint intrare ad regem, ut possint negotia sua et causas pertractare. *submo-*
uentes cum uirgis. *ambitus* ambientes uel ambitiosi. *concubiae* Prima uigilia noctis 25
Fol. 143ᵇ.   fax appellatur, secunda concubium uel conticinium, tertia nox intempesta, quarta
galli cantus siue gallicinium, quinta antelucanum. *sane* .i. certe. *intromittuntur* ad
cenam regiam. *ydraulica* i. musica ab ydor quod est aqua. unde ydraulia .i. organum,
ydor enim aqua, aule cannulae. Aqua enim multum iuuat organum, quod in ydraulia
potest uideri. unde in musa dicitur quasi moysa. Moys enim aqua. Vnde Moyses dicitur 30
aquaticus quia de aqua fuit sublatus. *subfonasco* r. dicitur 'suschant' a sub et fonos quod
est sonus. *achroama* r. 'surchant' i. altum et melodum. Tria enim sunt genera artis
musicae. s. chromaticum diatonicum et enharmonicum. Quorum mollissimum est chromaticum. *lyristes* a lira. *eburaules* qui ducit choream. *mesochorus* qui de medio choro
ceteros ad cantandum inuitat. *fidibus* .i. chordis. *gazae* sunt diuitiae, sed hic ponitur 35
pro militibus.

1. infra.   4. teca.   forello] forellus uagina *Du Cange*.   5. cordam.   conatis *i. q.*
furcatis. q. d.   6. fallatur.   8. profestis] *Paul. Diac.* Profesti dies procul a religione
numinis diuini.   9. reg.   10. cisforum.   11. peri patasmatum.   cortinarum]
'curtains.'   16. ciffi.   17. ytalam.   21. indignatur. thessaras.   23. pulsā.   24. submo.
25. ambicientes.   32. r. *i.e.* romanice.   33. cromaticum, enermoniacum.   34. coraules.
coream. mesocorus. coro.   35. cordia. gaze.

GLOSSAE IN SIDONIVM.

I. 3.

Filimatio.

oscitare proprium est desidiosorum os aperire. os citare enim est os aperire et dictum est ab otio. *desidiosus* .i. ignauus .i. piger. Inde desidia et ignauia idem est quod pigritia siue segnities. Vnde segnis dicitur quasi sine igne. *mussitat* mussare .i. murmurare siue dubitare et inde mussitare frequentatiuum uerbum. *suspicere* .i. sursum 5 aspicere. *despicere* deorsum aspicere. *obiter* .i. interim. *antiquare* .i. antiquum facere. *priuilegium* .i. priuata lex. *stertere* dicuntur illi qui obmurmurant et tractum est a more dormientium. Qui cum firmiter dormiunt stertunt quod romanice dicitur 'Rute.' *perniciter* .i. cito, antepenultima producta, et deriuatur a per et nitor, pernix pernicis ante penultima producta. correpta significat detrimentum a nece deriuata. *sarcire* .i. re- 10 parare et *resarcire* .i. redintegrare.

I. 4.

Syd. Gaudentio Sat.

Macte esto .i. aucte. Istam epistolam mittit Gaudentio. De quo locutus est in priore epistola illum commendans quod ex plebeia familia factus sit summus magistratus et uituperans nobiles ignauos qui prae ignauia sunt absque honore. *sic adolescentium.* 15 Hic reddit rationem quare patres eorum castigabant. Videbant enim patres puerorum comparationem quamdam et similitudinem inter pannos textiles et eloquia puerorum. Quoniam sicut panni textiles post texturam facilius contrahuntur quam extenduntur, sic facilius pueri a magnis reuocantur quam ad magna inuitantur et ideo patres eorum eos castigabant. *declamatiunculas* .i. causas. 20

I. 5.

Syd. Heronio.

Secundum conuentionem .i. secundum quod disposueramus domi. *auspicor* .i. diuinare. *Rodanusiae* .i. Lugduni. Quae sic uocatur quoniam supra Rodanum sita est. *uered orum* ueredi sunt equi qui portant uel trahunt redam. Veredarii autem sunt magistri redarum, et tamen unum saepissime ponitur pro altero. *silex* .i. rupis. Inde silicernus .i. curuus a 25 cernendo terram. *fornix* idem est quod testudo arcuata siue criptica a cripta. tae quod est proprie 'cruste.' *commessaliter* ad mensam. *Phaetontiadas* accusatiuus Graecus ponitur pro Phaetontiades et sunt Phaetontiades sorores Phaetontis. Quae flentes pro lapsu fratris a caelo membra eius collegerunt a fluuio in quem cecidit et ibi mutatae sunt in arbores. *commenticias* .i. fictas et fabulosas a commentor. taris quod est componere. *uluosum.* Vlua 30 dicitur herba quaedam quae recte uocatur 'chenapie.' *acernisque nemoribus uestiebantur.* Acernis .i. de acere arbore unde habetur haec acer et hoc acer. haec acer, dum stat

1. Filimatio *sic Laud.* 104.   4. sine igne.   5. frequentatiuum uerbum] *Addit codex haec* Et inde amussis quod est perpendiculum caementariorum quo perpenditur maceriei aequalitas et dicitur amussis quasi sine duhitatione et amussim .i. indubitanter et inde Musio .i. fatuus. *Quae quamquam ridenda uidentur, conspirant cum Paulo Diac. s. u.* Amussim regulariter, tractum a regula ad quam aliquid exaequatur quae amussis dicitur. Quidam amussim dicunt esse non tacite, quod muttire interdum dicitur loqui.   18. extendantur.   19. inuitentur.   22. conguentionem *uulgo legitur* commune consilium.   25. silicernus] *Fulg. Exp. Serm. Antiq.* 560 silicernios dici uoluerunt senes iam incuruos quasi iam sepulchrorum suorum silices cernentes.

GLOSSAE IN SIDONIVM. 31

crescendo in uiriditate, hoc acer huius aceris ipsa excisa. Vnde uersus auctoris Vile fuistis acer. *scirpis enodis* .i. iuncis sine nodis. *dexterior* .i. melior. Sicut enim a sinistra dicitur sinisterior pars .i. deterior ita a dextra pars dexterior .i. melior. *discerptus* .i. separatus et quandoque ponitur discerpere pro dilaniare. Vnde dicitur Poenis discerpitur iste. *pulte* puls pultis recte dicitur ' puz ' sed hic ponitur pro cloaca quia tenax est. *lin-* 5 *trium* .i. scapharum. *glutino* hoc glutinum .i. gluten .i. ' giu ' sed hic ponitur pro cloaca. *glarea* glarea .i. lutum illud tenax quod sub †marinis fluuiis latet. Sed tamen proprie ponitur pro lapillis harenosis in aquis iacentibus. *cisterna defaecabilis* sine faece. *fons irriguus* .i. currens. *puteus illimis* sine limo. *alternante* ' entrecaniant.' Quoniam qui febricitat modo calores patitur modo frigora. *alternante* .i. ' entrecangant ' unde sequi- 10 tur *ne spiritu aeris uenenatis flatibus inebriato et modo calores alternante modo frigora uaporatum corpus inficiatur. uaporatum* .i. calidum uel tepidum. *thermas* thermae sunt loca calida ad balneandum. *naumachium*† naumachian† dicebatur locus publicus ubi erant aquae turbidae pluuis congregatae. Et dicitur naumachia a naue et machia quod est pugna. *membris male fortibus* .i. debilibus. *explosum languorem* .i. extra collisum uel 15 percussum. Complodere .i. simul collidere. Vnde Complosis manibus .i. simul collisis uel percussis. Diplodere idem. unde uersus Nam diplosa sonat quantum uesica pepedit. *pauxillum* .i. parum a paulo. *paxillum* paxillus a palo .i. sude .i. ' pel.' *exarabantur* scribebantur. *festenminus* .i. cantus. *macellum* .i. ' mazazerre.' Inde macellarius .i. ' mazerre ' a mactando sic dictus. *talassia*. Talassia sunt maria. Talassa enim Graece Latine dicitur 20 mare. Inde bitalassum .i. duplex mare, ubi duo .s. maria concurrunt .i. ubi quaedam terra se extendit in mare ita ut acutum terrae illius mare habeat ex utraque parte sui. Vnde dicitur quod Paulus apostolus naufragatus est in bitalasso .s. acumine
                                      .i. truillerias
terrae sic extensae in mare. Inde talassia .i. loca maritima, *inter scurrilitates hystrionum* .i. lenocinium lecatorum. *totus actionum seriarum* .i. ' discretariun.' Inde dicitur Serio 25 agit et intendit .i. discrete. Idem est seriatim aduerbium. *palmata* est uestis quaedam nobilium quae dabatur alicui ob aliquam palmam .i. uictoriam quam fecerat. *ciclas* cicladis .i. ' ciclatun.' *pronuba* est illa quae cum noua nupta ad domum nubentis domini uenit. *paranimphus* est ille qui cum nubente marito ad domum uenit sicut pronuba cum nupta. *inglorius* .i. ignobilis .i. sine gloria. *molimina* .i. machinamenta a molior . liris. 30

I. 6.   Sydonius Eutropio salutem.

domestici (sic) .i. familiaris. Vnde dicuntur domestici illi qui in intima domo nutriuntur et comedunt. *capessenda* .i. frequenter capienda. *munia* .i. officia et munera non a manu dicta sed a munio. *trabeatis* trabea quaedam uestis est pretiosa quasi ultra alias uestes beans et pacificans. *iuuenta* .i. iuuentus. *subulci*. Sicut dicuntur bubulci qui 35 custodiunt boues, sic dicuntur subulci qui custodiunt sues et porcos. *runcantes*. Run-

1. auctoris *Ouid. Am. I.* 11. 28.   2. cirpis enodis. iunctis.   4. penis discerpitur iste] *non repperi*.   12. termas terme *uulgo legitur* formas.   16. conplosis manibus *Petron. S.* 18 *et* 137.   17. uersus *Hor. S. I.* 8. 46 *ubi* pepedi.   19. secenninus.   20. talassa. 25. lecatorum *i. e.* parasitorum.   32. ima.   33. cupienda.   34. *Irid. Orig. XIX.* 24. 8. 36. sues et boues porcos. runcā.

GLOSSAE IN SIDONIVM.

care est aliquam herbam nociuam euellere. Sicut auencare est proprie auenas extirpare et ponitur pro euellere. *curuus* .i. inclinus. *populari* deuastare. *cernuus* pronus uel humilis. *expergiscere* expergiscor gisceris .i. 'aueiller' uel 'ebruscer.' *eneruis* .i. sine neruis uel sine uiribus. *marcidus* a marceo ces. *effetis* .i. sine fetu .i. inutilibus ad proelia. *ligone* quod romanice dicitur 'picois.' *musta* noua uina. *uinetis* .i. locis ubi crescunt uineae. 5 Vnde dicitur *multiplicatis tibi spumabunt musta uinetis. mulctram.* Haec mulctra uas in quo mulgetur. *olida* olentia a uerbo oleo les. Vnde dicitur Iste cibus bene olet. *caula* 'faude' .i. oulle. *pinguis* pastor .i. propter pinguia pascua et pinguia armenta. *faeculento com.* .i. pleno faece. Inde faeculentia. *mauis ut aiunt* homines. *Epicuri* genitiui

Fol. 144ª. casus. *dogmatibus copulari* uel implicari. *testor maiores* .i. duco in testimonium. *huic* 10 *me noxae non esse confinem* et non inputabitur mihi culpa haec.

I. 7.
Angit .i. 'Destreint' Inde angor 'Destresce.' *queror* .i. conqueror. *non insultatorie* .i. ex affectu reprehendendi. Vel *insul.* .i. derisorie. Vnde *insultare* est deridere. *ludibrium* .i. ridiculum siue deliramentum. Vnde dicitur Ad poenae ludibrium .i. derisum. 15 *miseraremur.* Misereri superiorum est quando miseriam habent cum aliquo. Miserari autem omnium est quando .s. aliquis de aliquo quandam habet miseriam et doloris conpassionem. Et construitur transitiue cum accusatiuo casu. *popularitas* .i. adulatio. Vnde dicitur *praefecturam primam gubernauit cum magna popularitate. populatione* .i. deuastatione dictum a populor laris. *successuros.* Timebat enim ne propter aes alienum 20 remoueretur a praefectura et ei substitueretur aliquis fortis et nobilis. *aemulabatur* .i. inuidebat. *uallatus* circumdatus quoniam uallum romanice dicitur 'balie.' *destinatus* .i, missus. *interceptas litteras* .i. extortas et raptas a scriptore ubi eas scripsit uel ubi eas ab Aruando dictatas legit. *Intercipere* uero proprie *interrecipere* ut Interceptus aquis. *perimachiam* circumpugnationem et machinamenta accusatorum. Peri circum, machia 25 pugna. Vnde monomachia .i. singularis pugna. *occulere* celare. in *actionibus repetundarum.* Actio repetundarum est propria appellatio cuiusdam actionis quam intendere potest quis aduersus illum qui aliena rapuit et possidet. *subdolis* .i. dolosis. Vnde dicitur Nihil loquamur subdolum .i. dolosum. *bullas.* Bullae autem sunt quando gutta pluulae cadit in aliquam aquam et facit aquam inferiorem resilire, et sunt plenae aeris 30 et uacuae et inanes. *crepantes* .i. sonantes quoniam *cum* franguntur sonant. *serica* .i. 'seie.' *trapezitarum* Trapezitae sunt monetarii siue cambiatores. *inuolucra* .i. ludicra sicut anulos monilia et cetera huiusmodi quia inuoluuntur in saccis nec semper exponuntur emptoribus ne deturpentur pluuia et uento et alia intemperie. *Inuolucrum* uero proprie est 'trusse.' *pumicatus* .i. planatus leuigatus cum pumice. *pumicatus* a 35

---

6. spumabant u *in* a *mutata.* 12. I. 7. *titulus deest.* 15. Ad pene ludibrium.
18. acusatiuo. 21. emulabatur. 24. arueno. Interceptus aquis] *Stat. Theb. IX.* 509.
25. acusatorum. 26. oculere. 29. Nihil loquamur subdolum.] *ex hymno* Lux ecce surgit aurea, *Breuiar. Rom. Part. Aest. Fer. V. Ad laudes, quem locum indicauit mihi amicus A. Robertson.* 31. cum om. 32. Trapezetarum. trapezete.

GLOSSAE IN SIDONIVM. 33

puniceo colore .i. rubeo. *semipullati* .i. seminigri. pullus la lum idem est quod niger. *concreti* .i. non tonsis capillis. Sed concretus est proprie coaceruatus uel coniunctus. Inde concretio .i. conmassatio .i. in unam massam conpositio. *Concitato* .i. citato. *collegis* .i. sociis. Collega enim est uicinus uel socius. *paenitudo* .i. paenitentia. *fascibus* honoribus. *exauctoratus* spoliatus .i. extra auctoritatem positus. *politum* .i. leuigatum 5 uel planatum. *addictus* duplicem habet significationem. Dicitur enim addictus .i. coactus. Vnde Horatius (Epp. I. 1. 14) Nullius addictus iurare in uerba magistri. Dicitur etiam addictus adiudicatus. Vnde Addictus est morti (Cic. de Off. III. 10. 45). *accuratus* est ille qui maximam curam habet de se ut bene uestiatur et pulcre. *delibutum* unctum perfusum. *ergastulum* .s. locus ubi damnati stabant ad laborandum. *mulctatus* 10 punitus. Vnde multatus capite dicitur, quoniam multa est poena. *deuenustatus* deturpatus. *nausea* est appetitus uomendi. *unco* .i. 'Croc.' Vnde uncinum pomorum et Cum unco trahebatur. *carnifices* tortores qui praesunt reis puniendis. *Augusti* dicebantur antiquitus omnes Imperatores. *notas inustas* cauterio inustas. Cauterium autem est ferrum calidum quo fit nota aliqua in damnatis. 15

I. 8.   Sydonius Candidiano Salm.

Exprobrare .i. 'repruuer.' *uerna* seruiens uel cliens uel seruus uel uernaculus. *Padano culice.* Candidianus cum in municipio esset Rauennae cotidie sero et mane audiuit ranas garrientes in palude circa illud castellum et culices. *culex* autem est illa musca quae dispergit boues eos pungendo et dicitur alio nomine oestrum. *domicilia* .i. 20 domus. Vel domicilia .i. cilicia domus quod romanice est 'seuerunde.' *territorium* dicitur praedia omnia quae circa aliquod municipium est. *dote* .i. dotalicio.

I. 9.   Sydonius Heronio.

Euentilatas opes .i. expensas. *laribus* .i. domibus. *comiter* .i. 'curteisement.' Vnde *comis* .i. 'curteis.' Vnde uersus prouerbialis Carne canore comis me Tallit femina comis. 25 *aenigmata* .i. obscura dicta. *schemata* .i. figuras. *Commata* membra siue distinctiones. Quia tria sunt *cola, comma, periodus*. *Periodus* est quando finitur uersus. *Comma* quando suspensiua est oratio per metrum. *Cola* quando .s. oratio profertur cum distinctionibus, punctis .s. interpositis. *mecanemata*. Sciunt citharizare cum digitis et simphonizare et alia per musica instrumenta. *cunctatio* mora. Vnde cunctanter .i. morose et incunctanter .i. 30 sine mora. *fastigatissimi* .i. altissimi et primates a fastigio dicti. *seposita praerogatiua partis armatae* seposita .i. seorsum posita praerogatiua .i. 'eslitte' .i. exceptis militibus

---

4. sotiis. sotius. penitudo. penitentia. 6. dupplicem. 8. acuratus. 10. *Praecedunt in codice haec* Ergastulum Ergas labor unde *quae omisi tamquam nimis inscita*. dampnato. dampnati. 11. pena. 12. unccinum. 15. dampnatis. 21. *Cf. Roquefort Glossaire de la Langue Romane*. 'Seueronde, seuerons, seueronde, subgronde: La partie inférieure d'une couverture de maison: celle qui est en saillie sur la rue, pour jeter les eaux pluviales hors du mur.' 26. scemata. comata. 27. coma. 29. puctis. 30. *Post* instrumenta *addita sunt haec* Mecaneuma dicitur ab artibus mecanicis et neuma quod est cantus dulcis. Alii dicunt quod mecaneumata sunt solsationes *cf. Du Cange* Solfizare notas musicales canere.

F   [1 5.]

GLOSSAE IN SIDONIVM.

imperatoris. *genii.* Genius est deus naturae qui praeest nascentibus. Vnde genialis .i. naturalis. *succinctius fabor* .i. breuiter. *sera* .i. tarda. Sera ae obstaculum cum quo serantur ostia. Hoc serum .i. 'wege.' Vnde caseus dicitur quasi carens sero. *illicet* .i. ilico. *fastis* fasti sunt libri annales. Vt kalendaria et in quibus facta nobilium scribebantur. Aliquando accipiuntur fasti pro honoribus. *carminantem* cantantem carmina. 5 *seria* .i. utilia. *serietas* utilitas. Vnde in eadem epistola dicitur *Reditum est in publicam serietatem. rostra.* Rostra nauium hostium deuictorum in foro ponebantur publico ubi praetores ius dicebant. *contionante* .i. loquente et recitante in contione. *lati claui.* Clauus est quoddam genus pallii ex purpura facti et est latum et magnum. Quo induebantur nobiles. *quisquilias* .i. turpe carmen meum. Quoniam quisquiliae sunt sordes et 10 rudera .i. purgamenta quae a domo eiciuntur. *Clios* Musa. *phalerae* proprie sunt ornamenta equorum et hic ponitur pro coloribus rhetoricis et flosculis. *epitaphistarum* .i. eorum qui scribunt epitaphia supra mortuos. *Epitaphium* uero dicitur super sepulcrum ab epi supra et taphos sepulcrum. *neniis* .i. cantibus qui cantabantur supra mortuos.

I. 10.   Sydonius Campaniano Salutem.   15

Accepi per praefectum. Campanianus iste quaestor erat a senatu Romae constitutus .s. ut senatui in adquirenda annona tempore famis seruiret. *sane* certe. *raptim* cito. Vnde uersus Nam data raptim etc.

I. 11.   Montio.

Fol. 144ᵇ.

Petis. Iste Montius rogauit Sydonium ut ei mitteret quandam inuectionem quam 20 fecisse dicebatur de Paeonio qui plebeius erat genere et ad honores per scelera sua et factiones ascenderat. Quia ut filiam suam nobili uiro daret dedit cum ea infinitam pecuniam. Qui etiam semel cum imperator mortuus esset et esset regnum sine domino sua auctoritate inuasit Gallos regendos. *disertissime* sapientissime. Vnde *disertus* sapiens. *perperam* malum et iniquum uel fraudulenter. *themati* materiae. *Calaber* Horatius. 25 *suditate.* Ille nude loquitur qui de rebus obscenis loquitur. Obscenum autem dicitur a caeno quod est lutum. Vnde obscenius .i. foedius. *capessendo* .i. cupiendo. *factione* coniuratione in malum uel deceptione. *fascibus* honoribus. *interregnum.* Vna est dictio et est inter regnum .s. illud spatium quod est post mortem praecedentis regis et ante electionem futuri. *numerariorum.* Numerarii sunt, siue nummularii, qui numerant publi- 30 cum nummum. *codicillis.* Codicillos hic appellat epistolas in quibus solebant scribere Romani aliquibus gentibus ut hunc siue illum reciperent imperatorem uel praefectum uel in aliquem alium magistratum. *tribunal* sedes iudicis. *uitricus* dicitur qui habet matrem alterius in uxorem. Vnde uersus Vitricus et gladiis et acuta dimicat hasta. *praeconia* .i. laudes. Vnde praeconor naris .i. commendare. *postridie* aduerbium .i. post 35 triduum. *edulium* .i. prandium ab edendo. *Caesaris.* Omnes principes antiquitus dice-

8. concionante.   9. clauum.   12. rethoricis.   14. cantibustantur.   15. Campaniano *sic cod. Laud.*   18. Nam data raptim] *Non repperi.*   21. peonio.   22. accenderat.   23. domina.   25. temati.   26. obcenis *et sic semper.*   33. uictricus.   34. uersus] *Ouid. Rem.* 27 *ubi* dimicet Victricus. preconia.   36. Cesaris.

bantur Caesares. *cachinnus* .i. cum risu derisio. *stipadium* a stipe pandenda uel a stipando dicitur. Est enim tabula rotunda super quam fercula panduntur uice stipis. *decernas* .i. iudices. *simultatibus* .i. latentibus odiis. *exertum* .i. extractum. Vnde *mucro exertus*. Est autem exero ris idem quod extendo unde dicitur Ingessit se super exertam ceruicem .i. extensam. *pressus* .i. coactus. *conglobatorum* in congerie circumpositorum 5 et dicitur a globo quod est congeries uel aceruus uel strues uel agger unde aggero ras.

II. 1.   Hecdicio.

Duo nunc. Hanc epistolam scribit Sidonius Hecdicio, fratri uxoris Sydonii, fortissimo .s. militi, inuitans eum ut in Aruerniam redeat ad expugnandum et expellendum Seronatum crudelissimum tirannum qui Aruerniam depopulabatur cum eam regere 10 deberet. Seronatus proprium nomen est et dicitur Seronatus per antifrasim quasi nimis cito natus quia tirannus numquam deberet nasci. *propinare* est proprie potum afferre uel ministrare. *ex asse* perfecte. *dissimulati.* Quia mos est tirannorum antequam habeant honores aliquos simulare se esse simplices et iustos. Cum autem ad honores peruenerint statim ostendunt sub qua pelle prius latuerunt. *per dies* .i. De die in diem et magis et 15 magis. *seruiliter* .i. uiliter .i. citra honestum modum. *addicit* iudicat. *ructat* 'ruter' romanice dicitur. Inde ructus tus tui. Vnde dicitur Ructu uesano. Eructare uero producere. Vnde Eructauit cor m. u. bon. *apicibus* litteris .i. elementis primis. Et dicitur apex quod superscribitur litterae uel summitas cuiuslibet litterae. *comparauit* emit. *numerarii* sunt qui publicum nummum recipiunt et in scripta redigunt quid acceperint. 20

II, 2.   Sydonius Domitio suo sal.

Ruri in rure. *causaris* conquereris. *decedit* .i. cedit .i. dat ei locum. ponitur tamen decedere pro mori uel pro migrare ab hoc saeculo. *axem scithicum* .i. polun septemtrionalem. *squalet* .i. durescit. *Squama* est illud uillosum et durum quo tegitur piscis. *biuleis* .i. apertis ab hiando. *carbaso* .i. uelo .i. lineo panno. Quia carbasa sunt ex lino. 25 *bombice* .i. ueste serica. Quoniam bombix est uermis qui sericum emittit. *endromidatus* uestitus pellibus siue pellicea grossa ex ouibus facta. *auenter* Id est auide ab aueo aues quod est cupere. Inde auidus quod est cupidus uel improbus. *caedua* dicitur illa silua quae si caedatur cito succrescit alia. *strues* lignorum est fasciculus simul ligatus. *imbricarentur* imbrices sunt stillicidia in quibus aqua imbrium recipitur, et concaua sunt. 30 *lacunar* est †illa summitas domus. *lubrici* pugiles .i. athletae qui inunguunt se oleo ut facilius elabi possint a manibus oppugnantium. *palaestritae* .i. luctantes. Quoniam palaestra est lucta. *gimnasiarchae* dicuntur magistri gimnasii .i. scholae palaestricae.

1. caesares. stipadium] *sic etiam in Laud.* 104 *scriptum est* a stipe uel a stipando dicitur pandenda. 3. mucro exertus *etiam Stat. Theb. X.* 412 *reperitur*. 9. aruenniam. 10. serenatum. aruenniam. 13. dissimilati. 18. Eructauit cor. m. u. bon. *Psalm. XLIV.* 1. 19. comparauit *immo* comparat. 21. II. 2. Domicio. 25. hyando. lineo. 26. bombex. endromedatus. 29. *Cf. Dig. L.* 16. 30 Silua caedua est, ut quidam putant, quae in hoc habetur, ut caederetur. Seruius eam esse quae succisa rursus ex stirpibus aut radicibus renascitur. 31. †illa] *Notandus hic usus pronominis, ubi nos dicimus* 'so and so' *uel* 'one,' *ut ex compluribus locis Digestorum ostendit H. I. Roby, Introduction to Iustinian's Digest; p.* 145. allete. 32. palestrite.

GLOSSAE IN SIDONIVM.

genuino conchylio .i. naturali rubore. *tugurria* .i. domus pastorum. *mapalia* sunt domus paruae mercatorum dictae a manu et palo. Differentia inter *pilam* et *columnam*. columna fit ex uno solo lapide uel ligno, pila ex multis lignis uel lapidibus simul appositis. Vnde dicitur pila pontis et monasterii. *Columna* uero medius lapis in fenestra supportans superluminare. *canales* sunt ubi aquae currunt in plumbis. Haec iuba .i. ' creste ' et 5 proprie dicitur equorum. *collirium* dicitur a lirin Graece quod est uarium Latine. Inde collirium quasi ex pluribus commixtum. *extimus* .i. extremus. *appendicium* .i. 'Appentiz.' *animatus* .i. ' espris.' *fuligo* ' soth.' *camino* .i. ' chemenee.' *abstemius* abstinens a uino. Vnde temulentus quasi plenus temeto .i. uino. *cubicularius* ' chamberlene.' *dormitare* frequenter dormire. *dormire* uero notat magnum somnum. *uolupe* 10 .i. uoluptuose. Vel *uolupedales cicadae* .i. ' grisilim.' Quia uolant circa pedes. Sicut *nudipedales homines* quia nudis incedunt pedibus. *oscines corui* quia nimis clamando os aperiunt. *philomela* ' Russenole.' *Prognen* hirundinem quia mutata erat in hirundinem. *minurientem* .i. uocem minutim proferentem. *armentalem camoenam* .i, ' frestel.' Et sunt foramina illa sic proportionaliter facta ut amoene canat. *insomnes* uigiles. *titiri* pastores 15 a Titiro Virgiliano pastore. *greges tinnibulatos* .i. sonantes cum tintinnabulis. *per depasta buceta* .i. per pinguem pasturam quoniam ibi pascuntur boues. Quia oues de nocte pascuntur in loco ubi in die boues pascebantur. *Lenocinabuntur* .i. exercebunt lenocinium .i. libidinem. Sed in hoc loco dicitur *sopori tuo lenocinabuntur* .i. allicient te sopori. Quoniam lenones romanice sunt ' amacheurs.' *uulgare* publicare. *tilia* .i. 20 quoddam genus arboris quod romanice dicitur ' teil.' *alluuio* .i. latens aquae incrementum. *humectare* .i. facere humidum. *coalescit* coagulat. *algidis* frigidis. *litoribus algosis* .i. lutosis. Quoniam alga est quod mare eicit et in mare crescit. *turgescit* .i. tumescit. *salebratim* .i. saltuatim. Quoniam salebrae sunt loca aspera et saxosa. *per cola subterranea* .i. per meatus. *abdomen* minis .i. pinguedo. *lemborum* .i. scapharum. 25 *lubrici scirporum cirri* cirrus Romanice ' loc.' *lubrici* ex aqua. *uluarum* quaedam herbae sunt quae in uiuariis super enatant. quas si detrudas in aquas statim resurget sicca. *salicum glaucarum* quia glaucum colorem habent .i. pallidum. *naualibus giris* .i. circuitionibus. *Scrupulus* dicitur esse in quaestionibus difficilibus. Dicitur etiam scrupulus lapis qui calcantibus molestiam infert. Inde dicitur scrupulosus animus .i. molestus. Inde 30 scrupulosa res aspera et difficilis.

Labirintum .i. domus Daedali.

7. *appendicium*] *sed codices Sidonii habent* appendix, *quamquam* appendicium *reperitur apud Hieronymum.* 10. sompnum. 11. uel uolupedales] *Videtur esse coniectura glossatoris.* 12. Nudipedalia *uocabulum Tertulliani et Hieronymi. Fuerunt sacra nudis pedibus facta ut pluuia eliceretur. Petron.* 44. Antea stolatae ibant nudis pedibus in cliuum ... et Iouem aquam exorabant. Itaque statim urceatim plouebat; aut tunc aut numquam; et omnes redibant udi tamquam mures. 12. Oscines] *Varro L. L. VI.* 76 Oscines quae ore faciunt auspicium. 13. philomena. prognem. 14. camenam. 15. amene. insompnes. 22. Coaggulat. 23. Algoso litore *legitur ap. Auson. Epist. VII.* 2. 43. littoribus. in mare crescit] *Vnde hoc sumpsit? Ipse* in mari *dicturus erat.* 26. cirporum. lubrici.

GLOSSAE IN SIDONIVM.

II. 7.

Ex solido .i. ex toto.

II. 8.

Iustitium dicitur quasi iuris statio. *Vispiliones*. Quidam dicunt esse differentiam inter uispiliones .i. latrones qui ui spoliant et uispillones qui mortuos ad tumulandum 5 deportant, sed unum trahitur ab alio .i. romanice 'ribauz.' *sandapila* .i. feretrum. Vnde *sandapilarii* portantes feretrum. *libitina* .i. feretrum, per contrarium sic dictum quia minime libeat. *ueniam* .i. cantum supra mortuos. *Prensitare* .i. prendere. *decimam trieteridem* .i. xxx annum. Quoniam eteris est annus. Inde trieteris .i. spatium trium annorum. 10

II. 9.

Sidonius Dionisio Sal.

Quaeris interrogas. *prodere* propalare. *destinatis* .i. missis. *exploratores* .i. 'espies.' *aucupari* .i. aues capere. *pastoria diuerticula* .i. locus ubi pastores diuertebantur propter pluuiam. *culina* .i. coquina. *lancem* .i. libram uel discum. *catastropharum* cata iuxta strophos conuersio. Inde catastropha dicitur *sphaera* quae uersatur in manibus. *com-* 15 *petitiones* .i. interpellationes. *tesserarum* .i. talorum. Inde *tesserarii* .i. magistri talorum. *affatim* .i. habunde. *pluteos* .i. 'karoles' supra quos scribunt clerici. *machaera* gladius longus ex una tantum parte acutus. Inde *archymachyrus* uir habens potestatem faciendi iuris. *clepsydra* .i. horologium aquaticum dictum a clepo pis quod est furari. *iurulenta caro* .i. caro elixa, a iure .s. in quo caro decoquitur. Ius autem plures habet significa- 20 tiones. Dicitur enim ius necessitudinis .i. sanguinis. Vnde Iste iure necessitudinis .i. consanguinitatis contingit mihi. (Dig. I. 1, 12.) Locus etiam in quo ius redditur (Dig. I. 1, 11) dicitur ius. Vnde Confessi in iure pro conuictis habentur. Ius etiam dicitur potestas. (Dig. XXVI, 1, 1, Inst. I. 13. 1.) Vt cum dicitur Iste est sui iuris. Ius quoque dicitur instrumentum uel forma petendi. Vt Actio est ius per se quaerendi 25 quod sibi debetur .i. forma uel instrumentum quo quisque quod suum est petit. (Dig. XLIV. 7, 51.) Ius quoque dicitur iuris rigor. Vt ibi Inter ius et aequitatem etc. Ius praeterea dicitur cibus delicatior quem nos uulgariter dicimus salsamentum uel condimentum. Vnde Terentius Panem atrum in iure hesterno deuorauit. Vnde uersus Vt facias offas in iure meo tibi do fas. Nam et aqua crassior in qua carnes sunt 30 elixae non simpliciter ius sed ius carnium dicitur. Ius quoque dicitur meritorium. Sicut habes in distinctione iustitiae. Vnde Iustitia est constans et perpetua uoluntas

---

4. Iusticium. 7. Sandapili. 9. trieteridem. teris. triateris. 11. Dionisio] *Cod. Laud.* Donidio. salt. 15. sphaera] *aperte uitiosa interpretatio.* 17. machaera] *Isid. Orig. XVIII.* 6, 2. 18. Archimacherus magister coquinae *affertur a Du Cangio ex reg. cod. Paris.* 7679. *Addit codex* Sed saepissime ponitur pro seneschallo et hic et in benefy. *At nihil ap. Senecam de archimachiro, sed uidetur respicere locum de Benef. V.* 24. 19. clepsedra. 25. ius per se quaerendi] *immo persequendi ut ex Inst. IV.* 6. 1, *Dig. XLIV.* 7. 51 *ostendit mihi T. E. Holland, cui hos locos omnes ex Inst. et Dig. debeo.* 29. Terentius] Eun. V. 4. 17 Quo pacto ex iure hesterno panem atrum uorent *ubi Bembinus habet* deuorent *teste Vmpfenbachio.*

GLOSSAE IN SIDONIVM.

ius suum cuique tribuens .i. meritum. (Dig. I. 1. 10.) *paulisper* .i. parumper. *marcida* .i. 'flestrie.' Vnde hic dicitur *Torpore meridiano paulisper equitabamus quo facilius pectora marcida cibis cenatoriae fami exaecueremus. asseclarum* .i. famulorum .i. uernulorum. Dicitur enim uernulus et uernula. *stridere* .i. 'Crustre.' *quamprimum* .i. cito.

II. 10.

Vsque quaque .i. perfecte. *postquam ab alterutro discessimus* ego a te et tu a me. *pronuba*. Pronuba est illa quae cum noua nupta domum uiri nupti petit ut eam custodiat et ei seruiat. *stupula* romanice 'stuble.' *culmus* .i. 'caume' .i. stipula. *bractea*. Bractea est lamina spissa auri. Vnde habetur in hymno quodam quod tres magi optulerunt domino tus et mirram et bracteam. *prasinum* uiride quod romanice dicitur 'prasine.' Vnde *uitrum prasinum* (u. 15). *esseda* dorum uehicula sunt. *moderator* dicitur magister redae. *belciariorum* .i. monachorum. Vnde hic dictum *Curuorum chorus belciariorum* (u. 25). *amnicum celeuma*. Celeuma dicitur cantus nauticus. *oppido* .i. ualde. *meminens* .i. 'remembrant.' *depretior* aris .i. 'despreiser.' Vnde *appretior* est pretio emere.

II. 11.

Discretione separatione a discerno nis quod est separare. Vnde dicitur Discernit Graecum a Latino.

II. 12.

Lembum .i. scapham.

II. 13.

Fascium .i. honorum. *uertiginem*. Vertigo est in capite morbus quo uexatus putat domum circa se rotari. *anterius* .i. prius. *cinnamomum* romanice 'canele.' *Tantalio*. Tantalus secundum fabulam in aqua et inter poma est et cum uoluerit bibere effugit aqua et cum prandere effugiunt poma. Igitur inter copiam perit. Et talis est poena auari.

II. 14.

Iani .i. ianuarii. *Numae* .i. februarii quoniam illum mensem addit Pompilius. *ninguidos* quoniam tunc ningit et dicitur a niue.

III. 1.

Semirutis a semi quod est dimidium et ruo is. *indefessim* .i. indesinenter. *redbibetur* .i. iterum habetur.

8. culmus] An culmis *legit glossator pro eo quod habent MSS.* tubis? 9. hymno] *de Natiuitate Domini Tom. VI. p. 251 ed. Pisaur. Poetarum Lat.* Tus Deo, myrrham trocleten humando, Bracteas regi chryseas tulere. *Sed et in hymno ap. Daniel Thes. Hymnologicum, p. 80 est* Tus myrrham et auri bracteas Larga obtulere munera. 10. thus. Prasinum. 11. prassinum. 12. belchiariorum. 14. Depretior. Apprecior. 22. cinnamomum] *vulgo editum est* cinnamo. 23. Tantalus] *Videtur glossator respicere uersus* Non bibit inter aquas poma aut pendentia carpit Tantalus infelix *qui et ap. Petron. 82 et Fulgent. Myth. II.* 18 *extant.* 24. et igitur. 27. Nume.

GLOSSAE IN SIDONIVM. 39

III. 3.

Ferme .i. fere. *calx* cis .i. 'talun' et *calx* pro resoluta terra .i. 'cauz.' Et ponitur pro fine ut in calce libri. Idem est et *cardo*, ponitur enim quandoque pro fine, et est proprie id quo uertitur ostium. *duodeuiginti* .i. duo minus quam .xx. .i. .x. et .viii. *sellarum equestrium* .i. equorum. *madefacta sudoribus fulcra* .i. 'feutremenz.' *liues-* 5 *centibus* .i. 'Empallisanz' a liuesco. Vnde urina liuida .i. pallida. Dicitur et liuida cesaries .i. 'bloie' non quia alba ex toto sit sed modicam speciem candoris habet ad modum palloris. *tripudiantes* .i. gaudentes. Vnde tripudium .i. 'Tresche' et tripudiare .i. gaudere et terram pedibus terere. *inopinatis* .i. non putatis. *nox succincta* .i. breuis et aestiua. *decceruicatis* .i. decollatis. Quoniam ceruix est ubi capud et collum con- 10 ueniunt in occipite. *uillis crinitum* .i. crinibus. *rogalibus fragmentis* .i. torribus quod romanice dicitur 'tisun.'

III. 6.

Iactitant .i. iactanter dicunt. *liuidi* .i. inuidi.

III. 7.

15

Garrio .i. murmuro .i. 'iangler.' Inde garrulus .i. romanice 'ianglur.' Vnde *Garrulo* [*respondere uel*] *non respondere conuitium est. facilitas* est in paruis rebus, *facultas* in magnis. Vel *facilitas* .i. facile est *scribere paupertinum sermonem* sed non est *facultas* .i. ars, quoniam artes facultates dicuntur. *summa censura* .i. iudicium. Quoniam censere est iudicare. *Par comitas* .i. facetia. *tantisper* .i. tantum. *dies ninguidus* .i. niuis. *nox* 20 *illunis* .i. sine luna.

III. 9.
Fol. 145ᵇ.

Inconciliantur .i. inimicantur quoniam inconciliari est inimicari. *Sarcina* .i. honus *argutus* tres habet significationes. Dicitur enim argutum .i. sonorum. Vnde Argutum forum (A. A. I. 80). Iterum argutum .i. astutum. Inde argutia .i. astutia. Iterum 25 argutum .i. strictum uel angustum uel breue. Vnde Argutum foramen. *gerulus epistolarum* .i. portitor. Vnde componitur *nugigerulus* (Sid. VII. 7) .i. portitor nugarum .i. uanae locutionis et scurrilitatis. *contumax* est ille qui uocatus in ius uenire contemnit.

III. 11.

Summates .i. summi uiri. Vnde magnates .i. magni uiri. *praeconia* dicuntur a prae- 30 cone. Vnde praeconari .i. laudare.

III. 12.

Bustualibus fauillis .i. combustis. *Scrobem* .i. foueam. *sidentibus* .i. 'abeisanz' a sido dis vnde gemina super arbore sidunt (Aen. VI. 203). *lapicida* siue lapidicida lapidis caesor. *fors* .i. forte. *postumo* .i. posteriore. *inferias* obsequia mortuorum ab inferis. *manibus* 35 .i. animabus et dicuntur manes apud inferos, umbra circa corpus, anima in corpore.

III. 13.

Pensi .i. ponderis uel librati. *signifer* dicitur primipilarius .i. uexillarius. *gurges* est ubi in aliquo loco angustato maxima aqua defluit ut in molendinis. *concinnato*.

17. facillitas. 25. hastutum. hastutia. 30. magnates. 34. lapidicia. lapidiscida. 38. libᵃti. 39. concinnato] *Non.* 59 Cinnus est commixtio plurimorum, unde concinnare dicitur.

GLOSSAE IN SIDONIVM.

Cinnus est quaedam confectio ex multis speciebus. Vnde dicitur Concinnabat dolum .i. componebat. *dicax* quia uerba eius nullum habent saporem. *ridiculus* quia multotiens fingit risum uel *ridiculus* quia facit alios ridere. Vnde Parturiunt montes nascetur ridiculus mus (Hor. *A. P.* 139). *osor ieiuniorum* .i. habens ieiunium exosum. *in uomicas* .i. in nauseas. *si fatiget* s. alios conuitia dicendo. *si fatigetur* ab aliis, .s. quasi diceret, si alii 5 derideant illum, tunc .s. *fertur in furias. obsonia* dicuntur xenia .i. munera quae post somnum offeruntur. *faeculentiae* .i. plenae faece. *enimuero* .i. sed. *cadauer rogale* dicitur quod in rogo ponitur ad ardendum. *fascibus* .i. ' brandun ' .s. torribus ardentibus. *sidente* .i. ' abeisant.' *strue* .i. congerie. *torrium* .i. ' tisuns.' *pirae* .i. rogo a pir quod est ignis. *pollinctor* magister rogi qui corpora uel cadauera mortuorum ignibus imponit. 10 *barrinas* aures .i. elefantinas. Quoniam barrus est elefans qui maximas aures habet. *nodis tofosis.* Tofus est quidam lapis cauernosus, foraminosus, aptus ad testudines faciendas, quoniam cauernis suis bene recipit caementum et calcem. qualem lapidem Turonis habent. *simum* .i. pandum .i. curuum. *gingiuae* sunt illae carnes quae protuberant circa dentes. *uerrucis* .i. ' uerrues ' .i. ' wetten.' *spurcat* .i. coinquinat. Vnde spurcus 15 .i. sordidus uel immundus. *esculenta* .i. plena cibis uel escis. *sentina* dicitur locus clocae, unde inferior pars nauis, ubi totae sordes sunt nauis, dicitur sentina nauis. *umbrae larunles* dicuntur lemures .i. nocturnae fantasiae. Vnde dictum est de Sancto Cudberto quod multas effugauit laruas .i. umbras demoniorum. *uibex* uibicis est uestigium uirgae apparens in dorso uel alibi. *chiragrica manus.* Idem quod est in pedibus podagra idem est 20 in manibus chiragra a chiros quod est manus inde chirotheca. *cataplasma.* Cata iuxta plasma formatio. Inde cataplasma .s. emplastrum eo quod cum manui apponitur, morbose eandem formam contrahat quam habet manus, sicut cera accipit formam sigilli. *alarum* romanice ' essele ' idem est acella .s. fossicula illa quae sub brachiis est. *specubus* .i. antris siue fossiculis. *hircosis* .i. fetidis ab hyrco quod est fetidissimum animal. *acet-* 25 *centibus* romanice 'en egrisanz' ab aceto. *uallatus* .i. circumdatus a uallo quod romanice dicitur ' bailli.' *Ampsancti* .i. illius faetoris. Vel Ampsanctus potest appellari uligo proueniens ex locis palustribus illius fluuii .s. qui dicitur xanctus et ab am quod est circum. *duplicis* quoniam faetor alarum eius .i. acellarum in duplo uincebat faetorem Ampsanticum. *aruinae* pinguedinis. *casses* retia, sed hic uocat casses plicaturas 30 uentris et sulcos qui in uentre pingui reperiuntur. *ruga* dicitur complicatio siue contractio pellis humanae proueniens ex nimio labore uel senectute. *abdomen* .i. pinguedo .i. ' seim.' *clunes* .i. nates. Vnde dicitur Clunes agitant (*Iuuen.* II. 21). Inde clunabulum .i. gladius paruus sic dictus quod religetur ad clunes (*Isid. Orig. XVIII.* 6. 6). *inpetere* .i. inuadere. *cuniculis.* Cuniculi dicuntur quaedam animalia quae romanice dicuntur 35 ' cunis.' Et cuniculi dicuntur illorum foueae. Vnde prouerbium Sidonii Qui alium .i. discordiae
non *potest machinis apertae simultatis inpetere, cuniculis clandestinae proditionis impugnat* .i.

1. concinnabat dolum] *non repperi.* Concinnare ambages *legitur ap. Apul. M. VIII.* 12.
6. exenia.   7. sompnum. feculentie. fece.   8. (fascibus] an facibus?   14. simum]
Non extat in hac epistula, ubi tamen per marginem curuum protuberantibus.   25. acessentibus.
29. dupplicis.   31. repperiuntur.

GLOSSAE IN SIDONIVM. 41

Qui non potest aperte detrahere detrahit occulte. *prostitutio* meretricatio. Vnde pros-
tituuntur meretrices. *Hisco* .l. hiare, unde *debisco* .i. aperio. Vnde fatisco .l. multum
hisco a fatis quod est multum. Vnde affatim .i. habunde, ab ad et fatis.

IV. 1.

Necessitudo .i. consanguinitas uel uinculum amoris. *meracius* .i. purius. *contro-* 5
uersantur .i. confligunt. Vnde controuersia .i. certamen. *fratres patrueles* .i. filii duorum
fratrum, fratres autem patrueles magis solent se diligere quam duo fratres, quia inter duos

Fol. 146ª. fratres maxima solet esse inuidia super paterna hereditate diuidenda; sed fratres
patrueles non habent aliquam hereditatem corporalem. *comicus* .i. a comedia. *lepidus*
a lepore .i. a facetia. *liricus* .i. uaria metra componens a lirin quod est uarium. *pane-* 10
girista. Panegiricus est laus ficta principum. *epigrammatista* est ille qui scribit et materiis
inponit metrum lasciuum uel profani lasciuiam, ut Hodie cum pretio cras sine pretio.
Hoc supra scriptum erat in balneis quasi sophistice. *categorias* .i. praedicamenta. *atti-*
cissabas ab Attico .i. Graeco .i. graecissabas, vnde Attice .i. Graece. *fibra* .i. uena.
egelidare .i. extra gelu ponere. congelidare .i. simul gelare. *ferociam* .i. saeuitiam. *stolidi-* 15
tatem .i. stultitiam. *brutescit* more brutorum animalium. *perennare* .i. perpetuare .i.
facere perpetuum.

IV. 2.

Enimuero sed. *prodigis* .i. erogas large et dicitur a prodigalitate. *exoccupatu* .i.
magna occupatione. Quoniam exoccupatus est una dictio et ex ibi positum significat 20
intensionem occupationis. Ex quandoque augmentatiue ponitur, quandoque priuatiue,
ut exauctoratus auctoritate priuatus. Augmentatiue ut hic exoccupatus. *praepedimen-*
tum .i. inpedimentum. *ambiguo caret* .i. dubio.

IV. 3.

Committi .i. 'forfere.' *pugillaribus* .i. paruis tabulis quae in pugno feruntur. Vnde 25
pugillus .i. paruus pugnus. *uolas* .i. palmas et inde *inuolare* .i. furari. *latialiter* .i.
latine. *rusticabuntur* .i. rusticitati deputabuntur. *astipulatur* attestatur. *probemiaris*
.i. in prohemio. *tribulosum* .i. spinosum. Vnde tribulos dicimus. *admittit* .i. recipit.
censura iudicium. *euentilata* discussa et intellecta. *scaturigines* proprie ebullitiones fontium.
hyperbolicas. Hyperbole est dictio fidem excedens ut aquilis ueluciores leonibus fortiores 30
(2 *Sam. I.* 23). *tapinomata.* Tapinoma est humilitas rei magnae. *baculo* quia baculo inni-
tuntur aegri. *Orpheo.* Orpheus quidam sapiens erat qui per citharam suam et eloquentiam
conuocauit in unum .i. in concordiam et humanitatem dura saxa .l. homines incultos.

3. fatis] *Seru. ad Aen. I.* 123 fatim abundanter dicimus, unde et adfatim, hiscere autem
aperiri, uerbum frequentatiuum ab hiare. *Placidi Glossae p.* 48. 3 *Deuerling* Fatisceret abunde
aperiretur. 10. lirin] *num Λειρίον quod ποικίλον interpretatur Hesychius?* panigirista. 11. pa-
nagiricus. 12. laciuiam. 20. exoccupatus est una dictio] *Verum hoc nec a quoquam,*
quantum scio, enotatum. 22. exauctoratus] *cf. Macrob. S. I.* 5. 3 Mille denique uerborum
talium est quae cum in ore priscae auctoritatis crebro fuerint, exauctorata tamen a sequenti
aetate repudiataque sunt. 30. yperbolicas. yperbole.

G [I. 5.]

GLOSSAE IN SIDONIVM.

horoscopi dicuntur qui horas natiuitatis hominum uel horas dierum speculantur. Vnde horoscopium .i. horologium ab hora et scopos quod est intendere. *circinum.* Perdix iuxta Ouidium repertor circini fuit et dicitur hic circinus quod est romanice ' Cumpas.' Vnde *circinari* .i. ' Cumpasser.' *Atlanta.* Atlans erat astronomicus. Vnde quidam mons dicitur Atlans quia altus est et uicinus sideribus (*Isid. Orig. XIV.* 17). *exertat* .i. prae- 5 parat exerto brachio et extenso, ab exero ris, quod est extra ponere. *simbolum* in neutro genere coniunctionem uel communionem significat quod romanice dicitur 'cumfre,' a sin quod est con et bolus quod est ' morsel.' *commessatio* idem est. *affluit* .i. habundat. *commaticus* .i. distincte in eo tractatur per commata. *phalerata* .i. ornata. *ampullosis uerbis* .i. grossis. Vnde dicitur ab ampulla, quod est ampla bulla. *tesqua* sunt loca 10 inamoena praerupta et aspera, et est tesqua nomen indeclinabile. Et sunt tesqua contraria tempe. *confraga* sunt loca montuosa in quae uenti undique concurrunt ac sese frangunt. *inpactae* professionis ab inpingo gis quia quodammodo inuitus factus fuerat Sidonius episcopus. Vnde dicitur uulgo Aduersitas inpacta est mihi. *uenula* .i. parua fibra. *cathedrarios* quoniam minores iudices sedent in cathedris, maiores autem 15 in tribunalibus. *rauula* dicitur calumpniator.

IV. 4.

Pariles .i. pares. *perindignum est* .i. ualde indignum.

IV. 6.

Cordicitus .i. usque ad cor. *difficulter* .i. grauate unde *nec difficulter.* Immo faciliter. 20 *album calculum.* Solebant antiqui in fine cuiuslibet diei in ollam quamdam lapillulum proicere. Si autem illis dies bonus esset album, si autem malus, nigrum. Et in fine anni solebant aperire ollam illam et computare an ibi essent plures lapides albi an nigri. Si autem plures essent albi, dicebant illum annum illis fuisse felicem. Si autem plures nigros inuenissent dicebant illum annum illis fuisse infelicem. *plectibili* .i. punienda. 25 *procax petitor* .i. inprobus. Inde procaciter. *cautos* .i. astutos. Vnde cautela .i. euitatio. Vnde †inuitas patrum legimus quod quidam frater ueniam de praeteritis postulabat delictis et fortitudinem ad cautelam futurorum .i. euitationem. *Sectatores litium* .i. placitatores litium .i. causarum. Vnde placitor idem est quod causari uel licitari.

IV. 7.

30

Admissus .i. receptus. *Et crapulis ceparum* crapula est superfluitas sumpti cibi. *ceparum* .i. 'vinnuns.' Et declinatur hoc cepe et pluraliter hae cepae parum. *apicios* .i. nobiles. *epulones* qui nobiliter comedunt. *chironomontas* .i. quasi mouentes manus.

IV. 8.

Artifex argentarius qui facit uel operatur illud. *ferrarius* qui ferrum. Sic *lignarius* 35

1. *Horoscopi*] Hesych. ὡροσκόπος ὁ σκοπῶν τὰς ὥρας. 2. Perdix] *nomen non est ap. Ouidium M. VIII.* 247–9, *sed uocatur filius germanae Daedali.* 9. comaticus. comata. 12. in qua uenti. 20. difficultas .i. grauedine. 22. prohicere. 26. hastutos. 32. he cepe. 33. chironomantas. senescalcos quasi.

GLOSSAE IN SIDONIVM. 43

qui operatur uel sculpit in ligno sculptura uel incisione aliqua. *patrocinari* .i. adiuuare.
Vnde *patrocinium*. *famulari* .i. obsequi.

IV. 9.

Paludamentum est insigne pallium imperatorum cocco purpura et auro distinctum
et dictum est paludamentum quia eo indutus imperator palam sedebat in diebus festiuis 5
et palam faceret bellum suum futurum.

IV. 11.

[*Extorquere* .i. extra ponere. Vnde dictum est Difficile est clauam extorquere a manibus Herculis.] *hoc schema* .i. ornamentum. Vnde est schemate uerborum etc. *phonascus*
modulator a phonos quod est sonus .i. cantor qui solebat antiphonam incipere. *classes*. 10

Fol. 146ᵇ. Classica sunt cornua quae conuocandi causa erant facta et a † kalon classica dicebantur.
antistes .i. ante stans. *fasce* .i. honore.

IV. 12.

Conformis .i. similis. *bilem* .i. iram. *inexoratus* .i. inflexibilis ad faciendum. *bal-
butire* .i. 'stamerie.' *caecutiret*. Caecutire est oculos prae confusione frequenter et citius 15
claudere et dicitur a caecitate. *replicare lectionem* est eam iterum recordari et relegere.
officiat .i. noceat.

IV. 13.

Cothurnus .i. crepida .i. 'bote.' *tensus* quoniam stricte sedebant circa pedem.

IV. 14.

20

Haec insiticia idem est quod insitio .i. 'entement.' Vnde Ouidius (*Rem*. 195)
Venerit insitio fac ramum ramus adoptet. Vnde Sidonius *Hanc inte ipse uirtutem si
naturalis est excole, si minus, ut insiticiam appone* .i. eam insere quod est Romanice
'enter.' Et dicitur ab insito insitiuus uel insiticius.

25

IV. 15.

Lectisternia sunt cubicula strata in area domus. *crepulo* .i. sonante a crepo pis.
fragore fragor arborum. *cocleatim*. Cocleae sunt altae et rotundae turres et dictae sunt
cocleae quasi ciclene eo quod in eis tanquam per circulum ascendatur et inde coclear
'cuillere.'

30

IV. 17.

Limitem .i. ueritatem quoniam limes rectus est. Vel *limitem* .i. finem. Vnde

1. adiuuari.   4. Paludamentum] *Isid. XIX*. 24. 9, *cf. Varro L. L. VII*. 37 Quae propterea
quod conspiciuntur qui ea habent ac fiunt palam paludamenta dicta.   8. Extorquere] *Ap.
Donat. Vit. Vergilii fin. et Macrob. V.* 3. 16 *prouerbium sic extat* clauam Herculi subripere
(subtrahere *Macrobius*), *non* extorquere, *quod unde sumptum sit nescio*.   9. scema.
11. Classica] *Isid. XVIII*. 4. 5.   a Kalon *cod. Isidori codices habent* a kalando.   26. *Post* in
area domus *codex addit haec* strata .i. ornata. Inde hoc stratum .i. ornamentum. Vnde Virgilius
(*immo* Claudianus *in Ruf*. I. 211) Fulgentibus illic Surgunt strata toris.   27. cocleae] *Isid.
XV*. 2. 38.   31. .L ueritatem] *mira interpretatio*.

G 2

44   GLOSSAE IN SIDONIVM.

collimitare .i. 'mancher.' *prothomista* dicitur a proto quod est primus et mista secretum. Inde prothomista dicitur persona primarie mistica intelligens. *euentilandae* .i. consumendae uel consummandae. Quoniam euentilare tamquam per uentum est dispergere.

IV. 18.

         Serraca sunt quoddam genus uehiculi. *Esseda* sunt redae.   5

IV. 20.

         Expetere .i. adire. *honusti* .i. honerati. *cocco* .i. purpura. *perone* .i. anglice 'riueling.' *setoso* quoniam in peronibus seta bouis adhuc manet. *surae* .i. tibiae. *uersicolor* .i. diuersicolor. *saga* 'saie' quoniam ex sago habebant clamides. *limbis* Romanice 'urles' 10 ex rubro panno et ideo subiungit *puniceis*. *renonibus* Renones sunt uelamenta humerorum et pectoris usque ad umbilicum atque intortis uillis adeo hispida ut imbrem respuant. Quae uulgus 'reptos' uocat eo quod longitudo uillorum quasi reptat. Dicuntur autem renones a Reno flumine Germaniae ubi his frequenter utuntur. *bullatis* a bulla aquae. Bulla autem potest dici omnis nodus rotundus. Vnde quaedam zona ex 15 corio facta dicitur bullam habere in capite pro buccula. Vnde hic dicuntur renones bullati quia quibusdam nodosis corrigiis circa latera hominis nectebantur ut eo facilius dilaqueari possent. *comebantur* .i. ornabantur. *uncatis* securibus .i. curuis.

IV. 22.

         Industrius .i. sapiens ab industria. *saties* .i. satietas. Veritas enim odium parit et 20 obsequium adulationis et falsitatis quandoque parit amicos.

IV. 23.

         Abdicatione .i. abnegatione. *culleo*. Culleus est quidam saccus corii in quo proiciebantur qui parentem suum occiderunt et cum eo simia et gallus et serpens et hoc totum in profluentem aquam proiciebatur. Vel secundum aliam litteram *eculeo*. Eculeus est 25 quoddam lignum in dorso acutum super quod equitabat reus ad cuius pedes aliqua ponderosa ligabantur. *suppliciis paricidalibus* a caedendo uel occidendo parem. *magnopere* summopere. *Mag.* .i. magna intentione. *summop.* .i. summa intentione.

IV. 24.

         Cauta dicitur esse pecunia feneratori .i. cautione confirmata. Cautio alia fideius- 30 soria, alia pignoraticia, alia hypothecaria, alia chirographaria. *executoris inprobitas* .i.

    8. anglice] a *codex*. Riueling] Halliwell's Dict. of Provincial and Archaic words s. u. Riveling a rough shoe formerly worn by the Scots.   11. renonibus] *Isid. XIX.* 23. 1. 4. 20. sacies. sacietas.   23. coreus. prohiciebantur.   25. prohiciebatur.   27. parem] *Paulus s. u.* Parici quaestores. Paricida non utique is qui parentem occidisset dicebatur, sed qualemcunque hominem indemnatum ita fuisse indicat lex Numae Pompilii regis (indemnatum. Ita fuisse C. O. *Mueller*).

GLOSSAE IN SIDONIVM. 45

executorum .i. creditorum. [Cui .s. committuntur causae .i. officiales.] *anterius* .i. prius. *factiose*. Factio est conspiratio in malum. *exactorum*. Exactores sunt illi qui uiolentia aliquid exigunt et ideo hic appellat creditores Turpionis exactores quia nimis perseuerant in petitione pecuniae suae. *indultis* .i. concessis. Indulgere autem plures habet significationes ponitur enim pro operam dare et pro condonare. *sub annis tutelaribus* degunt 5 .i. defensibilibus uel defensantibus, a tutela quod est defensio.

IV. 15.
    Per fragores parasiticos parasiticos a parapside. Vnde parasiti qui prope et iuxta mensam assident. *apice uotiuo* .i. illo episcopatu qui multum desideratur.

V. 1.
    Non uacans .i. non cessans. *Agnationis* Agnatio est parentela tantum per uirilem 10 sexum descendens. Et agnati secundum legem Romanam prius uocantur ad hereditatem quam cognati defunctorum. Qui cognati sunt descendentes per femininum sexum. *redibitio* a redibeo .i. iterum habeo.

V. 3.
    Miserrimum est ante docere quam discere . . . pro foliis. Quod restat. Vnde subiacere cor- 15 rectioni congruit *ne si in praeteritis criminibus manserimus incipiat ad animae potius pertinere mortem quod uiuimus.* Sterilis arbor non habet poma sed folia: ita qui docet et non facit quae docet.

V. 4.
    Inputo .i. inpono. *autumo* .i. existimo uel credo. *pessulum opponis* .i. 'pin.' *politis* 20 *affatibus dulcare* .i. 'enducer.'

V. 5.
Fol. 147ᵃ.
    Pronepos. Filius nepotis. *eufoniam* .i. bonam sonoritatem. *astupes* .i. stuporem habet. *curua senectus* quoniam senectus facit hominem curuum. Vnde quidam uersificator Me 25 reddit semper silicernum curua senectus. *arbitrum*. Arbiter est ille in quem se aduersae partes compromittunt.

V. 7.
    Manet .i. expectat. *addictos* .i. adiudicatos. *viatica*. Viaticum est quod datur alicui in uia ad cibum. *uredariis* .i. magistris redarum quoniam ueredus est equs ducens 30 redam. *portoria* .i. lucra quae accipiunt pro portandis honeribus. *tabellariis*. Tabellarii uel tabelliones sunt publicae personae in uilla quae in actis redigunt maiores actiones ciuitatis. *numerariis*. Numerarii uel nummularii sunt publicae personae quae publico nummo praesunt et in scriptis redigunt quanta acceperint et quanta militibus uel aliis dederint, quibus dari iusserit res publica. Et illis necessaria est dispositio et distinctio 35 et collatio acceptorum et datorum et deliberatio ut sic disponant actiones suas et

---

1. Cui .s. committuntur] *Videntur duae glossae coaluisse, altera quae executorem interpretetur creditorem, altera quae officialem, h. e. ministrum publicum.* 8. parasisti. 31. tabellariis] tabulariis *editiones Sidonii.* 36. acciones.

GLOSSAE IN SIDONIVM.

traditiones ut sibi praecaueant. Vel *dispositiones* quia qui solent numerare denarios, per aceruos multos .v. solidorum eos disponunt ut facilius post modum sciant quot libras numerauerint. *praetorianis* .i. executoribus praetorum uel iudicum. Nam executores sunt illi qui sententiam iudicis mancipauerint effectui. Et talibus dantur de iure ab actoribus quaedam munera quae uocantur *sportulae* .s. propter illorum laborem et operam. *publicanis*. Publicani sunt illi qui constituti (sunt) a re publica ut tributa regionum et prouinciarum et uectigalia quae inde sunt recipiant. *cinctis* .i. armatis. Vnde Lucanus (*I.* 348) Arma tenenti, Omnia dat qui iusta negat. *discinctis* .i. emeritis .s. ueteranis militibus qui post .l. annorum spatium non apti militiae priuilegiantur ut non de cetero pugnent. *castorinati* .i. ornati pelle castoria pretiosa. Et est castor Romanice 'beure.' *litanias* .i. rogationes ubi litania cantatur. *tractatibus* siue tractationibus .i. in causis tractandis. *cocleae* .i. tortuosi ad fallendum. Quoniam coclea romanice dicitur 'uiz' quasi ciclea ut supra dictum est. [Vel cocleae attrahentes, quoniam est conca cuiusdam piscis qui similiter dicitur coclea et illa coclea difficile aperitur.]

V. 10.

Acrimoniam sententiarum .i. acerbitatem. [*exacerbatus* .i. exasperatus.] *adquiesco* .i. concedo. [*exoculare* .i. oculum eruere.]

V. 11.

Puberes dicuntur a xiiii annis supra (*Inst. I.* 22).

V. 12.

Vti ut.

V. 13.

Eruderat .i. extra rudera ponit, quoniam rudera sunt quisquiliae domus. *indictionum* .i. exactionum uel tributorum ab indicendo. Vnde compotistae dicunt indictionem xv annorum spatium constare ex tribus lustris. [*elogium* dicitur et eulogium. Vnde uersus 25 Eulogium nobis sonat incrustatio laudis .i. iteratio uel multiplicatio laudis. Elogium uero sermo bonus ore latino.]

V. 14.

Iecorosis .i. a iecore. Vnde iecorosus morbus. *epaticis* [Cels. iv. 15 (8)] ab epate. Vnde morbus epaticus et est idem iecur et epar in homine sed non in nomine. *munitio-* 30 *num* .i. castellorum.

V. 16.

Titulis .i. honoribus uel laudibus. *manubiis* uictorialibus uestimentis uel armis.

1. denarios] *ð cod.* 2. quod. 6. sunt *om.* 8. iuste negat. 9. priuilegiuntur. 11. letanias. letania. 13. cocleae attrahentes] *num significantur* 'snapping cockles?' Sed uidetur Sidonius idem significare quod Plautus Poen. *III.* 1. 29 uicistis cochleam tarditudine. 14. apperitur. 17. exoculare] *non habet quo referatur.* Verbum Plautinum est Rud. *III.* 4. 26. 25. elogium] *aliunde inuectum est.* 26. Elogium nobis. 30. sed non in homine. 33. manubiae] *Isid. Orig. XVIII.* 2. 8 Manubiae eo quod manibus detrahantur. Hae et exuuiae ab exuendo dictae quia exuuntur.

GLOSSAE IN SIDONIVM. 47

Quoniam cum quis Romanorum hostem deuincebat assumpsit illius uestes et arma et in signum uictoriae *su*spendit illa in aliquo loco publico, et dicuntur manubiae quasi manuuiae .i. exuuiae quae manibus capiebantur. [*obsidere* .i. 'Assegger' .i. 'purser.'] *amita* .i. soror patris. *matertera* .i. soror matris.

V. 17.

Mulcedine a mulceo ces. *psalmicenes* canentes psalmos. *torreo* .i. ferueo calore. Vnde Feruida torruit aestas. *palmitis* arboris uineae. *stipites*. Stipitem hic appellat ipsius uineae arborem .i. robur quod in terra crescens supra sursum palos et laquearia huc et illuc dis*t*enditur. Vel *stipites* hic appellat palos qui supra et deorsum uineam sustinent. *torpore* .i. marciditate uel pigritia. Vnde Torpescunt .i. pigrescunt. Hoc *linteum* .i. 10 gausape uel manutergium. *uillis* .i. 'frenges.' *bonustum* plenum ab honore, uel uillis quia gausape illud uillosum erat. *troclea* dicitur 'pulie' Romanice per quam facilius cborda labitur et hoc gausape tamquam troclea erat circa quemdam baculum cuius baculi duo capita pendebant iuncta cuidam funi et duo capita ipsius gausapis consuta Fol. 147ᵇ. simul erant ut rotari posset gausape circa baculum illum. Quale gausape in claustris 15 religiosorum inuenitur. *ambio* .i. cupio.

V. 19.

Soluas .i. dissoluas. Et soluere .i. resoluere. Vnde Horatius Soluitur acris hyemps. *inquilinatu*. Inquilinus est ille qui sub alio domos habet. Sed hic accipitur inquilinatus pro seruitute uel pro originali colono, quia iam dicet hunc seruum esse colonum quem 20 nunc dicit inquilinum. Et est originarius colonus qui ab origine colona*r*iae condicioni est subiectus. Qui non potest a gleba remoueri inuitus nec se remouere inuito domino. *tributario* quoniam huiusmodi coloni domino sua tributa reddunt et annuum censum, qui et tributarii dicuntur.

VI. 1.

Specula. Specula est aliquis altus locus a quo undique aspici possit. *procul ambiguo* .i. procul dubio .i. certe. *desudare* .i. laborare a sudore .s. quoniam qui lahorat aliquando sudat prae labore, et *desudare* pro sudare. Vnde Ex eius tumba desudat oleum. *primipilarem*. Quoniam apostolicus primipilaris ad illa quae ad Dominum pertinent, reges autem uel alii potentes primipilares sunt ad illa quae ad saeculum pertinent. 30 Et est primipilaris qui fert ante pugnantes primum pilum .i. telum uexilla deportans. *apostolici* autem *uexilla crucis* sunt insignia primipilaria. *sequestratus* .i. separatus. *calones* sunt portitores lignorum et hic accipiuntur calones .i. peccatorum portitores. *extimos* .i. extremos. *trabariorum* Traharii sunt qui aliqua bonera trahunt. Sed hic accipiuntur traharii qui a carnis suae desideriis trahuntur. Virgilius Trahit sua quemque 35 uoluptas. Sidonius ergo se et alios peccatores uocat traharios qui propter uxores suas ad carnis sarcinas trahuntur adhuc. Apotheca repositione. *propinare* propinare est potum a penu ferre. *detrecto* .i. detraho uel contempno.

2. pendit. 6. ferueo] immo feruefacio. 7. feruida torruit aestas] *Luc. I.* 214 *ubi tamen* canduit. 9. distunditur. 10. gausape .i. lintheum. 18. *Hor. C. I.* 4. 20. iam dicet] *sequitur enim* plebeiam potius incipiet habere personam quam colonariam. 35. *Verg. Ecl. II.* 65.

48   GLOSSAE IN SIDONIVM.

VI. 2.
    Alienum sicut fecerant Nadab et Abiu filii Aaron et ideo quia ignem prohibitum
tulerunt ad altare domini igne caelesti combusti erant. *uadimonia reddo* uadi meo.
Et est usualis locutio. *uadis* .i. fideiussor.   Vnde cautio fideiussoria.

VI. 3.   5
    Testamentarium. Quoniam aliquis moriens in testamento suo †ei legata uel fidei
commissa uel hereditatem relinquit. *togatorum.* Idem sunt togati et aduocati et patroni
causarum. *perperam* aduerbium .i. strophose .i. fraudulenter a stropha quod est fraus.
aduocatio. Consilium aduocatorum .i. togatorum.

VI. 4.   10
    Distractam .i. uenditam. *negotiatoris* .i. emptoris .i. institoris. *defungitur* moritur.
Nam cum dicitur, aliquis defunctus est, nihil aliud est quam a corpore liberatus est,
quoniam idem est defungi et liberari. *nundinas* emptiones uel uenditiones.

VI. 5.
    Causam clientem libertum, nam relatiua sunt cliens et patronus.   Et patronus est ille 15
qui manumittit, sicut et ille qui est patronus causae .i. aduocatus.

VI. 6.
    Adeps pinguedo. *aruina* pinguedo intestinorum.

VI. 7.
    Cicatricentur .i. cicatricibus †ulcerentur.   20
VI. 8.
    Credulis quia libenter creditores credunt illi pecuniam suam sine pignore .i. sine
cautione pignoraticia. *intimos agunt* ponitur haec dictio *intimos* hic aduerbialiter.
propediem .i. cito et est una dictio et aduerbium, et inuenitur similiter hoc modo posita
in fine Tullii de officiis (III. 33. 121). *Fontem mercatorum.* Fons mercatorum est fons 25
aquae frigidae. Quoniam mercatores cum in mercimoniis suis proficiscuntur in aliquam regionem, frequentius ex aqua bibunt quam iuxta uiam reperiunt quam ex uino.

VI. 9.
    Adornauit Romanice 'apprester.' *gnauiter* .i. caute.
                                                                                          30
VI. 10.
    Domesticis. Domestici fidei sunt omnes Christiani et aliquando uocamus do. fi.
clericos ex eadem ecclesia uel ex eadem parochia parochianos. *opipare* .i. laudabiliter.

VI. 12.
    Miseratus. Nota quod aliud est misertus, atque aliud miseratus, quoniam unum
descendit a misereor eris quod est superiorum, sicut dicitur Miserere mei deus, aliud 35

                         defunctus
    11. defungitur moritur] cf. VII. 6 mortuus *codex.*   20. ulcerentur] *num* indurentur?
    22. qui.   25. Fontem mercatorem] *interpretatio uix sana.*   32. parrochianos.

GLOSSAE IN SIDONIVM.

autem descendit a miseror raris, quod est omnium hominum, *s.* ut possint habere in cordibus suis quamdam miseriam et quamdam pietatem de incommodis et calamitatibus alterius. *indagine* .i. inquisitione. Quoniam indago Romanice dicitur 'parc' s. ubi cerui includuntur. Et nota quod idem est indago nis et indages gis. *pudor* est uerecundia uirtuosa. *in inficias* .i. in negationes ab inficior quod est negare. *commercio* .i. 5 emptione uel uenditione. *significibus* .i. facientibus signa.

VII. 1.

Fol. 148ᵃ.

Animositas .i. Romanice 'ardiesce.' *putrem* .i. ex uetustate putridam. *cratem* .i. 'cleie.' Solebant enim obsessi, ut muri ciuitatis illaesi obseruarentur a machinis obsidentium, crates muris appendere. *propugnacula* .i. 'kernans.' *initiari.* Initior aris quadam 10 sua significatione est sacrificare uel sacrificationem incipere habere. Vt alibi dicitur Beelfegor deo initiatur .i. illa ciuitas deo sacrificium libat. *scenae* .i. umbrae .i. theatra. *exinanito* .i. euacuato. *ammonitio.* Ammonitio, ut in Macrobio legitur, est [propter peccata hominum] alicuius futuri incommodi denunciatio. *conuitiaretur* .i. conuitia inferret. *diuinae* .s. ammonitioni. [*perhemdie* .i. perhempto uno die.] 15

VII. 2.

Primore .i. primo uel *primorum* primatum .i. meliorum. *circumscriptus erat* .i. circumuentus .i. deceptus, et tractum est hoc a littera quae damnatur circumductione lineae. *palatino* a palatio. *diuersorio* .i. hospitio. *friuola* .i. uana, nugis plena. *mimica largitate* .i. ioculari, quoniam mimi .i. loculatores de magnis maiora loquuntur (*Iuuen.* 20 *IV.* 17). A nomine quod est mimus dicitur mimicus uel mimica. *conuasatis* .i. collectis. *munificentiae socrualis.* Vnde differentia est inter nurum et socrum. Nurus est uxor filii, socrus est mater puellae. *matrimonialibus* .i. nuptialibus quoniam matrimonium et nuptiae idem sunt. *non paruo* .i. magno. *Corollario.* Corollarium est, ut dicunt geometrae, gratuitum donum quod post debitum confertur gratis. *praestigiator* .i. incanta- 25 tor. *perhyperbolicis* .i. ualde hyperbolicis. *instrumentis.* Continebantur enim in tabulis nuptialibus tanta quae uix possent credi s. quae acceperat Amantius a socru sua et quae Amantius promisit uxori suae in donationibus propter nuptias. Et est hyperbole figura, quando maiora dicuntur de minoribus, ut existimationem hominum supergrediatur. *repetundarum* appellatio est cuiusdam actionis quando aliquis repetit quae 30 alius ab eo acceperit. *mancipiorum* .i. seruorum quia manu capiuntur; quasi diceret, Socrus eius flebat quod filia sua tam pauca .i. nulla mancipia uel alia munera quae capiuntur manu acceperat ab Amantio in donationibus propter nuptias. *sponsaliciae donationis* propter nuptias. *eximii* nobilis et magni. *Attice* .i. Graece.

1. possit. 9. solent. 13. Macrobio] *Videtur respicere Somn. Scip. I. 7.* 1 Non aduertunt hanc habere legem omnia uel signa uel somnia, ut de aduersis oblique aut denuntient aut minentur aut moneant. Et ideo quaedam cauendo transimus ... Nam ubi ammonitio est, uigilantia cautionis euaditur. 15. perhemdie] *aliunde inrepsit.* 18. dampnatur. 19. hospicio. 24. Corolario. Corolarium. *Boetius de Cons. Philos. III.* 11 Super haec igitur ueluti geometrae solent demonstratis propositis aliquid inferre, quae πορίσματα ipsi uocant, ita ego quoque tibi ueluti corollarium dabo. 26. peryperbolicis. yperbolicis. 28. yperbole. 30. accionibus.

H [I. 5.]

GLOSSAE IN SIDONIVM.

VII. 3.   Sydonius papae Migetio Salutem.

Diu multumque. Migetius iste rogauit Sidonium ut illi mitteret librum suum epistolarum uel panegiricum suum. Sed quia Migetius iste mirabilis erat clericus deliberauit diu Sydonius an tanto clerico suas nugas mittere auderet. Tandem tamen instantia Migetii ipsius sua scripta ei transmisit. *destinarem* .i. mitterem .i. delegarem. *pinniculo* 5 *Apellen*, etc. q. d. Etsi haberemus pinniculum quod est instrumentum pingendi non tamen essemus Apelles qui optimus erat pictor. *Apellen* accusatiuus Graecus. *caelum* hoc caelum ut hoc celte celtis instrumentum est quo caelatur .i. sculpitur. *malleo.* Malleus est instrumentum aurifabri. *Fidian* accusatiuus Graecus quoniam Fidias erat optimus sculptor et Policlitus aurifaber. *praesumptioni* quoniam tibi praesumpsi 10 mittere friuola mea. *examini* .i. iudicio. *ritu* consuetudine. *edat.* Edere aliquod scriptum est quando illud est dignum editione et recitatione. *birriant* inter dentes murmurent quod Anglice dicitur ' grunie.'

VII. 4.   Papae Fonteio.

Digressis .i. euntibus. *quoquo* .i. ubicumque. *fastigium* .i. sublimitatem. *comitate* 15 quia comis es et facetus et omnibus bonis comes. *inardesco* .i. uehementer cupio.

VII. 5.   Sydonius papae Agroetio Salutem.

Bituricas .i. ciuitas quae Romanice uocatur 'Buhuries.' De illa tamen ciuitate alibi legitur quod aliud nomen habet, sicut dicitur Dicitur urbs Bituris pro binis turribus istis. *decreto* uoluntate et mandato. *classicum.* Romanice dicitur 'glas.' Sonauerunt 20 enim classicum ut conuenirent clerici et laici ad eligendum episcopum. *consulas* quaeras. *fucata* .i. fuco tincta. *impudentia* quia nullum pudorem habuerunt rogandi uel emendi si possent illum episcopatum. *nundinam* uenditionem et emptionem quia nundinae sunt publicae mercationes. Dicuntur *prouinciales* episcopi qui metropolitano .i. archiepiscopo subiecti sunt, quia metropolis est mater ciuitatum. *sufficitur* .i. subrogatur .i. substituitur, 25 quasi sufficienter ministratur, quoniam sufficere est ministrare.

VII. 6.   Sydonius domino papae Basilio salutem et benedictionem.

Caula .i. ouile. *saginatur* .i. incrassatur. *clandestino morsu* necdum intellecti dentis .i. secreto uel priuato uel latenti, quia latenter decipit homines. *arrodat* .i. corrodat. *insultet* .i. derideat. *discutere* .i. indicare. *sinister interpres* .i. malus interpretator. 30 *Aegiptus* interpretatur lacrimae. *Pharao.* Pharao erat rex Aegipti et interpretatur rex lacrimarum. *Israelita* .i. filii Israel .i. Iudaei et interpretatur Iudaeus uere paenitens. Israel uero uidens deum interpretatur. *cum cophino.* Israhelitae enim, cum Pharao rex Aegipti eos cepisset, ei seruiebant in luto et latere et cum cophinis suis honera deportabant. *spiritualem* .i. deplangamus quod tam remoti sumus a caelo propter 35 nostra peccata. *Assur* .i. Nabugodonosor quia ipse erat rex Assiriorum et Chaldaeorum

3. panagiricum. 6. Appellen. 7. Appelles. Appellen acusatiuus *bis.* 8. celte celtis] *Notandum hoc lexicographis. Pro certo enim habeo ex grammatico aliquo sumptum fuisse.* 9. malleum est. 10. polliclitus. 13. murmurant. 20. Sonauerunt] *sic codex.* 29. Necdum intellecti dentis *post* decipit homines *codex.* 31. Pha erat. 32. renitens. 33. uidens deum] *immo* Ieriel.

GLOSSAE IN SIDONIVM. 51

ubi est Babilon. *fastu* .i. superbia. *futurarum* in caelo. *praesentium* in terra. *quod* .i. quia. *quae merear*. Quia per peccata mereor in gehennam mitti. *dein* .i. deinde. *trituretur* .i. teratur sicut triticum. *acet* .i. acescit .i. acida est. *ut ambigas* .i. dubites. *ualitudinem* .i. aegritudinem. Vnde senes ualitudinarii dicuntur .i. infirmi, quoniam ualitudinarii dicuntur infirmi. Vnde Terentius (*And. IV.* 2. 14) Valeant qui inter nos 5 discidium uolunt .i. pereant. Vnde dictum est de sancto Cudberto quod multiplicium morborum ualitudines depulit .i. pericula. Et ponitur ualitudo quandoque pro sanitate. Vnde dictum est uale. Similiter in principio Tullii de amicitia (*Lael. II.* 8) indifferenter ponitur ualitudo. *subfectis* .i. substitutis. *subrogantur* .i. substituuntur. *haeresiarcas*. Haeresiarca est princeps haereticorum. *inflectere* .i. trahere ad haeresim suam. *intercisae* 10 .i. interruptae et uiolatae. *diocesibus* haec diocesis est pluraliter hae dioceses sunt episcoporum et inferiorum sacerdotum parochiae. *ueprium* .i. 'Runces.' *fruticibus* 'Buissuns.'

VII. 7.

Amantius proprium nomen lectoris cuiusdam de quo habita est mentio supra in 15 duabus epistolis ad istum eundem Graecum papam missis. *uicissim* .i. quandoque uel e conuerso. *rimis cauernis*. *indiscretis* .i. indiuisis. *iactura* .i. amissio uel damnum. *praestigiae* incantationes. *comprouincialium* .i. compatriotarum. Et sunt compatriotae de una patria. *tradimur* .i. seducimur. Vnde dicitur Iudas traditor .i. proditor .i. seductor. 20

VII. 9.

Sicut diximus in praecedenti epistola Sidonius inuitabatur ut Bituricas ueniret ut ibi ille cum aliis episcopis eligeret Simplicium ei ciuitati in episcopum et illum ordinaret. *exacte* .i. perfecte. *schemata* .i. figuras et licita figmenta. *suggerebat mihi*. Suggerere duas habet significationes. Vna ponitur pro suadere uel instigare. Altera 25 pro subministrare, Spiritus sanctus suggeret nobis omnia .i. subministrabit. *uorago* .i. uortex. Et potest dici uorago a uorando, sicut terra paludosa et lutosa et aquosa. Vnde dictum est de Petro, Qui Petri pedibus marinos uortices inclinauit. *uolutabra*. Porcorum est uolutabrum, unde dictum est Canes reuertuntur ad uomicas et porci uolutantur in uolutabro suo. (2 *Pet.* 2. 22.) *prouincialis*. Quoniam Syd. erat prouin- 30 cialis episcopus et non metropolitanus .i. archiepiscopus, quoniam metropolis est mater ciuitatum. *procacis* .i. inprobi, vnde procacitas .i. proteruia. *penditote* .i. librate a penso
.i. erronea
uel a pondere. *erratum* .i. errorem, vnde Erratica prauitas. *opinionis* .i. famae. *obloqui* .i. detrahere, unde obloquium .i. detractio. *obloquentium* .i. contra loquentium. *scillas* .i. pericula marina sabulosa. *officium*. Quoniam officium est abbatis semper flere. Vnde 35 dicitur quod monachus dolentis habet officium. Sed episcopus quisque duplicem gerit

---

3. acessit.   5. unde Terentius] Persius *codex Nimirum et* ualitudo *et ualeant hoc habent commune quod modo in bonam partem, modo in malam dicuntur. Nam interdum* ualeant *per* εὐφημισμὸν *idem est quod pereant.* (*Donat. ad And. IV.* 3. 14.)   12. parrochie.   28. fort. inclinauit uortices.   32. proteruia Vnde proteruus *codex.* pensa.   33. oppinionis.   34. obloquentium] obloquiorum *codices Sidonii.*   35. sabulosa] *num* fabulosa?   36. dupplicem.

H 2

GLOSSAE IN SIDONIVM.

Fol. 145ᵃ.   personam quoniam regit ecclesiastica et regalia. *seueritas* uirtus est cum mediocris est. *superstitiosus* auarus quoniam auariria mala religio est. *abstemium* .i. sobrium .i. abstinentem a temeto .i. uino. *inpetitur* .i. accusatur. *inuncabuntur* unco .i. troco curuo trahentur. *ceruicosi* sunt elati et superbi et dicuntur ceruicosi quia ceruicem suam .i. caput alte supportant. *factione.* Factio est conspiratio in malum, unde Macrobius, Epicureorum tota 5 factio. *aemulationum* .i. inuidiarum. *assertione* confirmatione. *karisma* .i. donum. *fastigatur* uel a fastigio quod est altitudo uel a fastu quod est superbia. *opinaretur* Symon magus uidens Petrum apostolum miracula multa facientem optulit Petro multa donaria ut doceret illum talia miracula facere. Et quia putauit Symon magus pretio posse emi miracula Sancti Spiritus damnauit illum Petrus et omnes postea Symoniacos. 10 *tribunalibus* .i. iudicialibus. *canone* regula decretali. *efficax* dicitur quasi effectus capax. *rudimentis.* Rudimenta paruorum proprie sunt, ut alphabetum et alia talia quae in initio erudiuntur. *Solimis* .i. in Ierusalem, quoniam prius dicebatur ciuitas illa Solime et postea a quodam rege qui ibi regnauit, qui dicebatur Iebus, dicebatur ciuitas illa Iebosolime et sic mutata .b. in .r. propter kacenfaton dicebatur Ierosolime et postea Ierusalem, ab 15 alio rege Palaestinorum Palaestina prouincia. Ex Saba uenit quaedam sapientissima regina ad Salomonem regem propter eius sapientiam .s. ut ipsa temptaret sapientiam Salomonis. Salomon autem dixit illi quicquid illa aenigmatibus quibusdam quaesiuit uel mente cogitauit. Salomonisque scientiam admirata infinitam pecuniam auri et argenti ad templum construendum ei donauit. In Salomonis autem curia quaedam 20 arbor crescebat quam quotienscumque regina illa uidebat genua flexit illam adorans. De qua arbore lignum erat crucis Dominicae. Omnes autem admirabantur quare illam arborem adoraret. Postea uero cum regina illa remearet in patriam suam renunciauit Salomoni quod in curia eius quaedam arbor cresceret in qua passurus erat mortem rex Iudaeorum. Salomon autem hoc audito illam arborem in uisceribus terrae abscondit. 25 Sed in tempore natiuitatis Christi in probatica piscina supernatauit. *cumulauerit* auxerit.

VII. 10.

   Discretos diuisos. *Sed de bis. Quasi dicat,* Nolo plus loqui de miseria mea quoniam qui miseriam suam recolit eo magis dolet.

VII. 12.
                                                                                                                30
   Hic excusat se Syd. quod nullas litteras prius Ferriolo isti misit nec quod illi hunc suum librum nomine illius intitulauit. *affinitatis* .i. uicinitatis. Vnde Per Bethleem confinia .i. per uicinas illas patrias. *patrias infulas* .i. dignitates uel potestates. *triumfalibus adoreis* .i. uictoriis et est ador nomen indeclinabile frumenti. *stemmatibus* genealogiis parentum sicut alibi dicitur Stemmata quid faciunt (*Iuuen. VIII.* 1). Item 35 stemma est ordo uel series generationis. Stemma autem dicebatur filum quo sacerdotes tempore aestiuali capita ligabant non ualentes portare pilleos. Et frequenter pro corona accipitur. *exinaniretur* .i. euacuaretur. *incolumes* .i. alacres .i. in pace. *acuminaretur*

   2. auaricia.   3. themeto.   5. Macrobius] *Comm. in Somn. Scip. I.* 2. 3.   10. dampnauit.   13. erudiunt.   15. mutatata.   16. a palestina prouintia.   21. adhorans.   23. adhoraret.

GLOSSAE IN SIDONIVM. 53

.i. acueretur. *bebetatus* .i. 'rebuche' .i. induratus. *exbaustus* .i. pauperatus propter tributa quae dederat prius Gothis.

VII. 13.

Hymerius antistes. Haec epistola continet laudes sacerdotis Hymerii filii .s. †Simplicii papae. *opinione* .i. fama. *uenustate* .i. pulcritudine. *sale* .i. sapientia, quo- 5 niam iiii habet significationes hoc nomen sal. Significat enim ipsam substantiam salis, et dicta saporata, et reprehensoria, et sapientiam, sicut dictum est Accipe sal sapientiae. *consulitur* qum aliquis quaerit consilium ab illo. *consulit* quando ille consilium quaerit ab alio. *celeritas*. Quoniam si aliquis pauper coram illo causam habet agendam, uel etiam aliquis diues aliquando protrahit illam causam, cito eam 10 expedit, prout uiderit expedire illi qui iniuriam patitur. *rependatur* .i. soluatur. Vnde rependit qui pro inpenso beneficio retribuit. *credulus* est ille qui omnia dicta sibi credit.

VII. 14.

Peruicaciter. Peruicax est ille qui peruertit uices rerum .s. iustum pro iniusto et 15 uerum pro falso asserendo. *controuersarentur* .i. confligerent. *sicut facile conuinci ita difficile compesci* possunt. *Conuinci facile*, quoniam falsum et inprobabile dicentes possunt facile falsitatis argui. *difficile compesci*, quia semper uolunt blaterare .i. garrire. *dumtaxat* .i. tantummodo. *uultuum* quoniam laici illi magis laudant speciem corporis quam animae uirtutem. Indignatus igitur Sid. iterum probat multis modis quod magis 20 diligendus est Filagrius propter commoda animae suae quam propter commoda corporis. Quoniam etiam bruta animalia ipsis hominibus fortiora sunt et uelociora et maiora et multas uirtutes corporis habent quas homo habere non potest. *nouercari* .i. insidiari ad modum nouercae. Vnde dictum est Iste nouercatur mihi .i. insidiando aduersatur, et Sidonius *Inbecillitati nostrae nouercabor*. *noctua* .i. 'fresale' .i. quaedam auis magna ut 25 coruus quae tota nocte cantat. *uultur* est auis quae Anglice uocatur 'grip' in cuius ouo ponuntur reliquiae. De quo sic dicitur †Vulturis in siluis miserum mandebat homonem. *symio* nam dicitur hic symius et haec symia.

VII. 15.

Quotiens Viennam. Nomen ciuitatis ubi erat episcopatus. *inputationem* .s. quod ei non 30 possum inputare nec illum culpare. ·*serius* .i. tardius.

VII. 16.

Succiduo a succedendo .i. a successione continua unde Sid. *angore succiduo*. *libertos* .i. manumissos qui a seruitute sunt suspensi.

VII. 17. 35

Desides .i. pigros et negligentes. *incudibus* romanioe 'enclume.' *obsecundabo* .i. obsequar

5. †Simplicii] *immo* Sulpicii. oppinione. 10. causam aliquando cito. 27. Vulturis] Ennius *ap*. Priscian. *I*. 206 *Herts, Seru. ad Aen. VI*. 595. *Poeta uidetur scripsisse* Volturus; *sed cum glossatore nostro boni codices Prisciani* Vulturis. 33. succeduo. continuo. anguore.

GLOSSAE IN SIDONIVM.

uel obtemperabo, *truculenti* .i. pleni crudelitate. *lemurum* .i. nocturnarum fantasiarum quae in somno apparent. *daemonas* .i. daemones et est accusatiuus Graecus. *Helissae*. Helissa erat Dido cui rex Hyarchas dedit tantum terrae quantum corio taurino posset circumdari. Dido autem corium quoddam taurinum in minutissimas corrigias scidit, et illis maximum terrae amplexa est in qua fecit Cart*h*aginem. *Birsica tecta* .i. Cart*h*a- 5 ginem a birsa quod est corium taurinum. Vnde uersus *Spernis Elisseae birsica tecta domus* (*u.* 16) Mediolanum. Cum autem Mediolanum iam factum fuerat, dubitatur quod nomen illi ciuitati inponeretur. Et apparuit statim illis hominibus dubitantibus quidam aper ex media parte setam habens et ex media lanam. Illi autem qui ex una parte fuerunt dicebant esse ouem. Alii ex alia parte dicebant esse porcum. Et ideo propter 10 hanc nouitatem aliquid significantem inposuerunt urbi illi nomen Mediolanum. *paupertinus* pauper. *culmo* .i. stipula.

VII. 18.

Animi seruitutem. Ille patitur animi seruitutem cui aliquis conuitia ingerit .i. infert et postea conuitiatori nec conuitia infert nec satyra se uindicat quod romanice dicitur 15 'mauues daunger.' Eodem modo ille patitur animi seruitutem qui uitiosos non audet satyra reprehendere.

VIII. 1.

Tu quidem pulcre .s. facis. *lenocinaris* .i. blandiris. *suspicabamur* .i. putabamus. *uulgatu* .i. diuulgatu. *cauendum est ne in aliquos fortuitu* .i. forsitan *incidamus uituperones* 20 .i. uituperatores a uituperio. *quorum linguas cote liuoris acuminatas fugere* necessarium est. *derogatores* dicuntur turpiloqui unde dictum est iste derogat mibi .i. 'mesdit.'

VIII. 3.

Scedium est nouum scriptum nondum ex asse emendatum uel limatum. *opaca* .i. obscura. *inpluuio*. Inpluuium aliquando pro stillicidio ponitur, ut hic *inpluuio cubiculi* 25 *mei*, aliquando pro lu*mi*nario .i. fenestra domus quae in medio tecto domus pendet : ut

Fol. 149ᵇ.

in fabula. Nam in fabulis dicitur quod Dan*a*e pulcherrima puella fuit et ideo clausa erat in quadam eminentissima turri ne aliquis ad eam posset accedere. Tandem Iupiter eius amore accensus transformauit se in aurum et descendit per inpluuium domus in gremium Dan*a*es tamquam pluuia. *Pythicas* Foebeas .i. Apollinis qui deus erat sapientiae, 30 Et dicuntur Pythic*a*e lauri a Pythone serpente quem Ph*o*ebus occidit. *lauros* .i. sententias et colores r*h*etoricos. Nam Phoebus solebat coronari foliis lauri. *penitissime* a penitus. *domesticum* .i. priuatum. *atauo* hi sunt gradus parentum ascendendo pater auus proauus abauus atauus tritauus. Similiter descendendo pater filius nepos pronepos abnepos trinepos. *alabastrum* est uas unguentarium album ad modum albi marmoris 35

---

1. truculenti] *Codices Sidonii* truculentae. Videtur glossator legisse regis. fantasyarum. 2. sompno. demonas. demones. acusatiuus. 3. hyarchas] *sic codex*. 10. .i. diuulgatu] *addit codex* uel uulgatu. Vulgatum est res uilis uel uulgo digna. fortuitu] forsitan *Cod. Laud.* 104. 24. opaca] *sic codices plerique Sidonii, non* opica. 26. iuuario. ut in (fabula] *Non sunt haec uerba Sidonii*. 27. dane. 29. in ingremium danes tamquam. 30. phiticas. 31. phitice. phitone.

GLOSSAE IN SIDONIVM. 55

uel cristalli. Vnde alibi legitur alabastrum nardi pistici. *delibutarum* .i. inunctarum. *satrapas* satrapae lingua Syriorum duces uel principes .i. sapientes uocantur. *malo*bath*ratos.* Malobat*ò*rum est quoddam latum folium ut dicunt medici quod in Nilo repperitur supernatans. Et dicunt phisici quidam quod folium illud est folium ligni aloes quae crescit in paradiso et cum Nilo exit. Hoc autem mal*o*bat*ò*rum apponunt 5 medici pre*t*iosis unguentis et electuariis. *squalore* a squama piscis quae est hirsuta et dura et aspera et uillosa. Et ponitur squalor frequenter pro duritia siue pro sorde ut squalor carceris. *forsfuat* .i. dubium est uel dubitet aliquis.

VIII. 4.

Vnquamne. Ne .i. an. Sydonius in hac epistola desiderat ut aliquando detur sibi copia 10 uidendi Consentium istum et eius domum libris refertam et eius rus multis commodis et diuitiis plenum. *thymum.* T*h*ymus est quidam flos suauissimum habens odorem unde poeta (*Geor. IV.* 169) Redolentque t*h*imo flagrantia mella. *donaria* sunt dona quae donantur. *prodigimus* .i. large damus.

VIII. 5.

Hybericarum .i. Hyspanicarum quoniam Hiberi sunt Hispani.

VIII. 6.

Ducalius .i. melius et fortius a duce. *mutuo* .i. alternatim. *inficias* .i. negationes. *luculentis* .i. luce plenis. *trabeatus.* Trabea erat species togae ex purpura et cocco qua operti reges Romanorum procedebant. Et dicta trabea quod in maiorem gloriam 20 hominem ultra ceteros transbearet. *sportula.* Sportula est munus quod datur praeconibus et aliis praetorianis ministris et executoribus causarum. Et dicuntur executores qui rem iudicatam mancipant effectui. *fasti* .i. honores. Nam proprie fasti sunt libri annales in quibus scribuntur festa, et inde dicuntur translatiue honores fasti, quia in libris annalibus statim scribebatur tempus quando aliquis ad honorem peruenerat et sub 25 quo imperatore. *ante lucanas horas* .i. ante diem. *disposite* .i. ordinate .i. 'assisement.' *crepitantia* .i. sonantia. *segmenta.* Segmenta sunt quaedam Indumenta parua circa collum per humeros usque ad pectus dependentia quae possunt appellari 'scapelarie.' Et sunt segmenta inserta et referta gemmis pretiosis et auro. *palmatam* palmata est quaedam uestis pretiosa quae dabatur alicui ob uictoriam. *per ipsum fere tempus* usualis 30 est locutio .i. fere in illo tempore .i. parum ante illud tempus. Contigit quod Nicetius quamdam promulgauit legem de praescriptione longi temporis omni populo illi fauente et collaudante. Et nota quod aliud est praescriptio atque aliud est usucapio, usucapio enim est de rebus mobilibus, praescriptio autem de rebus est *non* mobilibus. Praescriptio autem est adquisitio dominii per continuationem longi temporis lege diffiniti. *abolita* .i. 35

---

3. Malobratos. malobatrum. 5. malobotrum. 6. preciosis. hyrsuta. 10. *sibi*] ei *codex.* 12. tymum. tymus. 13. timo. 14. prodigimus] *Num sic legit glossator pro eo quod codices habent* agimus? 20. praecedebant. 23. festa] *Fortasse ex Paul. Diac. fluxit haec glossa* Fastorum *libri appellantur, in quibus totius anni fit descriptio.* Fasti *enim dies festi sunt.* 26. assisement] *h. e.* conuenablement. 29. preciosis. 32. promulgauit] *intra Gallias scilicet.* de praescriptione] *sc. tricennaria, de qua Nouella extat Valentiniani XXVI. De xxx annorum praescriptione omnibus caussis opponenda* (p. 213 *ed. Haenelianae*). 34. *non*] om. *codex.*

56   GLOSSAE IN SIDONIVM.

deleta. *peremptoriis* quoniam omnem actionem in fine quinti decimi anni perimebat. Vnde dicitur dies peremptorius et institutorius: peremptorius quando aliquis peremptus est, ut ita dicam, .i. depositus ab officio in quo prius fuerat; cuius officium peremptum est quodam modo .i. ab eo sublatum uel ablatum. Et ille dies dicitur institutorius quando aliquis post alium instituitur uel ille qui ibi prius fuit uel alius subsequens. 5 *indidit* .i. demonstrauit. *edidit* .i. promulgauit. *decetero* .i. amodo. *capreas*. Nota quod aliud est capra, aliud caprea. Nam caper .i. *aedus* et capra simul iunguntur. Caprea autem est de feris bestiis. Et sunt illarum ferarum tria genera. Minimum inter illa est capreolus et caprea, maius uero animal damma. et est damma communis generis ad marem et ad feminam; maximum autem est ceruus et cerua quae romanice dicitur 10 'bisse.' *dereliquo* .i. de cetero .i. a modo. *scrupeas* .i. scopulosas et cauernosas. *lustris* .i. cubilibus ferarum. *circumuenire* .i. cauillari et decipere. *opacandis* .i. celandis quia opacitas .i. tenebrae celant .i. abscondunt. *canes ueloces* dicuntur canes leporarii qui lepores capiunt, uel alii canes qui ceruos et alias feras capiunt. Canes uero rustican̄i sunt qui in domibus rusticorum sunt, qui caulas ouium de nocte custodiunt ab incursione 15 luporum. *lepusculis* leporibus. *classicum* romanice 'glas.' Solebant enim milites cum socios ad bellandum conuocarent aut cum praedam aut hostes caperent cum cornibus suis classicum sonare. Et dicitur a clangendo unde clangor. *classe* .i. nauigio. *pandos* .i.

Fol. 150ᵃ.   curuos. *archypiratas* .i. principes piratarum; [et dicuntur piratae praedones maris .i. 'Robburs' a pir quod est ignis quia per ignem alias naues deperdant]. *discriminibus* 20 .i. periculis. *mioparones*. Paro dicitur a piratis. Vnde parunculus per diminutionem et mioparo quasi minimus paro. Est enim scapha ex uiminibus facta quae contexta crudo corio genus nauigii praebet quo utuntur Germanorum piratae in Oceani litoribus uel paludibus propter agilitatem (*Isid. Orig. XIX*, 1. 21). *remiges* qui remo nauigant.

VIII. 7.   25

Macte .i. mactus et ponitur aliquando pro nominatiuo ut dicit Priscianus (*XVII*, 208), ut Esto macte .i. sis mactus .i. uirtuosus quasi magis auctus, uel Macte .i. o macte. *misericordiae causas* quoniam de miserias patiente et paupere et damnato miseriam habemus, sed de superiore inuidiam, quoniam Perflant altissima uenti (*Ouid. Rem.* 369). *iusto principe* .i. 'iusto buore' de quo dictum est Iustius inuidia nihil est quae protinus 30 ipsum Auctorem rodit excruciatque suum.

VIII. 8.

Tesserarum .i. talorum. *instrumenta Cerealia* .i. carruca. *Cerealia* a Cerere quae est dea segetis. *bibernis noualibus*. Noualibus .i. 'warez'; et est nouale terra

---

1. perimebat] *Dig. V.* 1. 70 Tunc peremptorium impetret. Quod inde hoc nomen sumpsit, quod peremerit disceptationem, hoc est ultra non pateretur aduersarium tergiuersari.   6. amodo] *h. e.* posthac.   12. cauillare.   13. canes ueloces] *Spectant haec et quae secuntur de canibus ad uerba Sidonii* Namque apros frustra in uenabula uocas quos canibus misericordissimis . . . mouere potius quam commouere consuesti.   20. pir] *etymologia uere inepta.*   22. contexta] contecta *nonnulli codices Isidori.*   30. Iustius inuidia] *Extant ap. Hieronymum VII.* p. 568 *Vall. unde in codicem Sangallensem* 899 *f.* 132ᵇ *et Einsiedelensem* 326 *f.* 90 *uenerunt. Vide Baehrensii Poet. Lat. Min. III. p.* 169.   31. suum] animum *Hieronymus.*

GLOSSAE IN SIDONIVM. 57

antiqua uel pratum aliquod nuper aratum et sic iacet per totam hiemem absque semine et contra aestatem iterum aratur et tunc primo inseminatur. *ligonis* .i. 'picois.' *antibus*. Antes sunt pedamenta uinearum quae in anteriori parte uineam sustinent. Vel antes sunt extremi ordines uinearum. Vnde Virgilius (*Geor. II.* 417) Iam canit †affectus extremi uinitor antes. Vnde Sydonius *quousque pondus ligonis* 5 *optusi nec perfossis antibus ponis? stiuam* caudam aratri. *parce* .i. desine rusticari. *in inuidiam* .i. in odium nobilitatis, quoniam nobiles iam habebuntur odiosi, sicut alii rustici, quoniam magis intendunt agriculturae et lucro quam militiae. Et nota quod multotiens ponitur inuidia pro odio, ut in Tullio de amicitia, ut ibi Qui ad uiuum resecant sibi nomen amicitiae inuidiosum et obscurum sapientiam habent. Vel melius 10 *ad inuidiam nobilium* .i. ad increpationem nobilium, quoniam nobiles omnes increpabuntur et eis detrahetur propter rusticitatem tuam. Et †quod inuidia aliquando ponitur pro increpatione, hoc est exemplum auarorum increpantium deum quod plura eis non det. Vnde poeta Inuidiam fecere deis etc. *torques bracteatae*. Nam bractea est idem quod grossa et spissa lamina auri. *fastos* honores. *profecto* .i. certe. *industrium* industrius 15 est ille qui industriam habet .i. scientiam; unde industrie aduerbium.

VIII. 9.

Cum primum Burde. Nomen ciuitatis. Iste Lampridius mirae fuit facundiae et sapientiae, ut inferius in hoc libro dicetur, et semel ille cum Sydon. expulsus a terra sua simul exulauerunt. Tandem renocatus est a rege Francorum, qui eum expulerat, Lampridius, 20 et post illum remansit solus Sydon. in exilio, ibi multas aduersitates patiens, nec unquam a rege potuit licentiam habere redeundi. Mandauit postmodum Lampridius Sydonio adhuc in exilio posito ut illi aliquod metrum destinaret quod ipse posset cum tibiis et modulatione uocis cantare. Sidonius autem illi metrum sequens mittit, primo tamen excusans se quod non composite et tam decenter factum sit sicut deberet. Nam 25 Sidonius in exilio positus tristis erat. Et non potest tristis animus composite scribere. *nectaris* .i. pigmenti. *hoe*. Ebrii ad honorem Bacchi solebant in festis ipsius clamare *hoe bacche*. *poetarum* q. d. nullus qui metra scribit composite scribere potest nisi laetus sit. *amiciuntur* .i. cooperiuntur. Vnde alibi Amictus stola candida. Et dicitur amicior amiciris amictus sum et c^a., quia omnino differunt amicior et amicor. *lemma*. Lemma 30 potest dici tenor siue compositio siue sillogismus. Vnde per compositionem dilemma dicitur cornutus sillogismus, qui in rhetorica dicitur complexio. *ineptiae*. Ineptia inportunitas idem est. *olorinorum*. Olor est cignus. Vnde Cantus olorinus .i. Cignorum. *amiciuntur* .l. cooperiuntur. Vnde Sydonius *Nosti probe laetitiam poetarum quorum sic ingenia macroribus ut pisciculi retibus amiciuntur. Et si quid asperum est aut triste non statim se* 35

9. amicicia.] *De Amicit. V.* 18 Sed hoc primum sentio nisi in bonis amicitiam esse non posse: neque id ad uiuum reseco, *et mox* Quare sibi habeant sapientiae nomen et inuidiosum et obscurum. 12. Et quod inuidia] *Haec uitiosa sunt. Fortasse legendum est* Et nota quod inuidia aliquando ponitur pro increpatione; hoc est exemplum, auarorum increpantium deum quod plura eis non det. Vnde poeta, κ.τ.λ. 14. Inuidiam fecere deis] *Ouid. M. IV.* 547 Inuidiam fecere deae. *Stat. Theb. III.* 197 Inuidiam planxere deis. 18. lapridius. 21. exilium. 27. bachi. 29. cooperiuntur. 32. rethorica. 33. olor est cignus *om*. 34. leticiam. 35. meroribus.

I   [I. 5.]

poetica teneritudo a uinculo incursi angoris elaqueat. pantomimorum. Pantomimorum illorum
.s. qui per regiones discurrunt cantatores. Et dicitur pantomimus a pan quod est totum
et mimus ioculator et inde pantomimus quasi totus ioculator. *camenas.* Musas quasi
canentes am*o*ene. *tripodas* .i. tripodes et est accusatiuus gr*ae*ecus. *gripbas* .i. griphes
et est accusatiuus graecus. Et sunt griphes aues qu*a*edam magn*a*e corpulenti*a*e, 5
dedicatae Apollini, quia nimis alte contra radium solis uolare possunt. Vel griphes,
quoniam griphes, ut dictum est, monstruosae aues sunt et n*i*mis inimicantur equis et
animalia alia unguibus rapiunt. Et ideo hic griphes enumerat Sydonius inter illa quae
pertinent ad Apollinem, quia Apollo arcu suo monstra interficiebat et griphes. Vnde
Apollo dicitur p*y*thicus a pythone serpente quem ipse interfecit. *duplaeque frontis* .i. 10
habens duplam frontem sicut Apollo. Nam Apollo solebat ante et retro coronari fructu
lauri et fructu heder*a*e, quoniam laurus et hedera semper uirent quemadmodum debent
ingenia philosophorum. Haec *bacca* huius bacc*a*e est fructus lauri. *corimbus* corimbi
est fructus heder*a*e. *mirtos* mirtus est quaedam arbor paruula dedicata Veneri propter
eius calorem ex qua fit medo. *platanus* est quaedam arbor lata habens folia et inde 15
platanona .i. †loci ubi crescunt platani et est graecum. *barbitos* .i. citharam, quia
barbiton est cithara quae fit ex ossibus barri .i. elefantis. *per extimas* .i. per extremas.
elicit .i. extrahit. Vnde phisicus, Menstruus elicitur muliebri e corpore sanguis, et alibi,
Qui fortiter emungit nasum elicit sanguinem. *algoso profundo.* Alga est sordes maris .i.
herba uilissima quam proicit mare. *de podio.* Podium est lignum super quod homines ad 20
spectandum siue ad audiendum, ut modo pluribus habetur in ecclesiis, sese sustentant
atque suppodiant.

VIII. 10.   *Vt uera laus ornat ita falsa castigat. Quo loci tamen.* Hic monstrat Sydonius
quod Ruricius eum sic laudauit ut ingenium suum et scientiam probaret in difficili 25
materia et falsa, et ad hoc probandum multa exempla inducit. Verbi gratia bonus
agricola probari potest in sterili terra et bonus orator in difficili et falsa materia et
medicus in maxima alicuius *a*egritudine. *Materiae sterilis argumentum.* Argumentum
nullum habuisti quare essem bonorum morum, et argumentum tuum ieiunat, non habens
materiam fecundam sed sterilem et feram. Sed nota quod in omnibus dictionibus his 30
respicit ad similitudinem. *scaturit* habundat et proprie ponitur pro ebullire. *praecedentia pericula* .i. praecedentia experimenta. Nam periculum quandoque pro experientia
ponitur. Vnde poeta Insidior uobis uestrosque periclitor actus .i. experior. Sed tunc
deri*u*atur periculum a peritia .i. sapientia, unde dicit Sidonius *Nam moris est eloquentibus
uiris ingeniorum facultatem negotiorum probare difficultatibus, et illic stilum peritum quasi* 35
Fol. 150ᵇ.   *quemdam fecundi pectoris uomerem figere, ubi materiae sterilis argumentum uelut arida
cespitis macri gleba ieiunat. Scaturit mundus similibus exemplis. Medicus in desperatione,
gubernator in tempestate cognoscitur. Horum omnium famam praecedentia pericula extollunt,
quae profecto delitescit nisi ubi probetur inuenerit. Sic et magnus orator si negotium aggredia-*

4. amene. acusatiuos grecus *bis*.   5. griphes] *Seruius ad Ecl. VIII.* 27 griphes equis
uehementer infestis, Apollini consecrati.   7. nmis.   10. phiticus.   15. medo] *Anglice*
'mede.'   25. eum laudauit ut sic *codex*.   33. poeta] *Non repperi.*   34. deruatur.
35. fac difficultatibus (*sic*).

tur angustum, tunc amplum plausibilius manifestat ingenium. De centum uirali suggestu .i. de tribunali centum uirorum iudicum. Centumuir est qui habet centum uiros sub se. Semper fere nomina huiusmodi duumuir triumuir decemuir centumuir ponuntur pro iudicibus. *suggestum* romanice 'deis.' *domum retulit* .i. portauit et est usualis locutio. *decipulam* romanice 'calchetrappe' qualis est illa in qua aues capiuntur. Et decipula a decipiendo; sic muscipula quia mures capit. *indulges* .i. intendis. Vnde dicitur Auarus indulget qu*ae*stui .i. intendit .i. operam dat.

VIII. 11.
     Altrinsecus .i. alternatim. *matrimonium.* Idem est hic matrimonium quod dos quam uir cum uxore accipit. Sed tamen alibi aliter accipitur matrimonium ut inter istos contractum est matrimonium .i. coniugium uel nuptiae. *egeries* ab extra et gerendo. *Bibliotheca* .i. repositio librorum a †biblis quod est liber et t*h*eca quod est positio. *plectris* .i. citharis [Pecten dicitur quod pexos faciat capillos. Vnde poeta Incompti capitis pectuntur pectine crines. Pecten etiam ponitur pro plectro citharae, siue pro ipsa cit*h*ara, unde legitur in †Virgilio de Orpheo Commouit pectine manes. Pecten uero ponitur pro 'plaix' quodam pisce. Vnde †Iuuenalis Pectinibus patulis iactat se molle Tarentum .i. aqua uel flumen. Pecten uero ponitur pro rastro unde alius poeta Sparsim diffusas lustrabo pectine spicas]. *procella* dicitur quod percellat .i. percusiat. *uitta* .i. 'bendello.' *Rugas tibi profundi sirmatis Succingant hederae expeditiores. Rugas* quoniam sirma est proprie rugosum. *profundi* .i. longi usque ad terram. *hedera* est arbor semper uirens. *Ansae* et *ansulae* aliculus rei sunt illa eminentia in illa re per quam capi possit .i. 'stale.' *pernix* .i. uelox a nitor niteris. *parato hospitio* .i. si uoluerit me hospitari .i. 'herberger.' *manu osculata* hic notatur triplex osculum. Nam cum uenimus ad apostolicum Romanum osculamur eius pedem. Cum uero ad episcopum, osculamur eius manum; cum uero ad aequalem, osculamur eius os. *serpilliferis catenis* caldariorum .i. portantibus serpillum et est serpillum herba quaedam quae iuxta terram serpit, quae uocatur romanice 'puliol' et est aptissima ad salsamenta condenda. *crepitantibus* .i. sonum facientibus, unde crepitare .i. sonare. *cieo* cies ciui ciere producta media idem est quod suscitare uel commouere. *excitus* .i. excitatus media correpta .i. euigilatus uel expergefactus. *camena* .i. cantu. *susurrare* .i. murmurando detrahere. Vnde susurrones. *O necessitas.* Hic persequitur Sidonius uitia ipsius Lampridii et postmodum eius uirtutes, dicens quod aliquantulum iracundus erat et cito mouebatur ad iram, et quod ita seuerus esset quod putabant eum homines esse crudelem et ideo redarguebant eum crudelitatis. Sed Sidonius semper eum excusauit, dicens quod illam iram magis haberet Lampridius ex materia et complexione et natura quam aliquo alio uitio animi. Postea dicit Sidonius quod ille erat maximae uirtutis

---

2. centum uiros sub se] *Videlicet ipse inter centum est.* 14. Incompti] *Non repperi.* 15. Virgilio] *nusquam legitur.* 16. Iuuenalis] *immo Horatius S. II.* 4. 34. 18. Sparsim] *Non repperi.* 19. percuciat. 20. rugosum] *Post hoc addit codex* et est proprie sirma anglice 'hem' .i. margo femineae uestis. 22. *parato hospitio*] om. *codex.* 25. serpilliferis. 26. cathenis. caldariorum *h. e. fasciculis serpylli quales in caldariis ad ius condiendum inmittuntur.* 27. condenda] *num* condienda?

GLOSSAE IN SIDONIVM.

et auctoritatis et reuerentiae apud quoslibet, et qualiter instructus fuit in oratoria facultate. *naturam* hic uocat complexionem uel naturam .s. ex progenie deriuatam. *seueritas* uirtus est grauis personae. *emacularetur* .i. extra maculam poneretur. *poemata* poema dicitur a poesis quod est figmentum. Inde poeta qui in uersibus suis quandoque ad delectationem intermiscet falsa ueris unde Aut prodesse uolunt aut delectare poetae 5 (Hor. A. P. 333). Et alius uersus Scribimus indocti doctique poemata passim (Hor. Epp. II. 1. 117). *oppido exactos* .i. ualde perfectos. *exametros uersus* .i. vi pedum. *recurrentes* .i. retrogrados, sicut Roma tibi subito motibus ibit amor. Hii nimirum sunt recurrentes uersus qui metro stante neque litteris loco motis ut ab exordio ad terminum sic a fine releguntur ad summum. Sicut est illud antiquum Roma tibi subito et cetera quae 10 praedicuntur et iterum illud Sole medere pede. ede perede melos. (Sid. IX. 14.) *bucolica* Virgilius fecit Bucolica in quibus loquitur de bobus et introducit pastores custodientes boues. *Georgica* a †geos quod est terra et inde Georgica quae docent colere terram qualia sunt Georgica Virgilii. *distico* tenore duorum uersuum a †dia quod est duo et

sticos quod est uersus. *tetrastico* tenore iiii uersuum. *oda* uel *odos* dicitur laus uel cantus. 15 *citus* dicitur propter uelocitatem pedis. *scripturiret*. Verbum meditatiuum est .i. semper fuit in meditatione scribendi. *matbematicos* .i. astronomicos. *sanguinaria genitura* .i. sanguine plena. *strangulatus* romanice 'estrangle.' *paricidales* .i. in paricidio consentientes. *obtutu* .i. uisu. *exanimati* .i. anima exspoliati. *animare* uero aliud significat, quod est uiuificare uel inducere. *cadauer* est corpus sine anima. *extortae* ui raptae. 20 *protuberantes* grossi. *tabo deciduo* .i. tabe quae decidebat ab ore et a naribus. Et nota quod hoc nomen tabo non habet in declinatione nisi ablatiuum. *inconsulte* .i. stulte. VIII. 12. *consultat* .i. quaerit. *interdicta* prohibita.

Crocodili sunt animalia quaedam crudelissima in Nilo habitantia et homines necantia 25 et deuorantia. *Sirticus*. Sirtes sunt quaedam loca arenosa in mari ita, ut nec omnino sint nec omnino aqua cooperta; sed alicubi sunt sicca ut per ea transire possit quis siccis pedibus. Vocat igitur Sydonius agrum Sirticum .i. arenosum et sabulosum quia in ea ciuitate potest quis perire propter habundantiam sabuli et est ibi *pedestre naufragium*. *per anadiplosim*. Anadiplosis est geminatio dictionis ex ultimo loco prae- 30 cedentis uersus et principio sequentis ut *pulcherrimus Astur Astur equo fidens etc.* (Verg. Aen. X. 180). *suda* .i. clara. *Auras*. Aurae sunt quando aer aliquantulum mouetur ex minimo inpulsu parui uenti. *enixius* .i. fortius et melius, a nitor niteris. *temperies* aer temperatus. *opipare* nobiliter ab opibus paratis. *mugilibus* mugiles sunt nobiles pisces qui romanice uocantur 'mulesz.' 35

11. sole medere pede] *immo* Sole medere pedes. Bubolica. 19. ex anima spoliati. 25. Cocodrilli. 27. possit] potest. 30. Anadiplosis] *Charis*. 281 *Keil* Anadiplosis est cum eadem dictio et in clausula uersus et in principio sequentis ponitur ut Sequitur pulcherrimus Astor A. e. f. et uernicoloribus armis. *Diomed*. 445 *Keil*. Anadiplosis est cum ultima prioris uersus dictio initio sequentis iteratur ut Sequitur pulcherrimus Astyr, Astyr equo fidens.

GLOSSAE IN SIDONIVM.

VIII. 13.
  Conducibilius .i. compendiosius et melius.

VIII. 14.
  Nadab et Abiud isti duo conflagrati sunt caelesti igne .i. combusti sunt, quia trecesserant contra mandatum Domini, quia iusserat eis Dominus ut numquam alium ignem ponerent in turibulis suis ad incensendum altare quam illum ignem qui perpetuo reseruabatur in tabernaculo. Quodam autem die spreto domini mandato alienum ignem ponebant in turibulis suis et conflagrati sunt, quod totum significat quod omnes catholici mundam debent habere conscientiam et amorem purum apud deum et sanctum spiritum in corde suo et non alienum .i. malignum.

VIII. 16.
  Coactorum .i. coadunatorum. Vnde Virgilius Tityre coge pecus. *leuigatur* .i. conplanatur uel politur. Vnde Sidonius *pumices muscidos* dicit .i. habentes muscum. Et est muscus anglice ' musse ' uel ' mosse.'

IX. 9.
  Thematis. Thema dicitur similitudo uel materia uel positio uel etiam causa. Vnde dicit Sidonius *thematis ante inauditi operam peruulgat.*

IX. 13.
  Genialis apparatus .i. naturalis. *crepula bucca* .i. sonora. [Lux crepera .i. dubia. Vnde Res crepera .i. anceps dubium me facit (Symm. Epp. I. 1).] *Quaestus* tus tui .i. romanice ' purcaz.' [Vnde Symmachus Quaestus uester in meum currit commodum (Symm. Epp. I. 6). *Inpatientes* dicuntur quasi sine patientia. Vnde Symmachus Solent inpatientes esse dilectionis qui sperant in se aliquid muneris conferendum (Symm. Epp. I. 6).]

  8. catholicus. 19. crepera] *Varro L. L. VI.* 5 In Reatino crepusculum significat dubium : ab eo res dictae dubiae creperae quod crepusculum dies etiam nunc sit an iam nox, multis dubium. *Ib. VII.* 77 dubiae res creperae dictae. *Symmach. Epp. I.* 1 ita res crepera atque anceps dubium me habet. 21. Questus. Symacus. *Codices Symmachi habent* cucurrit quaestus uester in meum commodum. 22. Inpacientes. pacientia. Symachus. 23. inpacientes *Codices Symmachi habent* Solent inpatientes dilationis esse (*non* dilectionis) qui sperant in se aliquid muneris conferendum.

Fol. 145ᵃ.

[ADDENDUM.]

Leccatorum multa genera. Quidam enim dicuntur mimi, quidam balatrones, quidam nebulones, quidam nepotes, quidam scurrae, quidam lenones, quidam histriones, quidam parasiti, quidam farmacopol*ae*, a †farmaca quod est unguentum et †pole quod est uendere. De mimis dicit Horatius in Sermonibus (S. I. 2. 1) Ambubaiarum collegia 5 farmacopol*ae* Mendici mimi balatrones hoc genus omne Maestum ac sollicitum est †mei pro morte Tigelli. Et notandum quod *balatrones* dicuntur a baratro quod est infernus. Dicitur autem baratrum quasi uoratrum quia omnia deuorat. Inde balatrones quasi uoratores, quia propria deuorant et aliena consumunt. Dicuntur *nebulones* a nebula quia ad modum nebulae transit gloria eorum. Vel quia aliena uitia per suas 10 adulationes obc*a*ecant. Dicuntur *nepotes* a nepa serpente quae suos fetus deuorat. *Scurra* proprie appellatur uagus qui de domo ad domum discurrit ut uentrem sa*t*iet. De quibus bene dicitur, Quorum deus uenter est (Paulus ad Philipp. 111. 19). Vnde Magister Serlo Scurrae ieiuni te contra guttura muni. *Lenones* dicuntur conciliatores stupri. Vnde quidam egregius uersificator Leno ferre pedem talem non debet in 15 aedem. Hac habitare domo debet honestus homo. *Histrio* dicitur ab †historon quod est adulari. Vnde quidam in cantilena sua Meretur histrio uirtutis praemium, Dum palpat uitium †dulci mendacio. *Parasiti* dicuntur quasi parantes situs hominum uel quasi iuxta parapsidem siti.

5. collegio. 6. farmacopole. mendices. mestum. 7. †mei pro] *cantoris Horatius* dicuntur a baratro] *Acron ad Hor. S. I.* 2. 2 Barathrones qui bona sua lacerant, id est in barathrum mittunt. 9. a nebula] *Acron ad Hor. Epist. I.* 2. 28 Nebulones leues ut nebula, perditi luxuriosi molles inepti. *Paulus Diac. p.* 164 *M.* Nebulo dictus est qui non pluris est quam nebula, aut qui non facile perspici possit, qualis sit. 11. a nepa] *Placidus s. u. Nepa p.* 70 *Deuerling* Nepa scorpius quae natos consumit nisi eum qui dorso eius inhaeserit. Rursum ipse, qui seruatus fuerit, consumit patrem. Vnde homines qui bona parentum per luxuriam consumunt, nepotes dicuntur. 14. lenones] conciliatoris stupri, qui proprie leno dicitur, *Acron ad Hor. Epist. II.* 1. 272. Serlonis] *Non repperi in Serlonis carminibus editis a Thoma Wright* (Anglo-Latin Satirical Poets of the Twelfth Century, Tom. II). 16. †historon] *hoc quid sit uix expedias.* 18. dulci] *fortasse* dulico. situs] *h. e.* σίτους.

Clarendon Press Publications.

Anecdota Graeca Oxoniensia. Edidit J. A. CRAMER, S.T.P. Tomi iv. 8vo. 22*s*.

Anecdota Graeca e Codd. MSS. Bibliothecae Regiae Parisiensis. Edidit J. A. CRAMER, S.T.P. Tomi iv. 8vo. 22*s*.

Heracliti Ephesii Reliquiae. Rec. I. BYWATER, M.A. Appendicis loco additae sunt Diogenis Laertii Vita Heracliti, Particulae Hippocratei De Diaeta Libri primi, Epistolae Heracliteae. 8vo. 6*s*.

Herculanensium Voluminum Partes II. 8vo. 10*s*.

Scholia Graeca in Iliadem. Edited by Prof. W. DINDORF, after a new collation of the Venetian MSS. by D. B. Monro, M.A., Provost of Oriel College. 8vo.

    Vols. I, II, 24*s*.   Vols. III, IV, 26*s*.
    Vols. V, VI. Edited by E. MAASS, Phil. Doc. [*In the Press.*]

Scriptores rei metricae. Edidit THOMAS GAISFORD, S.T.P. Tomi iii. 8vo. 15*s*.

Catulli Veronensis Liber. Iterum recognovit, apparatum criticum prolegomena appendices addidit, ROBINSON ELLIS, A.M. 8vo. 16*s*.

A Commentary on Catullus. By ROBINSON ELLIS, M.A. 8vo. 16*s*.

P. Ovidii Nasonis Ibis. Ex novis codicibus edidit, Scholia vetera Commentarium cum Prolegomenis Appendice Indice addidit, R. ELLIS, A.M. 8vo. 10*s*. 6*d*.

The Book of Hebrew Roots, by Abu'l-Walîd Marwân ibn Janâh, otherwise called Rabbi Yônâh. Now first edited, with an Appendix, by AD. NEUBAUER, M.A. 4to. 47*s*. 6*d*.

Libri Prophetarum Majorum, cum Lamentationibus Jeremiae, in Dialecto Linguae Aegyptiacae Memphitica seu Coptica. Edidit cum Versione Latina H. TATTAM, S.T.P. Tomi ii. 8vo. 17*s*.

The Psalter, or Psalms of David, and certain Canticles; with a Translation and Exposition in English, by Richard Rolle of Hampole. Edited by H. R. BRAMLEY, M.A. With an Introduction and Glossary. 8vo. 21*s*.

        OXFORD: CLARENDON PRESS.
        LONDON: HENRY FROWDE;
  OXFORD UNIVERSITY PRESS WAREHOUSE, AMEN CORNER.

Anecdota Oxoniensia.

The English Manuscripts of the Nicomachean Ethics, described in relation to Bekker's Manuscripts and other Sources. By J. A. STEWART, M.A. 3*s*. 6*d*.

Aristotle's Physics, Book VII. Collation of various MSS.; with Introduction by R. SHUTE, M.A. 2*s*.

Nonius Marcellus. de Compendiosa Doctrina, Harleian MS. 2719. Collated by J. H. ONIONS, M.A. 3*s*. 6*d*.

Bentley's Plautine Emendations. From his copy of Gronovius. By E. A. SONNENSCHEIN, M.A. 2*s*. 6*d*.

Commentary on Ezra and Nehemiah. By Rabbi Saadiah. Edited by H. J. MATHEWS, M.A. 3*s*. 6*d*.

The Book of the Bee. The Syriac Text, edited, with an English Translation, by E. A. W. BUDGE, B.A. [*In the Press.*]

Buddhist Texts from Japan.

I. Vagrakkhedikâ. Edited by F. MAX MÜLLER, M.A. 3*s*. 6*d*.

II. Sukhâvatî Vyûha. Description of Sukhâvatî, the Land of Bliss. Edited by F. MAX MÜLLER, M.A., and BUNYIU NANJIO, Priest of the Eastern Hongwanri in Japan. 7*s*. 6*d*.

III. The Ancient Palm-leaves containing the Pragñâ-Pâramitâ-Hrïdaya-Sûtra and the Ushnisha-Vigaya-Dhâranî, edited by F. MAX MÜLLER, M.A., and BUNYIU NANJIO, M.A. With an Appendix by G. BÜHLER. 10*s*.

IV. *In the Press*.

The Sarvânukramanî. Edited by A. A. MACDONELL, M.A. [*In the Press.*]

Sinonoma Bartholomei; A Glossary from a Fourteenth-Century MS. in the Library of Pembroke College, Oxford. Edited by J. L. G. MOWAT, M.A. 3*s*. 6*d*.

The Saltair Na Rann. A collection of Early Middle-Irish Poems. Edited from a MS. in the Bodleian Library, by WHITLEY STOKES, LL.D. 7*s*. 6*d*.

Cath Finntrága; The Battle of Ventry Bay. Edited by KUNO MEYER, Phil. Doc. [*In the Press.*]

Also, uniform with the above:

Old-Latin Biblical Texts, No. 1: The Gospel according to St. Matthew, from the St. Germain MS. (g₁). Edited with Introduction and Appendices by the Rev. JOHN WORDSWORTH, M.A. 6*s*. [*Parts II and III in the Press.*]

The Editio Princeps of the Epistle of Barnabas, by Archbishop Ussher, as printed at Oxford, A.D. 1642, and preserved in an imperfect form in the Bodleian Library. With a Dissertation on the Literary History of that Edition, by the Rev. J. H. BACKHOUSE, M.A. 3*s*. 6*d*.

OXFORD: CLARENDON PRESS.

LONDON: HENRY FROWDE;

OXFORD UNIVERSITY PRESS WAREHOUSE, AMEN CORNER.

Anecdota Oxoniensia

TEXTS, DOCUMENTS, AND EXTRACTS

CHIEFLY FROM

MANUSCRIPTS IN THE BODLEIAN

AND OTHER

OXFORD LIBRARIES

CLASSICAL SERIES. VOL. I—PART V

HARLEIAN MS. 2610, OVID'S METAMORPHOSES I, II, III. 1–622
XXIV LATIN EPIGRAMS FROM BODLEIAN OR OTHER MSS.
LATIN GLOSSES ON APOLLINARIS SIDONIUS
FROM MS. DIGBY 172

COLLATED AND EDITED BY

ROBINSON ELLIS, M.A., LL.D.

Oxford
AT THE CLARENDON PRESS

[UNDER the general title of *Anecdota Oxoniensia*, it is proposed to publish materials, chiefly inedited, taken direct from MSS., those preserved in the Bodleian and other Oxford Libraries to have the first claim to publication. These materials will be (1) unpublished texts and documents, or extracts therefrom, with or without translations; or (2) texts which, although not unpublished, are unknown in the form in which they are to be printed in the *Anecdota*; or (3) texts which, in their published form, are difficult of access through the exceeding rarity of the printed copies; or (4) collations of valuable MSS.; or (5) notices and descriptions of certain MSS., or dissertations on the history, nature, and value thereof. The materials will be issued in four Series:—

 I. *The Classical Series.*
 II. *The Semitic Series.*
 III. *The Aryan Series.*
 IV. *The Mediaeval and Modern Series.*]

www.ingramcontent.com/pod-product-compliance
Lightning Source LLC
Chambersburg PA
CBHW030734230426
43667CB00007B/711